suse

SUSE LINUX

ADMINISTRATION GUIDE

9. Edition 2004

Authors:	Frank Bodammer, Stefan Dirsch, Olaf Donjak, Roman Drahtmüller, Torsten Duwe, Thorsten Dubiel, Karl Eichwalder, Thomas Fehr, Stefan Fent, Werner Fink, Kurt Garloff, Carsten Groß, Andreas Grünbacher, Franz Hassels, Andreas Jaeger, Klaus Kämpf, Hubert Mantel, Johannes Meixner, Lars Müller, Matthias Nagorni, Anas Nashif, Siegfried Olschner, Peter Pöml, Heiko Rommel, Marcus Schäfer, Nicolaus Schüler, Klaus Singvogel, Hendrik Vogelsang, Klaus G. Wagner, Christian Zoz
Translators:	Olaf Niepolt, Tino Tanner
Editors:	Jörg Arndt, Antje Faber, Berthold Gunreben, Roland Haidl, Jana Jaeger, Edith Parzefall, Ines Pozo, Thomas Rölz, Thomas Schraitle, Rebecca Walter
Layout:	Manuela Piotrowski, Thomas Schraitle
Setting:	DocBook-XML und LaTeX

This book has been printed on 100 % chlorine-free bleached paper.

Contents

II Configuration 63

Welcome

The SUSE LINUX Administration Guide provides background information about the way your SUSE LINUX operates. This book introduces Linux system administration basics such as file systems, kernels, boot processes, an Apache web server, and secure authentication.

The SUSE LINUX Administration Guide comprises five major categories:

Installation Details about special installation types, updates, LVM, and RAID.

Configuration Configuration of the boot loader, X Window System, printer operation, and mobile computing with Linux.

System Special characteristics of a SUSE LINUX system, details about the kernel, boot concepts, and init processes.

Network Integration in (heterogeneous) networks, configuring an Apache web server, file synchronization, and security aspects.

Appendices File Systems and Access Control Lists

The digital versions of the SUSE LINUX manuals are available in the directory `/usr/share/doc/manuals/`.

New Features in the Administration Guide

Changes in the documentation since SUSE LINUX 9.0:

- The chapter about using mobile devices has been complemented by a detailed section about the use of Bluetooth (see Section 7.4 on page 172).
- The power management chapter has been expanded with information about the powersave package (see Section 8.5 on page 191 and Section 8.6 on page 198).
- The Apache chapter has been optimized for the use of Apache 2 (see Section 14 on page 339).
- The Samba section has been optimized for the use of Samba 3 (see Section 16.1 on page 384).
- The chapter about printing now focuses on CUPS (see Chapter 5 on page 87).
- The X Window System contains a detailed section about the use of fonts in SUSE LINUX (see Section 4.2 on page 78).

Typographical Conventions

The following typographical conventions are used in this guide:

- YaST: programs
- `/etc/passwd`: file or directory names
- ⟨*placeholder*⟩: replace ⟨*placeholder*⟩ with the actual value
- `PATH`: the environment variable PATH
- `ls`: commands
- `--help`: options and parameters
- `user`: users

- Alt: a key to press
- 'File': menu items, buttons
- "Process killed": system messages

Acknowledgment

With a lot of voluntary commitment, the developers of Linux cooperate on a global scale to promote the development of Linux. We thank them for their efforts — this distribution would not exist without them. Furthermore, we want to thank Frank Zappa and Pawar. Last but not least, special thanks to LINUS TORVALDS!

Have a lot of fun!

Your SUSE Team

Part I

Installation

Installation

SUSE LINUX can be installed in a number of ways. The possibilities range from a graphical quick installation to a text-based installation allowing numerous manual adaptions. The following sections cover various installation procedures and the use of diverse installation sources (CD-ROM, NFS). This chapter also features information about resolving problems encountered during the installation and a detailed section about partitioning.

Note

This chapter focuses exclusively on special installation procedures. Refer to the *User Guide* for a comprehensive description of the standard graphical installation procedure.

Note

1.1 Text-Based Installation with YaST

In addition to installing with the assistance of a graphical interface, SUSE LINUX can also be installed with the help of the text version of YaST (console mode). All YaST modules are also available in this text mode. The text mode is especially useful if you do not need a graphical interface (e.g., for server systems) or if the graphics card is not supported by the X Window System. The visually impaired can also benefit from this text mode.

1.1.1 The Start Screen

First, set the boot sequence in the BIOS to enable booting from the CD-ROM drive. Insert the DVD or CD 1 in the drive and reboot the machine. The start screen is displayed after a few seconds.

Use ↑ and ↓ to select 'Manual Installation' within ten seconds to prevent YaST from starting automatically. If your hardware requires special parameters, which is not usually the case, enter these in `Boot Options`. The parameter `textmode=1` can be used to force YaST to run in text mode.

Use F2 ('Video Mode') to set the screen resolution for the installation. If you expect your graphics card to cause problems during the installation, select 'Text Mode'. Then press Enter. A box appears with the progress display `Loading Linux kernel`. The kernel boots and linuxrc starts. Proceed with the installation using the menus of linuxrc.

Other boot problems can usually be circumvented with kernel parameters. If DMA causes difficulties, use the start option 'Installation – Safe Settings'.

If your CD-ROM drive (ATAPI) crashes when booting the system, refer to Section 1.5 on page 21.

The following kernel parameters may be used if you experience problems with ACPI (Advanced Configuration and Power Interface).

acpi=off This parameter disables the complete ACPI subsystem on your computer. This may be useful if your computer cannot handle ACPI at all or if you think ACPI in your computer causes trouble.

acpi=oldboot Switch off ACPI for everything but those parts that are necessary to boot.

acpi=force Always enables ACPI, even if your computer has an old BIOS dated before the year 2000. This parameter also enables ACPI if it is set in addition to `acpi=off`.

pci=noacpi Prevents ACPI from doing the PCI IRQ routing.

Also refer to the SDB article `http://portal.suse.com/sdb/en/2002/10/81_acpi.html`.

If unexplainable errors occur when the kernel is loaded or during the installation, select 'Memory Test' in the boot menu to check the memory. Linux requires the hardware to meet high standards, which means the memory and its timing must be set correctly. More information is available at `http://portal.suse.com/sdb/en/2001/05/thallma_memtest86.html`. If possible, run the memory test overnight.

1.1.2 The Basis: linuxrc

The linuxrc program can be used to specify settings for the installation and load needed drivers as kernel modules. Finally, linuxrc launches YaST, starting the actual installation of the system software and other applications.

Use ↑ or ↓ to choose menu items. Use ← or → to select a command, such as 'Ok' or 'Cancel'. Execute the command by pressing Enter. A detailed description of linuxrc is provided in Section 11.4 on page 232.

Settings

The linuxrc application automatically begins with the language and keyboard selection. Select the language for the installation (for example, 'English') and confirm with Enter. Next, select the keyboard layout.

If linuxrc does not offer the desired keyboard layout, select an alternative layout. Once the installation is completed, the layout can be changed with YaST.

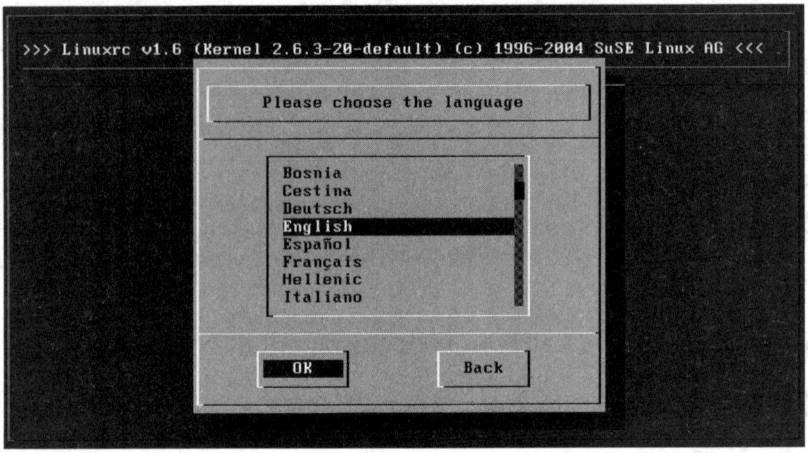

Figure 1.1: Language Selection

Main Menu of linuxrc

The main menu of linuxrc opens, as shown in Figure 1.2 on the next page. The following options are offered here:

'Settings' Select the language, screen, and keyboard.

'System Information' Shows information about the hardware as detected by the kernel or activated by loaded modules.

'Kernel modules (hardware drivers)'
Here, load any modules needed for your hardware. Also use this to load modules for additional file systems, such as ReiserFS. Normally, you do not need to use this if both your hard disks and the CD drive (ATAPI) are connected to an (E)IDE controller, as (E)IDE support is integrated in the kernel. Details for module selection is presented later.

'Start Installation or System' Proceeds to the actual installation.

'Exit or Reboot' Cancels the installation.

'Power off' Halts the system and switches the power off.

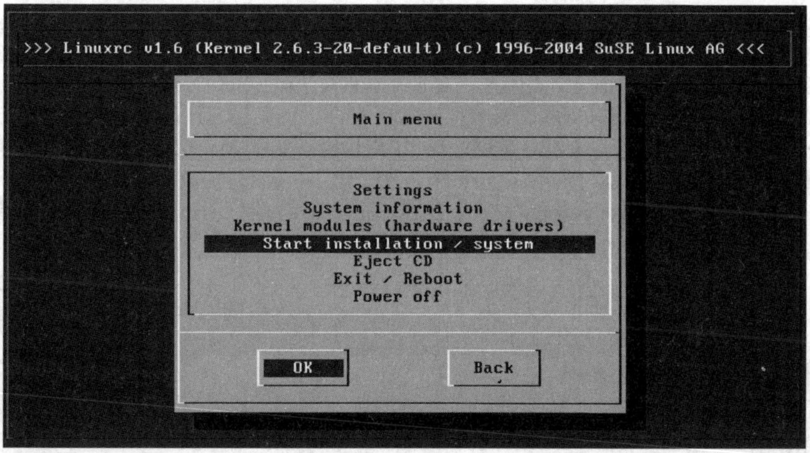

Figure 1.2: The Main Menu of linuxrc

Hardware Integration with Modules

Only load kernel modules by means of 'Kernel modules' if you need support for special system properties, such as SCSI, network cards, or PCMCIA, or if the CD-ROM drive used for the installation is not an ATAPI drive. Meanwhile, other components have been separated (e.g., IDE) or added (e.g., USB, FireWire, and file systems). Information about how modules are loaded is provided in Section 11.4 on page 232. Select the modules to load in the following submenu:

SCSI Module For SCSI hard disks or SCSI CD-ROM drives.

CD-ROM Module This is required if your CD-ROM drive is *not* connected to the (E)IDE-Controller or the SCSI controller. This especially applies to older CD-ROM drives that are connected to the machine by way of a proprietary controller.

Network Module For installing via NFS or FTP; see Section 1.3.2 on page 15.

File Systems For file systems such as ReiserFS or ext3.

Note

If your installation medium (proprietary CD-ROM drive, parallel port CD-ROM drive, network card, PCMCIA) is not listed among the standard modules, check the additional drivers on a module disk. See Section 1.4 on page 17 for information about how to create such a floppy disk. When ready, select 'More Modules'. linuxrc prompts you to insert the module disk.

Note

Starting the Installation

Select 'Start Installation or System' then press Enter to proceed with the installation.

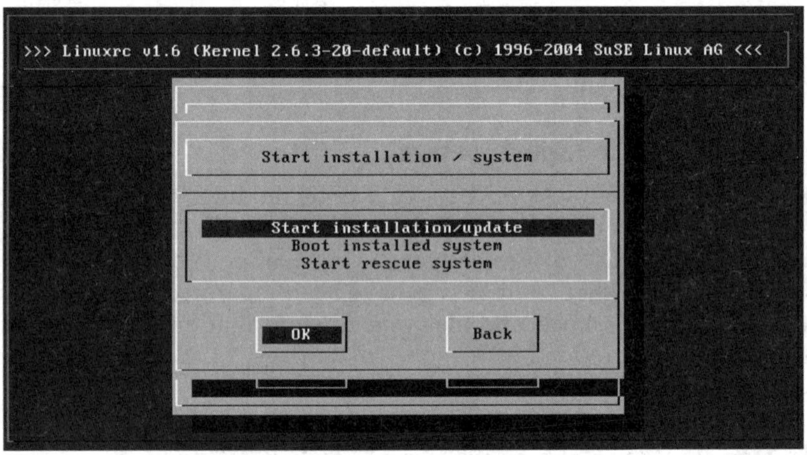

Figure 1.3: linuxrc Installation Menu

To begin the installation, select 'Start Installation or Update' then press Enter. Then select the source medium. Usually, the cursor can be left at the default selection: 'CD-ROM'.

Now press Enter. The installation environment will be loaded directly from CD 1. As soon as this procedure is completed, YaST starts in the text-based (ncurses) version. The installation then continues as described in *User Guide*, Chapter *Installation*.

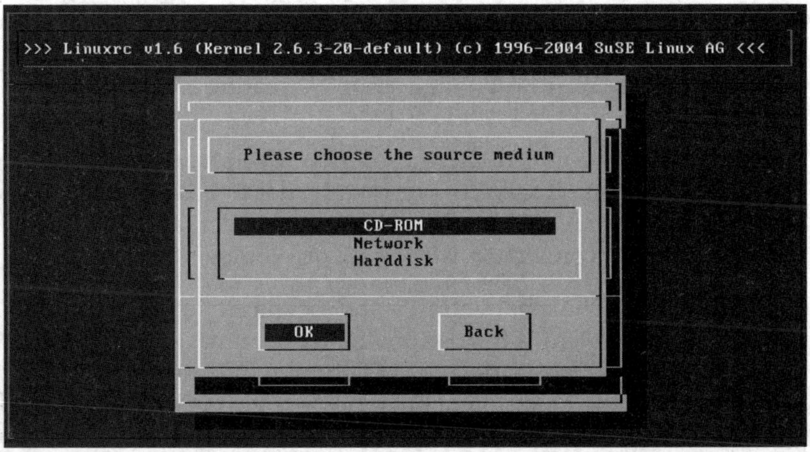

Figure 1.4: Selecting the Source Medium in linuxrc

Possible Problems

- If the SCSI adapter is not detected, try loading a module for a compatible driver. Alternatively, use a kernel with the appropriate integrated SCSI driver. This kernel would need to be custom-built.
- The ATAPI CD-ROM drive hangs when reading the data. See Section 1.5 on page 21.
- Problems sometimes occur when loading data to the RAM disk, preventing YaST from starting. If this situation arises, the following procedure can often lead to efficient results:

  Select 'Settings' -> 'Debug (Experts)' in the linuxrc main menu. There, select 'no' in 'Force root image'. Then return to the main menu and restart the installation.

1.2 Starting SUSE LINUX

Following the installation, decide how to boot Linux for daily operations. The following overview introduces various alternatives for booting Linux. The most suitable method depends on the intended purpose.

Boot Disk You can boot Linux from a *boot disk*. This approach will always work and is easy. The boot disk can be created with YaST. See the *User Guide* manual, 'YaST — Configuration': 'Creating a Boot, Rescue, or Module Disk'.

The boot disk is a useful interim solution if you have difficulties configuring the other possibilities or if you want to postpone the decision regarding the final boot mechanism. A boot disk may also be a suitable solution in connection with OS/2 or Windows NT.

Linux Boot Loader The most versatile and technically elegant solution for booting your system is the use of a Linux boot manager like GRUB (GRand Unified Bootloader) or LILO (LInux LOader), which both allow selection from different operating systems prior to booting. The boot loader can either be configured during installation or later with the help of YaST.

Caution

There are BIOS variants that check the structure of the boot sector (MBR) and erroneously display a virus warning after the installation of GRUB or LILO. This problem can be easily solved by entering the BIOS and looking for corresponding adjustable settings. For example, you should switch off 'virus protection'. You can switch this option back on again later. It is unnecessary, however, if Linux is the only operating system you use.

Caution

A detailed discussion of various boot methods, especially of GRUB and LILO, can be found in Section 6 on page 135.

1.2.1 The Graphical SUSE Screen

Starting with SUSE LINUX 7.2, the graphical SUSE screen is displayed on the first console if the option "vga=<value>" is active as kernel parameter. If you install using YaST, this option is automatically activated in accordance with the selected resolution and the graphics card.

Disabling the SUSE Screen

Basically there are three ways to achieve this:

- Disabling the SUSE screen whenever necessary. Enter the command `echo 0 >/proc/splash` on the command line to disable the graphical screen. To activate it again, enter `echo 0x0f01 >/proc/splash`.
- Disabling the SUSE screen by default. Add the kernel parameter `splash=0` to your boot loader configuration. 6 on page 135 provides more information about this. However, if you prefer the text mode which was the default in previous versions, set `vga=normal`.
- Completely disabling the SUSE screen. Compile a new kernel and disable the option 'Use splash screen instead of boot logo' in the menu 'framebuffer support'.

> **Note**
>
> Disabling framebuffer support in the kernel will automatically disable the splash screen as well. SUSE cannot provide any support for your system if you run it with a custom kernel.
>
> **Note**

1.3 Special Installation Procedures

1.3.1 Installation Without CD-ROM Support

What if a standard installation via CD-ROM drive is not possible? For example, your CD-ROM may not be supported because it is an older proprietary drive. A secondary machine, like a notebook, might not have any CD-ROM drive at all, only an ethernet adapter. SUSE LINUX offers the possibility of performing the installation on machines without a CD-ROM drive over a network connection. Usually this is done by means of NFS or FTP over ethernet. The following section describes the procedure.

1.3.2 Installation from a Network Source

No installation support is available for this approach. Therefore, the following procedure should only be applied by experienced computer users.

To install SUSE LINUX from a network source, two steps are necessary:

1. The data required for the installation (CDs, DVD) must be made available on a machine that will serve as the installation source.
2. The system to install must be booted from floppy disk or CD and the network must be configured.

Configuring a Network Installation Source

Prepare the network share by copying the installation CDs to individual directories and make these available on a system with NFS server functionality. For example, on an existing SUSE LINUX machine, copy the individual CDs with `cp -a /mnt/cdrom /suse-share/`.

Then rename the directory, for example, to *CD1*, with a command like `mv /suse-share/cdrom /suse-share/CD1`. Repeat this procedure for the other CDs. Then export the `/suse-share` directory via NFS. For information, see Section 13.9 on page 325.

Booting for the Network Installation

Insert the boot medium in the drive. The creation of the boot disk is described in Section 1.4.1 on the next page and 1.4.2 on page 19. The boot menu will appear after a short time. Select 'Manual Installation'. You can also specify additional kernel parameters. Confirm the selection with (Enter). The kernel will be loaded and you will be prompted to insert the first module disk.

After a short while, linuxrc will appear and ask you to enter a number of parameters:

1. Select the language and the keyboard layout in linuxrc.
2. Select 'Kernel modules (hardware drivers)'.
3. Load the IDE, RAID, or SCSI drivers required for your system.
4. Select 'Load network card modules' and load the needed network card driver (e.g., `eepro100`).
5. Select 'Load file system driver' and load the needed drivers (e.g., `reiserfs`).
6. Select 'Back' then 'Start installation / system'.

7. Select 'Start installation/update'.
8. Select 'Network' then the network protocol (e.g., NFS).
9. Select the network card to use.
10. Specify the IP addresses and other network information.
11. Specify the IP address of the NFS server providing the installation data.
12. Enter the path of the NFS share (e.g., /suse-share/CD1).

Now linuxrc will load the installation environment from the network source and start YaST. Proceed with the installation as described in the *User Guide* manual, Chapter *Installation*.

Troubleshooting

- The installation is terminated before it actually starts. The installation directory of the *other* machine was not exported with exec permissions. Do this now.
- The server does not recognize the host on which to install SUSE LINUX. Enter the name and IP address of the host to install in the /etc/hosts file of the server.

1.4 Tips and Tricks

1.4.1 Creating a Boot Disk in DOS

You need formatted 3.5" HD floppy disks and a bootable 3.5" floppy disk drive. The boot directory on CD 1 contains a number of disk images. With a suitable utility, these images can be copied to floppy disks. A floppy disk prepared in this way is referred to as a boot disk.

The disk images also include the loader SYSLINUX and the program linuxrc. SYSLINUX enables the selection of a kernel during the boot procedure and the specification of any parameters needed for the hardware used. The program linuxrc supports the loading of kernel modules for your hardware and subsequently starts the installation.

Creating a Boot Disk with rawwritewin

In Windows, boot disks can be created with the graphical utility rawwritewin. In Windows, find this utility in the directory `dosutils/rawwritewin/` on CD 1.

On start-up, specify the image file. The image files are located in the `boot` directory on CD 1. At the least, you will need the images "bootdisk" and "modules1". To list these images in the file browser, set the file type to "all files". Then insert a floppy disk in your floppy disk drive and click "write". To create several floppy disks, repeat the same procedure.

Creating a Boot Disk with rawrite

The DOS utility `rawrite.exe` (CD 1, directory `dosutils/rawrite` can be used for creating SUSE boot and module disks. To use this utility, you need a computer with DOS (such as FreeDOS) or Windows.

In Windows XP, proceed as follows:

1. Insert SUSE LINUX CD 1.
2. Open a DOS window (in the start menu, select 'Accessories' ->'Command Prompt').
3. Run rawrite.exe with the correct path specification for the CD drive. The example assumes that you are in the directory `Windows` on the hard disk `C:` and your CD drive is `D:`.

   ```
   d:\dosutils\rawrite\rawrite
   ```

4. On start-up, the utility asks for the source and destination of the file to copy. The image of the boot disk is located in the directory `boot/` on CD 1. The file name is `bootdisk`. Remember to specify the path for your CD drive.

   ```
   d:\dosutils\rawrite\rawrite
   RaWrite 1.2 - Write disk file to raw floppy diskette

   Enter source file name: d:\boot\bootdisk
   Enter destination drive: a:
   ```

After you enter the destination drive `a:`, rawrite prompts you to insert a formatted floppy disk and press Enter. Subsequently, the progress of the copy action is displayed. The process can be terminated with Ctrl + C.

The other disk images (`modules1`, `modules2`, `modules3`, and `modules4`) can be created in the same way. These floppy disks are required if you have USB or SCSI devices or a network or PCMCIA card that you want to address during the installation. A module disk may also be needed if using a special file system during the installation.

1.4.2 Creating a Boot Disk in a UNIX-Type System

On a UNIX or Linux system, you need a CD-ROM drive and a formatted floppy disk. Proceed as follows to create boot disks:

1. If you need to format the disks first, use:

   ```
   fdformat /dev/fd0u1440
   ```

2. Mount CD 1 (for example, to `/media/cdrom`):

   ```
   mount -tiso9660 /dev/cdrom /media/cdrom
   ```

3. Change to the `boot` directory on the CD:

   ```
   cd /media/cdrom/boot
   ```

4. Create the boot disk with the following command:

   ```
   dd if=/media/cdrom/boot/bootdisk of=/dev/fd0 bs=8k
   ```

The `README` file in the `boot` directory provides details about the floppy disk images. You can read these files with `more` or `less`.

The other disk images, `modules1`, `modules2`, `modules3`, and `modules4`, can be created in the same way. These floppy disks are required if you have USB or SCSI devices or a network or PCMCIA card that you want to address during the installation. A module disk may also be needed to use a special file system during the installation.

To use a custom kernel during the installation, the procedure is a bit more complex. In this case, write the default image `bootdisk` to the floppy disk then overwrite the kernel `linux` with your own kernel (see Section 10.7 on page 215):

```
dd if=/media/cdrom/boot/bootdisk of=/dev/fd0 bs=8k
mount -t msdos /dev/fd0 /mnt
cp /usr/src/linux/arch/i386/boot/vmlinuz /mnt/linux
umount /mnt
```

1.4.3 Booting from a Floppy Disk (SYSLINUX)

The boot disk can be used for handling special installation requirements (for example, if the CD-ROM drive is not available). See Section 1.4.1 on page 17 or Section 1.4.2 on the page before for more information about creating boot disks.

The boot procedure is initiated by the boot loader SYSLINUX (`syslinux`). When the system is booted, SYSLINUX runs a minimum hardware detection that mainly consists of the following steps:

1. The program checks if the BIOS provides VESA 2.0–compliant framebuffer supports and boots the kernel accordingly.
2. The monitor data (DDC info) is read.
3. The first block of the first hard disk (MBR) is read to map BIOS IDs to Linux device names during the boot loader configuration. The program attempts to read the block by means of the the lba32 functions of the BIOS to determine if the BIOS supports these functions.

Note

If you keep Shift pressed when SYSLINUX is started, all these steps will be skipped. For troubleshooting purposes: if you insert the line

```
verbose 1
```

in `syslinux.cfg`, the boot loader tells you which action is currently being performed.

Note

If the machine does not boot from the floppy disk, you may have to change the boot sequence in the BIOS to `A, C, CDROM`.

1.4.4 Using CD 2 for Booting

CD 2 is also bootable. In contrast to CD 1, which uses a bootable ISO image, CD 2 is booted by means of 2.88 MB disk image. Use CD 2 if you are sure you can boot from CD, but it does not work with CD 1 (fallback solution).

1.4.5 Supported CD-ROM Drives

Most CD-ROM drives are supported.

- ATAPI drives should work smoothly.
- The support of SCSI CD-ROM drives depends on whether the SCSI controller to which the CD-ROM drive is connected is supported. Supported SCSI controllers are listed in the Hardware Database at `http://cdb.suse.de`. If your SCSI controller is not supported and your hard disk is also connected to the controller, you have a problem.
- Many vendor-specific CD-ROM drives are supported in Linux. Nevertheless, problems may be encountered with this kind of drives. If your drive is not explicitly listed, try using a similar type from the same vendor.
- USB CD-ROM drives are also supported. If the BIOS of your machine does not support booting from USB devices, start the installation by means of the boot disks. For details, refer to Section 1.4.3 on the facing page. Before you boot from the floppy disk, make sure all needed USB devices are connected and powered on.

1.5 ATAPI CD-ROM Hangs While Reading

If your ATAPI CD-ROM is not recognized or it hangs while reading, this is most frequently due to incorrectly installed hardware. All devices must be connected to the EIDE controller in the correct order. The first device is master on the first controller. The second device is slave on the first controller. The third device should be master on the second controller, and so forth.

It often occurs that there is only a CD-ROM besides the first device. The CD-ROM drive is sometimes connected as master to the second controller (secondary IDE controller). This is wrong and can cause Linux not to know what to do with this *gap*. Try to fix this by passing the appropriate parameter to the kernel (`hdc=cdrom`).

Sometimes one of the devices is just *misjumpered*. This means it is jumpered as slave, but is connected as master, or vice versa. When in doubt, check your hardware settings and correct them where necessary.

In addition, there is a series of faulty EIDE chipsets, most of which have now been identified. There is a special kernel to handle such cases. See the `README` in `/boot` of the installation CD-ROM.

If booting does not work immediately, try using the following kernel parameters:

`hdx=cdrom` x stands for a, b, c, d, etc., and is interpreted as follows:

- a — Master on the first IDE controller
- b — Slave on the first IDE controller
- c — Master on the second IDE controller

An example of `parameter to enter` is `hdb=cdrom`. With this parameter, specify the CD-ROM drive to the kernel, if it cannot find it itself and you have an ATAPI CD-ROM drive.

`idex=noautotune` x stands for 0, 1, 2, 3, etc., and is interpreted as follows:

- 0 — First IDE controller
- 1 — Second IDE controller

An example of `parameter to enter` is `ide0=noautotune`. This parameter is often useful for (E)IDE hard disks.

1.6 Assigning Permanent Device File Names to SCSI Devices

When the system is booted, SCSI devices are assigned device file names in a more or less dynamic way. This is no problem as long as the number or configuration of the devices does not change. However, if a new SCSI hard disk is added and the new hard disk is detected by the kernel before the old hard disk, the old disk will be assigned new names and the entries in the mount table `/etc/fstab` will no longer match.

To avoid this problem, use `boot.scsidev`. `boot.scsidev` handles the setup of the SCSI devices during the boot procedure and enters permanent device names under `/dev/scsi/`. These names can be used in `/etc/fstab`.

In the expert mode of the runlevel editor, activate `boot.scsidev` for level `B`. The links needed for generating the names during the boot procedure are then created in `/etc/init.d/boot.d`.

1.7 Partitioning for Experts

This section provides detailed information for tailoring system partitioning to your needs. This information is mainly of interest for those who want to optimize a system for security and speed and who are prepared to reinstall the entire existing system if necessary.

The procedures described here require a basic understanding of the functions of a UNIX file system. You should be familiar with mount points and physical, extended, and logical partitions.

First, consider the following questions:

- How will the machine be used (file server, application server, compute server, stand-alone machine)?
- How many people will work with this machine (concurrent logins)?
- How many hard disks are installed? What is their size and type (EIDE, SCSI, or RAID controllers)?

1.7.1 Size of the Swap Partition

Many sources state the rule that the swap size should be at least twice the size of the main memory. This is a relic of times when 8 MB RAM was considered a lot. In the past, the aim was to equip the machine with about 30 to 40 MB of virtual memory (RAM plus swap). Modern applications require even more memory. For normal users, 256 MB of virtual memory is currently a reasonable value. Never configure your system without any swap memory.

1.7.2 Suggested Partitioning Schemes

A Stand-Alone Machine

The most common use for a Linux machine is as a stand-alone system. To give you an idea of possible values, the following paragraphs present a number of example configurations that you can adopt for home or office use. Table 1.1 on the next page provides an overview of the various installation scopes for different Linux systems.

Table 1.1: Estimated Disk Space Requirements for Different Installations

Installation	Required Disk Space
minimum	180 MB to 400 MB
small	400 MB to 1500 MB
medium	1500 MB to 4 GB
large	more than 4 GB

Example: Standard Workstation (Small)

To install Linux on a 500 MB hard disk, use 64 MB for the swap partition and the rest for / (root partition).

Example: Standard Workstation (Average)

If you have 2 GB available for Linux, use a small boot partition (`/boot`) of 5–10 MB or 1 cylinder, 128 MB for swap, 800 MB for `/`, and the rest for a separate `/home` partition.

Example: Standard Workstation (Deluxe)

If you have more than 2 GB or more on several hard disks available, there is no standard way to partition. Read Section 1.7.3 on the facing page.

A File Server

Here, hard disk performance is crucial. Use SCSI devices if possible. Keep in mind the performance of the disk and the controller. A file server is used to save data, such as user directories, a database, or other archives, centrally. This approach greatly simplifies the data administration.

Optimizing the hard disk access is vital for file servers in networks of more than twenty users. Suppose you want to set up a Linux file server for the home directories of 25 users. If the average user requires 100–150 MB for personal data, a 4 GB partition mounted under `/home` is probably sufficient. For fifty users, you would need 8 GB. If possible, split `/home/` to two 4 GB hard disks that share the load (and access time).

Note

Web browser caches should be stored on local hard disks.

Note

A Compute Server

A compute server is generally a powerful machine that carries out extensive calculations in the network. Normally, such a machine is equipped with a large main memory (more than 512 RAM). Fast disk throughput is only needed for the swap partitions. If possible, distribute swap partitions to multiple hard disks.

1.7.3 Optimization

The hard disks are normally the limiting factor. To avoid this bottleneck, combine the following three possibilities:

- Distribute the load evenly to multiple disks.
- Use an optimized file system, such as `reiserfs`).
- Equip your file server with a sufficient amount of memory (at least 256 MB).

Parallel Use of Multiple Disks

The total amount of time needed for providing requested data consists of the following elements:

1. Time elapsed until the request reaches the disk controller.
2. Time elapsed until this request is send to the hard disk.
3. Time elapsed until the hard disk positions its head.
4. Time elapsed until the media turns to the respective sector.
5. Time elapsed for the transmission.

The first item depends on the network connection and must be regulated there. Item two is a relatively insignificant period that depends on the hard disk controller itself. Items three and four are the main parts. The positioning time is measured in ms. Compared to the access times of the main memory, which are measured in ns, this represents a factor of one million. Item four depends on the disk rotation speed, which is usually several ms. Item five depends on the rotation speed, the number of heads, and the current position of the head (inside or outside).

To optimize the performance, the third item should be improved. For SCSI devices, the *disconnect* feature comes into play. When this feature is used, the controller sends the command *Go to track x, sector y* to the connected device (in this case, the hard disk). Now the inactive disk mechanism starts moving. If the disk is smart (if it supports disconnect) and the controller driver also supports this feature, the controller immediately sends the hard disk a disconnect command and the disk is disconnected from the SCSI bus. Now, other SCSI devices can proceed with their transfers. After some time (depending on the strategy or load on the SCSI bus) the connection to the disk is reactivated. In the ideal case, the device will have reached the requested track.

On a multitasking, multiuser system like Linux, these parameters can be optimized effectively. For example, examine the following excerpt of the output of the command `df` (see Example 1.1).

Example 1.1: *Example df Output*

```
Filesystem Size Used Avail Use% Mounted on
/dev/sda5 1.8G 1.6G 201M 89% /
/dev/sda1 23M 3.9M 17M 18% /boot
/dev/sdb1 2.9G 2.1G 677M 76% /usr
/dev/sdc1 1.9G 958M 941M 51% /usr/lib
shmfs 185M 0 184M 0% /dev/shm
```

To demonstrate the advantages, consider what happens if `root` enters the following in `/usr/src`:

```
tar xzf package.tgz -C /usr/lib
```

This command extracts `package.tgz` to `/usr/lib/package`. To do this, the shell runs tar and gzip (both located in `/bin` on `/dev/sda`) then `package.tgz` is read by `/usr/src` (on `/dev/sdb`). Finally, the extracted data is written to `/usr/lib` (on `/dev/sdc`). Thus, the positioning as well as the reading and writing of the disks' internal buffers can be performed almost concurrently.

This is only one of many examples. As a general rule, if you have several hard disks (with the same speed), `/usr` and `/usr/lib` should be placed on separate disks. `/usr/lib` should have about seventy percent of the capacity of `/usr`. Due to the frequency of access, / should be placed on the disk containing `/usr/lib`.

Processor Speed and Main Memory Size

In Linux, the size of main memory is often more important than the processor speed. One reason, if not the main reason, for this is the ability of Linux to create dynamic buffers containing hard disk data. For this purpose, Linux uses various tricks, such as *read ahead* (reading of sectors in advance) and *delayed write* (postponement and bundling of write access). The latter is the reason why you should not simply switch off your Linux machine. Both factors contribute to the fact that the main memory seems to fill up over time and that Linux is so fast. See Section 11.2.6 on page 225.

1.8 LVM Configuration

This professional partitioning tool enables you to edit and delete existing partitions and create new ones. Access the Soft RAID and LVM configuration from here.

Note

Background information and partitioning tips can be found in Section 1.7 on page 23.

Note

In normal circumstances, partitions are set up during installation. However, it is possible to integrate a second hard disk in an existing Linux system. First, the new hard disk must be partitioned. Then it must be mounted and entered into the `/etc/fstab` file. It may be necessary to copy some of the data to move an `/opt` partition from the old hard disk to the new one.

Use caution repartitioning the hard disk in use — this is essentially possible, but you will have to reboot the system right afterwards. It is a bit safer to boot from CD then repartition it.

'Experts. . . ' opens a pop-up menu containing the following commands:

Reread Partition Table Rereads the partitioning from disk. For example, you need this for manual partitioning in the text console.

Adopt Mount Points from Existing /etc/fstab
This is only relevant during installation. Reading the old `fstab` is useful for completely reinstalling your system rather than just updating it. In this case, it is not necessary to enter the mount points by hand.

Delete Partition Table and Disk Label

This completely overwrites the old partition table. For example, this can be helpful if you have problems with unconventional disk labels. Using this method, all data on the hard disk is lost.

1.8.1 Logical Volume Manager (LVM)

Starting from kernel version 2.6, you can use LVM version 2, which is downward-compatible with the previous LVM and enables the continued management of old volume groups. When creating new volume groups, decide whether to use the new format or the downward-compatible version. LVM2 does not require any kernel patches. It makes use of the device mapper integrated in kernel 2.6. This kernel only supports LVM version 2. Therefore, when talking about LVM, this chapter always refer to LVM version 2.

Instead of LVM2, you can also use EVMS (Enterprise Volume Management System), which offers a uniform interface for logical volumes as well as RAID volumes. Like LVM2, EVMS makes use of the device mapper in kernel 2.6.

The Logical Volume Manager (LVM) enables flexible distribution of hard disk space over several file systems. As it is difficult to modify partitions on a running system, LVM was developed. It provides a virtual pool (Volume Group — VG for short) of memory space from which logical volumes (LV) can be generated if needed. The operating system accesses these instead of the physical partitions.

Features:

- Several hard disks or partitions can be combined to a large logical partition.
- Provided the configuration is suitable, a LV (such as `/usr`) can be enlarged when the free space is exhausted.
- Using LVM, even add hard disks or LVs in a running system. However, this requires hot-swappable hardware that is capable of such actions.
- Several hard disks can be used with improved performance in the RAID 0 (striping) mode.
- The snapshot feature enables consistent backups (especially for servers) in the running system.

Implementing LVM already makes sense for heavily used home PCs or small servers. If you have a growing data stock, as in the case of databases, MP3 archives, or user directories, LVM is just the right thing for you. This would allow file systems that are larger than physical hard disk. Another advantage of the LVM is that up to 256 LVs can be added. Keep in mind that working with LVM is very different than working with conventional partitions. Instructions and further information about configuring LVM is available in the official LVM HOWTO at `http://tldp.org/HOWTO/LVM-HOWTO/`.

LVM Configuration with YaST

Prepare the LVM configuration in YaST by creating an LVM partition when installing. To do this, click 'Partitioning' in the suggestion window then 'Discard' or 'Change' in the screen that follows. Next, create a partition for LVM by first clicking 'Add' -> 'Do not format' in the Partitioner then clicking '0x8e Linux LVM'. Continue partitioning with LVM immediately afterwards or wait until after the system is completely installed. To do this, highlight the LVM partition in the partitioner then click 'LVM...'.

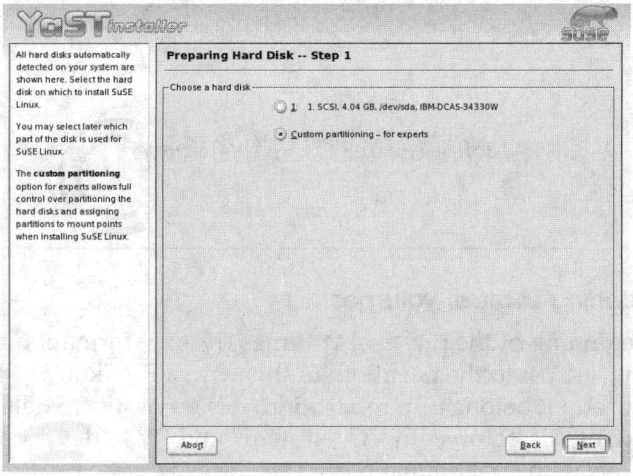

Figure 1.5: Activating LVM During Installation

LVM — Partitioning

After selecting 'LVM...' in the partitioning section, continue automatically to a dialog in which to repartition your hard disks. Delete or modify existing partitions here or add new ones. A partition to use for LVM must have the partition label 8E. These partitions are indicated by "Linux LVM" in the partition list.

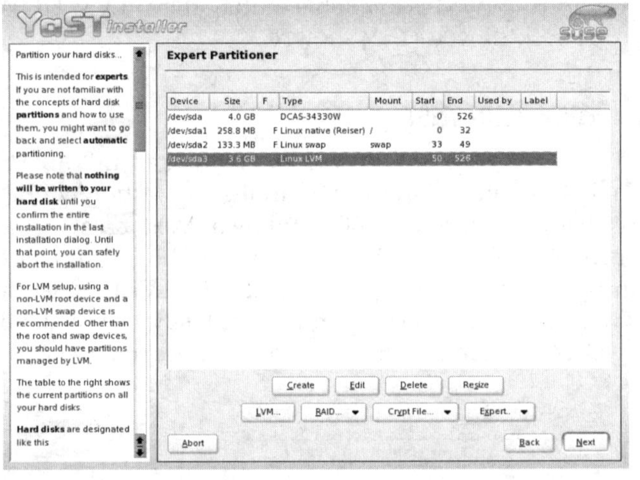

Figure 1.6: YaST: LVM Partitioner

> **Note**
>
> **Repartitioning Logical Volumes**
>
> At the beginning of the physical volumes (PVs), information about the volume is written to the partition. In this way, a PV "knows" to which volume group it belongs. To repartition, it is advisable to delete the beginning of this volume. In VG "system" and PV "/dev/sda2", this can be done with the command `dd if=/dev/zero of=/dev/sda2 bs=512 count=1`.
>
> **Note**

You do not need to set the 8E label for all partitions designated for LVM. If needed, YaST automatically sets the partition label of a partition assigned to an LVM volume group to 8E. For any unpartitioned areas on your disks, create LVM partitions in this dialog. These partitions should then be designated the partition label 8E. They do not need to be formatted and no mount point can be entered.

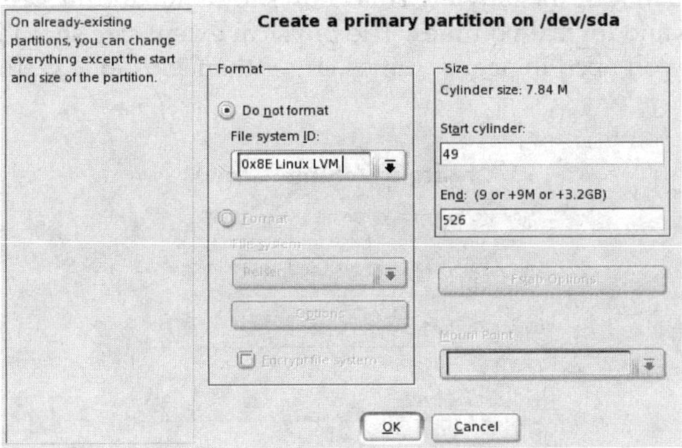

Figure 1.7: *Creating LVM Partitions*

If a working LVM configuration already exists on your system, it is automatically activated as soon as you begin configuring the LVM. If this is successfully activated, any disks containing a partition belonging to an activated volume group can no longer be repartitioned. The Linux kernel will refuse to read the modified partitioning of a hard disk as long as only one partition on this disk is used.

Repartitioning disks not belonging to an LVM volume group is not a problem at all. If you already have a functioning LVM configuration on your system, repartitioning is usually not necessary. In this screen, configure all mount points not located on LVM Logical Volumes. The root file system in YaST must be stored on a normal partition. Select this partition from the list and specify this as root file system using the 'Edit' button. In view of the flexibility of LVM, we recommend that you place all additional file systems in LVM logical volumes. After specifying the root partition, exit this dialog.

LVM — Configuring Physical Volumes

In the dialog 'LVM', the LVM volume groups are managed. If no volume group exists on your system yet, you will be prompted to add one. `system` is suggested as a name for the volume group in which the SUSE LINUX system files are located. Physical extent size (PE Size) defines the maximum size of a physical and logical volume in this volume group. This value is normally set to four megabytes. This allows for a maximum size of 256 GB for physical and logical volumes. The physical extent size should only be increased if you need logical volumes larger than 256 GB (e.g., to 8, 16, or 32 MB).

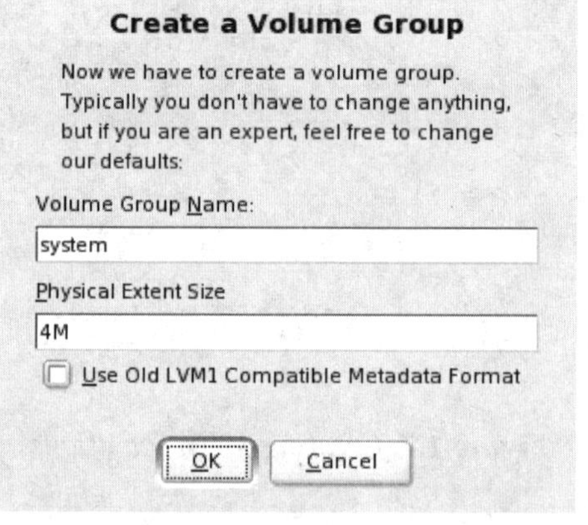

Figure 1.8: Adding a Volume Group

The following dialog lists all partitions with either the "Linux LVM" or "Linux native" type. No swap or DOS partitions are shown. If a partition is already assigned to a volume group, the name of the volume group is shown in the list. Unassigned partitions are indicated by "--".

The volume group currently being edited can be modified in the selection box to the upper left. The buttons in the upper right enable creation of additional volume groups and deletion of existing volume groups. Only volume groups to which no partitions are assigned can be deleted. No more than one volume group needs to be created for a normally installed SUSE LINUX system. A partition assigned to a volume group is also referred to as a physical volume (PV).

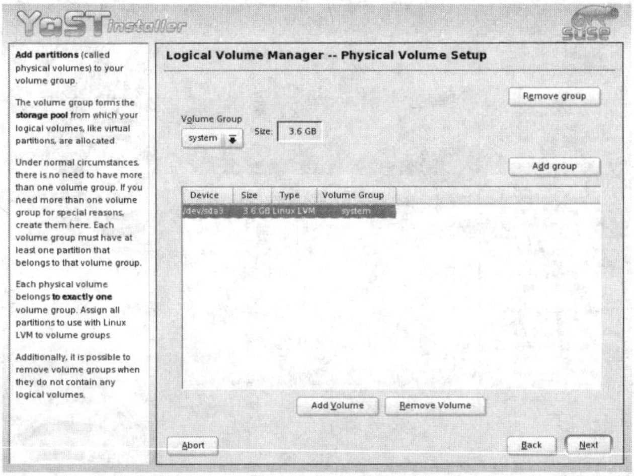

Figure 1.9: Partition List

To add a previously unassigned partition to the selected volume group, first click the partition then 'Add Volume'. At this point, the name of the volume group is entered next to the selected partition. Assign all partitions reserved for LVM to a volume group. Otherwise, the space on the partition will remain unused. Before exiting the dialog, every volume group must be assigned at least one physical volume.

Logical Volumes

This dialog is responsible for managing logical volumes. Assign one logical volume to each volume group. To create a striping array when you create the logical volumes, first create the LV with the largest number of stripes. A striping LV with n stripes can only be created correctly if the hard disk space required by the LV can be distributed evenly to n physical volumes. If only PVs are available, an LV with three stripes is impossible.

Normally, a file system is created on a logical volume (e.g., reiserfs, ext2) and is then designated a mount point. The files stored on this logical volume can be found at this mount point on the installed system. All normal Linux partitions to which a mount point is assigned, all swap partitions, and all already existing logical volumes are listed here.

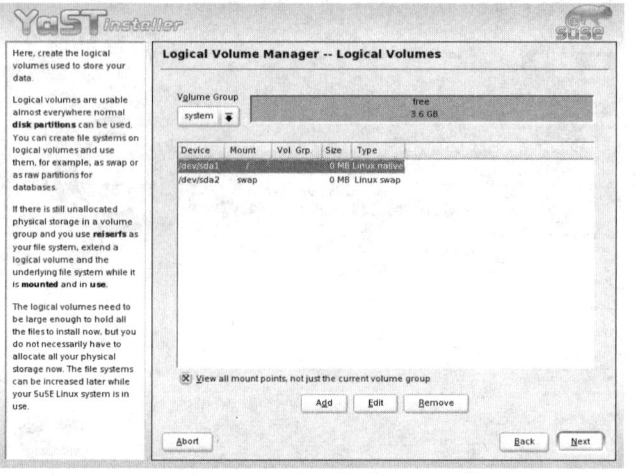

Figure 1.10: Logical Volume Management

Caution

Using LVM might be associated with increased risk factors, such as data loss. Risks also include application crashes, power failures, and faulty commands. Save your data before implementing LVM or reconfiguring volumes. Never work without a backup.

Caution

If you have already configured LVM on your system, the existing logical volumes must be entered now. Before continuing, assign the appropriate mount point to these logical volumes. If you are configuring LVM on a system for the first time, no logical volumes are displayed in this screen yet. A logical volume must be generated for each mount point (using 'Add'). Also set the size, the file system type (e.g., reiserfs or ext2), and the mount point (e.g., `/var/`, `/usr/`, `/home/`).

If you have created several volume groups, switch between individual volume groups by means of the selection list at the top left. Added logical volumes are listed in the volume group displayed there. After creating all the logical volumes required, exit the dialog. If you are still in the installation process, you can proceed with the software selection.

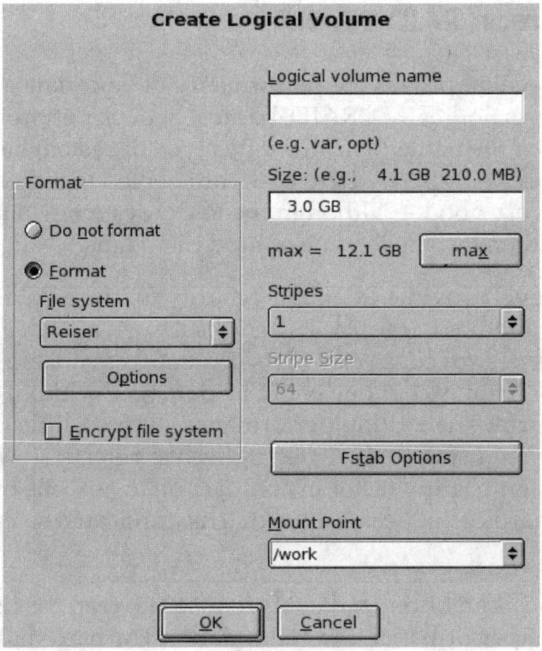

Figure 1.11: Creating Logical Volumes

1.9 Soft RAID

The purpose of RAID (redundant array of inexpensive disks) is to combine several hard disk partitions into one large *virtual* hard disk for the optimization of performance and data security. Using this method, however, one advantage is sacrificed for another. *RAID level* defines the pool and common triggering device of the all hard disks, the RAID controller. A RAID controller mostly uses the SCSI protocol, because it can drive more hard disks better than the IDE protocol. It is also better able to process commands running in parallel.

Like a RAID controller, which can often be quite expensive, soft RAID is also able to take on these tasks. SUSE LINUX offers the option of combining several hard disks into one soft RAID system with the help of YaST — a very reasonable alternative to hardware RAID.

1.9.1 Common RAID Levels

RAID 0 This level improves the performance of your data access. Actually, this is not really a RAID, because it does not provide data backup, but the name *RAID 0* for this type of system has become the norm. With RAID 0, two hard disks are pooled together. The performance is very good — although the RAID system will be destroyed and your data lost if even one of hard disks fails.

RAID 1 This level provides adequate security for your data, as the data is copied to another hard disk 1:1. This is known as *hard disk mirroring*. If a disk is destroyed, a copy of its contents is available on another one. All of them except one could be damaged without endangering your data. The writing performance suffers a little in the copying process when using RAID 1 (ten to twenty percent slower), but read access is significantly faster in comparison to any one of the normal physical hard disks, because the data is duplicated so can be parallel scanned.

RAID 5 RAID 5 is an optimized compromise between the two other levels in terms of performance and redundancy. The hard disk space equals the number of disks used minus one. The data is distributed over the hard disks as with RAID 0. *Parity blocks*, created on one of the partitions, are there for security reasons. They are linked to each other with XOR — enabling the contents, via XDR, to be reconstructed by the corresponding parity block in case of system failure. With RAID 5, no more than one hard disk can fail at the same time. If one hard disk fails, it must be replaced as soon as possible to avoid the risk of losing data.

1.9.2 Soft RAID Configuration with YaST

Access Soft RAID configuration with the 'RAID' module under 'System' or via the partitioning module under 'Hardware'.

First Step: Partitioning

First, see a list of your partitions under 'Expert Settings' in the partitioning tool. If the Soft RAID partitions have already been set up, they appear here. Otherwise, set them up from scratch. For RAID 0 and RAID 1, at least two partitions are needed — for RAID 1, usually exactly two and no more. If RAID 5 is used, at least three partitions are required. It is recommended to take only partitions of the same size. The RAID partitions should be stored on various hard disks to decrease the risk of losing data if one is defective (RAID 1 and 5) and to optimize the performance of RAID 0.

Second Step: Setting up RAID

Click 'RAID' to open a dialog in which to choose between RAID levels 0, 1, and 5. In the following screen, assign the partition to the new RAID. 'Expert Options' opens the settings options for the *chunk size* — for fine-tuning the performance. Checking 'Persistent Superblock' ensures that the RAID partitions are recognized as such when booting. After completing the configuration, you will then see the `/dev/md0` device and others indicated with *RAID* on the expert page in the partitioning module.

1.9.3 Troubleshooting

Find out whether a RAID partition has been destroyed by the file contents `/proc/mdstats`. The basic procedure in case of system failure is to shut down your Linux system and replace the defective hard disk with a new one partitioned the same way. Then restart your system and give the `raidhotadd /dev/mdX /dev/sdX` command. This enables the hard disk to be integrated automatically into the RAID system and be fully reconstructed.

1.9.4 For More Information

Configuration instructions and more details for Soft RAID can be found in the HOWTOs at:

- `/usr/share/doc/packages/raidtools/Software-RAID-HOWTO.html`
- `http://en.tldp.org/HOWTO/Software-RAID-HOWTO.html`

Linux RAID mailing lists are also available, such as `http://www.mail-archive.com/linux-raid@vger.rutgers.edu`.

Updating the System and Package Management

SUSE LINUX provides the option of updating an existing system without completely reinstalling it. There are two types of updates: *updating individual software packages* and *updating the entire system*. Packages can also be installed by hand using the package manager RPM.

2.1 Updating SUSE LINUX

Software tends to *grow* from version to version. Therefore, we recommend first taking a look at the available partition space with df *before* updating. If you suspect you are running short of disk space, secure your data before updating and repartition your system. There is no general rule of thumb regarding how much space each partition should have. Space requirements depend on your particular partitioning profile, the software selected, and the version numbers of SUSE LINUX.

Note

It is recommended to read README and, in DOS and Windows, README.DOS on your CD. Find notes there regarding any additional changes made *after* this manual went to print.

Note

2.1.1 Preparations

Before you begin your update, copy the old configuration files to a separate medium just to be on the safe side. Such media can include streamers, removable hard disks, or ZIP drives. This primarily applies to files stored in /etc. Also, review the configuration files in /var/lib. Furthermore, you may want to write the user data in /home (the HOME directories) to a backup medium. Back up this data as root. Only root has read permission for all local files.

Before starting your update, make note of the root partition. The command df / lists the device name of the root partition. In the example shown in Output 2.1, the root partition to write down is /dev/hda2 (mounted as /).

***Example 2.1:** List with df -h*

```
Filesystem  Size  Used  Avail Use% Mounted on
/dev/hda1   1,9G  189M  1.7G  10%  /dos
/dev/hda2   8,9G  7,1G  1,4G  84%  /
/dev/hda5   9,5G  8,3G  829M  92%  /home
```

Possible Problems

PostgreSQL Before updating PostgreSQL (`postgres`), it is usually best to *dump* the databases. See the manual page of `pg_dump`. This is, of course, only necessary if you actually used PostgreSQL prior to your update.

Promise Controller The hard disk controller manufactured by Promise is currently found on high-end motherboards in numerous computer models, either as a pure IDE controller (for UDMA 100) or as an IDE-RAID controller. As of SUSE LINUX 8.0, these controllers are directly supported by the kernel and treated as a standard controller for IDE hard disks. The additional kernel module `pdcraid` is required before you can aquire RAID functionality.For some updates, hard disks on the Promise controller may be detected before disks on the standard IDE controller. If so, the system will no longer boot following a kernel update and usually exit with `Kernel panic: VFS: unable to mount root fs`. In this case, the kernel parameter `ide=reverse` must be passed when booting to reverse this disk detection process. See Section 1.1.1 on page 8. To apply this parameter universally when using YaST, enter it in the boot configuration. See the *User Guide*.

Caution

Only the controllers activated in the BIOS are detectable. In particular, subsequently activating or deactivating the controllers in the BIOS has a direct effect on the device names. Use caution or risk being unable to boot the system.

Caution

*Technical Explanation*The controller sequence depends on the motherboard. Each manufacturer wires its supplementary controllers differently. The `lspci` shows this sequence. If the Promise controller is listed before the standard IDE controller, the kernel parameter `ide=reverse` is required after updating. With the previous kernel (without direct Promise support), the controller was ignored so the standard IDE controller was detected first. The first disk was then `/dev/hda`. With the new kernel, the Promise controller is detected immediately and its (up to four) disks are registered as `/dev/hda`, `/dev/hdb`, `/dev/hdc`, and `/dev/hdd`. The previous `/dev/hda` disk becomes `/dev/hde` so is no longer detectable in the boot process.

2.1.2 Updating with YaST

Following the preparation procedure outlined in Section 2.1.1 on page 40, you can now boot:

1. Boot the system for the installation (see *User Guide*). In YaST, choose a language then select 'Update Existing System'. Do not select 'New Installation'.
2. YaST will determine whether there are several root partitions. If there is only one, continue with the next step. If there are several, select the right partition and confirm with 'Next' (`/dev/hda7` was selected in the example in Section 2.1.1 on page 40). YaST reads the *old* `fstab` on this partition to analyze and mount the file systems listed there.
3. Then you have the possibility to make a backup copy of the system files during the update. This option slows down the update process. Use this option if you do not have a recent system backup.
4. In the following dialog, either choose to update only the software that is already installed or to add important new software components to the system (upgrade mode). It is advisable to accept the suggested composition (e.g., 'Standard System'). Adjustments can be made later with YaST.

2.1.3 Manual Update

Updating the Base System

Because basic system components, such as libraries, must be exchanged when updating a base system, an update cannot be run from within a currently running Linux system. First, set up the update environment. This is normally done using the CD or DVD or with a custom boot disk. If you are carrying out manual modifications during the update or prefer to perform the entire update with YaST in text mode, follow the steps already described in detail in Section 1.1 on page 8. Below is a summary of this procedure.

1. Immediately after booting the kernel from the boot disk or from the CD or DVD, linuxrc automatically starts.
2. In linuxrc, specify the language and keyboard settings under 'Settings' and click 'OK' to confirm each setting.

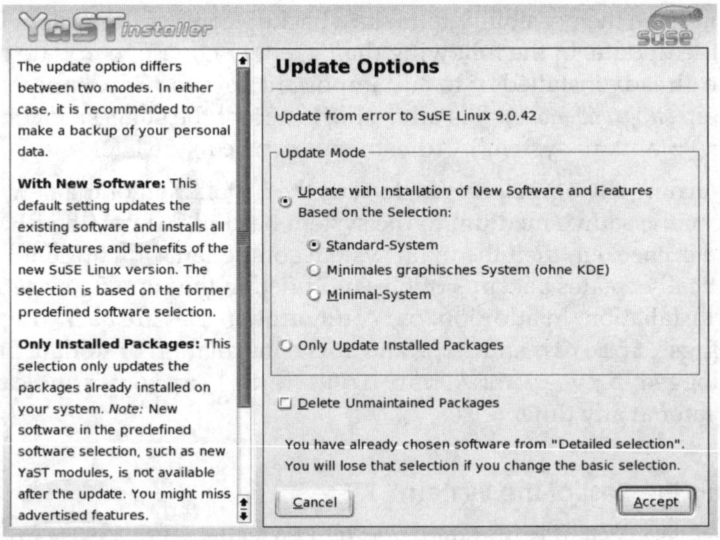

Figure 2.1: Updating the Software

3. You might need to load the required hardware and software drivers via 'Kernel Modules'. See Section 1.1.2 on page 9 for more details of how to proceed and Section 11.4.4 on page 234 for a description of linuxrc.

4. Go to 'Start Installation or System' -> 'Start Installation or Update' to select the source medium (see 11.4.6 on page 235).

5. The installation environment is loaded from linuxrc then YaST starts.

Following the selection of a language and the hardware detection by YaST, select 'Update Existing System' in the YaST opening screen.

Next, YaST attempts to determine the root partition and displays the result for selection or confirmation. Select your root partition from the list (example: `/dev/hda2`). In this way, prompt YaST to read the *old* `fstab` from this partition. YaST will analyze and mount the file systems listed there.

Then you have the possibility to make a backup copy of the system files during the update. In the following dialog, either choose to update only the software already installed or to add important new software components to the system (*upgrade mode*). It is advisable to accept the suggested composition (e.g., 'Standard system'). Adjustments can be made later with YaST.

In the warning dialog, select 'Yes' to start the installation of the new software from the source medium to the system hard disk. First, the RPM database is checked, then the main system components are updated. YaST automatically creates backups of files modified in the running system since the last installation. In addition, old configuration files are backed up with the endings `.rpmorig` and `.rpmsave`. The installation or update procedure is logged in `/var/adm/inst-log/installation-*` and can be viewed later at any time.

Updating the Rest of the System

After the base system is updated, you will be switched to YaST's update mode. This mode allows you to tailor the rest of the system update to your needs. Complete the procedure as you would a new installation. Among other things, select a new kernel. The available options are presented by YaST.

Possible Problems

If certain shell environments no longer behave as expected after the update, check to see if the current *dot* files in the home directory are still compatible with your system. If not, use the current versions in `/etc/skel`. For example, `cp /etc/skel/.profile  /.profile`

2.1.4 Updating Individual Packages

Regardless of your overall updated environment, you can always update individual packages. From this point on, however, it is your responsibility to ensure that your system remains consistent. Update advice can be found at `http://www.suse.de/en/support/download/updates/`.

Select components from the YaST package selection list according to your needs. If you select a package essential for the overall operation of the system, YaST issues a warning. Such packages should be updated only in the update mode. For instance, numerous packages contain *shared libraries*. If you update these programs and applications in the running system, things might malfunction.

2.2 Software Changes from Version to Version

The individual aspects changed from version to version are outlined in the following sections in detail. This summary indicates, for example, whether basic settings have been completely reconfigured, whether configuration files have been moved to other places, or whether common applications have been significantly changed. The modifications that affect the daily use of the system at either the user level or the administrator level are mentioned below. The list is by no means complete.

Problems and special issues of the respective versions are published online as they are identified. See the links listed below. Important updates of individual packages can be accessed at `http://www.suse.de/en/support/download/`.

2.2.1 From 7.3 to 8.0

Problems and Special Issues:
`http://portal.suse.com/sdb/en/2002/04/bugs80.html`

- Boot disks are shipped only as floppy images (previously `disks` directory, now `boot`). A boot disk is only required if you cannot boot from CD. Depending on your hardware or installation preferences, you can also create floppies from the images `modules1`, `modules2`, etc. Read Section 1.4 on page 17 or Section 1.4.2 on page 19 for information about creating these disks.
- YaST2 has completely replaced YaST1, even in the text and console mode. When the text says *YaST*, it always refers to the new version.
- Some BIOSes require the kernel parameter `realmode-power-off`, which was known as `real-mode-poweroff` up to kernel version 2.4.12.
- The `START` variables of the `rc.config` for launching services are no longer required. Services are started if the respective links exist in the runlevel directories. These links are created with `insserv`.
- System services are configured by variable lines in the files located under `/etc/sysconfig`. The settings in `/etc/rc.config.d` will be applied to the update.

- /etc/init.d/boot has been split into several scripts and moved to other packages, where this made sense (see kbd, isapnp, lvm, etc.). See Section 12.4 on page 251.
- Some changes have been made in the network area. Read Section 13.4 on page 289 for more information.
- logrotate is used to manage log files. /etc/logfiles is no longer necessary. See Section 11.2.3 on page 222.
- The root login over telnet or rlogin can be permitted by entering settings in the files under /etc/pam.d. Due to security risks, ROOT_LOGIN_REMOTE can no longer be set to yes.
- PASSWD_USE_CRACKLIB can be activated with YaST.
- If NIS files for autofs will be distributed over NIS, the YaST NIS client module should be used for configuration. There, select 'Start Automounter'. This aspect has made the USE_NIS_FOR_AUTOFS variable obsolete.
- The locate tool for quickly finding files is no longer included in the standard software installation. If desired, install it (find-locate). If installed, the updatedb process will be started automatically about fifteen minutes after the computer is booted, just as in previous versions.
- The mouse support for pine is activated. This means that pine in an xterm can also be operated with a mouse (or a similar input device) by clicking the menu items. This, however, also means that cut and paste only works by using Shift when the mouse support is activated. This is deactivated with a new installation. It is, however, not excluded that the function is still active following an update (when an older ~/.pinerc is present). The option enable-mouse-in-xterm can be deactivated in the configuration for pine.

2.2.2 From 8.0 to 8.1

Problems and Special Issues:

http://portal.suse.com/sdb/en/2002/10/bugs81.html

- Changes in the user and group names: To comply with UnitedLinux, some entries in /etc/passwd and /etc/group have been adjusted accordingly.

- ▷ Changed users: ftp is now in group ftp (not in daemon).
- ▷ Renamed groups: www (was wwwadmin), games (was game).
- ▷ New groups: ftp (with GID 50), floppy (with GID 19), cdrom (with GID 20), console (with GID 21), utmp (with GID 22).

- Changes related to FHS (see Section 11.1.2 on page 220):
  - ▷ An example environment for HTTPD (Apache) is created at /srv/www (formerly /usr/local/httpd).
  - ▷ An example environment for FTP is created at /srv/ftp (formerly /usr/local/ftp). ftpdir is required for this purpose.
- To ease access to the desired software, the single packages are not stored in a few bulky series any more, but rather in accessible *RPM groups*. This also means the CDs no longer contain cryptic directories under suse, but only few directories named after architectures, for example, ppc, i586, or noarch.
- The installation status of the following programs has changed for a new installation:
  - ▷ The boot loader GRUB, which offers more possibilities than LILO, is installed by default. However, LILO is retained if the system is updated.
  - ▷ The mailer postfix instead of sendmail.
  - ▷ The modern mailing list application mailman is installed instead of majordomo.
  - ▷ Select harden_suse manually if needed and read the enclosed documentation.
- Split packages: rpm to rpm and rpm-devel, popt to popt and popt-devel, libz to zlib and zlib-devel.
  yast2-trans-* is now split by languages: yast2-trans-cs (Czech), yast2-trans-de (German), yast2-trans-es (Spanish), etc. Not all languages are installed to save hard disk space. Install the required packages for the YaST language support as needed.
- Renamed packages: bzip to bzip2.
- Packages no longer supplied: openldap, use openldap2; su1, use sudo.

2.2.3 From 8.1 to 8.2

Problems and Special Issues:
`http://portal.suse.com/sdb/en/2003/04/bugs82.html`

- 3D support for nVidia-based graphics cards (changes): The RPM `NVIDIA_GLX/NVIDIA_kernel` (including the script `switch2nvidia_glx`) is no longer included. Download the nVidia installer for `Linux IA32` from the nVidia web site (`http://www.nvidia.com`), install the driver with this installer, and use SaX2 or YaST to activate 3D support.
- During a new installation, xinetd is installed instead of inetd and configured with secure values. See directory `/etc/xinetd.d`. However, during a system update, inetd is retained.
- The current PostgreSQL version is 7.3. When switching from version 7.2.x, perform a *dump/restore* with `pg_dump`. If your application queries the system catalogs, additional adaptions are necessary, as schemas were introduced in version 7.3. For more information, visit `http://www.ca.postgresql.org/docs/momjian/upgrade_tips_7.3`.
- Version 4 of stunnel no longer supports any command-line options. However, the enclosed script `/usr/sbin/stunnel3_wrapper` can convert the command-line options into a configuration file that is suitable for stunnel and use it when the program is started (replace `OPTIONS` with your options):

  ```
  /usr/sbin/stunnel3_wrapper stunnel OPTIONS
  ```

  The generated configuration file will be printed to the default output, enabling the use of these specifications for generating a permanent configuration file.
- If your own applications depend on the directory `jade_dsl` and the files previously installed there, adapt them to the new directory `/usr/share/sgml/openjade` or create a link as `root`:

  openjade (`openjade`) is the DSSSL engine currently used instead of jade (`jade_dsl`) when db2x.sh (`docbook-toys`) is run. For compatibility reasons, the individual programs are also available without the prefix `o`.

  In case you own applications depend on the directory `jade_dsl` and the files previously installed there, the applications must be adapted to the new directory /usr/share/sgml/openjade or a link can be created as root:

```
cd /usr/share/sgml rm jade_dsl ln -s openjade jade_dsl
```

To avoid a conflict with rzsz, the command-line tool sx continues to be called s2x, sgml2xml, or osx.

2.2.4 From 8.2 to 9.0

Problems and Special Issues:
http://portal.suse.com/sdb/en/2003/07/bugs90.html

- Version 4 of the RPM package manager is now available. The functionality for building packages has been shifted to the separate program rpmbuild. rpm continues to be used for the installation, updates, and database queries. See Section 2.3 on page 52.
- The package foomatic-filters is now available for printing. The content was split from the cups-drivers, as it can be used for printing even if CUPS is not installed. In this way, YaST supports configurations that are independent of the print system (CUPS, LPRng). The configuration file for this package is /etc/foomatic/filter.conf.
- The packages foomatic-filters and cups-drivers are now also required for LPRng and lpdfilter.
- The XML resources of the enclosed software packages can be accessed by means of the entries in /etc/xml/suse-catalog.xml. This file should not be edited with xmlcatalog, as this would result in the deletion of structural comments required for correct updates. /etc/xml/suse-catalog.xml is accessed by means of a nextCatalog statement in /etc/xml/catalog, enabling XML tools like xmllint or xsltproc to find the local resources automatically.

2.2.5 From 9.0 to 9.1

Problems and Special Issues:
http://sdb.suse.de/sdb/de/html/bugs91.html

- SUSE LINUX is now based entirely on kernel 2.6. The predecessor version 2.4 should no longer be used, as the enclosed applications may not work with kernel 2.4. Moreover, note the following details:
  - ▷ The loading of modules is now configured by means of the file `/etc/modprobe.conf`. The file `/etc/modules.conf` is obsolete. YaST will try to convert the file (see also script `/sbin/generate-modprobe.conf`).
  - ▷ Modules now have the suffix `.ko`.
  - ▷ The module `ide-scsi` is no longer needed for burning CDs.
  - ▷ The prefix `snd_` has been removed from the ALSA sound module options.
  - ▷ `sysfs` now complements the `/proc` file system.
  - ▷ The power management (especially ACPI) has been improved and can now be configured by means of a YaST module.
- See the above-mentioned portal articles for changes in the input devices.
- Applications linked against NGPT (*Next Generation POSIX Threading*) do not work with glibc 2.3.x. All affected applications that are not shipped with SUSE LINUX must be compiled with linuxthreads or with NPTL (*Native POSIX Thread Library*). NPTL is preferred, as this is the standard for the future.

  If NPTL causes difficulties, the older linuxthreads implementation can be used by setting the following environment variable (replace ⟨*kernel-version*⟩ with the version number of the respective kernel):

  ```
  LD_ASSUME_KERNEL=kernel-version
  ```

  The following version numbers are possible:

  2.2.5 (i386, s390): linuxthreads without floating stacks

  2.4.1 (AMD64, IPF, s390x, i686): linuxthread with floating stacks

  Notes regarding the kernel and linuxthreads with floating stacks:

  Applications using `errno`, `h_errno`, and `_res` must include the header files (`errno.h`, `netdb.h`, and `resolv.h`) with `#include`. For C++ programs with multithread support that use *thread cancellation*, the environment variable `LD_ASSUME_KERNEL=2.4.1` must be used to prompt the use of the linuxthreads library.

- SUSE LINUX 9.1 contains the thread package NPTL (*Native POSIX Thread Library*). NPTL is binary-compatible with the older linuxthreads library. However, areas in which linuxthreads violates the POSIX standard require NPTL adaptions. This includes the following: signal handling, `getpid` returns the same value in all threads, and thread handlers registered with pthread_atfork do not work if `vfork` is used.
- Currently, the default encoding for the system is `UTF-8`. Thus, when performing a standard installation, a locale is set with `.UTF-8` encoding (e.g., `en_US.UTF-8`).
- In the default setting, shell tools from the `coreutils` package (`tail`, `chown`, `head`, `sort`, etc.) no longer comply with the POSIX standard of 1992 but with the POSIX standard of 2001 (*Single UNIX Specification, version 3 == IEEE Std 1003.1-2001 == ISO/IEC 9945:2002*). The old behavior can be forced with an environment variable:

  ```
  _POSIX2_VERSION=199209
  ```

  The new value is 200112 and is used the default for `_POSIX2_-VERSION`. The SUS standard can be reviewed at the following URL (free of charge, but registration is required):

  `http://www.unix.org`

***Table 2.1:** Comparison POSIX 1992 vs. POSIX 2001*

POSIX 1992	POSIX 2001
chown tux.users	chown tux:users
tail +3	tail -n +3
head -1	head -n 1
sort +3	sort -k +3
nice -10	nice -n 10
split -10	split -l 10

> **Note**
>
> Third-party software may not yet comply with the new standard. In this case, set the environment variable as described above: `_POSIX2_VERSION=199209`.

- `/etc/gshadow` has been abandoned and removed, as this file is superfluous for the following reasons:
  - It is not supported by glibc.
  - There is no official interface for this file; even the shadow suite does not contain such an interface.
  - Most tools that check the group password do not support the file and ignore it for the said reasons.
- The FHS (see 11.1.2 on page 220) now requires XML resources (DTDs, stylesheets, etc.) to be installed in `/usr/share/xml`. Therefore, some directories are no longer available in `/usr/share/sgml`. If you encounter problems, modify your scripts or makefiles or use the official catalogs (especially `/etc/xml/catalog` or `/etc/sgml/catalog`).

2.3 RPM — the Package Manager

In SUSE LINUX, RPM (Red Hat Package Manager) is used for managing the software packages. Its main programs are `rpm` and `rpmbuild`. The powerful RPM database can be queried by the users, the system administrators, and package builders for detailed information about the installed software.

Essentially, `rpm` has five modes: installing, uninstalling, or updating software packages; rebuilding the RPM database; querying RPM bases or individual RPM archives; integrity checks of packages; and signing packages. `rpmbuild` can be used to build installable packages from pristine sources.

Installable RPM archives are packed in a special binary format. These archives consist of the program files to install and certain meta information used during the installation by `rpm` to configure the software package or stored in the RPM database for documentation purposes. RPM archives normally have the extension `.rpm`.

rpm can be used to administer LSB-compliant packages. Refer to Section 11.1.1 on page 220 for more information about LSB.

Note

For a number of packages, the components needed for software development (libraries, headers, include files, etc.) have been put into separate packages. These development packages are only needed if you want to compile software *yourself*, for example, the most recent GNOME packages. They can be identified by the name extension -devel, such as the packages alsa-devel, gimp-devel, and kdelibs-devel.

Note

2.3.1 Verifying Package Authenticity

SUSE LINUX RPM packages have a GnuPG signature:

```
1024D/9C800ACA 2000-10-19 SuSE Package Signing Key <build@suse.de>
Key fingerprint = 79C1 79B2 E1C8 20C1 890F  9994 A84E DAE8 9C80 0ACA
```

The command rpm --checksig apache-1.3.12.rpm can be used to verify the signature of an RPM package to determine whether it really originates from SUSE or from another trustworthy facility. This is especially recommended for update packages from the Internet. The SUSE public package signature key normally resides in /root/.gnupg/. Since version 8.1, the key is additionally located in the directory /usr/lib/rpm/gnupg/ to enable normal users to verify the signature of RPM packages.

2.3.2 Managing Packages: Install, Update, and Uninstall

Normally, the installation of an RPM archive is quite simple: rpm -i <package>.rpm With this command, the package will be installed — but only if its dependencies are fulfilled and there are no conflicts with other packages. With an error message, rpm requests those packages that need to be installed to meet dependency requirements. In the background, the RPM database ensures that no conflicts arise — a specific file can only belong to one package. By choosing different options, you can force rpm to ignore these defaults, but this is only for experts. Otherwise, risk compromising the integrity of the system and possibly jeopardize the ability to update the system.

The options `-U` or `--upgrade` and `-F` or `--freshen` can be used to update a package.

```
rpm -F <package>.rpm
```

This command will remove the files of the old version and immediately install the new files. The difference between the two versions is that `-U` installs packages that previously did not exist in the system, but `-F` merely updates previously installed packages. When updating, `rpm` updates configuration files carefully using the following strategy:

- If a configuration file was not changed by the system administrator, `rpm` will install the new version of the appropriate file. No action by the system administrator is required.
- If a configuration file was changed by the system administrator before the update, `rpm` saves the changed file with the extension `.rpmorig` or `.rpmsave` (backup file) and installs the version from the new package, but only if the originally installed file and the newer version are different. If this is the case, compare the backup file (`.rpmorig` or `.rpmsave`) with the newly installed file and make your changes again in the new file. Afterwards, be sure to delete all `.rpmorig` and `.rpmsave` files to avoid problems with future updates.
- `.rpmnew` files appear if the configuration file already exists *and* if the `noreplace` label was specified in the `.spec` file.

Following an update, `.rpmsave` and `.rpmnew` files should be removed after comparing them, so they do not obstruct future updates. The `.rpmorig` extension is assigned if the file has not previously been recognized by the RPM database.

Otherwise, `.rpmsave` is used. In other words, `.rpmorig` results from updating from a foreign format to RPM. `.rpmsave` results from updating from an older RPM to a newer RPM. `.rpmnew` does not disclose any information as to whether the system administrator has made any changes to the configuration file. A list of these files is available in `/var/adm/rpmconfigcheck`. Some configuration files (like `/etc/httpd/httpd.conf`) are not overwritten to allow continued operation.

The `-U` switch is *not* just an equivalent to uninstalling with the `-e` option and installing with the `-i` option. Use `-U` whenever possible.

Note

Following every update, check the backup copies with the extension `.rpmorig` or `.rpmsave`, which are created by `rpm`. These are your old configuration files. If necessary, adopt your modifications from the backup copies to the new configuration file then delete the old files with the extension `.rpmorig` or `.rpmsave`.

Note

To remove a package, enter `rpm -e` ⟨*package*⟩. `rpm` will only delete the package if there are no unresolved dependencies. It is theoretically impossible to delete Tcl/Tk, for example, as long as another application requires it. Even in this case, RPM calls for assistance from the database. If such a deletion is — for whatever reason and under unusual circumstances — impossible, even if *no* additional dependencies exist, it may be helpful to rebuild the RPM database using the option `--rebuilddb`.

2.3.3 RPM and Patches

To guarantee the operational security of a system, update packages must be installed in the system from time to time. Previously, a bug in a package could only be eliminated by replacing the entire package. Large packages with small bugs could easily result in large amounts of data. However, since SUSE 8.1, the SUSE RPM offers a new feature enabling the installation of patches in packages.

The most important considerations are demonstrated using pine as an example:

- Is the patch RPM suitable for my system?

  To check this, first query the installed version of the package. For pine, this can be done with

  ```
  rpm -q pine
  pine-4.44-188
  ```

  Then check if the patch RPM is suitable for this version of pine:

  ```
  rpm -qp --basedon pine-4.44-224.i586.patch.rpm
  pine = 4.44-188
  pine = 4.44-195
  pine = 4.44-207
  ```

This patch is suitable for three different versions of pine. The installed version in the example is also listed, so the patch can be installed.

- Which files are replaced by the patch?

  The files affected by a patch can easily be seen in the patch RPM. The `rpm` parameter `-P` allows selection of special patch features. Display the list of files with the following command:

  ```
  rpm -qpPl pine-4.44-224.i586.patch.rpm
  /etc/pine.conf
  /etc/pine.conf.fixed
  /usr/bin/pine
  ```

  or, if the patch is already installed, with the following command:

  ```
  rpm -qPl pine
  /etc/pine.conf
  /etc/pine.conf.fixed
  /usr/bin/pine
  ```

- How can a patch RPM be installed in the system?

  Patch RPMs are used just like normal RPMs. The only difference is that a suitable RPM must already be installed.

- Which patches are already installed in the system and for which package versions?

  A list of all patches installed in the system can be displayed with the command `rpm -qPa`. If only one patch is installed in a new system (as in this example), the list appear as follows:

  ```
  rpm -qPa
  pine-4.44-224
  ```

  If, at a later date, you want to know which package version was originally installed, this information is also available in the RPM database. For `pine`, this information can be displayed with the following command:

  ```
  rpm -q --basedon pine
  pine = 4.44-188
  ```

More information, including information about the patch feature of RPM, is available in `man rpm` and in `man rpmbuild`.

2.3.4 RPM Queries

With the `-q` option, `rpm` initiates queries, making it possible to inspect an RPM archive (by adding the option `-p`) and also to query the RPM database of installed packages. Several switches are available to specify the type of information required (see Table 2.2).

***Table 2.2:** The Most Important RPM Query Options (-q [-p] ...package)*

`-i`	Package information
`-l`	File list
`-f` ⟨*FILE*⟩	Query a package owned by ⟨*FILE*⟩ (the full path must be specified with ⟨*FILE*⟩)
`-s`	File list with status information (implies `-l`)
`-d`	List only documentation files (implies `-l`)
`-c`	List only configuration files (implies `-l`)
`--dump`	File list with complete details (to be used with `-l`, `-c`, or `-d`)
`--provides`	List features of the package that another package can request with `--requires`
`--requires`, `-R`	Capabilities the package requires
`--scripts`	Installation scripts (preinstall, postinstall, uninstall)

For example, the command `rpm -q -i wget` displays the information shown in Output 2.2.

***Example 2.2:** rpm -q -i wget*

```
Name        :wget                    Relocations: (not relocateable)
Version     :1.8.2                   Vendor: SuSE Linux AG, Nuernberg, Germany
Release     :301                     Build Date: Di 23 Sep 2003 20:26:38 CEST
Install date:Mi 08 Okt 2003 11:46:31 CEST Build Host: levi.suse.de
Group       :Productivity/Networking/Web/Utilities
Source RPM  :wget-1.8.2-301.src.rpm
Size        :1333235                           License: GPL
Signature   :DSA/SHA1, Di 23 Sep 2003 22:13:12 CEST, Key ID a84edae89c800aca
Packager    :http://www.suse.de/feedback
```

```
URL          :http://wget.sunsite.dk/
Summary      :A tool for mirroring FTP and HTTP servers
Description :
Wget enables you to retrieve WWW documents or FTP files from a server.
This can be done in script files or via the command line.
[...]
```

The option `-f` only works if you specify the complete file name with its full path. Provide as many file names as desired. For example, the following command

```
rpm -q -f /bin/rpm /usr/bin/wget
```

results in:

```
rpm-3.0.3-3
wget-1.5.3-55
```

If only part of the file name is known, use a shell script as shown in File 2.3. Pass the partial file name to the script shown as a parameter when running it.

Example 2.3: *Script to Search for Packages*

```
#! /bin/sh
for i in $(rpm -q -a -l | grep  $1); do
    echo "\"$i\" is in package:"
    rpm -q -f $i
    echo ""
done
```

The command `rpm -q --changelog rpm` displays a detailed list of information (updates, configuration, modifications, etc.) about a specific package. This example shows information about the package `rpm`. However, only the last five change entries in the RPM database are listed. All entries (dating back the last two years) are included in the package itself. This query only works if CD 1 is mounted at `/media/cdrom/`:

```
rpm -qp --changelog /media/cdrom/suse/i586/rpm-3*.rpm
```

With the help of the installed RPM database, verification checks can be made. These checks are initiated with the option `-V`, `-y`, or `--verify`. With this option, `rpm` shows all files in a package that have been changed since installation. `rpm` uses eight character symbols to give some hints about the following changes:

Table 2.3: RPM Verify Options

5	MD5 check sum
S	File size
L	Symbolic link
T	Modification time
D	Major and minor device numbers
U	Owner
G	Group
M	Mode (permissions and file type)

In the case of configuration files, the letter c is printed. Example for changes to /etc/wgetrc (wget):

```
rpm -V wget
S.5....T c /etc/wgetrc
```

The files of the RPM database are placed in /var/lib/rpm. If the partition /usr/ has a size of 1 GB, this database can occupy nearly 30 MB, especially after a complete update. If the database is much larger than expected, it is useful to rebuild the database with the option --rebuilddb. Before doing this, make a backup of the old database. The cron script cron.daily makes daily copies of the database (packed with gzip) and stores them in /var/adm/backup/rpmdb. The number of copies is controlled by the variable MAX_RPMDB_BACKUPS (default: 5) in /etc/sysconfig/backup. The size of a single backup is approximately 3 MB for 1 GB in /usr.

2.3.5 Installing and Compiling Source Packages

All source packages of SUSE LINUX carry a .src.rpm extension (source RPM).

Note

Source packages can be installed with YaST, like any other package. They will not, however, be marked as installed ([i]) in the package manager. This is because the source packages are not entered in the RPM database. Only *installed* operating system software is listed in the RPM database.

Note

The following directories must be available for `rpm` and `rpmbuild` in `/usr/src/packages` (unless you specified custom settings in a file like `/etc/rpmrc`):

SOURCES/ for the original sources (`.tar.gz` files, etc.) and for distribution-specific adjustments (`.dif` files)

SPECS/ for the *.spec* files, similar to a meta Makefile, which control the *build* process

BUILD/ all the sources are unpacked, patched, and compiled in this directory

RPMS/ where the completed *binary* packages are stored

SRPMS/ here are the *source* RPMs

When you install a source package with YaST, all the necessary components will be installed in `/usr/src/packages/`: the sources and the adjustments in `SOURCES/` and the relevant `.spec` file in `SPECS/`.

Caution

Do not experiment with system components (`glibc`, `rpm`, `sysvinit`, etc.), as this endangers the operability of your system.

Caution

The following example uses the `wget.src.rpm` package. After installing the package with YaST, you should have the following files:

```
/usr/src/packages/SPECS/wget.spec
/usr/src/packages/SOURCES/wget-1.4.5.dif
/usr/src/packages/SOURCES/wget-1.4.5.tar.gz
```

`rpmbuild -b ⟨X⟩ /usr/src/packages/SPECS/wget.spec` starts the compilation. ⟨X⟩ is a wild card for various stages of the build process (see the output of `--help` or the RPM documentation for details). The following is merely a brief explanation:

-bp Prepare sources in `/usr/src/packages/BUILD`: unpack and patch.

-bc Do the same as `-bp`, but with additional compilation.

-bi Do the same as `-bp`, but with additional installation of the built software. Caution: if the package does not support the BuildRoot feature, you might overwrite configuration files.

-bb Do the same as `-bi`, but with the additional creation of the binary package. If the compile was successful, the binary should be in `/usr/src/packages/RPMS`.

-ba Do the same as `-bb`, but with the additional creation of the source RPM. If the compilation was successful, the binary should be in `/usr/src/packages/SRPMS`.

--short-circuit Allows skipping specific steps.

The binary RPM created can now be installed with `rpm -i` or, preferably, with `rpm -U`. Installation with `rpm` makes it appear in the RPM database.

2.3.6 Compiling RPM Packages with build

The danger with many packages is that unwanted files are added to the running system during the build process. To prevent this, use `build`, which creates a defined environment in which the package is built. To establish this *chroot* environment, the `build` script must be provided with a complete package tree. This tree can be made available on the hard disk, via NFS, or from DVD. The respective position is specified with `build --rpms <path>`. Unlike `rpm`, the `build` command looks for the SPEC file in the source directory. To build wget anew (like in the above example) with the DVD mounted in the system under `/media/dvd`, use the following commands as `root`:

```
cd /usr/src/packages/SOURCES/
mv ../SPECS/wget.spec .
build --rpms /media/dvd/suse/ wget.spec
```

Subsequently, a minimum environment will be established at `/var/tmp/build-root`. The package will be built in this environment. Upon completion, the resulting packages are located in `/var/tmp/build-root/usr/src/packages/RPMS`.

The `build` script offers a number of additional options. For example, cause the script to prefer your own RPMs, omit the initialization of the build environment, or limit the `rpm` command to one of the above-mentioned stages. Access additional information can be accessed with `build --help` and `man build`.

2.3.7 Tools for RPM Archives and the RPM Database

Midnight Commander (`mc`) can display the contents of RPM archives and copy parts of them. It represents archives as virtual file systems, offering all usual menu options of Midnight Commander: the `HEADER` information can be displayed with F3, the archive structure can be viewed with the cursor keys and Enter, and archive components can be copied with F5.

A front-end for rpm is also available for Emacs. KDE offers the kpackage tool. GNOME offers gnorpm.

Using the Alien (`alien`) Perl script, it is possible to convert or install an *alien* binary package. This tries to convert *old* TGZ archives to RPM before installing. This way, the RPM database can keep track of such a package after it has been installed. Beware: `alien` is still *alpha* software, according to its author — even if it already has a high version number.

Part II

Configuration

YaST in Text Mode (ncurses)

This chapter is mainly intended for system administrators and experts who do not run an X server on their systems and depend on the text-based installation tool. It provides basic information about starting and operating YaST in text mode (ncurses). It also explains how to update your system online automatically.

3.1 Usage

Basically, the entire program can be controlled with Tab, Alt-Tab, Space, the arrow keys (↑ and ↓), Enter, and shortcuts.

3.1.1 The YaST Control Center

When YaST is started in text mode, the YaST Control Center appears first (see Figure 3.1).

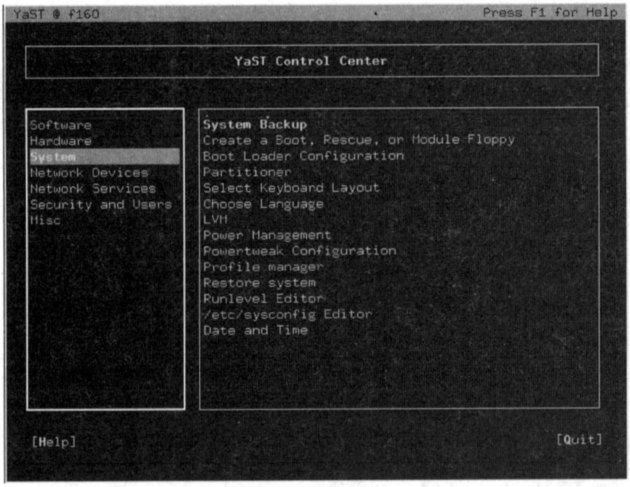

Figure 3.1: Main Window of YaST in Text Mode

The main window consists of three areas. The left frame, which is surrounded by a thick white border, features the categories to which the various modules belong. The active category is indicated by a colored background. The right frame, which is surrounded by a thin white border, provides an overview of the modules available in the active category. The bottom frame contains the buttons for 'Help' and 'Exit'.

When the YaST Control Center is started, the category 'Software' is selected automatically. Use ↓ and ↑ to change the category. To start a module from the selected category, press →. The module selection now appears with a thick border. Use ↓ and ↑ to select the desired module. Keep the arrow keys pressed to scroll through the list of available modules. When a module is selected, the module title appears with a colorful background and a brief description is displayed in the bottom frame.

Press Enter to start the desired module. Various buttons or selection fields in the module contain a letter with a different color (yellow by default). Use Alt-yellow_letter to select a button directly instead of navigating there with Tab. Exit the YaST Control Center by pressing the 'Exit' button or by selecting 'Exit' in the category overview and pressing Enter.

3.1.2 The YaST Modules

The following description of the control elements in the YaST modules assumes that all function keys and Alt key combinations work and are not assigned different global functions. Read Section 3.2 on the next page for information on possible exceptions.

Navigation among Buttons and Selection Lists
Use Tab and Alt-Tab or Shift-Tab to navigate among the buttons and the frames containing selection lists.

Navigation in Selection Lists Use the arrow keys (↑ and ↓) to navigate among the individual elements in an active frame containing a selection list (e.g., between the individual modules of a module group in the Control Center). If individual entries within a frame exceed its width, use Shift-→ or Shift-← to scroll horizontally to the right and to the left. Alternatively, use Ctrl-E or Ctrl-A. This combination can also be used if using → or ← would result in changing the active frame or the current selection list, as in the Control Center.

Buttons, Radio Buttons, and Check Boxes
To select buttons with empty square brackets (check boxes) or empty parentheses (radio buttons), press Space or Enter. Alternatively, radio buttons and check boxes can be selected directly with Alt-yellow_letter. In this case, you do not need to confirm with Enter. If you navigate to an item with Tab, press Enter to execute the selected action or activate the respective menu item (see Figure 3.2 on the following page).

Function Keys The F keys (F1 to F12) enable quick access to the various buttons. Which function keys are actually mapped to which buttons depends on the active YaST module, as the different modules offer different buttons (Details, Info, Add, Delete, etc.). Use F10 for 'OK', 'Next', and 'Finish'. Press F1 to access the YaST, help which shows the functions mapped to the individual F keys.

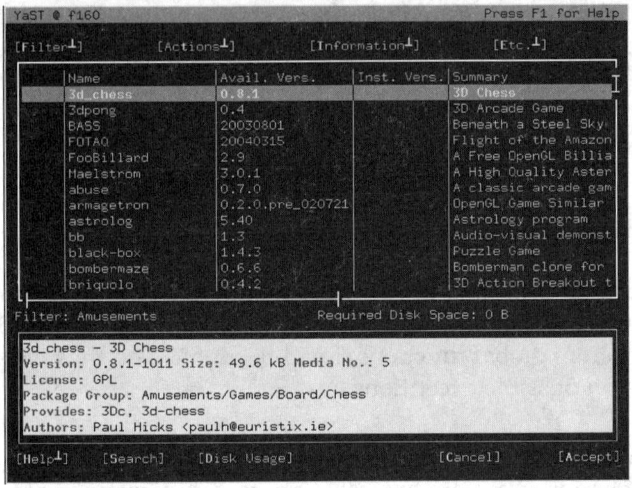

Figure 3.2: The Software Installation Module

3.2 Restriction of Key Combinations

If your window manager uses global Alt combinations, the Alt combinations in YaST might not work. Moreover, keys like Alt or Shift might be occupied by the settings of the terminal.

Replacing Alt with Esc: Alt shortcuts can be executed with Esc instead of Alt. For example, Esc–H replaces Alt–H.

Backward and Forward Navigation with Ctrl–F and Ctrl–B:
If the Alt and Shift combinations are occupied by the window manager or the terminal, use the combinations Ctrl–F (forward) and Ctrl–B (backward) instead.

Restriction of Function Keys: The F keys are also used for functions. Certain function keys might be occupied by the terminal and may not be available for YaST. However, the Alt key combinations and F keys should always be fully available on a pure text console.

3.3 Starting the Individual Modules

To save time, the individual YaST modules can be started directly. To start the modules, enter yast <module_name>. The network module, for example, is started with `yast lan`. A list of all module names available on your system can be viewed with the command `yast -l` or `yast --list`.

3.4 YaST Online Update

3.4.1 The YOU Module

The YaST Online Update (YOU) module can be started from the command line as `root` like any other YaST module:

```
yast online_update .url <url>
```

`yast online_update` starts the respective module. The option `url` can be used to specify the server (local or on the Internet) from which YOU should get all information and patches. If you do not specify a server when starting the module, select the server or the directory in the YaST dialog. The usage of the dialog corresponds to the usage of the graphical YaST module as described in the *User Guide*. Like in its graphical counterpart, cronjobs for automating the update can be configured with 'Configure Fully Automatic Update'.

3.4.2 Online Update from the Command Line

Using the command-line tool online_update, the system can be updated automatically (e.g., by means of scripts). For instance, you may want your system to search a specific server for updates and download the patches and patch information at a specified time in regular intervals. However, you may not want the patches to be installed automatically; rather, you may want to review the patches and select the patches for installation at a later time.

- Configure a cronjob that executes the following command:

```
online_update -u <URL> -g <type_specification>
```

`-u` introduces the base URL of the directory tree from which the patches should be downloaded. The following protocols are supported: `http`, `ftp`, `smb`, `nfs`, `cd`, `dvd`, and `dir`. `-g` downloads the patches to a local directory without installing them. Optionally, filter the patches by specifying the type: `security`, `recommended`, or `optional`. If no filter is specified, online_update downloads all new `security` and `recommended` patches.

- The downloaded packages can be installed immediately without reviewing the individual patches. online_update saves the patches in the directory `/var/lib/YaST2/you/mnt/`. To install the patches, execute the following command:

```
online_update -u /var/lib/YaST2/you/mnt/ -i
```

The parameter `-u` specifies the (local) URL of the patches to install. `-i` starts the installation procedure.

- To review the downloaded patches prior to the installation, start the YOU dialog:

```
yast online_update .url /var/lib/YaST2/you/mnt/
```

YOU starts and uses the local directory containing the downloaded patches instead of a remote directory on the Internet. Select the patches to install in the same way as packages for installation in the package manager.

For more information about online_update, enter `online_update -h`.

The X Window System

The X Window System (X11) is the de facto standard for graphical user interfaces in UNIX. Moreover, X11 is network-based, enabling applications started on one host to be displayed on another host connected over any kind of network (LAN or Internet).

This chapter presents optimization possibilities for your X Window System environment, background information about the use of fonts in SUSE LINUX, and the configuration of OpenGL and 3D. The YaST modules for configuring the mouse and keyboard are covered in the *User Guide*.

X11 was first developed as an enterprise of DEC™ (Digital Equipment Corporation™) and the Athena project at MIT™ (Massachusetts Institute of Technology™). The first version of X11R1 was released in September 1987. Since release 6, the X Consortium, Inc.™ has been responsible for the development of the X Window System.

XFree™ is a freely available implementation of X servers for PC UNIX systems (see `http://www.XFree86.org`). It was and continues to be developed by programmers all over the world who founded the XFree team in 1992. In 1994, this team established The XFree86 Project, Inc.™, whose aim is to continue research and development on XFree and to make it available to the public.

To use the available hardware (mouse, graphics card, monitor, keyboard) in the best way possible, the configuration can be optimized manually. Some aspects of this optimization are explained below. For detailed information about configuring the X Window System, review the various files in the directory `/usr/share/doc/packages/xf86` and `man XF86Config`.

Caution

Be very careful when configuring your X Window System. Never start the X Window System until the configuration is finished. A wrongly configured system can cause irreparable damage to your hardware (this applies especially to fixed-frequency monitors). The authors of this book and SUSE LINUX AG cannot be held responsible for damage. This information has been carefully researched, but this does not guarantee that all methods presented here are correct and will not damage your hardware.

Caution

4.1 Optimizing the Installation of the X Window System

The following paragraphs describe the structure of the configuration file `/etc/X11/XF86Config`. Each *section* starts with the keyword `Section <designation>` and ends with `EndSection`. Below is a rough outline of the most important sections.

The programs SaX2 and xf86config create the file `XF86Config`, by default in `/etc/X11`. This is the primary configuration file for the X Window System. Find all the settings here concerning your graphics card, mouse, and monitor.

`XF86Config` consists of several sections, each one dealing with a certain aspect of the configuration. A section always has the same form:

```
Section designation
entry 1
entry 2
entry n
EndSection
```

The following types of sections exist:

Table 4.1: Sections in /etc/X11/XF86Config

Type	Meaning
`Files`	This section describes the paths used for fonts and the RGB color table.
`ServerFlags`	General switches are set here.
`InputDevice`	Input devices, like keyboards and special input devices (touchpads, joysticks, etc.), are configured in this section. Important parameters in this section: `Driver` and the options defining the `Protocol` and `Device`.
`Monitor`	Describes the monitor used. The individual elements of this section are the name, which is referred to later in the `Screen` definition, the `bandwidth`, and the synchronization frequency limits (`HorizSync` and `VertRefresh`). Settings are given in MHz, kHz, and Hz. Normally, the server refuses any modeline that does not correspond with the specification of the monitor. This is to prevent too high frequencies from being sent to the monitor by accident.

`Modes`	The modeline parameters are stored here for the specific screen resolutions. These parameters can be calculated by SaX2 on the basis of the values given by the user and normally do not need to be changed. Intervene manually at this point, if, for example, you want to connect a fixed frequency monitor. An exact explanation of the individual parameters would be too much for this book. Find details of the meaning of individual number values in the HOWTO file `/usr/share/doc/howto/en/XFree86-Video-Timings-HOWTO.gz`.
`Device`	This section defines a specific graphics card. It is referenced by its descriptive name.
`Screen`	This section puts together a `Monitor` and a `Device` to form all the necessary settings for XFree. In the `Display` subsection, specify the size of the virtual screen (`Virtual`), the `ViewPort`, and the `Modes`) used with this screen.
`ServerLayout`	This section defines the layout of a single or multihead configuration. This section binds the input devices `InputDevice` and the display devices `Screen`.

`Monitor`, `Device`, and `Screen` are explained in more detail below. Further information about the other sections can be found in the manual pages of `XFree86` and `XF86Config`.

There can be several different `Monitor` and `Device` sections in `XF86Config`. Even multiple `Screen` sections are possible. The following `ServerLayout` section determines which one is used.

4.1.1 Screen Section

First, take a closer look at the screen section, which combines a monitor with a device section and determines the resolution and color depth to use. A screen section might resemble the example in File 4.1 on the next page.

Example 4.1: Screen Section of the File /etc/X11/XF86Config

```
Section "Screen"
  DefaultDepth  16
  SubSection "Display"
    Depth       16
    Modes       "1152x864" "1024x768" "800x600"
    Virtual     1152x864
  EndSubSection
  SubSection "Display"
    Depth       24
    Modes       "1280x1024"
  EndSubSection
  SubSection "Display"
    Depth       32
    Modes "640x480"
  EndSubSection
  SubSection "Display"
    Depth        8
    Modes       "1280x1024"
  EndSubSection
  Device        "Device[0]"
  Identifier    "Screen[0]"
  Monitor       "Monitor[0]"
EndSection
```

The line `Identifier` (here `Screen[0]`) gives this section a defined name with which it can be uniquely referenced in the following `ServerLayout` section. The lines `Device` and `Monitor` specify the graphics card and the monitor that belong to this definition. These are just links to the `Device` and `Monitor` sections with their corresponding names or *identifiers*. These sections are discussed in detail below.

Use the `DefaultDepth` setting to select the color depth the server should use unless it is started with a specific color depth. There is a `Display` subsection for each color depth. The keyword `Depth` assigns the color depth valid for this subsection. Possible values for `Depth` are 8, 15, 16, and 24. Not all X server modules support all these values.

After the color depth, a list of resolutions is set in the `Modes` section. This list is checked by the X server from left to right. For each resolution, a suitable `Modeline` is searched in the `Modes` section. The `Modeline` depends on the capability of both the monitor and the graphics card. Thus, the `Monitor` settings will determine the resulting `Modeline`.

The first resolution found is the `Default mode`. With Ctrl + Alt + + (on the number pad), switch to the next resolution in the list to the right. With Ctrl + Alt + − (on the number pad), switch to the left. This enables you to vary the resolution while X is running.

The last line of the `Display` subsection with `Depth 16` refers to the size of the virtual screen. The maximum possible size of a virtual screen depends on the amount of memory installed on the graphics card and the desired color depth, not on the maximum resolution of the monitor. Because modern graphics cards have a large amount of video memory, you can create very large virtual desktops. However, you may no longer be able to use 3D functionality if you fill most of the video memory with a virtual desktop. If the card has 16 MB video RAM, for example, the virtual screen can be up to 4096x4096 pixels in size at 8-bit color depth. Especially for accelerated cards, however, it is not recommended to use all your memory for the virtual screen, because this memory on the card is also used for several font and graphics caches.

4.1.2 Device Section

A device section describes a specific graphics card. You can have as many device entries in `XF86Config` as you like, as long as their names are differentiated, using the keyword `Identifier`. As a rule — if you have more than one graphics card installed — the sections are simply numbered in order. The first one is called `Device[0]`, the second one `Device[1]`, and so on. The following file shows an excerpt from the `Device` section of a computer with a Matrox Millennium PCI graphics card:

```
Section "Device"
  BoardName      "MGA2064W"
  BusID          "0:19:0"
  Driver         "mga"
  Identifier     "Device[0]"
  VendorName     "Matrox"
  Option         "sw_cursor"
EndSection
```

If you use SaX2 for configuring, the device section should look something like the above diagram. Both the `Driver` and `BusID` are dependent on the hardware installed in your computer and are detected by SaX2 automatically. The `BusID` defines the PCI or AGP slot in which the graphics card is installed. This matches the ID displayed by the command lspci. The X server needs details in decimal form, but lspci displays these in hexadecimal form.

Via the `Driver` parameter, specify the driver to use for this graphics card. If the card is a Matrox Millennium, the driver module is called `mga`. The X server then searches through the `ModulePath` defined in the `Files` section in the `drivers` subdirectory. In a standard installation, this is the directory `/usr/X11R6/lib/modules/drivers`. For this purpose, simply `_drv.o` is added to the name, so, in the case of the `mga` driver, the driver file `mga_drv.o` is loaded.

The behavior of the X server or of the driver can also be influenced through additional options. An example of this is the option `sw_cursor`, which is set in the device section. This deactivates the hardware mouse cursor and depicts the mouse cursor using software. Depending on the driver module, there are various options available, which can be found in the description files of the driver modules in the directory `/usr/X11R6/lib/X11/doc`. Generally valid options can also be found in the manual pages (`man XF86Config` and `man XFree86`).

4.1.3 Monitor and Modes Section

Like the `Device` sections, the `Monitor` and `Modes` sections describe one monitor each. The configuration file `/etc/X11/XF86Config` can contain as many `Monitor` sections as desired. The server layout section specifies which `Monitor` section is relevant.

Monitor definitions should only be set by experienced users. The modelines constitute an important part of the `Monitor` sections. Modelines set horizontal and vertical timings for the respective resolution. The monitor properties, especially the allowed frequencies, are stored in the `Monitor` section.

Caution

Unless you have an in-depth knowledge of monitor and graphics card functions, nothing should be changed in the modelines, as this could cause severe damage to your monitor.

Caution

If you want to develop your own monitor descriptions, read the documentation in `/usr/X11/lib/X11/doc`. The section covering the video modes deserves a special mention. It describes in detail how the hardware functions and how to create modelines.

The manual specification of the modelines is hardly ever needed nowadays. If you are using a modern multisync monitor, the allowed frequencies and optimal resolutions can, as a rule, be read directly from the monitor by the X server via DDC, as described in the SaX2 configuration section. If this is not possible for some reason, you can also use one of the VESA modes included in the X server. This will function with practically all graphics card and monitor combinations.

4.2 Installing and Configuring Fonts

The installation of additional fonts in SUSE LINUX is very easy. Simply copy the fonts to any directory that is located in the X11 font path (see Section 4.2.1 on page 82). To enable use of the fonts with the new `xft` font rendering system, the installation directory should be a subdirectory of the directories configured in `/etc/fonts/fonts.conf` (see Section 4.2.1 on the next page).

The font files can be copied manually (as `root`) to a suitable directory, such as `/usr/X11R6/lib/X11/fonts/truetype/`. Alternatively, the task can be performed with the KDE font installer in the KDE Control Center. The result is the same.

Instead of copying the actual fonts, you can also create symbolic links. For example, you may want to do this if you have licensed fonts on a mounted Windows partition and want to use them. Subsequently, run `SuSEconfig --module fonts`.

`SuSEconfig --module fonts` executes the script `/usr/sbin/fonts-config`, which handles the configuration of the fonts. To see what exactly this script does, refer to the manual page of the script (`man fonts-config`).

The procedure is the same for bitmap fonts, TrueType and OpenType fonts, and Type1 (PostScript) fonts. All these font types can be installed in any directory. Only CID-keyed fonts require a slightly different procedure. For this, see Section 4.2.1 on page 83.

4.2.1 Font Systems

XFree contains two completely different font systems: the old *X11 core font system* and the newly designed *Xft and fontconfig* system. The following sections briefly describe these two systems.

Xft

From the outset, the programmers of Xft made sure that scalable fonts including antialiasing are supported well. If Xft is used, the fonts are rendered by the application using the fonts, not by the X server as in the X11 core font system. In this way, the respective application has access to the actual font files and full control of how the glyphs are rendered. This constitutes the basis for the correct display of text in a number of languages. Moreover, direct access to the font files is very useful for embedding fonts for printing to make sure that the printout looks the same as the screen output.

In SUSE LINUX, the two desktop environments KDE and GNOME, Mozilla, and many other applications already use Xft by default. Thus, Xft is already used by more applications than the old X11 core font system.

Xft uses the fontconfig library for finding fonts and influencing how they are rendered. The properties of fontconfig are controlled by the global configuration file `/etc/fonts/fonts.conf` and the user-specific configuration file `~/.fonts.conf`. Each of these fontconfig configuration files must begin with

```
<?xml version="1.0"?>
<!DOCTYPE fontconfig SYSTEM "fonts.dtd">
<fontconfig>
```

and end with

```
</fontconfig>
```

To add directories to search for fonts, append lines such as the following:

```
<dir>/usr/local/share/fonts/</dir>
```

However, this is usually not necessary. By default, the user-specific directory `~/.fonts/` is already entered in `/etc/fonts/fonts.conf`. Accordingly, all you need to do to install additional fonts is to copy them to `~/.fonts`.

You can also insert rules that influence the appearance of the fonts. For example, enter

```
<match target="font">
 <edit name="antialias" mode="assign">
  <bool>false</bool>
 </edit>
</match>
```

to disable antialiasing for all fonts or

```
<match target="font">
 <test name="family">
  <string>Luxi Mono</string>
  <string>Luxi Sans</string>
 </test>
 <edit name="antialias" mode="assign">
 <bool>false</bool>
 </edit>
</match>
```

to disable antialiasing for specific fonts.

By default, most applications use the font names `sans-serif` (or the equivalent `sans`), `serif`, or `monospace`. These are not real fonts but only aliases that are resolved to a suitable font, depending on the language setting.

Users can easily add rules to `~/.fonts.conf` to resolve these aliases to their favorite fonts:

```
<alias>
 <family>sans-serif</family>
 <prefer>
  <family>FreeSans</family>
 </prefer>
</alias>
<alias>
 <family>serif</family>
 <prefer>
  <family>FreeSerif</family>
 </prefer>
</alias>
<alias>
 <family>monospace</family>
 <prefer>
  <family>FreeMono</family>
 </prefer>
</alias>
```

Because nearly all applications use these aliases by default, this affects almost the entire system. Thus, you can easily use your favorite fonts almost everywhere without having to modify the font settings in the individual applications.

Use the command `fc-list` to find out which fonts are installed and available for use. For instance, the command `fc-list ""` returns a list of all fonts. To find out which of the available scalable fonts (`:outline=true`) contain all glyphs required for Hebrew (:lang=he), their font names (family), their style (style), their weight (weight), and the name of the files containing the fonts, enter the following command:

```
fc-list ":lang=he:outline=true" family style weight file
```

The output of this command could appear as follows:

```
/usr/X11R6/lib/X11/fonts/truetype/FreeSansBold.ttf: FreeSans:style=Bold:weight=200
/usr/X11R6/lib/X11/fonts/truetype/FreeMonoBoldOblique.ttf: FreeMono:style=BoldOblique:weight=200
/usr/X11R6/lib/X11/fonts/truetype/FreeSerif.ttf: FreeSerif:style=Medium:weight=80
/usr/X11R6/lib/X11/fonts/truetype/FreeSerifBoldItalic.ttf: FreeSerif:style=BoldItalic:weight=200
/usr/X11R6/lib/X11/fonts/truetype/FreeSansOblique.ttf: FreeSans:style=Oblique:weight=80
/usr/X11R6/lib/X11/fonts/truetype/FreeSerifItalic.ttf: FreeSerif:style=Italic:weight=80
/usr/X11R6/lib/X11/fonts/truetype/FreeMonoOblique.ttf: FreeMono:style=Oblique:weight=80
/usr/X11R6/lib/X11/fonts/truetype/FreeMono.ttf: FreeMono:style=Medium:weight=80
/usr/X11R6/lib/X11/fonts/truetype/FreeSans.ttf: FreeSans:style=Medium:weight=80
/usr/X11R6/lib/X11/fonts/truetype/FreeSerifBold.ttf: FreeSerif:style=Bold:weight=200
/usr/X11R6/lib/X11/fonts/truetype/FreeSansBoldOblique.ttf: FreeSans:style=BoldOblique:weight=200
/usr/X11R6/lib/X11/fonts/truetype/FreeMonoBold.ttf: FreeMono:style=Bold:weight=200
```

Important parameters that can be queried with fc-list:

Table 4.2: Parameters of fc-list

Parameter	Meaning and Possible Values
family	Name of the font family, e.g., FreeSans.
foundry	The manufacturer of the font, e.g., urw.
style	The font style, e.g., Medium, Regular, Bold, Italic, Heavy.
lang	The language that the font supports, e.g., de for German, ja for Japanese, zh-TW for traditional Chinese, zh-CN for simplified Chinese.
weight	The font weight, e.g., 80 for regular, 200 for bold.
slant	The slant, usually 0 for none, 100 for italic.
file	The name of the file containing the font.
outline	true for outline fonts, false for other fonts.
scalable	true for scalable fonts, false for other fonts.
bitmap	true for bitmap fonts, false for other fonts.
pixelsize	Font size in pixels. In connection with fc-list, this option only makes sense for bitmap fonts.

X11 Core Fonts

Today, the X11 core font system supports not only bitmap fonts but also scalable fonts, like Type1 fonts, TrueType and OpenType fonts, and CID-keyed fonts. Unicode fonts have also been supported for quite some time. In 1987, the X11 core font system was originally developed for X11R1 for the purpose of processing monochrome bitmap fonts. All extensions mentioned above were added later.

Scalable fonts are only supported without antialiasing and subpixel rendering and the loading of large scalable fonts with glyphs for many language may take a long time. The use of Unicode fonts may also be slow and consume much more memory than necessary.

The X11 core font system has many other inherent weaknesses. It is hopelessly outdated and can no longer be extended meaningfully. Although it must be retained for reasons of backward compatibility, the more modern Xft/fontconfig system should be used if at all possible.

Remember that only directories meeting the following requirements are taken into account by the X server:

- Directories entered as `FontPath` in the `Files` section in the file `/etc/X11/XF86Config`.
- Directories that have a valid `font.dir` file (generated by SuSEconfig).
- Directories that are not disabled with the command `xset -fp` when the X server is active.
- Directories that are not enabled with the command `xset +fp` when the X server is active.

If the X server is already active, newly installed fonts in mounted directories can be made available with the command `xset fp rehash`. This command is executed by `SuSEconfig --module fonts`.

As the command `xset` needs access to the running X server, this will only work if `SuSEconfig --module fonts` is started from a shell that has access to the running X server. The easiest way to achieve this is to assume `root` permissions by entering `sux` and the root password. `sux` transfers the access permissions of the user who started the X server to the root shell. To check if the fonts were installed correctly and are available by way of the X11 core font system, use the command `xlsfonts` to list all available fonts.

By default, SUSE LINUX uses UTF-8 locales. Therefore, Unicode fonts should be preferred (font names ending with `iso10646-1` in `xlsfonts` output). All available Unicode fonts can be listed with `xlsfonts | grep iso10646-1`. Nearly all Unicode fonts available in SUSE LINUX contain at least the glyphs needed for European languages (formerly encoded as `iso-8859-*`).

CID-Keyed Fonts

In contrast to the other font types, you cannot simply install CID-keyed fonts in just any directory. CID-keyed fonts must be installed in `/usr/share/ghostscript/Resource/CIDFont/`. This is not relevant for Xft/fontconfig, but it is necessary for Ghostscript and the X11 core font system.

> **Note**
>
> See `http://www.xfree86.org/current/fonts.html` for more information about fonts under X11.
>
> **Note**

4.3 OpenGL — 3D Configuration

In Linux, the OpenGL interface is available for programs. Direct3D from Microsoft is not available in Linux.

4.3.1 Hardware Support

SUSE LINUX includes several OpenGL drivers for 3D hardware support. Table 4.3 on the next page provides an overview.

Table 4.3: Supported 3D Hardware

OpenGL Driver	Supported Hardware
nVidia	nVidia Chips: all except Riva 128(ZX)
DRI	3Dfx Voodoo Banshee, 3Dfx Voodoo-3/4/5, Intel i810/i815/i830M, Intel 845G/852GM/855GM/865G, Matrox G200/G400/G450/G550, ATI Rage 128(Pro)/Radeon

If you are installing with YaST for the first time, 3D acceleration can be activated during installation, provided YaST detects 3D support. For nVidia graphics chips, the nVidia driver must be installed first. To do this, select the nVidia driver patch in YOU (YaST Online Update). Due to license restrictions, the nVidia driver is not included in the distribution.

If an update is carried out instead of a new installation or a 3Dfx add-on graphics adapter (Voodoo Graphics or Voodoo-2) needs to be set up, the procedure for configuring 3D hardware support is different. This depends on which OpenGL driver is used. Further details are provided in the following section.

4.3.2 OpenGL Drivers

nVidia and DRI

These OpenGL drivers can configured easily with SaX2. For nVidia adapters, the nVidia driver must be installed first (see above). Enter the command `3Ddiag` to check if the configuration for nVidia or DRI is correct.

For security reasons, only users belonging to the group `video` are permitted to access the 3D hardware. Therefore, make sure that all local users are members of this group. Otherwise, the slow *Software Rendering Fallback* of the OpenGL driver will be used for OpenGL applications. Use the command `id` to check whether the current user belongs to the group `video`. If this is not the case, use YaST to add the user to the group.

4.3.3 The Diagnosis Tool 3Ddiag

The diagnosis tool 3Ddiag allows verification of the 3D configuration in SUSE LINUX. This is a command line tool that must be started in a terminal. Enter `3Ddiag -h` to list possible options for 3Ddiag.

To verify the XFree configuration, the tool checks if the packages needed for 3D support are installed and if the correct OpenGL library and GLX extension are used. Follow the instructions of 3Ddiag if you receive "failed" messages. If everything is correct, you will only see "done" messages on the screen.

4.3.4 OpenGL Test Utilities

For testing OpenGL, the program `glxgears` and games like `tuxracer` and `armagetron` (packages have the same names) can be useful. If 3D support has been activated, it should be possible to play these smoothly on a fairly new computer. Without 3D support, it is not possible to play these games or they run only very slowly. Use the `glxinfo` command to verify that 3D is active, in which case the output contains a line stating `direct rendering: Yes`.

4.3.5 Troubleshooting

If the OpenGL 3D test results are negative (the games cannot be smoothly played), use 3Ddiag to make sure no errors exist in the configuration ("failed" messages). If correcting these does not help or if failed messages have not appeared, take a look at the XFree86 log files.

Often, you will find the line `DRI is disabled` in the XFree86 4.x file `/var/log/XFree86.0.log`. The exact cause can only be discovered by closely examining the log file — a task requiring some experience.

In such cases, no configuration error exists, as this would have already been detected by 3Ddiag. Consequently, at this point, the only choice is to use the software rendering fallback of the DRI driver, which does not provide 3D hardware support. You should also go without 3D support if you get OpenGL representation errors or instability. Use SaX2 to disable 3D support completely.

4.3.6 Installation Support

Apart from the `software rendering fallback` of the DRI driver, all OpenGL drivers in Linux are in developmental phases and are therefore considered experimental. The drivers are included in the distribution because of the high demand for 3D hardware acceleration in Linux. Considering the experimental status of OpenGL drivers, SUSE cannot offer any installation support for configuring 3D hardware acceleration or provide any further assistance with related problems. The basic configuration of the graphical user interface X11 does not include 3D hardware acceleration configuration. If you experience problems with 3D hardware acceleration, it is recommended to disable 3D support completely.

4.3.7 Additional Online Documentation

- DRI: `/usr/X11R6/lib/X11/doc/README.DRI` (`XFree86-doc`)
- Mesa/Glide: `/usr/share/doc/packages/mesa3dfx/` (`mesa3dfx`)
- Mesa general: `/usr/share/doc/packages/mesa/` (`mesa`)

5

Printer Operation

This chapter discusses various aspects of the printing system in general. It should also help with finding solutions for problems related to network printers.

5.1 Printing Basics

On a Linux system, printers are managed with *print queues*. Before any data is printed, it is sent to the print queue for temporary storage. From there, the print spooler sends the data to the printer.

However, this data is predominantly not available in a form that can be processed by the printer. A graphical image, for example, first needs to be converted into a format the printer can understand. This conversion into a *printer language* is achieved with a *print filter*, a program run by the print spooler to translate data as needed so the printer can process it.

5.1.1 Important Standard Printer Languages

ASCII text Most printers are at least able to print ASCII text. The few devices that cannot print ASCII text directly should be able to understand one of the other standard printer languages mentioned below.

PostScript PostScript is the established printer language under Unix and Linux. PostScript output can be printed directly by PostScript printers. However, these printers are relatively expensive, because PostScript is a powerful yet complex language that requires a lot of computing in the PostScript printer before actually putting something on paper. Adding to the price of PostScript printers are licensing costs.

PCL3, PCL4, PCL5e, PCL6, ESC/P, ESC/P2, and ESC/P raster
If a PostScript printer is not available, the print filter uses the program Ghostscript to convert PostScript data into one of these other standard languages. Ghostscript uses different drivers for different printers to make use of specific features offered by the various models, such as color settings.

5.1.2 Processing Print Jobs

1. A print job is started by the user either from the command line or from an application.
2. The corresponding print data is temporarily stored in the print queue. It is retrieved from there by the print spooler, which sends it to the print filter.

3. The print filter performs the following steps:

   (a) The filter determines the format of print data.

   (b) If the print data is not in PostScript format, it is first converted to the standard language PostScript. Usually, ASCII text is also converted to PostScript.

   (c) The PostScript data is converted into another printer language, if necessary.

      - If the printer is a PostScript model, the data is sent to it with no further processing.
      - If the printer is not a PostScript printer, the program Ghostscript is run and uses one of its drivers to convert data into the language of the printer model. This generates the data that is finally sent to the printer.

4. As soon as all the data of the print job has been sent to the printer, the print spooler deletes it from the print queue.

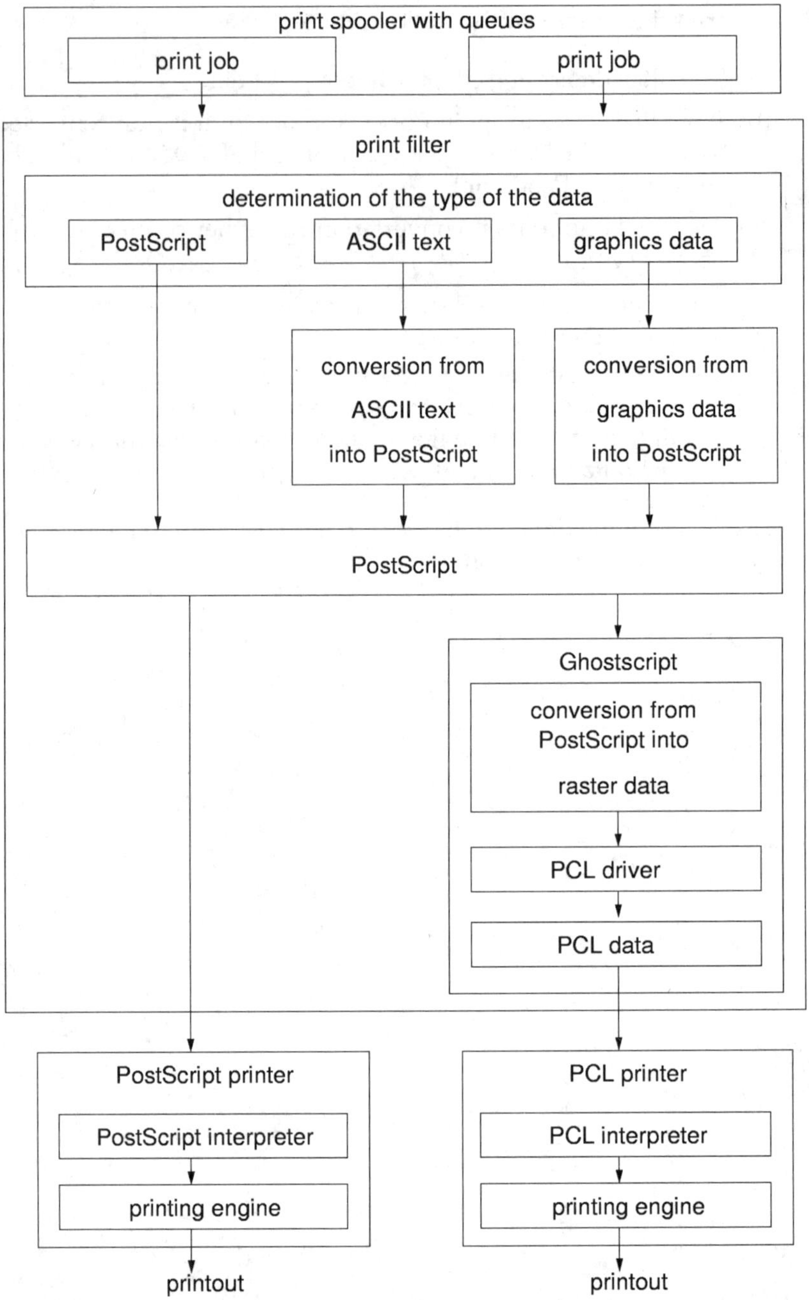

Figure 5.1: *The Printing Workflow*

5.1.3 Various Printing Systems

SUSE LINUX supports two different printing systems:

LPRng and lpdfilter This is a traditional printing system consisting of the print spooler LPRng and the print filter lpdfilter. The configuration of this system must be entirely defined by the system administrator. Normal users can only choose between different print queues that have already been configured. To allow users to choose between different options for a given printer, a number of print queues should be defined beforehand — each for a different printer configuration. For plain black-and-white printers, such as most laser printers, it is sufficient to define just one configuration (the standard queue). For modern color inkjet printers, define several configurations, for example, one for black-and-white printing, one for color printing, and maybe another one for high-resolution photograph printing. Setting up the printer with predefined configurations has the advantage that the system administrator has a lot of control over the way in which the device is used. On the other hand, there is the disadvantage that users cannot set up the printer according to the job at hand, so maybe they will not be able to use the many options offered by modern printers unless the administrator has defined the corresponding print queues beforehand.

CUPS CUPS allows users to set different options for each print job and does not require the entire configuration of the print queue to be predefined by the system administrator. With CUPS, printer options are stored in a PPD (PostScript printer description) file for each queue. These can be made available to users in printer configuration dialogs. By default, the PPD file gives users control over all printer options, but the system administrator may also limit printer functionality by editing the PPD file.

Under normal conditions, it is not possible to install these two printing systems *concurrently*, as there are conflicts between them. However, you can switch between the two print systems with YaST (see the information in *User Guide*).

5.2 Preconditions for Printing

5.2.1 General Requirements

- Your printer must be supported by SUSE LINUX. To see whether this is the case, consult the following sources:

  SUSE Printer Database `http://cdb.suse.de` or `http://hardwaredb.suse.de/` (click 'Englisch' to get the English version).

  The linuxprinting.org Printer Database
  `http://www.linuxprinting.org/` (*The Database* `http://www.linuxprinting.org/database.html` or `http://www.linuxprinting.org/printer_list.cgi`)

  Ghostscript `http://www.cs.wisc.edu/~ghost/`

  The SUSE LINUX Ghostscript Driver List
  `/usr/share/doc/packages/ghostscript/catalog.devices` This file lists the Ghostscript drivers enclosed with the respective version of SUSE LINUX. This is important, as the web pages sometimes refer to a Ghostscript driver not included in SUSE LINUX. For license reasons, SUSE LINUX comes with GNU Ghostscript. In most cases, GNU Ghostscript offers a suitable driver for your printer.

- The printer has been properly connected to the interface over which it will communicate.

- You should be using one of the standard kernels included on CD, not a custom kernel. If you have problems with your printer, install one of the SUSE standard kernels first and reboot before looking further into the problem.

- The 'Default System' is installed to make sure all required packages are available. As long as you have not uninstalled any of the packages of the standard system, things should be ready. Otherwise, install the 'Default System' with YaST. None of the 'Minimum System' selections are sufficient for printing.

5.2.2 Finding the Right Printer Driver

PostScript printers do not require a special printer driver (see Section 5.1.2 on page 88). Other printer types need a Ghostscript driver to produce the data. For non-PostScript devices, choosing the right Ghostscript driver and the right options for it has a big influence on output quality. The Ghostscript drivers available for specific models are listed in the sources mentioned in Section 5.2.1 on the preceding page.

If you cannot find a Ghostscript driver for your printer, ask the manufacturer which printer language your model understands. Some manufacturers supply special Ghostscript drivers for their printers. Even if the manufacturer is not able to provide any Linux-specific information on your printer model, he can still provide the following information to facilitate the selection of a suitable printer driver:

- Find out whether your printer is compatible with a model supported by Linux. You may then be able to use the driver for the compatible model. For printers to be *compatible*, they must be able to work correctly using the same binary control sequences. Both printers must understand the same language on the hardware level without relying on additional driver software to emulate it.

  A similar model name does not always mean the hardware is really compatible. Printers that appear very similar on the outside sometimes do not use the same printer language at all.

- Check if your printer supports a standard printing language by asking the manufacturer or checking the technical specifications in the printer manual.

  PCL5e or PCL6 Printers that understand the *PCL5e* or *PCL6* language natively should work with the ljet4 Ghostscript driver and produce output at a resolution of 600x600 dpi. Often, PCL5e is mistaken for PCL5.

  PCL4 or PCL5 Printers that understand the *PCL4* or *PCL5* language natively should work with one of the following Ghostscript drivers: laserjet, ljetplus, ljet2p, or ljet3. Output resolution is limited to 300x300 dpi, however.

  PCL3 Printers that understand the *PCL3* language natively should work with one of these Ghostscript drivers: deskjet, hpdj, pcl3, cdjmono, cdj500, or cdj550.

  ESC/P2, ESC/P, or ESC/P raster Printers that understand *ESC/P2*, *ESC/P*, or *ESC/P raster* natively should work with the stcolor Ghostscript driver or with the uniprint driver in combination with a suitable `*.upp` parameter file (e.g., `stcany.upp`).

5.2.3 The Issue with GDI Printers

Because the printer drivers for Linux are usually not developed by the hardware manufacturer, it is crucial that the printer can be addressed with one of the common printer languages (*PostScript*, *PCL*, and *ESC/P*). Normal printers understand at least one of the common printer languages. However, *GDI printers* only work with the operating system versions for which the manufacturer has enclosed drivers, as they can only be addressed with special control sequences. As these printers cannot be addressed with any known standard, their use with Linux is impossible or difficult.

GDI is a programming interface developed by Microsoft for graphical devices. There is not much of a problem with the interface itself, but the fact that GDI printers can *only* be controlled through the proprietary language they use is an issue. A better name for them would be *proprietary-language-only printers*.

On the other hand, there are printers that can be operated both in GDI mode and in a standard language mode, but they need to be switched accordingly. If you use Linux together with another operating system, it may be possible that the driver set the printer to GDI mode when you last used it. As a result, the printer will not work under Linux. There are two solutions for this: switch the printer back to standard mode under the other operating system before using it under Linux or use only the standard mode, even under the other operating system. In the latter case, it may turn out that printing functionality is limited, such as to a lower resolution.

There are also some very special printers that implement a rudimentary set of a standard printer language, such as the commands needed for printing raster images. Sometimes these printers can be used in a normal way, as the Ghostscript drivers normally only use commands for printing raster images. In this case it may be impossible to print ASCII text directly. This should not be too much of a problem, however, as ASCII text is mostly printed through Ghostscript and not directly. However, printers that first must be toggled with special control sequences are problematic. This cannot be done with a normal Ghostscript driver, but requires a specially adapted driver.

For some GDI printers, you may be able to obtain Linux drivers directly from the manufacturer. There is no guarantee that such vendor-made drivers will work with other or future Linux versions.

In any case, the above is only true for GDI models. In contrast, printers that understand one of the standard languages do not depend on a particular operating system nor do they require a particular Linux version. However, they often produce the highest quality of output when used with a vendor-made driver.

To sum all this up, SUSE LINUX does support the GDI printers listed below. They can be configured using the printer configuration module of YaST. Be aware that their use will always be rather problematic. Some models might refuse to work at all or their functionality might be limited, for example, to low-resolution black-and-white printing. SUSE does not test GDI printers, so cannot guarantee this list is correct.

- Brother HL (720, 730, 820, 1020, 1040), MFC (4650, 6550, MC, 9050), and compatible models
- HP DeskJet (710, 712, 720, 722, 820, 1000) and compatible models
- Lexmark (1000, 1020, 1100, 2030, 2050, 2070, 3200, 5000, 5700, 7000, 7200), Z (11, 42, 43, 51, 52), and compatible models
- Oki Okipage (4w, 4w+, 6w, 8w, 8wLite, 8z, 400w) and compatible models
- Samsung ML-(200, 210, 1000, 1010, 1020, 1200, 1210, 1220, 4500, 5080, 6040) and compatible models

To our knowledge, the following GDI printers are *not supported* by SUSE LINUX (this list is not complete by any means):

- Brother DCP-1000, MP-21C, WL-660
- Canon BJC (5000, 5100, 8000, 8500), LBP (460, 600, 660, 800), MultiPASS L6000
- Epson AcuLaser C1000, EPL (5500W, 5700L, 5800L)
- HP LaserJet (1000, 3100, 3150)
- Lexmark Z(12, 22, 23, 31, 32, 33, 82), Winwriter (100, 150c, 200)
- Minolta PagePro (6L, 1100L, 18L), Color PagePro L, Magicolor 6100DeskLaser, Magicolor 2 DeskLaser Plus/Duplex
- Nec SuperScript (610plus, 660, 660plus)
- Oki Okijet 2010
- Samsung ML (85G, 5050G), QL 85G
- Sharp AJ 2100, AL (1000, 800, 840, F880, 121)

5.3 Configuring a Printer with YaST

5.3.1 Print Queues and Configurations

In most cases, you will want to set up more than one print queue. If you have more than one printer, you need at least one queue for each of them. The print filter can be configured differently for each print queue. By having different queues for one printer, operate it with different configurations. This is not necessary in CUPS, as the user can specify the desired settings. See Section 5.1.3 on page 91.

If your model is a plain black-and-white printer, such as most laser printers, it is sufficient to configure just one standard queue. For most color inkjets, on the other hand, it is useful to have at least two different configurations:

- A standard configuration for quick and inexpensive black-and-white printouts.
- A `color` configuration or queue used for color printing.

5.3.2 Printer Configuration with YaST: The Basics

Start the YaST printer configuration by selecting it from the YaST menus or by entering `yast2 printer` directly on a command line as `root`. Easily switch back and forth between CUPS and LPRng and lpdfilter using a the YaST printer configuration with 'Advanced'. However, switching the print system does not keep an existing configuration — a CUPS configuration is not transformed into an LPRng and lpdfilter configuration and vice versa.

The YaST printer configuration module offers the following printing system selections:

CUPS as server (default in standard installations)
: If a printer is connected locally, CUPS must be running in server mode. If no local queue is configured with YaST, the CUPS daemon cupsd is not started automatically. If you still want cupsd to start, the 'cups' service must be activated (normally for the runlevels 3 and 5). See Section 5.8.2 on page 115. The following packages are installed for this print system:

  - `cups-libs`

- cups-client
- cups
- footmatic-filters
- cups-drivers
- cups-drivers-stp

CUPS in Client-Only Mode If there is a CUPS network server in the local network (see Section 5.8.1 on page 114) and you exclusively want to print by way of its queues, run CUPS as a client — see Section 5.8.2 on page 115. The following packages are sufficient for this mode:

- cups-libs
- cups-client

LPRng Select this to use the LPRng and lpdfilter print system or if the network only has an LPD server (see Section 5.8.1 on page 114) whose queues you want to use for printing (see Section 5.8.2 on page 115). The following packages are required for this setup:

- lprng
- lpdfilter
- footmatic-filters
- cups-drivers

cups-client and lprng should not be installed concurrently. The package cups-libs must always be installed, as several packages (such as Ghostscript, KDE, Samba, Wine, and the YaST printer configuration) need the CUPS libraries.

The printing system as a whole requires a number of additional packages, although the 'Default system' should include them. The most important ones are:

- ghostscript-library
- ghostscript-fonts-std
- ghostscript-x11
- libgimpprint

The YaST printer configuration module displays all configurations that could be created without errors. As the configurations are not generated until the YaST printer configuration module is terminated, restart the YaST printer configuration to make sure everything is OK.

5.3.3 Automatic Configuration

Depending on how much of your hardware can be autodetected and on whether your printer model is included in the printer database, YaST either automatically configures your printer or offers a reasonable selection of settings that then need to be adjusted manually. If this is not the case, the user must enter the needed information in the dialogs. YaST can configure your printer automatically if the following conditions are fulfilled:

- The parallel port or USB interface was set up automatically in the correct way and the printer model connected to it was autodetected.
- Your printer's ID, as supplied to YaST during hardware autodetection, is included in the printer database. As this ID may be different from the actual model designation, you may need to select the model manually.

Each configuration should be tested with the print test function of YaST to see whether it works as expected. In many cases, configuration data not explicitly supported by the printer manufacturer must be used. For this reason, operability cannot be guaranteed for all settings. The YaST test page additionally provides important information about the respective configuration.

5.3.4 Manual Configuration

If one of the conditions for automatic configuration is not fulfilled or if you want your own customized setup, the configuration must be performed manually. The following is an overview of the options to set during manual configuration:

Hardware Port (Interface) If YaST was able to autodetect the printer model, safely assume that the printer connection works as far as the hardware is concerned. You may then leave this part untouched.If YaST has not autodetected the printer model, there may have been some problem on the hardware level. Some manual intervention is needed to configure the physical connection. Manual configuration requires specification of the port to which the printer is connected. `/dev/lp0` is the first parallel port. `/dev/usb/lp0` is the port for a USB printer. Always test this setting from within YaST to see whether the printer is actually responding at the selected interface. It is safest to connect a printer to the first parallel port. In this case, the BIOS settings for this port should look like this:

- I/O address: `378` (hexadecimal)
- Interrupt: (not relevant)
- Mode: `Normal`, `SPP`, or `Output-Only`.
- DMA: Disabled

If the printer does not respond at the first parallel port with these settings, you may need to change the I/O address to have the explicit form of `0x378` under the BIOS menu item that lets you configure the advanced settings for parallel ports. If your machine has two parallel ports with I/O addresses 378 and 278 (hexadecimal), change them to read `0x378` and `0x278`, respectively.

Queue Name The name of the queue is used frequently when issuing print commands. The name should be rather short and consist of lowercase letters (and maybe numbers) only.

Ghostscript Driver and Printer Language (Printer Model)
The Ghostscript driver and the printer language depend on the printer model and are determined by selecting a predefined configuration suitable for the printer model. It can be customized in a separate dialog, if necessary. In other words, the selection of the manufacturer and the model actually represents the selection of a printer language and a Ghostscript driver with suitable driver settings for your printer. For non-PostScript models, all printer-specific data is produced by the Ghostscript driver. Therefore, the driver configuration (both choosing the right driver and the correct options for it) is the single most important factor determining the output quality. Your settings affect the printer output on a queue-by-queue basis. If your printer was autodetected, which means the model is included in the printer database, you will be presented with a choice of possible Ghostscript drivers and with several output options such as:

- black-and-white printing
- color printing at 300 dpi
- color printing at 600 dpi

Each default configuration includes a suitable Ghostscript driver and, if available, a number of driver-specific settings related to the output quality. Any driver-specific settings can be customized in a separate dialog. Click the respective values to view and access any indented submenu entries. Not all combinations of driver options work with every printer model. This is especially true for higher resolutions. Always check whether your settings work as expected by printing the YaST test page. If the output is garbled (for example, with several pages almost empty), you should be able to stop the printer by first removing all sheets then stopping the test print from within YaST. However, in some cases the printer will refuse to resume work if you do so. It may be better to stop the test print first and wait for the printer to eject all pages itself. If your model was not found in the printer database, you can select one of the generic Ghostscript drivers for the standard printing languages. These are listed under a generic *manufacturer*.

Other Special Settings Unless you are sure about what these options mean, do not change the default settings. For the CUPS printing system, the following special settings are available:

- Restricting printer use for certain users.
- Queue status: whether the queue is started or stopped and whether it is ready to accept new print jobs.
- Banner page: whether to print out a banner (cover) page at the beginning of each print job and which one. Similarly, whether to add a banner page at the end of each print job and which one.

For the LPRng and lpdfilter printing system, change the following hardware-independent settings:

- The page layout can be changed for ASCII text printouts (but not for graphics or documents created with special application programs).
- You can define an `ascii` print queue for special cases. The `ascii` queue forces the print filter to produce ASCII text output, which may be necessary for some text files that the print filter does not automatically recognize as such, for example, PostScript source code.
- Country-specific settings can be changed to ensure the correct character encoding when sending ASCII text to the printer and when printing plain text in HTML pages from Netscape.

5.4 Configuring Applications

Applications use the existing queues for printing from the command line. In applications, printer options are not configured directly, but rather through the existing queues.

On the command line, you can print with one of the following commands:

```
lpr -P color <filename>
lp -d color <filename>
```

Replace ⟨*filename*⟩ with the name of the file to print. The options `-P` and `-d` can be used to specify the queue explicitly. `-P color` and `-d color` both select the queue named `color`.

In applications, the existing queues are often available from a print menu, in which case no further configuration is necessary. In some applications, you can (or may need to) specify or configure a print command. Normally this print command should be one of the two mentioned above, but without the ⟨*filename*⟩ part, so enter just `lpr -P color` or `lp -d color`.

5.5 The CUPS Printing System

5.5.1 Naming Conventions

Client or *client program* refers to a program that sends print jobs to a print daemon. A *print daemon* is a local service that accepts print jobs to forward them or to process them locally. *Server* refers to a daemon able to deliver print data to one or more printers. Each server functions as a daemon at the same time. In most cases, however, there is no special distinction to make between a server and a daemon, neither from the developer or from the user standpoint.

5.5.2 IPP and Server

Print jobs are sent to servers by CUPS-based programs, such as `lpr`, `kprinter`, or `xpp`, and with the help of the *Internet Printing Protocol*, IPP. IPP is defined in RFC-2910 and RFC-2911 (see `http://www.rfc-editor.org/rfc.html`). IPP is somewhat similar to HTTP with identical headers but different content data. It also uses its own dedicated communication port 631, which has been registered with IANA (the Internet Authority for Number Allocation).

Print data is transferred to a CUPS daemon, which is also acting as a local server in most cases. Other daemons can be addressed using the environment variable `CUPS_SERVER`.

With the help of the broadcast function of the CUPS daemon, locally managed printers can be made available elsewhere in the network (using UDP port 631). They then appear as print queues on all other daemons configured to accept and use these broadcast packets. This makes it possible to *see* printers on other hosts after booting without configuring them locally, something that may be quite useful in corporate networks. On the other hand, this feature may pose a security risk if the host is connected to the Internet. When enabling printer broadcasting, make sure the daemon broadcasts into the local network only, access is limited to clients on the LAN, and the public IP address (the one used for the Internet connection) is not within the local IP range. Otherwise, remote users relying on the same ISP would be able to *see* and use the broadcast printers as well. In addition to that, such broadcasts mean more network traffic so may increase connection costs. Prevent a local printer from broadcasting IPP packets into the Internet by configuring the SUSE Firewall (`SUSEfirewall2`) accordingly.

No extra configuration is needed to receive broadcast IPP packets. A broadcast address must only be specified for outgoing print jobs. This may be configured with YaST, for example.

IPP is used for the communication between a local and a remote CUPS daemon or server. More recent network printers also have built-in support for this protocol (there are a number of models from different makers). Find more information about this on the web pages of manufacturers or in your printer's manual. IPP is also supported by Windows 2000 and newer Microsoft systems, although originally the implementation was somewhat flawed. These problems may have disappeared or it may be necessary to install a Service Pack to repair them.

5.5.3 Configuration of a CUPS Server

There are many ways to set up a printer with CUPS and to configure the daemon: with command-line tools, with YaST, with the KDE Control Center, or even through a web browser interface. The following sections are limited to the command-line tools and YaST.

Caution

When using the web browser interface for CUPS configuration, be aware that there is a risk of compromising the `root` password. The password will be transmitted as plain text if the URL specified includes the real host name. Therefore, you should always use `http://localhost:631/` as the host address.

Caution

For the above reason, the CUPS daemon can only be accessed for administration if addressed as `localhost` (which is identical to the IP address `127.0.0.1`) by default. Entering a different address returns an error message, even if it is valid.

To configure a locally connected printer, first set up a CUPS daemon on the local host. To do so, install `cups` together with the PPD files provided by SUSE as included in `cups-drivers` and `cups-drivers-stp`. After that, start the server as `root` with the command `/etc/rc.d/cups restart`. If you configure it with YaST, the above steps are already covered by selecting CUPS as the printing system and installing a printer.

PPD (PostScript Printer Description) files contain options for printer models in the form of a standard set of PostScript commands. They are required for printer installation under CUPS. SUSE LINUX comes with precompiled PPD files for many printers from a number of manufacturers. Manufacturers may also offer PPD files for their PostScript printers on web sites and installation CDs (often in an area called something like *Windows NT Installation*).

The local daemon can also be started so printers of all broadcasting servers are available locally, although there is no local printer. This simplifies the use of these printers from within KDE applications and OpenOffice.org, for example.

Broadcasting can be enabled with YaST. Alternatively, enable it by setting the `Browsing` directive to `On` (the default) and the `BrowseAddress` directive to a sensible value, like `192.168.255.255`, in the file `/etc/cups/cupsd.conf`. After that, tell the CUPS daemon explicitly to grant access to incoming packets, either under `<Location /printers>` or, preferably, under `<Location />`, where you would have to include a line like `Allow From some-host.mydomain` (see `file:/usr/share/doc/packages/cups/sam.html`). When finished editing the file, tell the daemon to reread its configuration by entering the command `/etc/rc.d/cups reload` as `root`.

5.5.4 Network Printers

Network printers are printers that have a built-in print server interface (such as the JetDirect interface in some HP printers) or printers connected to a print server box or a router box enabled as a print server. Windows machines offering printer shares are not print servers in the strict sense (although CUPS can handle them easily in a way similar to print servers).

In most cases, a network printer supports the LPD protocol, which uses port 515 for communication. Check lpd availability with the command:

```
netcat -z <hostname>.<domain> 515 && echo ok || echo failed
```

If such a server is available, CUPS can be configured to access it under a *device URI*, an address in the form `lpd://server/queue`. Read about the concept of device URIs in `file:/usr/share/doc/packages/cups/sam.html`.

However, you should probably not use the LPD protocol for a network printer, but rather the printer's built-in port 9100 if available (HP, Kyocera, and many others) or port 35 (QMS). In this case, the device URI must have the form `socket://Server:Port/`.

To use printers made available through Windows, install `samba-client` first and configure this package — enable the correct work group and make other settings. A device URI for Windows printers may be specified in several ways, but the most frequent one has the syntax `smb://user:password@host/printer`. For other configurations, see `file:/usr/share/doc/packages/cups/sam.html` and `man smbspool`.

If you have a small network consisting of several (Linux) machines and have set up a print server for it, avoid configuring the printer for each and every client host by enabling the broadcast function of the daemon (see above). Thus, when you modify the configuration (for instance, to use the new standard paper size `Letter`), it is sufficient to do this once on the server side (also see Section 5.7.1 on page 111). Although the configuration is saved locally on the server side, it is propagated to all clients in the network with the help of the CUPS tools and the IPP protocol.

5.5.5 Internal CUPS Print Job Processing

Conversion into PostScript

Basically the CUPS daemon should be able to handle any file type, although PostScript is always the safest bet. CUPS processes non-PostScript files by identifying the file type according to `/etc/cups/mime.types` first then converting the file into PostScript by calling the appropriate conversion tool for it as defined in `/etc/cups/mime.convs`. With CUPS, files are converted into PostScript on the server side rather than on the client side. This feature was introduced to ensure that special conversion operations necessary for a particular printer model are only performed on the corresponding server machine.

Accounting

After conversion into PostScript, CUPS calculates the number of pages for each print job. This is done with the help of pstops (an internal version of the program located at `/usr/lib/cups/filter/pstops`). The accounting data for print jobs is written to `/var/log/cups/page_log`. Each line in this file contains the following information:

- printer name (for example, `lp`)

- user name (for example, `root`)
- job number
- date and time (in square brackets)
- current page number
- number of copies

Other Filtering Programs

CUPS can also use other, special filters, if the corresponding printing options have been enabled. These are the most important ones:

psselect Allows limiting the printout to certain pages of a document.

ps-n-up Allows printing several pages on one sheet.

Read `file:/usr/share/doc/packages/cups/sum.html` for information about how to enable the various options.

Conversion into the Printer-Specific Language

The next step is the launch of the filter needed for generating printer-specific data. These filters are located in `/usr/lib/cups/filter/`. The suitable filter is determined in the PPD file in the `*cupsFilter` entry. If this entry does not exist, the print system assumes that the printer is a PostScript model. All device-specific printing options, such as the resolution and paper size, are processed in this filter.

Writing a custom printer-specific filter script is not a trivial task; see the SDB article *Using Your Own Filters to Print with CUPS* (keywords: *cups + filter*).

Transferring Data to the Printer

As the final step, CUPS calls one of its back-ends. A back-end is a special filter that transfers print data to a device or to a network printer (see `file:/usr/share/doc/packages/cups/overview.html`). The back-end maintains the communication with the device or network printer (as specified through a device URI during configuration). If the back-end is `usb`, for example, CUPS runs `/usr/lib/cups/backend/usb`, which in turn opens (and locks) the corresponding USB device file, initializes it, and passes the data coming from the print filter. When the job is finished, the back-end closes the device and unlocks it.

The following back-ends are currently available: `parallel`, `serial`, `usb`, `ipp`, `lpd`, `http`, `socket` (included in `cups`). Also available are `canon` and `epson`, included in `cups-drivers-stp`, and `smb`, included in `samba-client`.

Filterless Printing

To print files without any filtering, use the `lpr` command with `-l` or use the `lp` command with the `-oraw` option. Usually, the printout will not work, as no printer-specific conversion is performed or other important filters are omitted. The options are similar for other CUPS tools.

5.5.6 Tips and Tricks

OpenOffice.org

When printing from OpenOffice.org applications, CUPS is supported such that a running CUPS daemon is autodetected and queried for available printers and options (this is different from StarOffice 5.2, where it was still necessary to perform a setup for each printer). An extra CUPS setup from within OpenOffice.org should not be necessary.

Printing to or from Windows

Printers connected to a Windows machine can be addressed through a device URI, such as `smb://server/printer`. To print from a Windows machine to a CUPS server, set the entries `printing = CUPS` and `printcap name = CUPS` in the Samba configuration file `/etc/samba/smb.conf` (this is preset in SUSE LINUX). Following modifications in `/etc/samba/smb.conf`, the Samba server must be restarted. See `file:/usr/share/doc/packages/cups/sam.html` for details.

Setting up a Raw Printer

A raw printer can be set up by leaving out the PPD file during configuration, which effectively removes all filtering and accounting features from CUPS. For this purpose, the data must be sent in the printer-specific data format.

Custom Printer Options

The configuration options, such as a different default resolution, can be modified and saved for each user. The configuration is saved in the file `~/.lpoptions`. If such a reconfigured printer is removed on the server side, it will still be visible in various tools, such as `kprinter` and `xpp`. You can still select it even if it no longer exists, which causes problems. Experienced users can easily remove the superfluous lines from `~/.lpoptions` with an editor. Refer to the Support Database article *Print Settings with CUPS* as well as Section 5.7.1 on page 111.

Compatibility with LPR

CUPS can also receive print jobs from LPR systems. The needed configuration in `/etc/xinetd.d/cups-lpd` can be handled manually or with YaST.

Troubleshooting in CUPS

By default, the configuration file `/etc/cups/cupsd.conf` contains the following section:

```
# LogLevel: controls the number of messages logged to the
# ErrorLog file and can be one of the following:
#
#     debug2    Log everything.
#     debug     Log almost everything.
#     info      Log all requests and state changes.
#     warn      Log errors and warnings.
#     error     Log only errors.
#     none      Log nothing.
#
LogLevel info
```

To detect errors in CUPS, set `LogLevel debug` and use `rccups restart` to have cupsd use the modified configuration file. Subsequently, `/var/log/cups/error_log` contains detailed messages that assist in detecting the cause of problems.

With the following command, print a label before starting to run the test:

```
echo "LABEL $(date)" | tee -a /var/log/cups/error_log
```

This label will be entered in `/var/log/cups/error_log`. This makes it easier to find the messages after the test.

5.6 Printing from Applications

Applications use the existing queues for printing from the command line. In applications, printer options are not configured directly, but rather through the existing queues.

To print from the command line, enter the command `lp -d color` ⟨*filename*⟩, where ⟨*filename*⟩ is the name of the file to print. The `-d` option can be used to specify the queue explicitly. `-d color` specifies that the queue named `color` should be used.

The `cups-client` package includes some command-line tools to print with CUPS, such as the `lp` program, so commands like the one mentioned above can also be used with CUPS (see Section 5.7 on the following page). However, to be able to enter print commands, the print dialog in KDE must be set to 'Print through an External Program (generic)' — see Section 5.8.2 on page 115.

In addition, graphical printer dialog programs, such as xpp or the KDE program kprinter, allow selecting a queue and modifying standard CUPS options and printer-specific options in the PPD file by means of graphical selection menus. To use kprinter as the default print dialog for various applications, enter the print command `kprinter` or `kprinter --stdin` in the print dialog of the applications. Subsequently, whenever you enter the application-specific print command, the kprinter dialog is displayed after the print dialog of the application, allowing you to specify the queue and other options. When using this approach, make sure there is no conflict between the settings in the print dialog of the application and those in kprinter. If possible, print settings should only be specified in kprinter.

5.7 Command-Line Tools for the CUPS Printing System

The command-line tools of the CUPS printing system and their manual pages are included in `cups-client`. Further documentation is provided by `cups` and installed in `/usr/share/doc/packages/cups`, in particular the *CUPS Software Users Manual*, found at `/usr/share/doc/packages/cups/sum.html` and the *CUPS Software Administrators Manual* at `/usr/share/doc/packages/cups/sam.html`. If a CUPS daemon runs locally on your host, you should also be able to access the documentation at `http://localhost:631/documentation.html`.

As a general rule, it is useful to remember that CUPS command-line tools sometimes require options be supplied in a certain order. Consult the corresponding manual pages if you are unsure about specific options.

5.7.1 Managing Local Queues

Printing Files

To print a file, enter the *System V style* print command `lp -d` ⟨*queuename*⟩ ⟨*file*⟩ or a *Berkeley style* command like `lpr -P`⟨*queuename*⟩ ⟨*file*⟩.

Additional information can be obtained with `man lpr` and `man lp` as well as in the section *Using the Printing System* of the *CUPS Software Users Manual* (`/usr/share/doc/packages/cups/sum.html#USING_SYSTEM`).

The `-o` parameter allows specification of a number of important options, some of which directly influence the type of printout. More information is available in the manual page of `lpr` and `lp` as well as in the section *Standard Printer Options* of the *CUPS Software Users Manual* (`/usr/share/doc/packages/cups/sum.html#STANDARD_OPTIONS`).

Checking the Status

To check the status of a queue, enter the *System V style* command `lpstat -o` ⟨*queuename*⟩ `-p` ⟨*queuename*⟩ or the *Berkeley style* command `lpq -P`⟨*queuename*⟩. If you do not specify a queue name, the commands display information about all queues.

With `lpstat -o`, the output shows all active print jobs in the form of a ⟨*queuename*⟩-⟨*jobnumber*⟩ listing. With `lpstat -l -o` ⟨*queuename*⟩ `-p` ⟨*queuename*⟩, the output is more verbose. `lpstat -t` or `lpstat -l -t` displays the maximum amount of available information.

For additional information, consult the manual page of `lpq`, `lpstat`, and the section *Using the Printing System* of the *CUPS Software Users Manual* (`/usr/share/doc/packages/cups/sum.html#USING_SYSTEM`).

Removing Jobs from the Queue

Enter the *System V style* command `cancel` ⟨*queuename*⟩-⟨*job number*⟩ or the *Berkeley style* command `lprm -P`⟨*queuename*⟩ ⟨*job number*⟩ to remove the job with the specified number from the specified queue. For additional information, consult the manual page of `lprm`, `cancel`, and the section *Using the Printing System* of the *CUPS Software Users Manual* (`/usr/share/doc/packages/cups/sum.html#USING_SYSTEM`).

Specifying Options for Queues

To see how to specify hardware-independent options that affect the type of printout, read the section *Standard Printer Options* in the *CUPS Software Users Manual* (`/usr/share/doc/packages/cups/sum.html#STANDARD_OPTIONS`). The section *Saving Printer Options and Defaults,* which is found at `/usr/share/doc/packages/cups/sum.html#SAVING_OPTION`, explains how to save option settings.

Printer-specific options affecting the type of printout are stored in the PPD file for the queue in question. List them with the command `lpoptions -p` ⟨*queuename*⟩ `-l`. The output has the following form:

```
option/text: value value value ...
```

The currently active setting is marked with an asterisk (`*`) to the left, for example:

```
PageSize/Page Size: A3 *A4 A5 Legal Letter
Resolution/Resolution: 150 *300 600
```

According to the above output, the `PageSize` is set to `A4` and the `Resolution` to `300` dpi.

The command lpoptions -p ⟨*queuename*⟩ -o option=value changes the value for the given option. With the above sample settings in mind, use the following command to set the paper size for the specified queue to Letter:

```
lpoptions -p <queuename> -o PageSize=Letter
```

If the above lpoptions command is entered by a normal user, the new settings are stored for that user only in the file ~/.lpoptions. In contrast, if the lpoptions command is entered by root, the settings specified are stored in /etc/cups/lpoptions and become the default for all local users of the queue. The PPD file is not touched by this, however.

If (and only if) you change the contents of a PPD file for a given queue, the new settings apply to all users in the local network who print through this queue. The system administrator can change the defaults of a PPD file with a command like:

```
lpadmin -p <queuename> -o PageSize=Letter
```

For more information, refer to the Support Database article *Print Settings with CUPS*.

5.7.2 Managing Remote Queues

For each of the commands explained below, replace ⟨*printserver*⟩ with the name or IP address of your print server. ⟨*queuename*⟩ must be a queue on the print server. This section merely covers the basic commands. Additional options and information sources are referred to in Section 5.7.1 on page 110.

Printing Files

You can use the *System V style* command lp -d ⟨*queuename*⟩ -h ⟨*printserver*⟩ ⟨*file*⟩ to generate a print job for the specified queue on the specified print server. This is only possible if the print server was configured to accept remote print jobs on its queues. This is not enabled by default in CUPS, but can easily be configured in the CUPS server settings in the YaST printer configuration module.

Checking the Status

Check the status of a queue on the print server with the *System V style* command lpstat -h ⟨*printserver*⟩ -o ⟨*queuename*⟩ -p ⟨*queuename*⟩.

Removing Jobs from the Queue

The *System V style* command `cancel -h` ⟨*printserver*⟩ ⟨*queuename*⟩-⟨*jobnumber*⟩ removes the print job with the specified job number from the specified queue on the print server.

5.7.3 Using Command-Line Tools for CUPS Troubleshooting

Print jobs will be kept in the printer queue if you shut down the system while a job is being processed. This means a broken print job will still be there even after rebooting and you need to remove it from the queue manually with the commands mentioned above.

Other problems occur if there is some fault in the physical data link between the computer and the printer. The printer may then be unable to make sense of the data it receives and start spitting out lots of pages with garbage on them.

1. To make sure the printer stops working, first remove all paper from it (in the case of inkjet printers) or open the paper trays (laser printers).
2. At this point, the print job will often still be in the queue, because jobs are only removed from the queue when all data has been sent to the device. Check which queue is currently printing by entering `lpstat -o` (or `lpstat -h` ⟨*printserver*⟩ `-o`) then remove the problematic print job with `cancel` ⟨*queuename*⟩-⟨*jobnumber*⟩ (or with `cancel -h` ⟨*printserver*⟩ ⟨*queuename*⟩-⟨*jobnumber*⟩).
3. Some data might still find their way to the printer in spite of the job having been deleted. To stop this, enter the command `fuser -k /dev/lp0` (for a printer at the parallel port) or `fuser -k /dev/usb/lp0` (for a USB printer). This kills any processes still using the printer device.
4. Do a complete reset of the printer by disconnecting it from power for some time. Then put in the paper and switch the printer back on.

You should also be aware that if data cannot get through to the printer or if there is some other major trouble with the data transfer (such as a longer interruption of the data link), the CUPS back-end responsible for the data transfer may abort with an error code. The exact circumstances of this depend on the back-end used (whether it is the back-end for the parallel or the USB port, for the LPD or the IPP server, or the one for direct data transfer via TCP sockets). If a back-end aborts, the CUPS server ceases to print via the queue affected and mark it as `disabled` or `stopped`. The system administrator, after having removed the cause of the trouble, must reenable these queues with the command `/usr/bin/enable` ⟨*queuename*⟩ (or with `/usr/bin/enable -h` ⟨*printserver*⟩ ⟨*queuename*⟩).

5.8 Printing in a TCP/IP Network

Find extensive documentation about the LPRng printing system in the *LPRng-Howto* in `/usr/share/doc/packages/lprng/LPRng-HOWTO.html` and on the CUPS printing system in the *CUPS Software Administrators Manual* in `/usr/share/doc/packages/cups/sam.html`.

5.8.1 Terminology

print server *Print server* refers to a complete, dedicated printing host with the required CPU power, memory, and hard disk space.

Print server box or network printer

- *Print server box* refers to a computer with relatively limited resources, which is equipped with both a TCP/IP network link and a local printer port. This includes *router boxes* with a built-in printer port.
- A *network printer* is a printer device with its own TCP/IP port. Basically, it is a printer with an integrated print server box. Network printers and print server boxes are handled in essentially the same way.

There is an important distinction to be made between a network printer or a print server box on the one hand and a true print server on the other. As a somewhat special case, there are large printer devices that have a complete print server included with them to make them network-capable. These are treated like print servers because clients will talk to the printer only through the server and not directly.

LPD server An *LPD server* is a print server that is addressed with the LPD protocol. This is the case if the print server runs the *LPRng* and *lpdfilter* print system (lpd, to be precise) or the *CUPS* print system configured in a way that the machine can be addressed with the LPD protocol (cups-lpd, to be precise).

IPP server or CUPS server An *IPP server* or *CUPS server* is a print server that is addressed with the IPP protocol. This is the case if the print server runs the CUPS print system (cupsd, to be precise).

CUPS network server The term *CUPS network server* refers to a CUPS server that was specifically configured to share its queues with other network hosts via UDP broadcast (via UDP port 631).

5.8.2 Quick Configuration of a Client Machine

Usually, client machines in a network do not have any locally connected printers. Rather, the client sends print jobs to a print server. If you have a print server and an additional local printer is connected to the client, you need a client configuration as well as a configuration for the local printer. The print system on the client machine should be selected in accordance with the print system on the print server.

Client Configuration for an LPD Server

If there is no CUPS network server in the network, but only an LPD server, use the LPRng and lpdfilter print system on the client. In this case, the client machine does not require any further configuration, as even remote queues can be addressed directly when using the LPRng spooler.

However, this is only possible if the LPD server was configured to allow the client to print to its queues. To print from applications, enter `lpr -P`⟨*queuename*⟩`@`⟨*printserver*⟩ in the application. However, no file name is specified.

Some applications are preconfigured to use CUPS and must be switched to LPRng. Especially KDE and the KDE printing program kprinter must be set to 'Print through an external program'. If this is not done, it will not be possible to enter the print command.

Client Configuration for a CUPS Network Server

If the print server is a CUPS network server, start the YaST printer configuration module, click 'Change' then 'Advanced' and select one of the following options:

CUPS as server (default in standard installations)
If no printer is connected locally, no local queue was configured with YaST2. In this case, cupsd is not started automatically, Activate the 'cups' service to start cupsd (normally for the runlevels 3 and 5).

The client machine does not require any further configuration, as a CUPS network server broadcasts its queues to all network hosts at regular intervals. Therefore, the queues of the network server will automatically be available on the client machine after a short time.

However, this is only possible if the broadcasting function is enabled on the CUPS network server, the broadcast address used is suitable for the client machine, and the client machine is permitted to print to the queues of the CUPS network server.

CUPS in client-only mode If you merely want to print via the queues of the CUPS network server, CUPS can be run in client-only mode. In the YaST2 *client-only* printer configuration, specify the name of the CUPS network server.

In this mode, the client machine does not run cupsd and the file `/etc/printcap` does not exist. However, applications that cannot be configured to use CUPS only offer the queues listed in the local `/etc/printcap`. In this case, it is advisable to run CUPS in server mode, as the local cupsd will automatically generate an `/etc/printcap` containing the queue names of the CUPS network server.

5.8.3 Protocols for Printing in TCP/IP Networks

The following lists the different methods that can be used to implement printing on a TCP/IP network. The decision of which one to use does not so much depend on the hardware, but more on the possibilities offered by each protocol. Accordingly, the YaST printer configuration asks you to select a protocol and not a hardware device when setting up network printing.

Nevertheless, the first step in the printer configuration with YaST is the selection of the hardware category for printing (e.g., via CUPS network server, via LPD network server, or direct printing on a network printer or print server box). Accordingly, available protocols are offered for selection. The protocol that should work in most cases is preselected. If only one protocol is possible, there is no selection. Examples:

- Print via CUPS Network Server
  - ▷ IPP protocol (single option)
- Print via LPD-Style Network Server
  - ▷ LPD protocol (single option)
- Print directly on a network printer or using a print server box
  - ▷ TCP socket
  - ▷ LPD protocol
  - ▷ IPP protocol

Data can only be transmitted from the sender to the recipient if both parties support the respective protocol. The software running on the sender and recipient must support the respective protocol.

Ultimately, it does not matter which kind of hardware and software is used, as long as both the sender and the recipient support the respective protocol. Depending on the protocol, print jobs or raw data are transmitted.

Apart from the print data, a print job contains additional information, such as the user on whose host the print job was generated, as well as any special print options (such as the paper size to use for printing, duplex mode, and so on).

Printing via the LPD protocol

The sender sends a print job to a queue on the recipient via the LPD protocol. According to the LPD protocol, the recipient is expected to receive print jobs on port 515. Therefore, a service receiving the print jobs on port 515 (normally this service is called lpd) and a queue in which received print jobs can be placed are needed on the receiving host.

Senders supporting the LPD protocol:

Linux host with LPRng print system:

- LPRng supports sending via the LPD protocol using lpd. On the sender host, a queue is needed from which the lpd of the sender takes the print job and forwards it to the lpd of the recipient.
- LPRng also supports sending via the LPD protocol without a local lpd. Using the LPD protocol, the lpr program in the lprng package can directly forward the print job to the lpd of the recipient.

Linux host with CUPS server print system:

- CUPS supports sending via the LPD protocol using the CUPS daemon (cupsd). On the sender host, a queue is needed from which cupsd takes the print job and forwards it to the lpd of the recipient.

Linux host with CUPS client print system:

- Sending via the LPD protocol is not supported by the CUPS client print system.

Host with non-Linux operating system:

- As the LPD protocol is very old, all operating systems should support this protocol at least as the sender. If the support is not available by default, suitable software may need to be installed.

Recipients supporting the LPD protocol:

Linux host with LPRng print system:

- LPRng supports reception via the LPD protocol using lpd.

Linux host with CUPS server print system:

- CUPS supports reception via the LPD protocol using the cups-lpd. cups-lpd must be activated by means of inetd or xinetd.

Linux host with CUPS client print system:

- The CUPS client print system does not support reception via the LPD protocol.

Print servers and print server boxes or network printers:

- As the LPD is very old, every normal print server, print server box, and network printer should support this protocol.
- For print server boxes and network printers, the name of the queue varies from model to model or there are several queues with different characteristics.

Printing via the IPP Protocol

The sender sends a print job to the queue on the recipient via the IPP protocol. According to the IPP protocol, the recipient is expected to receive print jobs on port 515. Therefore, a service receiving the print jobs on port 631 (in CUPS, this service is called cupsd) and a queue in which received print jobs can be placed are needed on the receiving host.

Senders supporting the IPP protocol:

Linux host with LPRng print system:

- LPRng does not support the IPP protocol.

Linux host with CUPS server or CUPS client print system:

- CUPS also supports sending via the IPP protocol without a local cupsd. The programs lpr or lp from the cups-client package, the program xpp, and the KDE program kprinter can forward the print job directly to the recipient via the IPP protocol.

Host with non-Linux operating system:

- The IPP protocol is relatively new, so support may not be available in all cases.

Recipients supporting the IPP protocol:

Linux host with LPRng print system:

- LPRng does not support the IPP protocol.

Linux host with CUPS server print system:

- CUPS supports reception via the IPP protocol using cupsd. On the receiving host, a queue is required in which cups-lpd can place the print job received from the sender.

Linux host with CUPS client print system:

- The CUPS client print system does not support reception via the IPP protocol.

Print servers and print server boxes or network printers:

- The IPP protocol is relatively new, so support may not be available in all cases.

Direct Remote Printing through TCP Sockets

With this method, no print job is sent to a remote queue, as there is no protocol (LPD or IPP) that can handle print jobs and queues. Rather, the raw data is sent directly to a remote TCP port via TCP socket. Usually, this approach is used for sending printer-specific data to print server boxes and network printers. In many cases, the TCP port 9100 is used for this purpose.

5

Printer Operation

Senders supporting printing directly via TCP socket:

Linux host with LPRng print system:

- LPRng supports sending directly via TCP socket using lpd. On the sender host, a queue is needed from which the lpd of the sender takes the print job and sends the print data to the TCP port of the recipient.
- With LPRng, this also works without a local lpd. Using the -Y option, the lpr program from the lprng package can send the print data directly to the TCP port of the recipient via TCP socket. Refer to the man page of lpr.

Linux host with CUPS server print system:

- CUPS supports sending directly via TCP socket using cupsd. On the sender host, a queue is needed from which cupsd takes the print job and sends the print data to the TCP port of the recipient.

Linux host with CUPS client print system:

- The CUPS client print system does not support direct sending via TCP socket.
- Nevertheless, data can be sent to a port on a host using a command such as the following:

```
cat <filename> | netcat -w 1 <host> <port>
```

Recipients supporting printing directly via TCP socket:

Linux host with LPRng, CUPS server, or CUPS client print system:

- No print system is required for receiving directly via TCP socket and there is no print system that supports this directly, as it makes little sense to send raw data when there is a print system that supports real print jobs and a suitable protocol (LPD or IPP).
- Nevertheless, in the CUPS print system data can be received via port 9100 and forwarded to a queue by entering in `/etc/inetd.conf`:

```
9100 stream tcp nowait lp /usr/bin/lp lp -d <queue>
```

If filtering is not wanted, append `-o raw` as an option.

- You can emulate the properties of a print server box that receives data via port 9100 and directly forwards them to the printer. To do this, append a line such as the following in `/etc/inetd.conf`:

```
9100 stream tcp nowait lp /bin/dd dd of=/dev/lp0
```

Print server box or network printer:

- The support status varies from case to case.
- The port depends on the model. For HP network printers and HP JetDirect print server boxes, the default port is 9100. For JetDirect print server boxes with two or three local printer ports, the ports are 9100, 9101, and 9102. The same ports are used by many other print server boxes. If you are not sure, ask the manufacturer or consult the printer manual to find out which port is used to address the printer directly. Additional information about this can be found in the `/usr/share/doc/packages/lprng/LPRng-HOWTO.html` (especially under `/usr/share/doc/packages/lprng/LPRng-HOWTO.html#SECNETWORK`, `/usr/share/doc/packages/lprng/LPRng-HOWTO.html#SOCKETAPI` and `/usr/share/doc/packages/lprng/LPRng-HOWTO.html#AEN4858`

Examples

Case 1: Several workstations, one print server, and one or more print server boxes or network printers:

Print server with LPRng print system:

- The workstations should also use the LPRng print system.
- A special queue is available on the print server for every network printer or every printer connected to a print server box.
- Via the LPD protocol, the workstations send the print jobs to the print server queue associated with the printer.
- Depending on which print server box or network printer supports which protocol, the print server uses the LPD protocol or direct data transmission via TCP socket for sending the print data to the print server box or network printer.

Print server with CUPS server print system:

- The workstations should also use the CUPS print system. In this case, the CUPS client print system is sufficient.
- A special queue is available on the print server for every network printer or every printer connected to a print server box.
- Via the IPP protocol, the workstations send the print jobs to the print server queue associated with the printer.
- Depending on which print server box or network printer supports which protocol, the print server uses the LPD protocol or direct data transmission via TCP socket for sending the print data to the print server box or network printer.

Case 2: A few workstations, no print server, and one or several print server boxes or network printers:

Workstations with LPRng print system or CUPS server print system:

- A special queue is available on each workstation for every network printer or every printer connected to a print server box. As all queues must be configured on all workstations, this only makes sense if there are only a few workstations.
- Depending on which print server box or network printer supports which protocol, the print server uses the LPD protocol or direct data transmission via TCP socket for sending the print data to the print server box or network printer.
- If several workstations concurrently send data to the same print server box or network printer, data loss and other problems may occur, especially if the LPD protocol is used for the data transmission. The implementation of the LPD recipient in the print server box or network printer is often inadequate, as there is usually not enough storage space for buffering several print jobs. If, however, the data transmission is performed exclusively via TCP socket, the system can be quite reliable, depending on the print server box or network printer.

5.8.4 Filtering for Network Printers

The previous section described how print jobs or raw data are transmitted from the workstation to the printer. The filtering process (the conversion of the original data to printer-specific data) is yet another subject. The conversion to printer-specific data for network printing occurs in the same way as for a printer locally connected to a stand-alone system. The print filter for network printing and a stand-alone system is identical, although the data flow from the workstation to the printer is more complicated and goes through several stages such as the following:

```
Workstation -> Print Server -> Print Server Box -> Printer
```

At this point in the chain, the source file must be converted into the format that the printer is able to print (PostScript, PCL, ESC/P). The conversion is handled by a print filter which should run on a machine with sufficient computing power and storage space — on the workstation or on a print server, but not in a print server box or network printer. Usually, print server boxes and network printers do not have any built-in print filter. Thus, they can only receive printer-specific data and forward it to the printer or printing unit.

A queue can configured with or without a filter. In the YaST printer configuration, the first step is the selection of the *Hardware* category for printing (e.g., via CUPS network server, via LPD network server, or direct printing on a network printer or print server box). Therefore, the default setting (with or without filtering) should normally work. If necessary, the default setting can be changed in the YaST printer configuration.

The default settings are as follows:

Print via CUPS Network Server: no filtering (as this is usually done on the CUPS network server)

Print via LPD-Style Network Server no filtering (as this is usually done on the LPD network server)

Print directly on a network printer or using a print server box: Filtering

If the queue is configured with filtering, the original data is buffered in the queue and subsequently filtered on the host on which the queue is located. Then the converted data is sent to the recipient (see Figure 5.2).

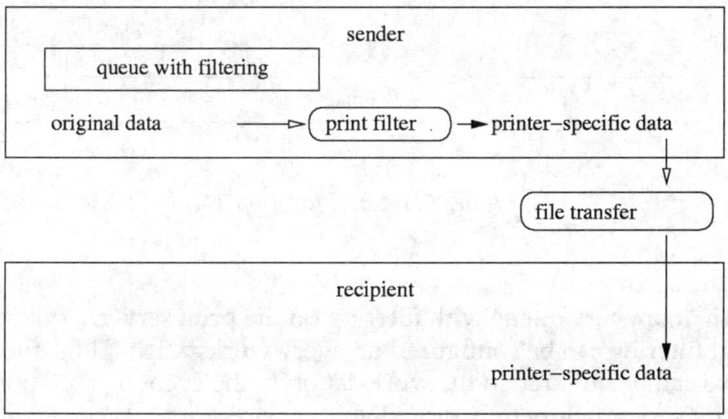

***Figure 5.2:** Overview of the Filtering Procedure*

The following paragraphs describe the filtering options for the above examples.

Case B1 Several workstations, one print server, and one or more print server boxes or network printers: The easiest and most suitable configuration is shown in Figure 5.3 on the following page.

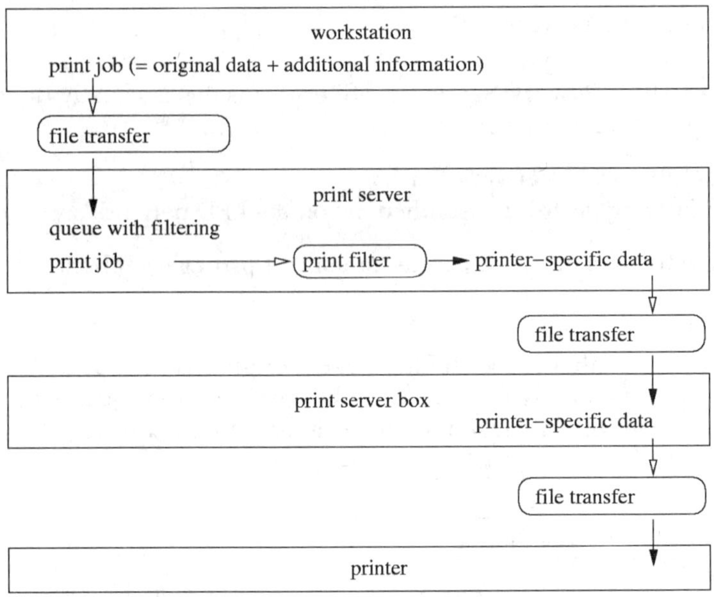

Figure 5.3: Configuration 1

Case B1b For every queue with filtering on the print server, a queue without filtering can be configured on every workstation. Thus, the print jobs can be buffered in the workstation in the event of a temporary print server failure or overload. In this way, printouts can always be generated on the workstations without having to wait until the print server is available. The disadvantage of this approach is that all queues have to be configured on all workstations (though without filtering) and certain modifications of the queues on the print server (such as renaming, addition, or deletion of queues) require an adaption of the configurations on all workstations. Changes in the filtering process do not require any adaption.This rather sophisticated configuration is shown in Figure 5.4 on the next page.

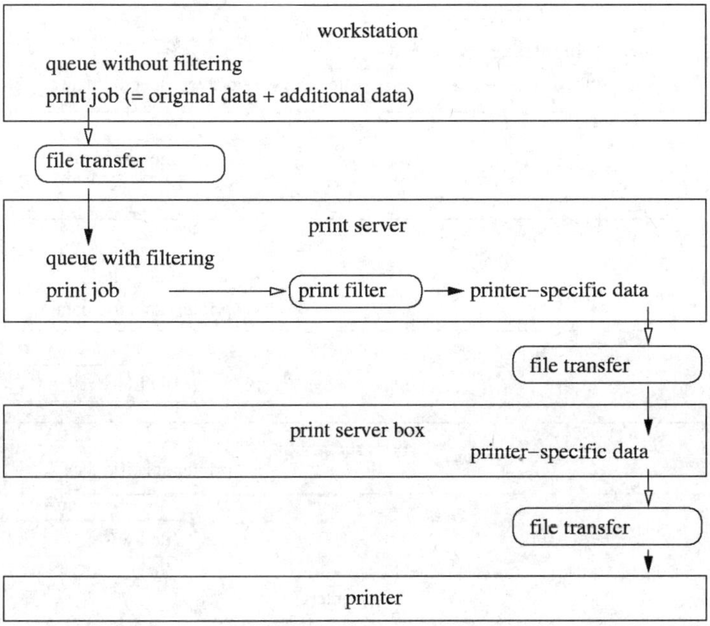

Figure 5.4: Configuration 2

Case B1c Theoretically, the filtering process could take place on the individual workstations. In this case, the only function of the print server would be the transmission of the printer-specific data to the print server boxes or network printers. However, this would degrade the print server to an oversized print server box, which is usually not very practical, unless the print server's performance is not sufficient for filtering. The disadvantage of this approach is that all queues must be configured on all workstations (with filtering) and all changes would require the adaption of the configurations on all workstations. Figure 5.5 on the following page shows this configuration.

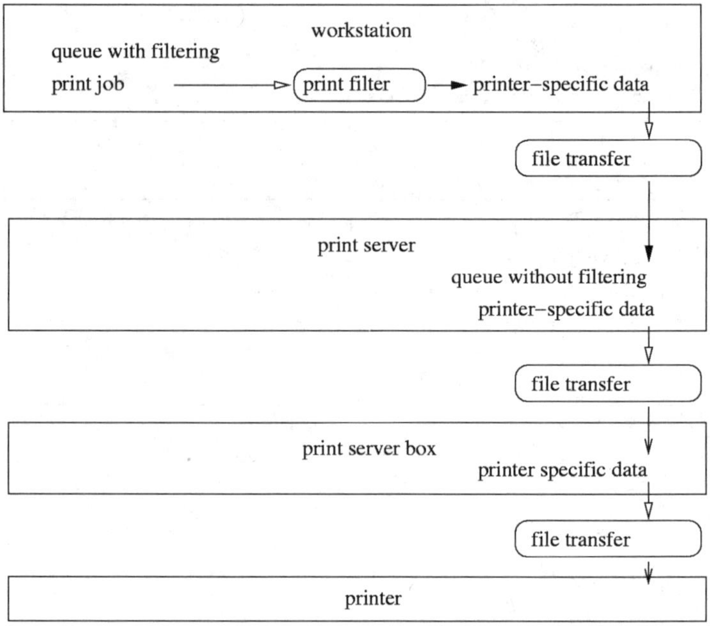

Figure 5.5: *Configuration 3*

Case B2 A few workstations, no print server, and one or several print server boxes or network printers:The only possible configuration is to have a queue with filtering for each printer on every workstation. The disadvantage of this approach is that all queues must be configured on all workstations (with filtering) and all changes would require the adaption of the configurations on all workstations. Figure 5.6 on the next page shows this configuration.

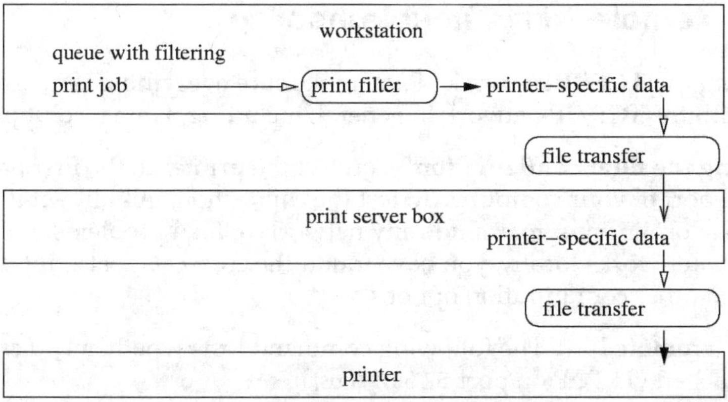

Figure 5.6: *Configuration 4*

Case B3 If you consider the above cases in reverse order, see the development from the configuration on a stand-alone system with a locally connected printer to a high-level configuration for several workstations with a print server for several print server boxes or network printers.

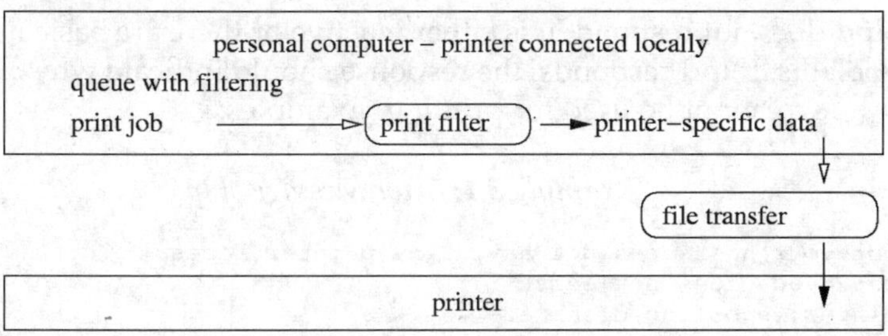

Figure 5.7: *Configuration 5*

The previous constellations looks almost the same as the configuration for a stand-alone system with a locally connected printer. Figure 5.7 shows the configuration for a stand-alone system.

5.8.5 Remote Printer Troubleshooting

Checking the TCP/IP network First, make sure everything is in order with the TCP/IP network in general, including name resolution.

Checking the filter configuration Connect the printer to the first parallel port of your computer. To test the connection, initially set it up as a local printer to exclude any network-related problems. If the printer works locally, you have found the correct Ghostscript driver and other configuration options.

Testing a remote lpd The following command tests whether `lpd` can be reached via TCP on port `515` of ⟨*host*⟩:

```
netcat -z <host> 515 && echo ok || echo failed
```

If `lpd` cannot be reached in this way, it is either not running at all or there is some basic network problem. This way you can get a (possibly very long) status report about the `queue` on the `host`, if `lpd` is running and the host is reachable. As `root`, enter the following command:

```
echo -e "\004<queue>" \
  | netcat -w 2 -p 722 <host> 515
```

If lpd does not respond, it is either inactive or there are basic network problems. If lpd responds, the response should indicate why `queue` on `host` cannot be used for printing. Examples:

Example 5.1: *Error Message of lpd*

```
lpd: your host does not have line printer access
lpd: queue does not exist
printer: spooling disabled
printer: printing disabled
```

If you receive such a response from the lpd, the problem is caused by the remote lpd.

Testing a remote cupsd By default, a CUPS network server broadcasts its queue every thirty seconds via the UDP port `631`. Thus, the following command can be used to test if a CUPS network server exists in the network:

```
netcat -u -l -p 631 & PID=$! ; sleep 40 ; kill $PID
```

By default, CUPS network servers broadcasts its queues via port 631 at thirty-second intervals. After waiting for forty seconds, the output should appear as follows if a broadcasting CUPS network server exists:

Example 5.2: *CUPS Network Server Broadcast*

```
... ipp://<host>.<domain>:631/printers/<queue>
```

The following command tests whether cupsd can be reached via TCP on port 631 of ⟨*host*⟩:

```
netcat -z <host> 631 && echo ok || echo failed
```

If cupsd cannot be reached in this way, it is either not running at all or there is some basic network problem.

```
lpstat -h <host> -l -t
```

With this command, get a (possibly very long) status report about all queues on ⟨*host*⟩, provided cupsd is running and the host is reachable.

```
echo -en "\r" \
| lp -d <queue> -h <host>
```

This command sends a print job consisting of a single carriage return character to test if the ⟨*queue*⟩ on ⟨*host*⟩ accepts any print jobs. This test command should not print out anything or only cause the printer to eject an empty page.

Testing a remote SMB server To test the basic operability of an SMB server, enter:

```
echo -en "\r" \
| smbclient '/<HOST>/<SHARE>' '<PASSWORD>' \
-c 'print -' -N -U '<USER>' \
 && echo ok || echo failed
```

For ⟨*HOST*⟩, enter the host name of the Samba server. For ⟨*SHARE*⟩, enter the name of the remote queue (i.e., the name of the Samba share). For ⟨*PASSWORD*⟩, enter the password string. Replace ⟨*USER*⟩ with the user name. This test command should not print out anything or only cause the printer to eject an empty page. The following command displays any shares on the ⟨*host*⟩ that are currently available. Details on this can be obtained from the manual page of `smbclient`.

```
smbclient -N -L <host>
```

Troubleshooting an unreliable network printer or print server box

Spoolers on print server boxes often become unreliable when having to deal with relatively high printing volumes. As the cause of this lies with the server-side spooler, there is mostly no way to fix this. As a workaround, however, circumvent the spooler on the print server box by using TCP sockets to directly stream data to the printer connected to the host. This turns the print server box into a mere data converter between the two different data streams (TCP/IP network and local printer line), which effectively makes the printer behave like a local printer although it is connected to the print server box. Without the spooler acting as an intermediary, this method also gives much more direct control over the printer device in general. To use this method, you need to know the corresponding TCP port on the print server box. If the printer is switched on and properly connected, you should be able to determine the TCP port a minute or so after booting the print server box with the program `nmap`. Running `nmap`⟨*`IP-address`*⟩ on the print server box may return an output similar to this:

```
Port        State        Service
23/tcp      open         telnet
80/tcp      open         http
515/tcp     open         printer
631/tcp     open         cups
9100/tcp    open         jetdirect
```

This output means:

- You can log in on the above print server box with `telnet` to look for important information or to change basic configuration options.
- The above print server runs an HTTP daemon, which can provide detailed server information or allow you to set specific printing options.

- The print spooler running on the print server box can be reached over the LPD protocol on port 515.
- The print spooler running on the print server box can also be reached over the IPP protocol on port 631.
- The printer connected to the print server box can be accessed directly via TCP sockets on port 9100.

By default, `nmap` only probes a number of common ports, as listed in `/usr/share/nmap/nmap-services`. To have all ports probed, use the command `nmap -p` ⟨*from_port*⟩-⟨*to_port*⟩ ⟨*IP-address*⟩ — which, however, might take quite some time. To learn more about this, have a look at the manual page with `man nmap`.

With a command like:

```
echo -en "\rHello\r\f" | netcat -w 1 <IP-address> <port>
cat <filename> | netcat -w 1 <IP-address> <port>
```

send entire strings or files straight to a given port, which is helpful when testing whether a printer can be addressed through that port.

5.8.6 Print Servers Supporting Both LPD and IPP

LPD, IPP, and CUPS

By default, the CUPS daemon only supports the IPP protocol. However, the program `/usr/lib/cups/daemon/cups-lpd` from the cups package enables the CUPS server to accept print jobs sent to port 515 via the LPD protocol. For this purpose, the respective service must be activated for `xinetd`. This can be done with YaST or manually by activating the respective line in the file `/etc/xinetd.d/cups-lpd`.

Supporting Both Protocols by Using LPRng and lpdfilter with CUPS

There may be situations where you want to run both LPRng and lpdfilter and CUPS on one system, maybe because you want to enhance the functionality of LPD with some CUPS features or because you need the LPRng and lpdfilter system as an add-on for certain special cases.

Running the two systems together on the same system leads to a number of problems, however. Below, we list the most important of these and briefly explain the limitations resulting from them. The topic is too complex to describe them in any greater detail here. There are several ways to solve these issues, depending on the individual case.

- You should not rely on YaST for configuration if you install both printing systems. The printer configuration module of YaST has not been written with this case in mind.
- There is a conflict between `lprng` and `cups-client`, because they contain a number of files with identical names, such as `/usr/bin/lpr` and `/usr/bin/lp`. You should, therefore, not install `cups-client`. This, however, means that no CUPS-based command-line tools are available, but only those included with LPRng. You are still able to print through CUPS print queues from the X Window System with `xpp` or `kprinter`, however, as well as from all application programs with built-in support for CUPS.
- By default, `cupsd` creates the `/etc/printcap` file when started and writes the names of CUPS queues to it. This is done to maintain compatibility with applications that expect queue names in `/etc/printcap` to offer them in their print dialogs. With both printing systems installed, disable this `cupsd` feature to reserve `/etc/printcap` for exclusive use by the LPRng and lpdfilter printing system. As a result, applications that get queue names only from `/etc/printcap` can use only these local queues, but not the remote queues made available by CUPS through the network.

6

Booting and Boot Managers

This chapter introduces various methods for booting the installed system. First, some of the technical details of the boot process are explained to help with understanding the various methods. This is followed by a detailed description of the default boot manager GRUB.

6.1 Booting a PC

After turning on your computer, the first thing that happens is that the BIOS (Basic Input Output System) takes control, initializes the screen and keyboard, and tests the main memory. At this point, no storage media or external devices are known to the system.

After that, the system reads the current date and time as well as information about the most important peripheral devices from the CMOS setup. After reading the CMOS, the BIOS should recognize the first hard disk, including details such as its geometry. It can then start to load the operating system (OS) from there.

To load the OS, the system loads a 512-byte data segment from the first hard disk into main memory and executes the code stored at the beginning of this segment. The instructions contained in it determine the rest of the boot process. This is why the first 512 bytes of the hard disk are often called the *Master Boot Record* (MBR).

Up to this point (loading the MBR), the boot sequence is independent of the installed operating system and is identical on all PCs. Also, all the PC has to access peripheral hardware are those routines (drivers) stored in the BIOS.

6.1.1 Master Boot Record

The layout of the MBR always follows a standard that is independent of the operating system. The first 446 bytes are reserved for program code. The next 64 bytes offer space for a partition table for up to four partitions (see Section 1.7 on page 23). Without the partition table, no file systems exist on the hard disk — the disk would be virtually useless without it. The last two bytes must contain a special *magic number* (`AA55`). An MBR containing a different number would be considered invalid by the BIOS and any PC operating system.

6.1.2 Boot Sectors

Boot sectors are the first sectors on a hard disk partition, except in the case of extended partitions, which are just *containers* for other partitions. Boot sectors offer 512 bytes of space and are designed to contain code capable of launching an operating system on this partition. Boot sectors of formatted DOS, Windows, and OS/2 partitions do exactly that (in addition, they contain some basic data about the file system structure). In contrast, the boot sector of a Linux partition is empty (even after creating a file system on it). Thus, a Linux partition cannot bootstrap itself, even if it contains a kernel and a valid root file system. A boot sector with a valid start code contains the same magic number as the MBR in its last two bytes (`AA55`).

6.1.3 Booting DOS or Windows

The DOS MBR of the first hard disk contains information that determines which partition of a hard disk is active (bootable). The active partition is searched for the operating system to boot. Therefore, DOS must be installed on the first hard disk. The DOS program code in the MBR is the first stage of the boot loader. It checks if the specified partition contains a valid boot sector.

If this is the case, the code in this boot sector can be loaded as the second stage of the boot loader, which in turn loads the system programs. Subsequently, the DOS prompt appears or the Windows user interface is started. In DOS, only one primary partition can be marked as active. This is why you cannot install the DOS system on logical drives in an extended partition.

6.2 Boot Concepts

The simplest boot concept involves only one machine with one operating system. The boot process for this case has already been outlined. The same boot concept can be used for a Linux-only machine. Theoretically, you do not need to install a boot loader for such a system. However, in this case you would not be able to pass additional parameters to the kernel at boot time. For a machine with multiple operating systems, the following boot concepts are possible:

Booting other operating systems from a floppy disk:
One operating system is booted from the hard disk. Other operating systems can be booted from the floppy disk drive.

- *Requirements:* bootable floppy disk drive
- *Example:* installation of Linux alongside Windows; booting of Linux from a boot disk
- *Advantage:* no boot loader needs to be installed
- *Disadvantage:* requires working boot disks and the boot process takes longer
- Depending on the purpose of the computer, it is an advantage or disadvantage that Linux cannot be booted without a disk.

Booting another operating system from a USB storage device: The system can also use a USB storage device to drive the boot process. This is very similar to the floppy method, except the necessary data is fetched from the USB memory stick.

Installing a boot manager: This allows you to use several operating systems on a single machine and to choose among the installed systems at boot time. Switching to another operating system requires a reboot. However, the boot manager must be compatible with all the operating systems installed on the machine. The boot managers of SUSE LINUX (LILO and its successor GRUB) can boot all common operating systems. By default, SUSE LINUX installs the preferred boot manager in the MBR, unless this setting is changed during the installation.

6.3 Map Files, GRUB, and LILO

The main obstacle for booting an operating system is that the kernel is usually a file within a file system on a partition on a disk. These concepts are unknown to the BIOS. To circumvent this, maps and map files were introduced. These maps simply note the physical block numbers on the disk that comprise the logical files. When such a map is processed, the BIOS loads all the physical blocks in sequence as noted in the map, building the logical file in memory.

In contrast to LILO, which relies entirely on maps, GRUB tries to gain independence from the fixed maps at an early stage. GRUB achieves this by means of the file system code, which enables access to files by way of the path specification instead of the block numbers.

Note

Boot Loader Selection

If you update from a previous version of SUSE LINUX in which LILO was the boot manager, the new system continues to use LILO. If you install SUSE LINUX from scratch, the system uses GRUB unless the root partition is installed on a RAID system of the following types:

- CPU-controlled RAID controllers, such as many Promise and Highpoint controllers
- software RAID
- LVM

For information about the installation of LILO, search for the keyword "LILO" in the Support Database (`http://portal.suse.de/sdb/en/index.html`).

Note

6.4 Booting with GRUB

GRUB (the Grand Unified Boot loader) consists of two stages. The first stage is only 512 bytes long. It is written to the MBR or to the boot sector of a disk partition or floppy disk. The second, larger stage is loaded after that and holds the program code. The only purpose of the first stage is to load the second one.

The second stage contains code for reading file systems. Currently supported are Ext2, Ext3, ReiserFS, JFS, XFS, Minix, and the DOS FAT file system used by Windows. GRUB has the ability to access file systems even before booting is finished, as long as they are on devices handled by the BIOS (floppies or hard disks).

All boot parameters can easily be changed *before* booting. If, for example, the menu file contains an error, it can be fixed. Boot parameters can be entered interactively at a prompt. GRUB offers the possibility to find the location of the kernel and initrd before booting. With this, you can even boot operating systems for which no entry exists in the boot menu.

6.4.1 The GRUB Boot Menu

GRUB displays a graphical splash screen or a text mode interface with a boot menu. The contents of this screen are controlled by the configuration file `/boot/grub/menu.lst`. This file contains all the information about the partitions or operating systems that can be selected from the boot menu.

This menu file is loaded by GRUB directly from the file system on each boot, so there is no need to update GRUB when the file has been modified. To reconfigure the boot loader, simply edit the file via YaST or with your favorite editor. Temporary changes can be made in the interactive edit mode.

The menu file contains commands GRUB should execute. Its syntax is quite simple. Each line consists of a command, optionally followed by arguments that must be separated by spaces, as is the case with shell commands. For historical reasons, there are some commands that allow an = before their first argument. Lines beginning with a hash (#) are comments.

To identify the menu item in the menu overview, specify a name or a `title` for every entry. The text (including any spaces) following the keyword `title` is displayed as a selectable option in the menu. All commands up to the next `title` are executed when this menu item is selected.

The simplest case is redirection to boot loaders of other operating systems. The command is `chainloader` and the argument is usually the boot block in another partition, written in GRUB block notation, for example:

```
chainloader (hd0,3)+1
```

The device naming scheme used by GRUB is explained in Section 6.4.1 on the facing page. The above example specifies the first block of the fourth partition on the first hard disk.

The command for specifying a kernel image is `kernel`. The first argument is the path to the kernel image on a partition. The remainder are parameters that are passed to the kernel when booting.

If the kernel does not have the needed built-in drivers for accessing the root partition, `initrd` must be specified. This is a separate GRUB command whose only argument is the path to the initrd file. As the loading address of the initrd is written to the loaded kernel image, the command `initrd` must follow immediately after the `kernel` command.

The `root` command simplifies specification of kernel and initrd files. The only argument for the command `root` is a device or partition (in GRUB notation). This device is used for all kernel, initrd, or other file paths for which no device is specified. This applies up to the next `root` command. The command is not used in the default `menu.lst` file created during the installation. It merely facilitates manual editing.

The `boot` command is implied and thus automatically executed at the end of each menu entry, so it does not need to be written into the menu file. If entering GRUB commands interactively at the prompt, remember to enter the `boot` command at the end. The command itself has no arguments. It merely boots the loaded kernel image or chain loader.

Once you have written all your menu entries, specify which entry to use as the `default`. Otherwise, the first one (number `0`) is booted by default. You can also specify a time-out in seconds after which this should occur. The `timeout` and `default` usually precede the menu entries. A sample configuration file is described in Section 6.4.1 on the next page.

Naming Conventions for Hard Disks and Partitions

GRUB names hard disks and partitions according to conventions that differ from the Linux device names, such as `/dev/hda1`. The first hard disk is always referred to as `/dev/hd0`. The floppy drive is called `/dev/fd0`. The four primary partitions allowed per disk are numbered from `0` to `3`. Logical partitions are counted beginning with `4`.

```
(hd0,0)    first primary partition on first hard disk
(hd0,1)    second primary partition
(hd0,2)    third primary partition
(hd0,3)    fourth primary partition (usually an extended partition)
(hd0,4)    first logical partition
(hd0,5)    second logical partition ...
```

GRUB does not distinguish between IDE, SCSI, or RAID devices. All hard disks detected by the BIOS or other disk controllers are counted according to the boot sequence set in the BIOS itself.

The fact that BIOS device names do not correspond to Linux devices is an issue resolved with algorithms that establish a mapping. GRUB stores the result in a file (`device.map`), which can be edited. For more information about `device.map`, refer to Section 6.4.2 on page 144.

For GRUB, a file name must be specified as a device name written in parentheses followed by the full path to the file and the file name. The path must always start with a slash. For example, on a system with a single IDE disk and Linux on the first partition, the bootable kernel might be specified with:

```
(hd0,0)/boot/vmlinuz
```

A Sample Menu File

The following example shows how the GRUB menu file works. This imaginary machine has a Linux boot partition on `/dev/hda5`, a root partition on `/dev/hda7`, and a Windows installation on `/dev/hda1`.

```
gfxmenu (hd0,4)/message
color white/blue black/light-gray
default 0
timeout 8

title linux
   kernel (hd0,4)/vmlinuz root=/dev/hda7 vga=791
   initrd (hd0,4)/initrd
title windows
   chainloader(hd0,0)+1
title floppy
   chainloader(fd0)+1
title failsafe
   kernel (hd0,4)/vmlinuz.shipped root=/dev/hda7 ide=nodma \
   apm=off acpi=off vga=normal nosmp maxcpus=0 3
   initrd (hd0,4)/initrd.shipped
```

The first part defines the splash screen configuration:

gfxmenu (hd0,4)/message The background image is located on `/dev/hda5` and has the name `message`.

color The color scheme: white as normal foreground, blue as normal background, black for the foreground of selected items, and light gray as the selection background. These colors do not affect the graphical splash screen as defined under `gfxmenu`, but the standard GRUB interface. On a SUSE LINUX system, this interface can be accessed from the splash screen by pressing Esc.

default 0 By default, the first menu entry `title linux` should be booted.

timeout 8 After 8 seconds without user input, GRUB will automatically boot the default entry.

The second, larger part defines the different operating systems to boot:

- The first entry (`title linux`) is responsible for booting SUSE LINUX. The kernel (`vmlinuz`) is located on the first hard disk on the first logical partition (which is the boot partition in this case). The appended arguments are kernel parameters, such as the root partition and the video mode. The root partition is specified according to the Linux convention (`/dev/hda7`), as this information is interpreted by the Linux kernel, not by GRUB. The `initrd` image is located on the same logical partition of the first hard disk.
- The second entry is responsible for booting Windows, which is installed on the first partition of the first hard disk (`hd0, 0`). The command `chainloader +1` causes GRUB to read and execute the first sector of the specified partition.
- The next entry enables booting from the floppy drive without changing any BIOS settings.
- The `failsafe` entry boots a Linux kernel with a number of kernel parameters that enable booting Linux even if the hardware is causing problems.

Changing the Hard Disk Sequence

Some operating systems, such as Windows, can only start from the first hard disk. If you have such an operating system installed on a different hard disk, you can implement a logical change for the respective menu entry. However, this only works if the operating system accesses the hard disks by way of the BIOS when booting.

```
...
title windows
   map (hd0) (hd1)
   map (hd1) (hd0)
   chainloader(hd1,0)+1
...
```

In this example, Windows is started from the second hard disk. For this purpose, the logical sequence of the hard disks is changed with `map`. This change does *not* affect the logic within the GRUB menu file. You still need to specify the second hard disk for `chainloader`.

Editing Menu Entries During the Boot Procedure

From the graphical boot menu of GRUB, use the cursor keys to select the operating system to boot. If you select a Linux system, you can add boot parameters. After pressing Esc and exiting the splash screen, n press E to edit individual menu entries directly. Changes made in this way only apply to the current boot procedure and will not be adopted permanently.

> **Note**
>
> **Keyboard Layout during the Boot Procedure**
>
> The US keyboard layout is the only one available at boot time.
>
> **Note**

After enabling the editing mode, use the arrow keys to navigate to the entry to change. To make the selected item editable, press E again. Adjust the entry as desired. Leave the editing mode with Enter and go back to the menu, where the changed entry can be booted by pressing E. In the lower part of the screen, GRUB displays further options.

6.4.2 The File device.map

The file `device.map` maps GRUB device names to Linux device names. This is only relevant when running the GRUB shell as a Linux program (command `grub`). For this purpose, the program reads the file `device.map`. See Section 6.4.4 on the next page for more information.

GRUB does not have access to the boot sequence information in the BIOS. If your system contains both IDE and SCSI hard disks, GRUB must try to determine the boot sequence by means of a special procedure. It saves the results of this check to the file `/boot/grub/device.map`. For a system that boots IDE devices before SCSI devices, the file `device.map` could look as follows:

```
(fd0) /dev/fd0
(hd0) /dev/hda
(hd1) /dev/hdb
(hd2) /dev/sda
(hd3) /dev/sdb
```

As the order of IDE, SCSI, and other hard disks depends on various factors and Linux is not able to identify the mapping, the sequence in the file `device.map` can be set manually. If you encounter problems when booting, check if the sequence in this file corresponds to the sequence in the BIOS and use the GRUB shell to modify it if necessary (see Section 6.4.4). Once you have successfully booted your Linux system, edit the file `device.map` permanently with the YaST boot loader module or an editor of your choice.

Any manual change to the `device.map` file requires that you update your GRUB installation. Use the following command:

```
grub --batch --device-map=/boot/grub/device.map < /etc/grub.conf
```

6.4.3 The File /etc/grub.conf

GRUB stores another important part of its configuration in the file `grub.conf`. This file defines the parameters and options needed by the `grub` command to install the boot loader correctly:

```
root (hd0,4)
install /grub/stage1 d (hd0) /grub/stage2 0x8000 (hd0,4)/grub/menu.lst
quit
```

The individual entries have the following meaning:

root (hd0,4) This command tells GRUB that all subsequent commands should be applied to the first logical partition on the first hard disk, where the boot files are located.

install `parameter` The command `grub` should be run with the parameter `install`. `stage1` of the boot loader should be installed in the MBR of the first hard disk (`/grub/stage1 d (hd0)`). `stage2` should be loaded to the memory address 0x8000 (`/grub/stage2 0x8000`). The last entry (`(hd0,4)/grub/menu.lst`) tells GRUB where to look for the menu file.

6.4.4 The GRUB Shell

GRUB actually consists of two parts: the boot loader and a normal Linux program (`/usr/sbin/grub`). This program is referred to as the *GRUB shell*. The functionality to install the boot loader on a hard disk or floppy disk is integrated into the GRUB shell through the internal commands `install` and `setup` — these commands can be executed using the GRUB shell on a running Linux system. However, these commands are also available while the system is booting with GRUB — before Linux is even running. This makes the repair of a defective system much easier.

6.4.5 Setting a Boot Password

Because GRUB is able to access file systems upon booting, it could also be used to read files that would not be accessible under normal circumstances — on a running system, users would need `root` permissions to read them. To put a stop to this, set a boot password. Such a password can be used to prevent unauthorized access to file systems at boot time and to prevent users from booting certain installed systems.

To create a boot password, log in as `root` and proceed as follows:

1. At the root prompt, enter `grub`.
2. In the GRUB shell, encrypt the password:

   ```
   grub> md5crypt
   Password: ****
   Encrypted: $1$lS2dv/$JOYcdxIn7CJk9xShzzJVw/
   ```

3. Paste the encrypted string into the global section of the file `menu.lst`:

   ```
   gfxmenu (hd0,4)/message
   color white/blue black/light-gray
   default 0
   timeout 8
   password --md5 $1$lS2dv/$JOYcdxIn7CJk9xShzzJVw/
   ```

   From now on, executing GRUB commands from the boot prompt is impossible without knowing the password. Permission to do so is only granted after pressing Ⓟ and entering the password. However, users can still boot all operating systems without any restriction.

4. To keep users from booting certain operating systems, add the entry `lock` for every section in `menu.lst` to prevent from being booted without entering a password. Example:

   ```
   title linux
     kernel (hd0,4)/vmlinuz root=/dev/hda7 vga=791
     initrd (hd0,4)/initrd
     lock
   ```

   After rebooting, trying to boot this entry from the menu would result in the following error message:

   ```
   Error 32: Must be authenticated
   ```

Return to the menu by pressing (Enter). From the menu, pressing (P) prompts for the password. The selected system (Linux in this case) should boot after typing the password and pressing (Enter).

Note

Boot Password and Splash Screen

Setting a boot password for GRUB disables the graphical splash screen as displayed by default.

Note

6.4.6 Boot Problems with GRUB

The geometry of attached hard disks is checked by GRUB only upon booting. In some cases, the BIOS returns inconsistent values, and GRUB reports *GRUB Geom Error* (see `http://portal.suse.com/sdb/en/2003/03/fhassel_geom-error.html`). In this case, use LILO or update the BIOS. Details on the installation, configuration, and maintenance of LILO is available in the Support Database article: `http://portal.suse.de/sdb/en/2004/01/lilo_overview.html>`.

6.4.7 For More Information

Extensive information about GRUB is available at `http://www.gnu.org/software/grub/`. If you have texinfo installed on your machine, view the GRUB info pages in a shell by entering `info grub`. You can also search for the keyword "GRUB" in the Support Database at `http://portal.suse.de/sdb/en/index.html` to get information about special issues.

6.5 Uninstalling the Linux Boot Loader

There are two ways to uninstall the Linux boot loader:

- Restore the backup of the original MBR by means of the YaST boot loader module. YaST creates this backup automatically. Refer to the installation section of the *User Guide* for details of the YaST boot loader module.

- Install a different boot loader or restore the DOS or Windows MBR.

Caution

A boot sector backup is no longer valid if the partition in question has a new file system. The partition table of an MBR backup becomes invalid if the hard disk has been repartitioned since the backup was created. Obsolete *backups* are time bombs. It is best to delete them from `/boot/backup.mbr` promptly.

Caution

6.5.1 Restoring the MBR (DOS, Win9x, or ME)

It is very simple to restore a DOS or Windows MBR. Just enter the MS-DOS command (available since DOS version 5.0) `fdisk /MBR`. These commands only write the first 446 bytes (the boot code) into the MBR and leave the partition table untouched, unless the MBR as a whole (see Section 6.1.1 on page 136) is treated as invalid due to an incorrect magic number. In this case, the partition table is set to zero. After restoring the MBR, mark the desired start partition as bootable (using fdisk again). This is required for the MBR routines of DOS and Windows.

6.5.2 Restoring the MBR of Windows XP

Boot from the Windows XP CD and press Ⓡ during the setup to start the recovery console. Select your Windows XP installation from the list and enter the administrator password. At the input prompt, enter the command `FIXMBR` and confirm with `y` when asked to do so. Then reboot the computer with `exit`.

6.5.3 Restoring the MBR of Windows 2000

Boot from the Windows 2000 CD and press Ⓡ then Ⓒ in the next menu to start the recovery console. Select your Windows 2000 installation from the list and enter the administrator password. At the input prompt, enter the command `FIXMBR` and confirm with `y` when asked to do so. Then reboot the computer with `exit`.

6.6 Creating Boot CDs

This concerns problems arising when attempting to boot a system with the LILO boot manager configured with YaST. The creation of a system boot disk fails with more recent SUSE LINUX versions because the space available on a floppy disk is no longer sufficient for the start-up files.

6.6.1 Procedure

It is possible to create a bootable CD-ROM containing the Linux start-up files if your system has an installed CD writer. This solution is only a workaround. It should normally be possible to configure LILO properly. Refer to the documentation about this subject in `/usr/share/doc/packages/lilo/README`, or read the man pages `man lilo.conf` and `man lilo`.

6.6.2 Boot CD with ISOLINUX

It is easiest to create a bootable CD with the ISOLINUX boot manager. The SuSE installation CDs are also made bootable with isolinux.

- Boot the installed system first using the following alternate procedure:
  - ▷ Boot from the installation CD or DVD as for installation.
  - ▷ Choose the preselected option 'Installation' during the boot sequence.
  - ▷ Choose the language and keyboard map next.
  - ▷ In the following menu, choose 'Boot installed system'.
  - ▷ The root partition is automatically detected and the system is booted from it.
- Install `syslinux` with YaST.
- Open a root shell. The following commands create a temporary directory and copy the files required for the booting of the Linux system (the isolinux boot loader as well as the kernel and the initrd) into it:

```
mkdir /tmp/CDroot
cp /usr/share/syslinux/isolinux.bin /tmp/CDroot/
cp /boot/vmlinuz /tmp/CDroot/linux
cp /boot/initrd /tmp/CDroot
```

- Create the boot loader configuration file `/tmp/CDroot/isolinux.cfg` with your preferred editor. Enter the following content:

  ```
  DEFAULT linux
  LABEL linux
    KERNEL linux
    APPEND initrd=initrd root=/dev/hdXY [boot parameter]
  ```

  Enter your root partition for the parameter `root=/dev/hdXY`. It is listed in the file `/etc/fstab`. Enter additional options for the setting `[boot parameter]`, which should be used during booting. The configuration files could, for example, look like this:

  ```
  DEFAULT linux
  LABEL linux
    KERNEL linux
    APPEND initrd=initrd root=/dev/hda7 hdd=ide-scsi
  ```

- The following command (entered at a command prompt) then creates an ISO-9660 file system for the CD.

  ```
  mkisofs -o /tmp/bootcd.iso -b isolinux.bin -c boot.cat
    -no-emul-boot -boot-load-size 4
    -boot-info-table /tmp/CDroot
  ```

  The complete command must be entered as one line.

- The file `/tmp/bootcd.iso` can be written to CD after that with either graphical CD writing applications, like K3b simply at a command prompt: `cdrecord -v speed=2 dev=0,0,0 /tmp/bootcd.iso -eject`

  The parameter `dev=0,0,0` must be changed according to the SCSI ID of the writer. This can be determined with the command `cdrecord -scanbus`. Also, refer to the man page `cdrecord`.

- Test the boot CD. Reboot the computer to verify whether the Linux system is started correctly from the CD.

7

Linux on Mobile Devices

This chapter focuses on the use of Linux on mobile devices — especially on laptops. It covers the configuration of PC cards (PCMCIA), the management of multiple system profiles with SCPM, and wireless communication with IrDA and Bluetooth.

7.1 PCMCIA

PCMCIA stands for *Personal Computer Memory Card International Association*. It is used as a collective term for all hardware and software involved.

7.1.1 The Hardware

The essential component is the PCMCIA card. There are two distinct types:

PC cards These are currently the most used cards. They use a 16-bit bus for data transmission. These cards are inexpensive and generally very well supported by Linux.

CardBus Cards This is a more recent standard. CardBus cards use a 32-bit bus, which makes them faster, but also more expensive. Because the data transfer rate is frequently restricted at another point, it is often not worth the extra cost. There are numerous drivers for these cards, but many of them still are unstable. Whether these cards are well supported also depends on the available PCMCIA controller.

If the PCMCIA service is active, determine the type of the inserted card using `cardctl ident`. A list of supported cards can be found in `/usr/share/doc/packages/pcmcia/SUPPORTED.CARDS` The most recent version of the PCMCIA HOWTO is available in the same directory.

The second essential component consists of the PCMCIA controller of the PC card or CardBus bridge. These establish the connection between the card and the PCI bus and, in older devices, the connection to the ISA bus as well. These controllers are almost always compatible with the Intel chip i82365. All common models are supported. Retrieve the controller type with `pcic_probe`. If it is a PCI device, `lspci -vt` provides additional information.

7.1.2 The Software

Differences between PCMCIA Systems

Currently there are two PCMCIA systems — external PCMCIA and kernel PCMCIA. The external PCMCIA system by David Hinds is the older one. It is quite well tested and development of this type of PCMCIA system continues. The sources of the modules used are not integrated in the kernel sources, which is why it is called an *external* system.

Starting with kernel 2.4, a set of alternative modules is contained in the kernel sources forming the *kernel* PCMCIA system. The basic modules were written by Linus Torvalds. Their support of more recent CardBus bridges is better than with external PCMCIA.

Unfortunately, the two systems are not compatible. They contain different sets of card drivers. Depending on the hardware involved, only one of the systems may be suitable. The default in SUSE LINUX is the more recent kernel PCMCIA. It is possible to change the system, however. To do this, give the variable `PCMCIA_SYSTEM` in the file `/etc/sysconfig/pcmcia/` either the value `external` or `kernel`. Then PCMCIA must be restarted with `rcpcmcia restart`. If intending to do just a temporary switch between systems, use `rcpcmcia restart external` or `rcpcmcia restart kernel`. If PCMCIA is not running, use the option `start` instead of `restart` to switch the PCMCIA system temporarily. Refer to `/usr/share/doc/packages/pcmcia/README.SuSE` for detailed information.

The Base Modules

The kernel modules for both systems are located in the kernel packages. In addition, the packages `pcmcia` and `hotplug` are required. When PCMCIA is started, the modules `pcmcia_core`, `i82365` (external PCMCIA) or `yenta_socket` (kernel PCMCIA), and `ds` are loaded. In some very rare cases, the module `tcic` is required instead of `i82365` or `yenta_socket`. They initialize the existing PCMCIA controller and provide basic functionality.

The Card Manager

As it is possible to change PCMCIA cards while the system is running, a deamon monitors any activity in the PCMCIA slots. Depending on the chosen PCMCIA system and hardware, this task is performed by the card manager or the hotplug system of the kernel. With external PCMCIA, only the card manager is used. For kernel PCMCIA, the card manager only handles PC Card cards. CardBus cards are handled by hotplug. The card manager is started by the PCMCIA start script after the base modules have been loaded. Because hotplug manages subsystems other than PCMCIA, it has its own start script.

If a card is inserted, card manager or hotplug determines the type and function of the card then loads the corresponding modules. If this is successful, card manager or hotplug starts certain initialization scripts. Depending on the function of the card, they establish a network connection, mount partitions from external SCSI hard drives, or carry out other hardware-specific actions. The scripts for the card manager are located in `/etc/pcmcia/`. The scripts for hotplug can be found in `/etc/hotplug/`.

If the card is removed, card manager or hotplug terminates all card activities using the same scripts. Finally, the modules that are no longer required are unloaded.

Both the start process of PCMCIA and card events are recorded in the system log (`/var/log/messages`). It records which PCMCIA system is currently used and which daemons have been used by which scripts to set up things. Removing a PCMCIA device should work smoothly, at least in theory. This works very well for network, modem, or ISDN cards as long as there are no active network connections. It does, however, fail if mounted partitions of an external hard drive or NFS directories are used. In such cases, ensure that these units are synchronized and cleanly unmounted. This is no longer possible if the card has already been removed. In case of doubt, `cardctl eject` can be helpful to safely eject the card.

This command deactivates all cards still in the laptop. To deactivate only one card, specify the slot number, for example, `cardctl eject 0`.

7.1.3 Configuration

Set whether PCMCIA or hotplug is started at boot time with the YaST runlevel editor or on the command line using `chkconfig`. In `/etc/sysconfig/pcmcia`, there are four variables:

`PCMCIA_SYSTEM` Specifies the PCMCIA system to use.

`PCMCIA_PCIC` Contains the name of the module that addresses the PCMCIA controller. Normally, the start script should detect the module automatically. If this automatic detection fails, enter the name of the desired module here. Otherwise, this variable should be left empty.

`PCMCIA_CORE_OPTS` This was originally designed to contain parameters for the `pcmcia_core` module, which are rarely used. Refer to the manual page of `pcmcia_core` for more information on these options.

PCMCIA_PCIC_OPTS Parameters for the module i82365. Refer to the manual page of i82365. If yenta_socket is used, these options are ignored, because yenta_socket has no options.

Card manager refers to the files /etc/pcmcia/config and /etc/pcmcia/*.conf for the assignment of drivers to PCMCIA cards. First, config is read then the *.conf files in alphabetical order. The last entry found for a card is used. Refer to the manual page of pcmcia for details on the syntax of these files.

Network Cards (Ethernet, Wireless LAN, and Token Ring)

These can be set up with YaST like normal network cards. Select 'PCMCIA' as the card type. All other details about setting up the network can be found in Section 13.4 on page 289. Read the notes there about hotpluggable cards.

ISDN

Even for ISDN PC cards, configuration is done to a large extent using YaST, as with other ISDN cards. It is not important which PCMCIA card offered there is chosen, but only that it is a PCMCIA card. When setting up hardware and provider, make sure the operating mode is set to hotplug and not to onboot.

ISDN modems also exist for PCMCIA cards. These are modem cards or multifunction cards with an additional ISDN connection kit. They are treated like an ordinary modem.

Modem

For modem PC cards, there are normally no PCMCIA-specific settings. As soon as a modem is inserted, it is available under /dev/modem.

There are also "soft modems" for PCMCIA cards. As a rule, these are not supported. If there is a driver, it must be individually integrated into the system.

SCSI and IDE

The corresponding driver module is loaded by the card manager or hotplug. When a SCSI or IDE card is inserted, the devices connected to it are available. The device names are detected dynamically. Information about existing SCSI or IDE devices can be found in `/proc/scsi/` or `/proc/ide/`.

External hard drives, CD-ROM drives, and similar devices must be switched on before the PCMCIA card is inserted into the slot. Use active termination for SCSI devices.

Caution

Removing IDE or SCSI Cards

If you intend to remove a SCSI or IDE card, properly unmount all partions on these devices. Otherwise you would not be able to access these devices after a reboot of the system.

Caution

You can also install Linux entirely on external hard drives. However, the boot process is a bit more complicated. You will always need a boot disk containing the kernel and an initial ramdisk (initrd). More information about this can be found in Section 11.3 on page 227.

The initrd contains a virtual file system that includes all required PCMCIA modules and programs. The boot disk (or rather the boot disk image) is designed in a similar fashion. Using these, you could always boot your external installation. It is, however, tiresome to load the PCMCIA support every time by hand. Advanced Linux users can create a customized boot disk for their own system. For more information on this topic refer to the PCMCIA HOWTO, section *Booting from a PCMCIA Device.*

7.1.4 Troubleshooting

Most problems arising with certain laptops or cards using PCMCIA can be solved with little trouble provided you approach the problem systematically.

Caution

Loading Kernel Modules by Hand

Kernel and external PCMCIA cannot be used at the same time, but they exist in parallel in SUSE LINUX. Keep this in mind when loading kernel modules by hand. The modules names of both PCMCIA systems are the same, but they are located in different subdirectories under `/lib/modules/<kernelversion>`. The subdirectories are called `pcmcia/` for kernel PCMCIA and `pcmcia-external/` for external PCMCIA. Thus, the subdirectory must be specified when loading modules manually:

```
modprobe -t <directory> <modulename>
```

Caution

First, find out if the problem is with the card or with the PCMCIA base system. For this reason, always start the computer first without the card inserted. Only insert the card when the base system appears to function correctly. Use `tail -f /var/log/messages` to monitor the system log while searching for the cause of the PCMCIA failure. With this approach, the problem is narrowed down to one of the two following cases.

Nonfunctional PCMCIA Base System

If the system hangs at boot time showing the message "PCMCIA: Starting services" or other strange things happen, PCMCIA can be prevented from being started at the next system boot by entering `NOPCMCIA=yes` at the boot prompt. To further isolate the error, load the three base modules of the PCMCIA system with the following commands by hand (as user `root`):

```
modprobe -t <dir> pcmcia_core
modprobe -t pcmcia-external i82365
```

for external PCMCIA or

```
modprobe -t pcmcia yenta_socket
```

for kernel PCMCIA
(in very rare cases, `modprobe -t <dir> tcic`)
and

```
modprobe -t <dir> ds
```

The critical modules are the first two.

If the error occurs while `pcmcia_core` is loaded, refer to the manual pages for `pcmcia_core` for further information. Use the options described there for a first testing with `modprobe`. As an example, switch off the APM support for the PCMCIA module. In a few cases, there could be problems with this. Use the setting `do_apm=0` to deactivate power management:

```
modprobe -t <dir> pcmciacore do_apm=0
```

If the chosen option is successful, write it to the variable `PCMCIA_CORE_-OPTS` in `/etc/sysconfig/pcmcia` to use it permanently:

```
PCMCIA_CORE_OPTS="do_apm=0"
```

Checking free I/O areas may lead to problems if other hardware components are disturbed by this. Avoid this by using `probe_io=0`.

If several options should be used, separate them by spaces:

```
PCMCIA_CORE_OPTS="do_apm=0 probe_io=0"
```

If errors occur while loading the `i82365` module, refer to the manual page of `i82365`.

A problem in this context is a resource conflict — if an interrupt, I/O port, or memory area is occupied twice. Although the module `i82365` checks these resources before they are made available to a card, sometimes just this check leads to problems. Checking the interrupt 12 (PS/2 devices) on some computers leads to the mouse or keyboard hanging. In this case, the parameter `irq_list=<List of IRQs>` can help. The list should contain all IRQs to use. For example, enter the command `modprobe i82365 irq_list=5,7,9,10` or permanently add the list of IRQs to `/etc/sysconfig/pcmcia`:

```
PCMCIA_PCIC_OPTS="irq_list=5,7,9,10"
```

In addition, there are `/etc/pcmcia/config` and `/etc/pcmcia/config.opts`. These files are evaluated by card manager. The settings made in them are only relevant when loading the driver modules for the PCMCIA cards. In `/etc/pcmcia/config.opts`, IRQs, I/O ports, and memory areas can be included or excluded. The difference from the option `irqlist` is that the resources excluded in `config.opts` are not used for a PCMCIA card, but are still checked by the base module `i82365`.

Improperly Functioning or Nonfunctional PCMCIA Card

Here, there are basically three variations: the card is not detected, the driver cannot be loaded, or the interface made available by the driver is set up incorrectly. Determine whether the card is managed by the card manager or hotplug. For external PCMCIA, card manager always takes control. For kernel PCMCIA, card manager manages PC card cards and hotplug manages CardBUS cards. Here, only the card manager is discussed.

Unrecognized Card The message "Unsupported Card in Slot x" in `/var/log/messages` indicates that card manager has failed to assign a driver to the card. The card and driver assignment is done by checking the files `/etc/pcmcia/config` or `/etc/pcmcia/*.conf`. They function as the driver database. This driver database can be easily extended using existing entries as reference. Use `cardctl ident` to find out how the card identifies itself. Refer to the PCMCIA HOWTO (Section 6) and the manual page of `pcmcia` for further details on this procedure. After modifying `/etc/pcmcia/config` or `/etc/pcmcia/*.conf`, reload the driver assignment with the command `rcpcmcia reload`.

Driver Not Loaded Wrong assignments of cards and drivers in the driver database may result in a driver not being loaded. This may happen if a vendor uses a different chip in an apparently unchanged card. Alternative drivers may also offer better support for a particular card than the default assignment. In these cases, precise information on the card is required. If needed, obtain further help from the Advanced Support Service or by asking on a mailing list.

A resource conflict may be another reason for a driver not being loaded. For most PCMCIA cards, it is irrelevant with which IRQ, I/O port, or memory area they are operated, but there are exceptions. First test only one card and, if necessary, switch off other system components, such as the sound card, IrDA, modem, or printer. The allocation of system resources can be monitored with the command `lsdev` (it is quite normal that several PCI devices share the same IRQ).One possible solution would be to use a suitable option for the module `i82365` (see `PCMCIA_PCIC_OPTS`). Many card driver modules also have options. Find these using the command `modinfo /lib/modules/<pcmciaădirectory>/<driver>.o` (the complete path is needed to locate the correct driver). Most of the modules ship with a manual page. `rpm -ql pcmcia | grep man` lists all manual pages contained in the `pcmcia` package. To test the options, the card drivers can also be unloaded manually. Again, ensure that the module is using the correct PCMCIA system. When a solution has been found, the use of a specific resource can, be allowed or forbidden in the file /etc/pcmcia/config.opts. You may even specify option for card drivers. If, for example, the module pcnet_cs should be exclusively operated with IRQ 5, the following entry is required:

```
module pcnet_cs opts irq_list=5
```

One problem that sometimes occurs with 10/100-Mbit network cards is incorrect automatic identification of the transmission method. Use the command ifport or mii_tool to view and modify the transmission method. To have these commands run automatically, the script /etc/pcmcia/network must be adjusted.

Incorrectly Configured Interface In this case, it is recommended to check the configuration of the interface to eliminate configuration errors. For network cards, the verbosity of the network scripts can be increased by assigning the value DEBUG=yes to the variable in /etc/sysconfig/network/config. For other cards or if this is of no help, there is still the possibility of inserting the line set -x into the script run by card manager (see /var/log/messages). With this, each individual command of the script is recorded in the system log. If you have found the critical part in a script, the corresponding commands can be entered in a terminal and tested.

7.1.5 Installation with PCMCIA

PCMCIA is already required for installation if you want to install over a network or if the CD-ROM relies on PCMCIA. To do this, start with a boot floppy. In addition, one of the module floppy disks is required.

After booting from floppy disk (or after selecting 'Manual Installation' booting from CD), the program linuxrc is started. Select 'Kernel Modules (Hardware Drivers)' -> 'Load PCMCIA Module'. Two entry fields appear in which to enter options for the modules pcmcia_core and i82365. Normally, these fields can be left blank. The manual pages for pcmcia_core and i82365 are available as text files on the first CD in the directory docu/.

SUSE LINUX is then installed with the external PCMCIA system. During the installation, system messages are sent to various virtual consoles. Switch to them using Alt + function key. Later, when a graphical interface is active, use Ctrl + Alt + function key.

During installation, several terminals are available on which commands can be run. As long as linuxrc is running, use console 9 (a very spartan shell). After YaST starts, a Bash shell and many standard system tools are available on console 2.

If the wrong driver module for a PCMCIA card is loaded during installation, the boot floppy must be modified manually. This requires a detailed knowledge of Linux, however. When the first part of the installation is finished, the system is partially or completely rebooted. In rare cases, it is possible that the system will hang when PCMCIA is started. At this point the installation has reached an advanced stage. You can then start Linux in text mode without PCMCIA using the `NOPCMCIA=yes` boot option. See also Section 7.1.4 on page 156. You may even change some system settings on the second console before the first part of the installation is completed to make sure the reboot will be successful.

7.1.6 Other Utilities

cardctl is an essential tool for obtaining information from PCMCIA and carrying out certain actions. In cardctl, find many details. Enter just `cardctl` to obtain a list of the valid commands.

The main functions can be controlled with the graphical front-end cardinfo. For this to work, the `pcmcia-cardinfo` package must be installed.

Additional helpful programs from the `pcmcia` package are `ifport`, `ifuser`, `probe`, and `rcpcmcia`. These are not always required. To find out about everything contained in the `pcmcia`, use the command `rpm -ql pcmcia`.

7.1.7 Updating the Kernel or PCMCIA Package

If you want to update the kernel, you should use the kernel packages provided by SUSE LINUX. If it is necessary to compile your own kernel, the PCMCIA modules must also be recompiled. It is important that the new kernel is already running when these modules are recompiled, because various information is extracted from it. The `pcmcia` package should already be installed, but not started. In case of doubt, run the command `rcpcmcia stop`. Install the PCMCIA source package and enter `rpm -ba /usr/src/packages/SPECS/pcmcia.spec`

The new packages will be stored in `/usr/src/packages/RPMS/`. The package `pcmcia-modules` contains the PCMCIA modules for external PCMCIA. This package must be installed with the command `rpm --force`, because the module files belong officially to the kernel package.

7.1.8 For More Information

For more information about specific laptops, visit the Linux Laptop home page at `http://linux-laptop.net`. Another good source of information is the Mobilix home page at `http://tuxmobil.org/`. The SUSE LINUX Support Database features several articles on the use of SUSE LINUX on mobile devices. Go to `http://portal.suse.de/sdb/en/index.html` and search for *laptop*.

7.2 SCPM — System Configuration Profile Management

Some situations require a modified system configuration of your computer. This would mostly be the case for mobile computers that are operated in varying locations. If a desktop system should be operated temporarily using other hardware components than usual, SCPM comes in handy. At any rate, restoring the original system configuration should be easy and the modification of the system configuration can be reproduced.

Up to the present, this problem had only been solved for PCMCIA hardware for which various configurations could be stored in distinct profiles. This approach has been further refined with the development of SCPM (*System Configuration Profile Management*), obsoleting the restriction to PCMCIA hardware. With SCPM, any desired part of the system configuration can be kept in a customized profile. This is like taking a snapshot of the system then being able to restore it at any point in time.

SCPM's main field of application is network configuration on laptops. Different network configurations often require different settings of other services, such as e-mail or proxies. Then other elements follow, like different printers at home and at the office, a separate X server configuration for the video beamer at conferences, special power-saving settings for the road, or the differing time zone in the agency abroad.

Increasing use of this tool leads to the continuous discovery of new requirements. Feel free to contact us and share your thoughts and ideas about SCPM. SCPM is based on a flexible framework in an effort to allow even server-based profile management. Send your wishes, inspirations, and error descriptions via our web front-end at `http://www.suse.de/feedback/`.

7.2.1 Basic Terminology and Concepts

The following are some terms used in SCPM documentation and in the YaST module.

- The term *system configuration* refers to the complete configuration of the computer. It covers all fundamental settings, like use of partitions, network settings, time zone selection, and keyboard mappings.
- A *profile*, also called *configuration profile*, is a state that has been preserved and can be restored at any time.
- *Active profile* refers to the profile last selected. This does not mean that the current system configuration corresponds exactly to this profile, because the configuration can be customized at any time.
- A *resource* in the SCPM context is an element that contributes to the system configuration. This can be a file or a softlink including its metadata, like user, permissions, or access time. This can also be a system service that runs in this profile, but is deactivated in another one.
- Every resource belongs to a certain *resource group*. These groups contain all resources that logically belong together — most groups would contain both a service and its configuration files. It is very easy to assemble resources managed by SCPM because this does not require any knowledge about the configuration files of the desired service. SCPM ships with a selection of preconfigured resource groups that should be sufficient for most scenarios.

7.2.2 SCPM YaST Module and Additional Documentation

A YaST module (package `yast2-profile-manager`) is a graphical front-end to SCPM that provides an alternative to the command line front-end. Because the functionality of both front-ends is substantially the same and the knowledge of the command line front-end is useful in many cases, only the latter is described here. Differences between the YaST front-end and the command line tool are mentioned wherever appropriate.

Refer to the info pages of SCPM for the most recent documentation. Read these with tools like Konqueror (with the command `konqueror info:scpm`) or emacs. On the console, use `info` or `pinfo`. Technical information is provided at `/usr/share/doc/package/scpm`. Running `scpm` without any arguments returns a command option summary.

7.2.3 Configuring SCPM

SCPM must be activated before use. By default, SCPM handles network and printer settings as well as the XFree86 configuration. If you need to manage special services or configuration files, activate appropriate resource groups. To list the predefined resource groups, use `scpm list_groups`. To see only the groups already activated, use `scpm list_groups -a`. Issue these commands as `root` on the command line. Activate or deactivate a group with `scpm activate_group NAME` or `scpm deactivate_group NAME`. Replace `NAME` with the relevant group name. All the resource groups can also be configured with the YaST profile manager.

Activate SCPM with `scpm enable`. When run for the first time, SCPM is initialized, which takes a few seconds. Deactivate SCPM with `scpm disable` at any time to prevent the unintentional switching of profiles. A subsequent reactivation simply resumes the initialization.

7.2.4 Creating and Managing Profiles

A profile named `default` already exists after SCPM has been activated. Get a list of all available profiles with `scpm list`. This only existing profile is also the active one, which can be verified with `scpm active`. The profile `default` is a basic configuration from which the other profiles are derived. For this reason, all settings that should be identical in all profiles should be made first. These modifications are then stored in the active profile with `scpm reload`. The profile `default` can be used, renamed, or deleted.

There are two possibilities to add a new profile. If the new profile (named `work` here) should be based on the profile `default`, create it with `scpm copy default work`. The command `scpm switch work` changes into the new profile, which can then be modified. Sometimes the system configuration was modified for special purposes that should be kept in a new profile. The command `scpm add work` creates a new profile by saving the current system configuration in the profile `work` and marking it as active. Running `scpm reload` then saves changes to the profile `work`.

Rename or delete profiles with the commands `scpm rename x y` and `scpm delete x`. For example, to rename `work` to `project` use `scpm rename work project`. Delete `project` with `scpm delete project`. The active profile cannot be deleted.

The YaST module only offers an 'Add' button. Pressing it opens a dialog in which to select whether an existing profile should be copied or the current system configuration should be saved. Use 'Edit' for renaming.

7.2.5 Switching Configuration Profiles

The command `scpm switch work` switches to another profile (the profile `work`, in this case). Switch to the active profile to save modified settings of the system configuration. Alternatively, use `scpm reload` to do this.

When switching profiles, SCPM first checks which resources of the active profile have been modified. It then queries whether the modification of each resource should be added to the active profile or dropped. If you prefer a separate listing of the resources (as in former versions of SCPM) use the switch command with the `-r` parameter: `scpm switch -r work`.

SCPM then compares the current system configuration with the profile to which to switch. In this phase, SCPM evaluates which system services need to be stopped or restarted due to mutual dependencies or to reflect the changes in configuration. This is like a partial system reboot that concerns only a small part of the system while the rest continues operating without change.

It is only at this point that the system services are stopped, all modified resources (e.g., configuration files) are written, and the system services are restarted.

7.2.6 Advanced Profile Settings

You can enter a description for every profile that is displayed with `scpm list`. For the active profile, set it with `scpm set description "text"`. Provide the name of the profile for inactive profiles, for instance, `scpm set description "text" work`. Sometimes it might be desirable to perform additional actions not provided by SCPM while switching profiles. Attach up to four executables for each profile. They are invoked at different stages of the switching process. These stages are referred to as:

prestop prior to stopping services when leaving the profile

poststop after stopping services when leaving the profile

prestart prior to starting services when activating the profile

poststart after starting services when activating the profiles

Switching from profile `work` to profile `home` thus proceeds as follows:

1. The prestop action of the profile `work` is executed.
2. The services are stopped.
3. The poststop action of the profile `work` is executed.
4. The system configuration is changed.
5. The prestart action of the profile `home` is executed.
6. The services are started.
7. The poststart action of the profile `home` is executed.

Attach these actions with the command `set` by entering `scpm set prestop <filename>`, `scpm set poststop <filename>`, `scpm set prestart <filename>`, or `scpm set poststart <filename>`. The call must be made to an executable — scripts must refer to the correct interpreter and must be executable at least for the superuser.

Query all additional settings entered with `set` with `get`. The command `scpm get poststart`, for instance, returns the name of the poststart call or simply nothing if nothing has been attached.

Reset such settings by overwriting with `""`. This means that the command `scpm set prestop ""` removes the attached prestop program.

All `set` and `get` commands can be applied to an arbitrary profile in the same manner as comments are added. For example, `scpm get prestop <filename work>` or `scpm get prestop work`.

Caution

These scripts or programs should not be modifiable by any user because they are executed with the rights of the superuser. It is recommended to make scripts only readable to the superuser because they can contain sensitive information. It is best to provide these programs with the permissions `-rwx---- root root` with the commands `chmod 700 variablefilename` and `chown root.root <filename>`.

Caution

7.2.7 Profile Selection at Boot

It is possible to select a profile during the boot process by providing the boot parameter `PROFILE=<name-of-the-profile>` at the boot prompt. In the boot loader configuration (`/boot/grub/menu.lst`), the option `title` reflects the name of the profile. For example:

Example 7.1: *The File /boot/grub/menu.lst*

```
gfxmenu (hd0,5)/boot/message
color white/green black/light-gray
default 0
timeout 8

title work
   kernel (hd0,5)/boot/vmlinuz root=/dev/hda6 PROFILE=work
   initrd (hd0,5)/boot/initrd

title home
   kernel (hd0,5)/boot/vmlinuz root=/dev/hda6 PROFILE=home
   initrd (hd0,5)/boot/initrd

title road
   kernel (hd0,5)/boot/vmlinuz root=/dev/hda6 PROFILE=road
   initrd (hd0,5)/boot/initrd
```

For systems that use LILO as the boot loader, refer to File 7.2 on the next page as an example. Then you can select the desired profile at the boot prompt.

Example 7.2: *File /etc/lilo.conf*

```
boot     = /dev/hda
change-rules
reset
read-only
menu-scheme = Wg:kw:Wg:Wg
prompt
timeout = 80
message = /boot/message

  image  = /boot/vmlinuz
  label  = home
  root   = /dev/hda6
  initrd = /boot/initrd
  append = "vga=0x317 hde=ide-scsi PROFILE=home"

  image  = /boot/vmlinuz
  label  = work
  root   = /dev/hda6
  initrd = /boot/initrd
  append = "vga=0x317 hde=ide-scsi PROFILE=work"

  image  = /boot/vmlinuz
  label  = road
  root   = /dev/hda6
  initrd = /boot/initrd
  append = "vga=0x317 hde=ide-scsi PROFILE=road"
```

7.2.8 Troubleshooting

In most cases, SCPM should function smoothly. There are, however, some pitfalls, which are described here.

SCPM is currently not able to survive a system update. The difficulty lies in the fact that, with a system update, the data stored in the profiles is not cleanly updated by the automatic mechanisms. SCPM then detects a system update and refuses to work. In this situation, you should get an error message from SCPM that contains "your operating system installation changed/is unknown, read man page!" In this case, reinitialize SCPM with `scpm -f enbale`. Your profiles, however, will be lost and you must reconfigure them.

It can also sometimes occur that SCPM stops working during a switch procedure. This may be caused by some outside effect, such as a user abort, a power fault, another similar problem, or even an error in SCPM itself. In this case, an error message saying SCPM is locked appears the next time you start SCPM. This is for system safety, because the data stored in its database may differ from the state of the system. To solve this issue, delete the lock file with `rm /var/lib/scpm/#LOCK` then update your database with `scpm -s reload`. After this procedure, proceed as usual.

There is no real problem with changing the resource group configuration of an already initialized SCPM. However, you must run `scpm rebuild` after adding or deleting groups. This adds new resources to all profiles and removes the deleted ones. The deleted ones are then lost to the system. If there are different configurations for the same resource in different profiles, the deletion of resources might cause serious problems. The current profile, which is not touched by SCPM, will not be affected. If you reconfigure your system with YaST, the rebuild is handled by YaST.

7.3 IrDA — Infrared Data Association

IrDA (*Infrared Data Association*) is an industry standard for wireless communication with infrared light. Many laptops sold today are equipped with an IrDA-compatible transceiver that enables communication with other devices, such as printers, modems, LANs, or other laptops. The transfer speed ranges from 2400 bps to 4 Mbps.

There are two IrDA operation modes. The standard mode, SIR, accesses the infrared port through a serial interface. This mode works on almost all systems and is sufficient for most requirements. The faster mode, FIR, requires a special driver for the IrDA chip. Not all chip types are supported in FIR mode because of a lack of appropriate drivers. Set the desired IrDA mode in the BIOS of your computer. The BIOS also shows which serial interface is used in SIR mode.

Information about IrDA can be found in the IrDA how-to by Werner Heuser at `http://tuxmobil.org/Infrared-HOWTO/Infrared-HOWTO.html`. Additionally refer to the web site of the Linux IrDA Project `http://irda.sourceforge.net/`.

7.3.1 Software

The necessary kernel modules are included in the kernel package. The package `irda` provides the necessary helper applications for supporting the infrared interface. The documentation can be found at `/usr/share/doc/packages/irda/README` after the installation of the package.

7.3.2 Configuration

The IrDA system service is not started automatically by the booting process. Use the YaST runlevel module to change the settings of the system services. Alternatively, use `chkconfig`. Every few seconds, IrDA sends out a "discovery packet" to detect other peripheral devices in its neighborhood. This consumes a considerable amount of battery power. For this reason, IrDA is disabled by default and should only be started when needed. Manually activate it with `rcirda start` or deactivate it with `rcirda stop`. All kernel modules needed are loaded automatically when the interface is activated.

The file `/etc/sysconfig/irda` contains only the one variable `IRDA_PORT`. This is where the interface used in SIR mode is set. The script `/etc/irda/drivers` of the infrared support package sets this variable.

7.3.3 Usage

Data can be sent to the device file `/dev/irlpt0` for printing. The device file `/dev/irlpt0` acts just like the normal `/dev/lp0` cabled interface, except the printing data is sent wireless with infrared light. Printers used with the infrared interface are installed just like printers connected to the parallel or serial ports. Make sure the printer is in visible range of the infrared interface and the infrared support is started.

Communication with other hosts and with mobile phones or other similar devices is conducted through the device file `/dev/ircomm0`. The Siemens S25 and Nokia 6210 mobile phones, for instance, can dial and connect to the Internet with the wvdial application using the infrared interface. Synchronizing data with a Palm Pilot is also possible, provided the device setting of the corresponding application has been set to `/dev/ircomm0`.

Only those devices that support the printer or IrCOMM protocols can be accessed without any further adjustments. Devices that support the IROBEX protocol, such as the 3Com Palm Pilot, can be accessed with special applications, like irobexpalm and irobexreceive. Refer to the IR-HOWTO on this subject. The protocols supported by the device are stated in brackets behind the name of the device in the output of irdadump. Ir-LAN protocol support is still a "work in progress" — it is not stable yet, but will surely also be available for Linux in the near future.

7.3.4 Troubleshooting

If devices connected to the infrared port do not respond, use the command `irdadump` (as `root`) to check if the other device is recognized by the computer. Something similar to Example 7.3 appears regularly when a Canon BJC-80 printer is in visible range of the computer:

Example 7.3: Output of irdadump

```
21:41:38.435239 xid:cmd 5b62bed5 > ffffffff S=6 s=0 (14)
21:41:38.525167 xid:cmd 5b62bed5 > ffffffff S=6 s=1 (14)
21:41:38.615159 xid:cmd 5b62bed5 > ffffffff S=6 s=2 (14)
21:41:38.705178 xid:cmd 5b62bed5 > ffffffff S=6 s=3 (14)
21:41:38.795198 xid:cmd 5b62bed5 > ffffffff S=6 s=4 (14)
21:41:38.885163 xid:cmd 5b62bed5 > ffffffff S=6 s=5 (14)
21:41:38.965133 xid:rsp 5b62bed5 < 6cac38dc S=6 s=5 BJC-80
                        hint=8804 [Printer IrCOMM ] (23)
21:41:38.975176 xid:cmd 5b62bed5 > ffffffff S=6 s=* earth
                        hint=0500 [ PnP Computer ] (21)
```

Check the configuration of the interface if there is no output or the other device does not reply. Verify that the correct interface is used. The infrared interface is sometimes located at `/dev/ttyS2` or at `/dev/ttyS3` and another interrupt than IRQ 3 is sometimes used. These settings can be checked and modified in the BIOS setup menu of almost every laptop.

A simple CCD video camera can also help in determining whether the infrared LED lights up at all. Most video cameras can see infrared light, whereas the human eye cannot.

7.4 Bluetooth — Wireless Connections

Bluetooth is a wireless technology for connecting various devices. Two important characteristics distinguish Bluetooth from IrDA: the individual devices do not need to "see" each other directly and several devices can be connected in a network with a maximum data rate of 720 Kbps (in the current version 1.1). Theoretically, Bluetooth is even capable of communicating through walls. However, in practice this largely depends on the properties of the walls and the device class. There are three device classes with maximum transmission ranges between ten and a hundred meters.

7.4.1 Profiles

In Bluetooth, services are defined by means of profiles, such as the file transfer profile, the basic printing profile, and the personal area network profile. To enable a device to use the services of another device, both must understand the same profile — a piece of information that is often missing on the device package and in the manual. Although some manufacturers strictly comply with the definitions of the individual profiles, others do not. Nevertheless, the communication between the devices usually works smoothly.

7.4.2 Software

To be able to use Bluetooth, you need a Bluetooth adapter (built-in or external), drivers, and a Bluetooth protocol stack. By default, the Linux kernel contains the basic drivers needed for using Bluetooth. The Bluez system is used as protocol stack. Additionally, install all packages associated with Bluetooth (`bluez-libs`, `bluez-bluefw`, `bluez-pan`, `bluez-sdp`, and `bluez-utils`), as these provide some necessary services and utilities.

7.4.3 Configuration

The configuration files described in this section can only be modified by the user `root`. Currently, there is no graphical user interface for setting the parameters. Therefore, the files must be modified with a text editor.

A PIN number provides basic protection against unwanted connections. Mobile phones usually query the PIN when establishing the first contact (or when setting up a device contact on the phone). For two devices to be able to communicate, both must identify themselves with the same PIN. On the computer, the PIN is located in the file `/etc/bluetooth/pin`. Currently, only one PIN is supported in Linux, regardless of the number of installed Bluetooth devices. Thus, multiple devices cannot be addressed with different PINs. Accordingly, you need to set the same PIN on all devices or deactivate the PIN authentication entirely.

Note

Security of Bluetooth Connections

Despite the PINs, the transmission between two devices may not be entirely secure.

Note

`/etc/bluetooth/hcid.conf`is main configuration file for Linux Bluetooth. Various settings, such as the device names and the security modes, can be modified in this file. Usually, the settings should be adequate. The file contains comments describing the options for the various settings.

`security auto;` is one of the most important settings. If necessary, a PIN is activated for the identification. If problems are encountered, the option `auto` disables the PIN. Depending on your preferences and your security needs, set this option to `none` never to use PIN numbers or to `user` to use PIN numbers.

Another important section is the one beginning with `device {`. In this section, define the name under which the host should be displayed on the other side. The device class (`Laptop`, `Server`, etc.), authentication, and encryption are defined in this section.

7.4.4 System Components and Useful Tools

The operability of Bluetooth depends on the interaction of various services. At least two background daemons are needed: hcid (*host controller interface*), which serves as an interface for the Bluetooth device and controls it, and sdpd (*service discovery protocol*), by means of which a device can find out which services the host makes available. If they are not activated automatically when the system is started, both hcid and sdpd can be activated with the command `rcbluetooth start`. This command must be executed as `root`.

The following paragraphs describe the main tools needed for working with Bluetooth. Currently, only command-line programs are available. Extensions for Konqueror (KDE desktop) and Nautilus (GNOME desktop) are under development. This functionality may have been implemented after the editorial deadline. In this case, the URL `sdp://` should display local Bluetooth devices (physically connected to the host) as well as remote Bluetooth devices (accessible by way of a wireless connection).

Note

Other functionalities of the above-mentioned Bluetooth applications can be viewed with `man <program_name>`.

Note

Some of the commands can only be executed as `root`. This includes the command `l2ping <device_address>` for testing the connection to a remote device.

hcitool

hcitool can be used to determine whether local and remote devices are detected. The command `hcitool dev` should list your devices. The output generates a line in the form `<interface_name> <device_address>` for every detected local device.

The command `hcitool name <device_address>` can be used to determine the device name of a remote device. If, for example, another computer is detected, the displayed class and device name corresponds to the information in the file `/etc/bluetooth/hcid.conf` on the remote computer. Local devices addresses generate an error output.

hciconfig

Get more information about the local device with `/sbin/hciconfig`. Search for remote devices (that are not connected physically to the host) with the command `hcitool inq`. Three values are displayed for every detected device: the device address, the clock offset, and the device class. The device address is important, as other commands use it for identifying the target device. The clock offset mainly serves technical purposes. In the class, the device type and the service type are encoded as a hexadecimal value.

sdptool

The program sdptool can be used to check which services are made available by a specific device. The command `sdptool browse <device_address>` returns all services of a device. The command `sdptool search <service_code>` can be used to search for a specific service. This command scans all accessible devices for the requested service. If one of the devices offers the service, the program prints the (full) service name returned by the device together with a brief description. A list of all possible service codes can be viewed by entering `sdptool` without any parameters.

7.4.5 Examples

The following two examples demonstrate some of the capabilities of Bluetooth.

Network Connection between Two Hosts

The first example shows the establishment of a network connection between two hosts with pand (*personal area networking*). The following commands must be executed by the user `root`. The description focuses on the Bluetooth-specific actions and does not provide a detailed explanation of the network command (ip):

Start pand with the command `pand -s` on one of the two hosts (referred to as *H1*). Determine the device address of the second host (*H2*) by running `hcitool inq` on this host. Run `pand -c <device_address>` to establish a connection. If you query the available network interfaces with `ip link show`, an entry such as the following should be displayed (the local device address should be displayed instead of `00:12:34:56:89:90`):

```
bnep0: <BROADCAST,MULTICAST> mtu 1500 qdisc noop qlen 1000
    link/ether 00:12:34:56:89:90 brd ff:ff:ff:ff:ff:ff
```

This interface must be assigned an IP address and activated. This can be done with the following two commands. On *H1*:

```
ip addr add 192.168.1.3/24 dev bnep0
ip link set bnep0 up
```

On *H2*:

```
ip addr add 192.168.1.4/24 dev bnep0
ip link set bnep0 up
```

Now *H1* can be accessed from *H2* under the IP `192.168.1.3`. Use the command `ssh 192.168.1.4` to access *H2* from *H1* (provided *H2* runs an sshd, which is activated by default in SUSE LINUX). The command `ssh 192.168.1.4` can also be run as a "normal" user.

File Transfer from a Mobile Phone to the Host

The second example shows how to transfer a photograph created with a mobile phone with a built-in digital camera to a computer (without incurring additional costs for the transmission of a multimedia message). Although the menu structure may differ on various mobile phones, the procedure is usually quite similar. Refer to the manual of your phone, if necessary. This example describes the transfer of a photograph from a Sony Ericsson mobile phone to a laptop. The service Obex-Push must be available on the computer and the computer must grant the mobile phone access. In the first step, the service is made available on the laptop. This is done by means of the opd daemon from the package `bluez-utils`. Start the daemon with the following command:

```
opd --mode OBEX --channel 10 --daemonize --path /tmp --sdp
```

Two important parameters are used: `--sdp` registers the service with the sdpd and `--path /tmp` instructs the program where to save the received data — in this case to `/tmp/`. You can also specify any other directory to which you have write access.

Now the mobile phone must "get to know" the computer. To do this, open the 'Connect' menu on the phone and select 'Bluetooth'. If necessary, click 'Turn On' before selecting 'My devices'. Select 'New device' and let your phone search for the laptop. If a device is detected, its name appears in the display. Select the device associated with the laptop. If you encounter a PIN query, enter the PIN specified in `/etc/bluetooth/pin`. Now your phone knows the laptop and is able to exchange data with the laptop. Exit the current menu and go to the image menu. Select the image to transfer and press 'More'. In the next menu, press 'Send' to select a transmission mode. Select 'Via Bluetooth'. The laptop should be listed as a target device. Select the laptop to start the transmission. The image is then saved to the directory specified with the opd command. In the same way, you can also transfer audio tracks to the laptop.

7.4.6 Troubleshooting

If you have difficulties establishing a connection, proceed as follows:

- Check the output of `hcitool dev`. Is the local device listed? If not, the hcid may not have been started at all or the device may not be recognized as a Bluetooth device (either because the driver is not able to do this or because the device is defective). Restart the daemon with the command `rcbluetooth restart` and check `/var/log/messages` to see if any errors occurred.
- Does the computer "see" other devices when you execute `hcitool inq`? Try the command twice — the connection may have been faulty, as the frequency band for Bluetooth is also used by other devices.
- Make sure that the PIN in `/etc/bluetooth/pin` is the same as the PIN of the remote device.
- Try to establish the connection from the other device. Check if this device sees the computer.
- The first example (network connection) does not work. This may be due to various reasons. Possibly one of the two hosts does not understand the ssh protocol. Try if `ping 192.168.1.3` or `ping 192.168.1.4` works. If it does, check if sshd is active. Another problem could be that you already have other addresses that conflict with the address `192.168.1.X` used in the example. If this is the case, try other addresses, such as `10.123.1.2` and `10.123.1.3`.
- In the second example, the laptop does not appear as the target device. Does the mobile device recognize the Obex-Push service on the laptop? In 'My devices', select the respective device and view the list of 'Services'. If Obex-Push is not displayed (even after the list is updated), the problem is caused by the opd on the laptop. Is the opd active? Do you have write access to the specified directory?
- Does the second example work in reverse order? If obexftp is installed, this should work with `obexftp -b <device_address> -B 10 -p <image>` on some devices (Siemens and Sony Ericsson have been tested, other devices may or may not support this action).

7.4.7 For More Information

An extensive overview of various instructions for the use and configuration of Bluetooth is available at `http://www.holtmann.org/linux/bluetooth/`.

Useful information and instructions:

Connection to PalmOS PDA:

`http://www.cs.ucl.ac.uk/staff/s.zachariadis/btpalmlinux.html`

Official howto for the integrated Bluetooth protocol stack in the kernel:

`http://bluez.sourceforge.net/howto/index.html`

8

Power Management

This chapter provides an overview of the various power management technologies in Linux. The configuration of all available APM (Advanced Power Management), ACPI (Advanced Configuration and Power Interface), and CPU frequency scaling settings are described in detail.

Unlike APM, which was previously used on laptops for power management only, the hardware information and configuration tool ACPI is available on all modern computers (laptops, desktops, and servers). On many types of modern hardware, the CPU frequency can be adapted to the respective situation, which helps save valuable battery time especially on mobile devices (*CPU frequency scaling*).

All power management technologies require suitable hardware and BIOS routines. Most laptops and many modern desktops and servers meet these requirements. APM had been used in many older computers. As APM largely consists of a function set implemented in the BIOS, the level of APM support may vary depending on the hardware. This is even more true of ACPI, which is even more complex. For this reason, it is virtually impossible to recommend one over the other. Simply test the various procedures on your hardware then select the technology that is best supported.

Note

Power Management for AMD64 Processors

AMD64 processors with a 64-bit kernel only support ACPI.

Note

8.1 Power Saving Functions

Although many of these functions are of general interest, they are especially important for mobile deployment. The following paragraphs describe the functions and which system offers them.

Standby This operating mode merely turns the display off. On some computers, the processor performance is throttled. This function is not available in all APM implementations. The corresponding ACPI state is *S1*.

Suspend (to memory) This mode writes the entire system state to the RAM. Subsequently, the entire system except the RAM is put to sleep. As the computer consumes very little power in this state, the battery may last anywhere from twelve hours to several days, depending on the device. The advantage of this state is the possibility to resume work at the same point within a few seconds, without having to boot and restart applications. Most modern devices can be suspended by closing the lid and activated by opening it. The corresponding ACPI state is *S3*. Support of this state largely depends on the hardware.

Hibernation (suspend to disk) This operating mode enables the computer to hibernate, as the entire system state is written to the hard disk and the system is powered off. The reactivation from the state of hibernation takes about 30 to 90 seconds. The state prior to the suspend will be restored. Some manufacturers offer useful hybrid variants of this mode in their APM (such as RediSafe in IBM Thinkpads). The corresponding ACPI state is *S4*.

Battery monitor In addition to monitoring the battery charge level, something must be done when power reserves are low. This control function is handled by ACPI or APM.

Automatic power-off Following a shutdown, the computer is powered off. This is especially important when an automatic shutdown is performed shortly before the battery is empty.

Shutdown of system components The most important component for saving power is the hard disk. Depending on the reliability of the overall system, the hard disk can be put to sleep for some time. However, the risk of losing data increases with the duration of the sleep periods. Other components can be deactivated via ACPI (at least theoretically) or permanently in the BIOS setup.

Processor speed control AMD PowerNow! and Intel SpeedStep are two concepts designed for reducing the power consumption of the overall system. For this purpose, the power consumption of the most power-hungry component — the processor — is reduced. A pleasant side-effect of the reduced processor speed is the reduced generation of heat. Thus, adjustable fans will also make less noise. This feature is controlled by the CPU frequency scaling functions of the Linux kernel. Basically, three different processor speed levels are distinguished:

performance Maximum processor performance for AC operation.

powersave Minimum processor performance for battery operation.

dynamic Dynamic adaption of the processor performance to the current processor load — this is the recommended setting for battery operation and AC operation in order to save battery power, reduce noise, and achieve optimum performance. Switching between the speed levels usually takes place seamlessly, unnoticed by the user.

See Section 8.5 on page 191 for more information about controlling the processor speed.

8.2 APM

Some of the power saving functions are performed by the APM BIOS itself. On many laptops, standby and suspend states can be activated with key combinations or by closing the lid, without any special operating system function. However, to activate these modes with a command, certain actions must be triggered before the system is suspended. To view the battery charge level, you need a suitable kernel and the respective packages.

By default, APM support is integrated in the kernels shipped with SUSE LINUX. However, APM is only activated if no ACPI is implemented in the BIOS and an APM BIOS is detected. To activate APM support, ACPI must be disabled with `acpi=off` at the boot prompt. Enter `cat /proc/apm` to check if APM is active. An output consisting of various numbers indicates that everything is OK. You should now be able to shut down the computer with the command `shutdown -h`.

Strange things may happen if the BIOS implementation does not fully comply with the standard. Some problems can be circumvented with special boot parameters (formerly kernel configuration options). All parameters are entered at the boot prompt in the form `apm=<parameter>`:

on or off Enable or disable APM support.

(no-)allow-ints Allow interrupts during the execution of BIOS functions.

(no-)broken-psr The "GetPowerStatus" function of the BIOS does not work properly.

(no-)realmode-power-off Reset processor to real mode prior to shutdown.

(no-)debug Log APM events in system log.

(no-)power-off Power system off after shutdown.

bounce-interval=⟨*n*⟩ Time in hundredths of a second after a suspend event during which additional suspend events are ignored.

idle-threshold=⟨*n*⟩ System inactivity percentage from which the BIOS function `idle` is executed (0=always, 100=never).

idle-period=⟨*n*⟩ Time in hundredths of a second after which the system activity is measured.

8.2.1 The APM Daemon (apmd)

The apmd daemon (package apmd) monitors the battery and can trigger certain actions when a standby or a suspend event occurs. Although it is not mandatory for operation, it may be useful for some problems.

apmd is not started automatically when the system is booted. If you want it started automatically, edit the settings for the system services with the YaST runlevel editor. Alternatively, this can also be done with the chkconfig utility. The daemon can be started manually with the command rcapmd start.

A number of configuration variables are available in /etc/sysconfig/powermanagement. As the file is commented, only some information is provided here:

APMD_ADJUST_DISK_PERF Adapts the disk performance to the power supply status. This can be done with a number of additional variables beginning with APMD_BATTERY (for battery operation) or APMD_AC (for AC operation).

APMD_BATTERY/AC_DISK_TIMEOUT
Disk inactivity period after which the disk is spun down. The values are described in Section 8.4 on page 190 or in the manual page for hdparm, option -S.

APMD_BATTERY/AC_KUPDATED_INTERVAL
Interval between two cycles of the kernel update daemon.

APMD_BATTERY/AC_DATA_TIMEOUT
Maximum age of buffered data.

APMD_BATTERY/AC_FILL_LEVEL
Maximum fill level of the hard disk buffer.

APMD_PCMCIA_EJECT_ON_SUSPEND
Although PCMCIA is implemented with APM support, difficulties may sometimes be encountered. Some card drivers do not resume correctly after a suspend (xirc2ps_cs). Therefore, apmd can deactivate the PCMCIA system prior to the suspend and reactivate it afterwards. To do this, set this variable to yes.

APMD_INTERFACES_TO_STOP Set network interfaces to stop prior to a suspend and restart afterwards.

APMD_INTERFACES_TO_UNLOAD
Use this variable if you also need to unload the driver modules of these interfaces.

APMD_TURN_OFF_IDEDMA_BEFORE_SUSPEND
Sometimes, resuming after a suspend may not work if an IDE device (hard disk) is still in DMA mode.

Other options include the possibility to correct the key repeat rate or the clock after a suspend or to shut down the laptop automatically when the APM BIOS send a "battery critical" event. To execute special actions, adapt the script `/usr/sbin/apmd_proxy` (performs the tasks listed above) to your needs.

8.2.2 Further Commands

apmd contains a number of useful tools. `apm` can be used to query the current battery charge level and to set the system to standby (`apm -S`) or suspend (`apm -s`). Refer to the manual page of `apm`. The command `apmsleep` suspends the system for a specified time. To watch a log file without keeping the hard disk spinning, use `tailf` instead of `tail -f`.

There are also tools for the X Window System. apmd contains the graphical utility xapm for displaying the battery charge level. If you use the KDE desktop or at least kpanel, use kbatmon to view the battery charge level and suspend the system. xosview is another interesting alternative.

8.3 ACPI

ACPI (Advanced Configuration and Power Interface) was designed to enable the operating system to set up and control the individual hardware components. Thus, ACPI supersedes both PnP and APM. Moreover, ACPI delivers information about the battery, AC adapter, temperature, fan, and system events like "close lid" or "battery low".

The BIOS provides tables containing information about the individual components and hardware access methods. The operating system uses this information for tasks like assigning interrupts or activating and deactivating components. As the operating system executes commands stored in the BIOS, the functionality depends on the BIOS implementation. The tables ACPI is able to detect and load are reported in `/var/log/boot.msg`. See Section 8.3.1 on page 188 for more information about troubleshooting ACPI problems.

8.3.1 ACPI in Action

If the kernel detects an ACPI BIOS when the system is booted, ACPI is activated automatically (and APM is deactivated). The boot parameter `acpi=on` may be necessary for some older machines. The computer must support ACPI 2.0 or later. Check the kernel boot messages in `/var/log/boot.msg` to see if ACPI was activated. If this is the case, there is a directory `/proc/acpi/`, which is described later.

Subsequently, a number of modules must be loaded. This is done by the start script of the ACPI daemon. If any of these modules causes problems, the respective module can be excluded from loading or unloading in `/etc/sysconfig/powersave/common`. The system log (`/var/log/messages`) contains the messages of the modules, enabling you to see which components were detected.

In `/proc/acpi/`, find a number of files that provide information on the system state or can be used to change some of the states actively. However, many features do not work yet, either because they are still under development or because they have not been implemented by the manufacturer.

All files (except `dsdt` and `fadt`) can be read with `cat`. In some files, settings can be modified by entering `echo X <file>` to specify suitable values for X (the objects in `/proc` are not real files on the hard disks but interfaces to the kernel). The most important files are described below:

/proc/acpi/info General information about ACPI.

/proc/acpi/alarm Here, specify when the system should wake from a sleep state. Currently, this feature is not fully supported.

/proc/acpi/sleep Provides information about possible sleep states.

/proc/acpi/event All events are reported here and processed by a daemon like `acpid` or `powersaved`. If no daemon accesses this file, events, such as a brief click on the power button or closing the lid, can be read with `cat /proc/acpi/event` (terminate with Ctrl + C).

/proc/acpi/dsdt and /proc/acpi/fadt
These files contain the ACPI tables DSDT (*differentiated system description table*) and FADT (*fixed ACPI description table*). They can be read with `acpidmp`, `acpidisasm`, and `dmdecode`. These programs and their documentation are located in the package `pmtools`. For example, `acpidmp DSDT | acpidisasm`.

/proc/acpi/ac_adapter/AC/state
Shows whether the AC adapter is connected.

/proc/acpi/battery/BAT*/{alarm, info, state}
Detailed information about the battery state. The charge level is read by comparing the `last full capacity` from `info` with the `remaining capacity` from `state`. A more comfortable way to do this is to use one of the special programs described below (see Section 8.3.1 on page 188). The charge level at which a battery event is triggered can be specified in `alarm`.

/proc/acpi/button This directory contains information about various switches.

/proc/acpi/fan/FAN/state Shows if the fan is currently active. The fan can be activated and deactivated manually by writing 0 (on) or 3 (off) into this file. However, both the ACPI code in the kernel and the hardware (or the BIOS) overwrite this setting when it gets too warm.

/proc/acpi/processor/CPU*/info
Information about the energy saving options of the processor.

/proc/acpi/processor/CPU*/power
Information about the current processor state. An asterisk next to 'C2' indicates that the processor is idle. This is the most frequent state, as can be seen from the `usage` figure.

/proc/acpi/processor/CPU*/performance
This interface is no longer used.

/proc/acpi/processor/CPU*/throttling
Enables further linear throttling of the processor. This interface is outdated. Its function has been taken over by the settings in `/etc/sysconfig/powersave/common` (see Section 8.5.2 on page 194).

/proc/acpi/processor/CPU*/limit
If the performance and the throttling are automatically controlled by a daemon, the maximum limits can be specified here. Some of the limits are determined by the system, some can be adjusted by the user. However, their function has been taken over by the settings in `/etc/sysconfig/powersave/common` (see Section 8.5.2 on page 193).

/proc/acpi/thermal_zone/ A separate subdirectory exists for every thermal zone. A thermal zone is an area with similar thermal properties whose number and names are designated by the hardware manufacturer. However, many of the possibilities offered by ACPI are rarely implemented. Instead, the temperature control is handled conventionally by the BIOS. The operating system is not given much opportunity to intervene, as the life span of the hardware is at stake. Therefore, some of the following descriptions only have a theoretical value.

/proc/acpi/thermal_zone/*/temperature
Current temperature of the thermal zone.

/proc/acpi/thermal_zone/*/state
The state indicates if everything is "ok" or if ACPI applies "active" or "passive" cooling. In the case of ACPI-independent fan control, this state will always be "ok".

/proc/acpi/thermal_zone/*/cooling_mode
Enables the selection of the passive (less performance, very economical) or active (full performance, uninterrupted fan noise) cooling method for full ACPI control.

/proc/acpi/thermal_zone/*/trip_points
Enables the determination of temperature limits for triggering specific actions like passive or active cooling, suspension ("hot"), or a shutdown ("critical").

/proc/acpi/thermal_zone/*/polling_frequency
If the value in `temperature` is not updated automatically when the temperature changes, the polling mode can be toggled here. The command `echo X > /proc/acpi/thermal_zone/*/polling_frequency` causes the temperature to be queried every X seconds. Set X=0 to disable polling.

The ACPI Daemon (acpid)

Like the APM daemon, the ACPI daemon processes certain events. Currently, the only supported events are the actuation of switches, such as the power button or the lid contact. All events are logged in the system log. The actions to perform in response to these events can be determined in the variables `ACPI_BUTTON_POWER` and `ACPI_BUTTON_LID` in `/etc/sysconfig/powermanagement`. For more options, modify the script `/usr/sbin/acpid_proxy` or the `acpid` configuration in `/etc/acpi/`.

Unlike `apmd`, little is preconfigured here, as ACPI in Linux is still in a very dynamic development stage. If necessary, configure `acpid` according to your needs. If you have any suggestions regarding preparatory actions, contact us through `http://www.suse.de/feedback`.

ACPI Tools

The range of more or less comprehensive ACPI utilities includes tools that merely display information, like the battery charge level and the temperature (acpi, klaptopdaemon, wmacpimon, etc.), tools that facilitate the access to the structures in `/proc/acpi` or that assist in monitoring changes (akpi, acpiw, gtkacpiw), and tools for editing the ACPI tables in the BIOS (package `pmtools`).

Troubleshooting

There are two different types of problems. On one hand, the ACPI code of the kernel may contain bugs that were not detected in time. In this case, a solution will be made available for download. More often, however, the problems are caused by the BIOS. Sometimes, deviations from the ACPI specification are purposely integrated in the BIOS to circumvent errors in the ACPI implementation in other widespread operating systems. Hardware components that have serious errors in the ACPI implementation are recorded in a blacklist that prevents the Linux kernel from using ACPI for these components.

The first thing to do when problems are encountered is to update the BIOS. This will solve many problems. If the computer does not boot properly, one of the following boot parameters may be helpful:

pci=noacpi Do not use ACPI for configuring the PCI devices.

acpi=oldboot Only perform a simple resource configuration. Do not use ACPI for other purposes.

acpi=off Disable ACPI.

> **Caution**
>
> **Problems Booting without ACPI**
>
> Some newer machines (especially SMP systems and AMD64 systems) need ACPI for configuring the hardware correctly. On these machines, disabling ACPI can cause problems.
>
> **Caution**

Take a closer look at the boot messages. This can be done with the command `dmesg | grep -2i acpi` (or all messages, as the problem may not be caused by ACPI) after booting. If an error occurs while parsing an ACPI table, the most important table — the DSDT — can be replaced with an improved version. In this case, the faulty DSDT of the BIOS will be ignored. The procedure is described in Section 8.5.4 on page 195.

In the kernel configuration, there is a switch for activating ACPI debug messages. If a kernel with ACPI debugging is compiled and installed, experts searching for an error can be supported with detailed information.

If you experience BIOS or hardware problems, it is always advisable to contact the manufacturer of the device. Although manufacturers may not always be able to provide assistance for Linux, it is still important that they hear the word "Linux" as often as possible. Manufacturers will only take the issue seriously if they realize that an adequate number of their customers use Linux.

Additional documentation and help:

- `http://www.columbia.edu/~ariel/acpi/acpi_howto.txt` (slightly outdated ACPI HowTo, incomplete)
- `http://www.cpqlinux.com/acpi-howto.html` (more detailed ACPI HowTo, contains DSDT patches)
- `http://www.intel.com/technology/iapc/acpi/faq.htm` (ACPI FAQ @Intel)
- `http://acpi.sourceforge.net/` (the ACPI4Linux project at Sourceforge)
- `http://www.poupinou.org/acpi/` (DSDT patches by Bruno Ducrot)

8.4 Rest for the Hard Disk

In Linux, a hard disk that is not used can be put to sleep. The hdparm utility modifies various hard disk settings. The option `-y` instantly switches the hard disk to the standby mode; the option `-Y` (caution) puts it to sleep. `hdparm -S <x>` causes the hard disk to be spun down after a certain period of inactivity. The placeholder ⟨x⟩ can be used as follows: `0` disables this mechanism, causing the hard disk to run continuously. Values from `1` to `240` are multiplied by 5 seconds. Values from `241` to `251` correspond to 1 to 11 times 30 minutes.

Often, it is not so easy to put the hard disk to sleep. In Linux, numerous processes write to the hard disk, waking it up repeatedly. Therefore, it is important to understand how Linux handles data that needs to be written to the hard disk. First, all data is buffered in the RAM. This buffer is monitored by the kernel update daemon (kupdated). When the data reaches a certain age limit or when the buffer is filled to a certain degree, the buffer content is flushed to the hard disk. The buffer size is dynamic and depends on the size of the memory and the system load. By default, kupdated is set to short intervals to achieve maximum data integrity. It checks the buffer every five seconds and notifies the bdflush daemon when data is older than thirty seconds or the buffer reaches a fill level of thirty percent. The bdflush daemon then writes the data to the hard disk. It also writes independently from kupdated if, for instance, the buffer is full. On a stable system, these settings can be modified. However, do not forget that this may have a detrimental effect on the data integrity.

Caution

Impairment of the Data Integrity

Changes to the kernel update daemon settings affect the data integrity. Do not touch these settings if you are not sure.

Caution

The settings for the hard disk time-out, the kupdated interval, the buffer threshold, and the age limit for data can be specified in `/etc/sysconfig/powermanagement` for battery operation and for AC operation. The variables are described in Section 8.2.1 on page 183 and in the file itself. Further information is available in `/usr/share/doc/packages/powersave`.

Apart from these processes, journaling file systems, like ReiserFS and Ext3, write their meta data independently from bdflush, which also prevents the hard disk from spinning down. To avoid this, a special kernel extension has been developed for mobile devices. See `/usr/src/linux/Documentation/laptop-mode.txt` for details.

Another important factor is the way active programs behave. For example, good editors regularly write hidden backups of the currently modified file to the hard disk, causing the disk to wake up. Features like this can be disabled at the expense of data integrity.

In this connection, the mail daemon postfix makes use of the variable `POSTFIX_LAPTOP`. If this variable is set to `yes`, postfix will access the hard disk far less frequently. However, this is irrelevant if the interval for kupdated was increased.

8.5 powersave

On laptops, the `powersave` package can be used to control the power saving function during battery operation. Some of the features of this package can also be used on normal workstations and servers (suspend, standby, ACPI button functionality, putting IDE hard disks to sleep).

This package comprises all power management features of your computer. It supports hardware using ACPI, APM, IDE hard disks, and PowerNow! or SpeedStep technologies. The functionalities from the packages `apmd`, `acpid`, `ospmd`, and `cpufreqd` (now `cpuspeed`) have been consolidated in the `powersave` package. For this reason, daemons from these packages should not be run together with the powersave daemon.

Even if your system does not have all hardware elements listed above (APM and ACPI are mutually exclusive), use the powersave daemon for controlling the power saving function. The daemon will automatically detect any changes in the hardware configuration.

Note

Information about powersave

Apart from this chapter, topical information about the powersave package is also available in `/usr/share/doc/packages/powersave/README_POWERSAVE`.

Note

8.5.1 Configuration of powersave

Normally, the configuration of powersave is distributed to several files:

`/etc/powersave.conf` The powersave daemon needs this file for delegating system events to the powersave_proxy. Additionally, custom settings for the behavior of the daemon can be made in this file.

`/etc/sysconfig/powersave/common`
This file provides the general configuration of the start-up script (`rcpowersave`) and the proxy. Usually, the default settings can be adopted as they are.

`/etc/sysconfig/powersave/scheme_*`
These are the various schemes or profiles that control the adaption of the power consumption to specific scenarios, some of which are already preconfigured and ready to use without any changes. Any custom profiles can be saved here.

8.5.2 Configuration of APM and ACPI

Suspend and Standby

In the file `/etc/sysconfig/powersave/common`, specify any critical modules and services that need to be unloaded or stopped prior to a suspend or standby event. When the system operation is resumed, these modules and services will be reloaded or restarted. The default settings mainly affect USB and PCMCIA modules.

POWERSAVE_SUSPEND_RESTART_SERVICES=""
List the services to restart after a suspend.

POWERSAVE_STANDBY_RESTART_SERVICES=""
List the services to restart after a standby.

POWERSAVE_UNLOAD_MODULES_BEFORE_SUSPEND=""
List the modules to unload before a suspend.

POWERSAVE_UNLOAD_MODULES_BEFORE_STANDBY=""
List the modules to unload before a standby.

Make sure that the following standard options for the correct processing of suspend, standby, occurrence, and resume are set (normally, these are the default settings following the installation of SUSE LINUX):

```
POWERSAVE_EVENT_GLOBAL_SUSPEND="prepare_suspend"
POWERSAVE_EVENT_GLOBAL_STANDBY="prepare_standby"
POWERSAVE_EVENT_GLOBAL_RESUME_SUSPEND="restore_after_suspend"
POWERSAVE_EVENT_GLOBAL_RESUME_STANDBY="restore_after_standby"
```

In `/etc/powersave.conf` (configuration file of the powersave daemon), these events are allocated to the `powersave_proxy` script. This script is executed when these events occur (default setting following the installation):

```
global.suspend=/usr/sbin/powersave_proxy
global.standby=/usr/sbin/powersave_proxy
global.resume.suspend=/usr/sbin/powersave_proxy
global.resume.standby=/usr/sbin/powersave_proxy
```

User-Defined Battery States

In the file `/etc/powersave.conf`, define three battery charge levels (in percent) that trigger system alerts or execute specific actions when they are reached.

```
POWERSAVED_BATTERY_WARNING=20
POWERSAVED_BATTERY_LOW=10
POWERSAVED_BATTERY_CRITICAL=5
```

The actions or scripts to execute when the charge levels drops under the specified limits are defined in `/etc/powersave.conf`. The action type is configured in `/etc/sysconfig/powersave/common`:

```
POWERSAVE_EVENT_BATTERY_NORMAL="ignore"
POWERSAVE_EVENT_BATTERY_WARNING="notify"
POWERSAVE_EVENT_BATTERY_LOW="notify"
POWERSAVE_EVENT_BATTERY_CRITICAL="suspend"
```

Further options are explained in this configuration file.

Adapting the Power Consumption to Various Conditions

The system behavior can be adapted to the type of power supply. Thus, the power consumption of the system should be reduced when the system is disconnected from the AC power supply and operated with the battery. In the same way, the performance should automatically be increased as soon as the system is connected to the AC power supply. The CPU frequency, the power saving function of IDE hard disks, and some other factors can be modified.

In /etc/powersave.conf, the execution of the actions triggered by the disconnection from or connection to the AC power supply is delegated to powersave_proxy. The scenarios (called schemes or profiles) to apply can be defined in /etc/sysconfig/powersave/common:

```
POWERSAVE_AC_SCHEME="performance"
POWERSAVE_BATTERY_SCHEME="powersave"
```

The schemes are located in files designated as scheme_<name of the scheme> in /etc/sysconfig/powersave/. The example refers to two schemes: scheme_performance and scheme_powersave. performance, powersave, and acoustic are preconfigured. The YaST Power Management module can be used to edit, create, and delete schemes or change their association with specific power supply states.

8.5.3 Additional ACPI Features

If you use ACPI, you can control the response of your system to *ACPI buttons* (Power, Sleep, Lid Open, Lid Closed). In /etc/powersave.conf, the execution of the respective actions is delegated to the powersave_proxy. The action itself is defined in the file /etc/sysconfig/powersave/common. The individual options are explained in this configuration file.

POWERSAVE_EVENT_BUTTON_POWER="wm_shutdown"
When the power button is pressed, the system responds by shutting down the respective window manager (KDE, GNOME, fvwm, etc.).

POWERSAVE_EVENT_BUTTON_SLEEP="suspend"
When the sleep button is pressed, the system is set to the suspend mode.

POWERSAVE_EVENT_BUTTON_LID_OPEN="ignore"
Nothing happens when the lid is opened.

POWERSAVE_EVENT_BUTTON_LID_CLOSED="screen_saver"
When the lid is closed, the screen saver is activated.

Further throttling of the CPU performance is possible if the CPU load does not exceed a specified limit for a specified time. Specify the load limit in `POWERSAVED_CPU_LOW_LIMIT` and the time-out in `POWERSAVED_CPU_-IDLE_TIMEOUT`.

8.5.4 Troubleshooting

The following items cover the most frequent problems in connection with powersave.

- **I have a problem, but I am not able to find the cause.**

  Take a look at `/var/log/messages`. All error messages and alerts are logged there. If you cannot find the needed information, use the variable `DEBUG` for powersave in the file `/etc/sysconfig/powersave/common` to increase the verbosity of the messages. Increase the value of the variable to 7 or even 15 and restart the daemon. The error messages in `/var/log/messages` will now be more detailed, enabling you to identify the error.

- **Although I activated ACPI, the battery states and buttons do not work as configured.**

  If you experience problems with ACPI, use the following command to search the output of `dmesg` for ACPI-specific messages: `dmesg|grep -i acpi`. A BIOS update may be required to resolve the problem. Go to the home page of your laptop manufacturer, look for an updated BIOS version, and install it. Request the manufacturer to comply with the latest ACPI specification. If the errors persist after the BIOS update, proceed as follows to replace the faulty DSDT table in your BIOS with an updated DSDT:

1. Download the DSDT for your system from `http://acpi.sourceforge.net/dsdt/tables`. Check if the file is decompressed and compiled as shown by the file extension `.aml` (ACPI machine language). If this is the case, continue with step 3.
2. If the file extension of the downloaded table is `.asl` (ACPI source language), it must be compiled with iasl (package `pmtools`). To do this, enter the command `iasl -sa <file>.asl`. The latest version of iasl (Intel ACPI Compiler) is available at `http://developer.intel.com/technology/iapc/acpi/downloads.htm`.
3. Copy the file `DSDT.aml` to any location (`/etc/DSDT.aml` is recommended). Edit `/etc/sysconfig/kernel` and adapt the path to the DSDT file accordingly. Start `mkinitrd` (package `mkinitrd`). Whenever you uninstall the kernel and use `mkinitrd` to create an initrd, the modified DSDT will be integrated and loaded when the system is booted.

- **CPU frequency does not work.**

  Refer to the kernel sources (`kernel-source`) to see if your processor is supported. You may need a special kernel module or module option to activate CPU frequency control. This information is available in `/usr/src/linux/Documentation/cpu-freq/*`. If a special module or module option is needed, configure it in the file `/etc/sysconfig/powersave/common` by means of the variables `CPUFREQD_MODULE` and `CPUFREQD_MODULE_OPTS`.

- **Suspend and standby do not work.**

  There are several kernel-related problems that prevent the use of suspend and standby on **ACPI** systems:

  - Currently, systems with more than 1 GB RAM do not (yet) support suspend.
  - Currently, multiprocessor systems and systems with a P4 processor (with hyperthreading) do not support suspend.

  The error may also be due to a faulty DSDT implementation (BIOS). If this is the case, install a new DSDT as described under *Although I activated ACPI, the battery states and buttons do not work as configured.*.

On **ACPI** and **APM** systems:

When the system attempts to unload faulty modules, the proxy is arrested and the suspend event is not triggered. The same can happen if you do not unload modules or stop services that prevent a successful suspend. In both cases, try to identify the modules causing the problem by manipulating the following settings in `/etc/sysconfig/powersave/common`:

```
POWERSAVE_UNLOAD_MODULES_BEFORE_SUSPEND=""
POWERSAVE_UNLOAD_MODULES_BEFORE_STANDBY=""
POWERSAVE_SUSPEND_RESTART_SERVICES=""
POWERSAVE_STANDBY_RESTART_SERVICES=""
```

- **When using ACPI, the powersave daemon does not notice when a certain battery limit is reached.**

  With ACPI, the operating system can request the BIOS to send a message when the battery charge level drops under a certain limit. The advantage of this method is that the battery state does not need to be polled constantly, which would impair the performance of the computer. However, this notification may not take place when the charge level drops under the specified limit, even though the BIOS supposedly supports this feature. If this happens on your system, set the variable `POWERSAVED_FORCE_BATTERY_POLLING` in the file `/etc/powersave.conf` to `yes` to force battery polling.

8.6 The YaST Power Management Module

The YaST Power Management module serves the configuration of all power management settings described above. When starting the module from the YaST Control Center ('System' → 'Power Management'), the first dialog of the module is displayed (see Figure 8.1). In this dialog, select the schemes to use for battery operation and AC operation.

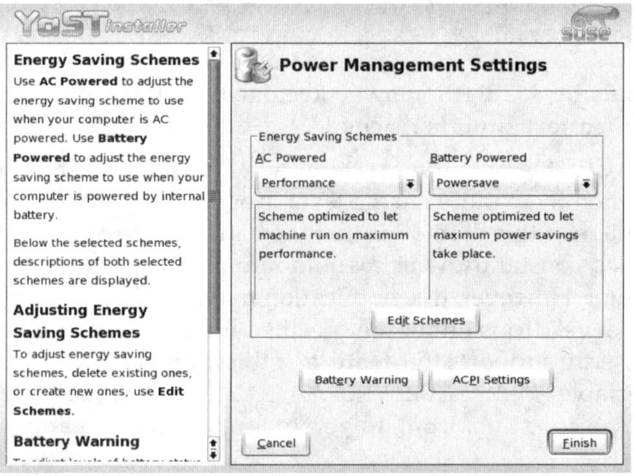

Figure 8.1: YaST Power Management: Scheme Selection

In this dialog, select one of the existing schemes or click 'Edit Schemes' to access an overview of the existing schemes. This is shown in Figure 8.2 on the facing page.

In the schemes overview, select a scheme and click 'Edit' to access the editing dialog (see Figure 8.3 on page 200). To create a new scheme, click 'Add'. The subsequent dialog is the same in both cases.

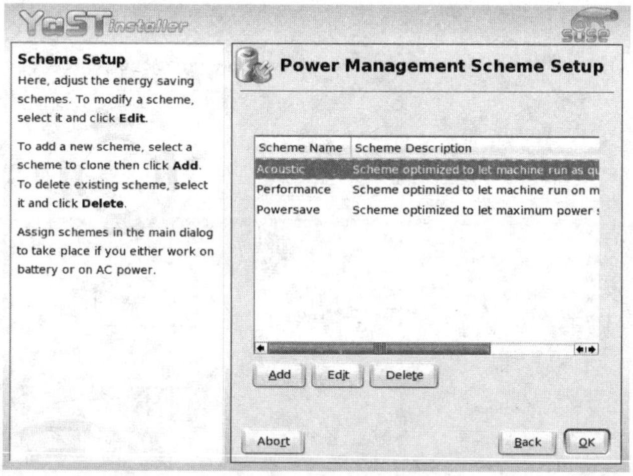

Figure 8.2: YaST Power Management: Overview of Existing Schemes

First, enter a suitable name and description for the new or edited scheme. For the hard disk, define a 'Standby Policy' for maximum performance or for energy saving. The 'Acoustic Policy' controls the noise level of the hard disk. Click 'Next' to enter the 'CPU' and 'Cooling Policy' dialog. 'CPU' comprises the options 'CPU Frequency Scaling' and 'Throttling'. Use these options to define if and to what extent the CPU frequency may be throttled. The 'Cooling Policy' determines the cooling method. Complete all settings for the scheme and click 'OK' to return to the start dialog (Figure 8.1 on the facing page). In the start dialog, assign the custom scheme to one of the two operating modes. To activate your settings, exit this dialog with 'OK'.

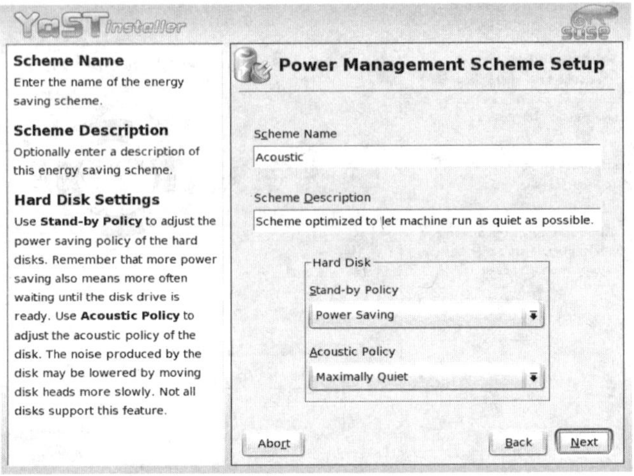

Figure 8.3: *YaST Power Management: Adding a Scheme*

Apart from selecting schemes for various operating modes, global power management settings can also be made from the start dialog using the 'Battery Warnings' or 'ACPI Settings' buttons (see Figure 8.1 on page 198). Click 'Battery Warnings' to access the dialog for the battery charge level, shown in Figure 8.4 on the facing page.

The BIOS of your system notifies the operating system whenever the charge level drops under certain configurable limits. In this dialog, define three limits: 'Warning Capacity', 'Low Capacity', and 'Critical Capacity'. Specific actions are triggered when the charge level drops under these limits. Usually, the first two states merely trigger a notification to the user. The third critical level triggers a suspend, as the remaining energy is not sufficient for continued system operation. Select suitable charge levels and the respective actions then click 'OK' to return to the start dialog. Access the dialog for configuring the ACPI buttons using the 'ACPI Settings' button. It is shown in Figure 8.5 on the next page.

The settings for the ACPI buttons determine how the system should respond to the actuation of certain switches. Configure the system response to pressing the Power button, pressing the Sleep button, and closing the laptop lid. Click 'OK' to complete the configuration and return to the start dialog (Figure 8.1 on page 198). Click 'OK' again to exit the module and confirm your power management settings.

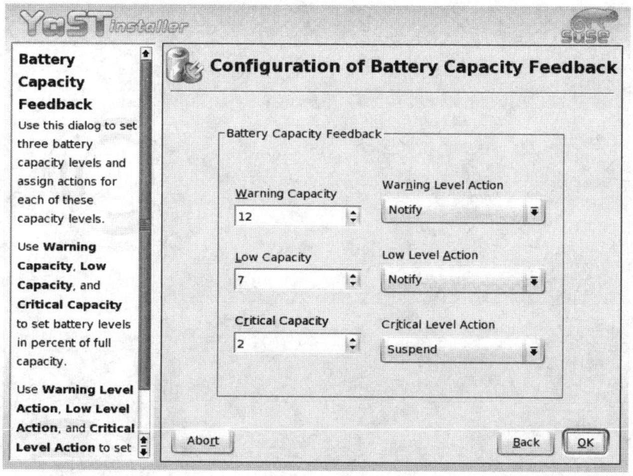

Figure 8.4: YaST Power Management: Battery Charge Level

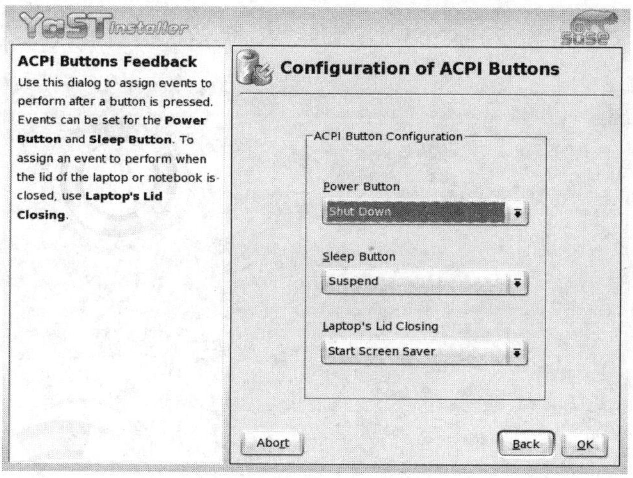

Figure 8.5: YaST Power Management: ACPI Settings

Part III

System

SUSE LINUX on AMD64 Systems

AMD presented its Athlon64 processor to the public in September 2003. This new processor is a 64-bit processor and is therefore able to execute new 64-bit AMD64 programs. It also supports the execution of existing 32-bit x86 programs at the same level of performance.

64-bit programs have a larger address space and offer better performance by providing modern calling conventions and additional registers that are only supported in 64-bit mode.

SUSE LINUX supports the new processor with this product in two ways.

- 32-bit SUSE LINUX for x86 supports this processor as 32-bit processor just like it supports the AMD Athlon and the Intel Pentium processors.
- The new 64-bit SUSE LINUX for AMD64 supports the processor in 64-bit mode. The execution as well as the development of 32-bit x86 programs is still supported.

Note

The output of `uname -m` is **x86_64** for historical reasons. This was the name of the first AMD specification.

Note

9.1 Hardware

From the perspective of the user, hardware relates to the AMD64 just like it does with AMD Athlon systems. The common interfaces and buses are the same on both platforms and are equally supported.

Because the hardware drivers for Linux on AMD64 must be 64-bit drivers, some of them still need to be adapted. While some older cards are currently not functional, the support of current hardware should be the same in 32-bit and 64-bit.

9.2 Software

Almost all packages are 64-bit on the software side. The execution of 32-bit programs is additionally supported. Dedicated 32-bit library packages were developed for this and are installed in the default installation. To enable installation of 32-bit and 64-bit libraries with the same name on one system, the 32-bit libraries are installed in the directory `/lib/` and the 64-bit libraries are installed in the `/lib64/` directory. This makes the installation of 32-bit RPMs possible without any modifications.

From the perspective of the administrator or the user, there is no directly discernable difference between 32-bit and 64-bit. All programs look and feel the same.

9.3 Running 32-bit Software

32-bit software that uses `uname` to probe for the architecture possibly may require an additional step to run properly. For this, use `linux32`, which changes the output of `uname -m`. Use it with the software by entering `linux32` , a space, then the command to run the software. This can be used to run a shell in which `uname` is modified, which can then be used to start any number of programs in the `linux32` environment.

9.4 Software Development in a 64-bit Environment

A SUSE LINUX for AMD64 system supports the development of 32-bit applications as well as 64-bit applications. The GNU compiler usually creates 64-bit AMD64 code. The switch `-m32` causes the creation of 32-bit x86 code, which then also runs on 32-bit AMD Athlon or Intel Pentium systems.

The 64-bit libraries must be used for the development of 64-bit code. The paths `/lib64/` and `/usr/lib64/` are always searched, but an option `-L/usr/X11R6/lib64` needs to be added for X11 code. Some adaptation of the Makefiles is thus necessary.

GDB can be used to debug the code. While the application for 64-bit AMD64 code is called gdb, it is called gdb32 for 32-bit x86 code. The strace tool can examine 32-bit as well as 64-bit programs and the library tracer ltrace also comes in a separate 32-bit version called ltrace32.

9.5 For More Information

The web sites of AMD (`www.amd.com`) and the project page of the Linux port to AMD64 (`www.x86-64.org`) provide additional information about the subject.

The Linux Kernel

The kernel manages the hardware of every Linux system and makes it available to the various processes. Although the information provided in this chapter will not make you a kernel hacker, you will learn how to perform a kernel update and how to compile and install a custom kernel. If you follow the instructions in this chapter, the previous kernel will remain functional and can be booted if necessary.

The kernel that is installed in the /boot/ directory is configured for a wide range of hardware. Normally, there is no need to compile a custom kernel, unless you want to test experimental features and drivers.

Several Makefiles are provided with the kernel to automate the process. Select the hardware settings and other kernel features. As you need to know your computer system pretty well to make the right selections, modifying an existing and working configuration file is recommended for your first attempt.

10.1 Kernel Update

To install an official SUSE update kernel, download the update RPM from the SUSE FTP server or a mirror like ftp://ftp.gwdg.de/pub/linux/suse/. To determine the version of your current kernel, look at the version string with cat /proc/version. Alternatively, check to which package the kernel (/boot/vmlinuz) belongs with rpm -qf /boot/vmlinuz.

Before installing this package, make a backup copy of the original kernel and the associated initrd. As root, enter the following two commands:

```
cp /boot/vmlinuz /boot/vmlinuz.old
cp /boot/initrd /boot/initrd.old
```

Then install the new kernel with the command rpm -Uvh <packagename>. Replace packagename with the name of the kernel RPM to install.

Since SUSE LINUX 7.3, reiserfs is the standard file system. It requires the use of an "initial ramdisk". Therefore, use the command mk_initrd to write the new initial ramdisk. In current SUSE LINUX versions this is done automatically when installing the new kernel.

To be able to boot the old kernel, configure the boot loader accordingly (for more information, refer to Chapter 6 on page 135). Finally, reboot to load the new kernel.

To reinstall the original kernel from the SUSE LINUX CDs, the procedure is almost the same, except you copy the kernel RPM from the directory boot/ on CD 1 or the DVD. Now, install as described above. If you receive an error message saying that a newer kernel rpm is already installed, add the option --force to the above rpm command.

10.2 Kernel Sources

To build a kernel, the package `kernel-source` must be installed. Additional packages, like the C compiler (package `gcc`), the GNU binutils (package `binutils`), and the include files for the C compiler (package `glibc-devel`), are selected for installation automatically by YaST.

After installation, the kernel sources are located in `/usr/src/linux-<kernel-version>/`. If you plan to experiment with different kernels, unpack them in different subdirectories and create a symbolic link to the current kernel source. As there are software packages that rely on the sources being in `/usr/src/linux/`, maintain this directory as a symbolic link to your current kernel source. YaST does this automatically.

10.3 Kernel Configuration

The configuration of the current kernel is stored in the file `/proc/config.gz`. To modify this configuration, go to the directory `/usr/src/linux/` as `root` and execute the following commands:

```
zcat /proc/config.gz > .config
make oldconfig
```

The command `make oldconfig` uses the file `/usr/src/linux/.config` as a template for the current kernel configuration. Any new options for your current kernel sources will be queried. If the file `.config` does not exist, the default configuration included in the kernel sources will be used.

10.3.1 Configuration on the Command Line

To configure the kernel, change to `/usr/src/linux` and enter the command `make config`. Choose the features you want supported by the kernel. Usually, There are two or three options: (y), (n), or (m). (m) means that this device will not be compiled directly into the kernel, but loaded as a module. Drivers needed for booting the system must be integrated into the kernel with (y). Press (Enter) to confirm the default settings read from the file `.config`. Press any other key to view a brief help text about the respective option.

10.3.2 Configuration in Text Mode

"menuconfig" is a more comfortable way to configure the kernel. If necessary, install `ncurses-devel` with YaST. Start the kernel configuration with the command `make menuconfig`.

For minor changes in the configuration, you do not have to go through all the questions. Instead, use the menu to access certain sections directly. The default settings are loaded from the file `.config`. To load a different configuration, select 'Load an Alternate Configuration File' and enter the file name.

10.3.3 Configuration in the X Window System

If you installed and configured the X Window System (package `xf86`) and Tcl/Tk (`tcl` and `tk`), you can use the command `make xconfig` to access a graphical user interface for the configuration. If you are not logged in to the X Window System as `root`, enter the command `xhost +` to give `root` access to the display. The default settings will be loaded from the file `.config`. As the configuration with `make xconfig` is not as well maintained as the other configuration possibilities, run the command `make oldconfig` after using this configuration method.

10.4 Kernel Modules

There is a wide variety of PC hardware components. To use this hardware properly, you need a "driver" with which the operating system (in Linux, the "kernel"), can access this hardware. There are basically two ways of integrating drivers into your system:

- The drivers can be compiled directly into the kernel. Such a kernel ("in one piece") is referred to as a *monolithic* kernel. Some drivers are only available in this form.
- Drivers can be loaded into the kernel on demand. In this case, the kernel is referred to as a *modularized* kernel. This has the advantage that only those drivers really needed are loaded and the kernel thus contains nothing unnecessary.

Which drivers to compile into the kernel and which to load as run-time modules is defined in the kernel configuration. Basically, components not required for booting the system should be built as modules. This makes sure the kernel does not become too big to be loaded by the BIOS or a boot loader. Drivers for `ext2`, the SCSI drivers on a SCSI-based system, and similar drivers should be compiled into the kernel. In contrast, items, such as `isofs`, `msdos`, or `sound`, which are not needed for starting your computer system, should definitely be built as modules.

Kernel modules are located in `/lib/modules/<version>/`. `Version` stands for the current kernel version.

10.5 Hardware Detection with the Help of hwinfo

hwinfo can detect the hardware of your system and select the drivers needed to run this hardware. Get a small introduction to this command with `hwinfo --help`. If you, for example, need information about your SCSI devices, use the command `hwinfo --scsi`.

All this information is also available in YaST in the hardware information module.

10.5.1 Handling Modules

The following commands are available:

insmod `insmod` loads the requested module after searching for it in a subdirectory of `/lib/modules/<version>/`. It is better, however, to use `modprobe` rather than `insmod`.

rmmod Unloads the requested module. This is only possible if this module is no longer needed. For example, the `isofs` module cannot be unloaded while a CD is still mounted.

depmod Creates the file `modules.dep` in `/lib/modules/<version>/` that defines the dependencies of all the modules. This is necessary to ensure that all dependent modules are loaded with the selected ones. This file will be built after the system is started if it does not exist.

modprobe Loads or unloads a given module while taking into account dependencies of this module. This command is extremely powerful and can be used for a lot of things (e.g., probing all modules of a given type until one is successfully loaded). In contrast to insmod, modprobe checks /etc/modprobe.conf and therefore is the preferred method of loading modules. For detailed information about this topic, refer to the corresponding man page.

lsmod Shows which modules are currently loaded as well as how many other modules are using them. Modules started by the kernel daemon are tagged with autoclean. This label denotes that these modules will automatically be removed once they reach their idle time limit.

modinfo Shows module information.

10.5.2 /etc/modprobe.conf

The loading of modules is affected by the files /etc/modprobe.conf and /etc/modprobe.conf.local and the directory /etc/modprobe.d. See man modprobe.conf. Parameters for modules that access hardware directly must be entered in this file. Such modules may need system-specific options (e.g., CD-ROM driver or network driver). The parameters used here are described in the kernel sources. Install the package kernel-source and read the documentation in the directory /usr/src/linux/Documentation/.

10.5.3 Kmod — the Kernel Module Loader

The kernel module loader is the most elegant way to use modules. Kmod performs background monitoring and makes sure the required modules are loaded by modprobe as soon as the respective functionality is needed in the kernel.

To use Kmod, activate the option 'Kernel module loader' (CONFIG_KMOD) in the kernel configuration. Kmod is not designed to unload modules automatically; in view of today's RAM capacities, the potential memory savings would be marginal. For reasons of performance, monolithic kernels may be more suitable for servers that are used for special tasks and need only a few drivers.

10.6 Settings in the Kernel Configuration

All the kernel's configuration options cannot be covered here in detail. Make use of the numerous help texts available on kernel configuration. The latest kernel documentation is always in /usr/src/linux/Documentation/.

10.7 Compiling the Kernel

Compiling a "bzImage" is recommanded. As a rule, this avoids the problem of the kernel getting too large, as can easily happen if you select too many features and create a "zImage". You will then get error messages like "kernel too big" or "System is too big".

After customizing the kernel configuration, start compilation by entering (remember to change into the directory /usr/src/linux/, first):

```
make clean
make bzImage
```

These two commands can be entered as one command line:

```
make clean bzImage
```

After a successful compilation, find the compressed kernel in /usr/src/linux/arch/<arch>/boot/. The kernel image — the file that contains the kernel — is called vmlinux.gz.

If you cannot find this file, an error probably occurred during the kernel compilation. In the Bash shell, enter the following command to launch the kernel compilation again and write the output to a file kernel.out:

```
make bzImage 2>&1 | tee kernel.out
```

If you have configured parts of your kernel to load as modules, launch the module compilation. Do this with make modules.

10.8 Installing the Kernel

After the kernel is compiled, it must be installed so it can be booted.

If you use LILO, LILO must be updated as well. To prevent unpleasant surprises, it is recommended to keep the old kernel (e.g., as /boot/vmlinuz.old), so you can still boot it if the new kernel does not function as expected:

```
cp /boot/vmlinuz /boot/vmlinuz.old
cp arch/i386/boot/bzImage /boot/vmlinuz
lilo
```

The Makefile target `make bzlilo` performs all three of these steps.

Note

If you use GRUB as the boot loader, it does *not* need to be reinstalled. Simply carry out the first two steps to copy the kernel to the right location in the system.

Note

Now the compiled modules need to be installed. Enter `make modules_install` to copy them to the correct target directories in `/lib/modules/<version>/`. If the kernel version is the same, the old modules will be overwritten. However, the original modules can be reinstalled together with the kernel from the CDs.

Note

To avoid unexpected effects, make sure that modules whose functionalities may now have been directly compiled into the kernel are removed from `/lib/modules/<version>/`. This is one of the reasons why inexperienced users are *strongly* discouraged from compiling the kernel.

Note

To enable GRUB or LILO to boot the old kernel (now `/boot/vmlinuz.old`), add an image entry with the label `Linux.old` in your `/boot/grub/menu.lst` or `/etc/lilo.conf` This procedure is described in detail in Chapter 6 on page 135. If you are using LILO as the boot loader, LILO must be reinstalled after modifications to `/etc/lilo.conf` with the command `lilo`. GRUB does not need to be reinstalled.

The file /boot/System.map contains kernel symbols required by the modules to ensure successful launching of kernel functions. This file depends on the current kernel. Therefore, once you have compiled and installed the kernel, copy /usr/src/linux/System.map to the directory (/boot/). This file is regenerated each time the kernel is recompiled. If you create your kernel using make bzlilo or make zlilo, this is done for you automatically. If you get an error message like "System.map does not match current kernel", System.map probably has not been copied.

10.9 Cleaning Your Hard Disk after Compilation

If you are low on hard disk space, delete the object files generated during kernel compilation using make clean in the /usr/src/linux/ directory. If you have plenty of disk space and plan to reconfigure the kernel on a regular basis, you might want to skip this. Recompiling the kernel is considerably faster then, because only the parts affected by changes will actually be recompiled.

Special Features of SUSE LINUX

This chapter provides information about the *Filesystem Hierarchy Standard* (FHS) and *Linux Standard Base* (LSB). Various software packages and special features, such as booting with *initrd*, linuxrc, and the rescue system, are described in detail.

11.1 Linux Standards

11.1.1 Linux Standard Base (LSB)

SUSE actively supports the efforts of the *Linux Standard Base* project. Up-to-date information about the project can be found at `http://www.linuxbase.org`. The currently valid LSB specification is at version 1.3.x. Apart from the File System Hierarchy Standard (FHS), which now forms part of it, the specification defines things like the package format and details of the system initialization (see Chapter 12 on page 247).

11.1.2 File System Hierarchy Standard (FHS)

In accordance with the LSB specification, SUSE LINUX is also compliant with the *File System Hierarchy Standard* or FHS (package `fhs`). Also see `http://www.pathname.com/fhs/`. For this reason, in some cases it was necessary to move files or directories to their *correct* places in the file system, as specified by the FHS.

For example, one aim of the FHS is to define a structure with the help of which `/usr` can be mounted *read-only*.

11.1.3 teTeX — TeX in SUSE LINUX

TeX is a comprehensive typesetting system that runs on various platforms. It can be expanded with macro packages, like LaTeX, and consists of numerous files that have to be organized according to the *TeX Directory Structure* (TDS) (see `ftp://ftp.dante.de/tex-archive/tds/`). teTeX is a compilation of current TeX software. On a SUSE LINUX system, teTeX is installed in a way that ensures compliance with the requirements of both the TDS and the FHS.

11.1.4 Example Environment for FTP Server

To make it easier to set up an FTP server, the `ftpdir` package includes an example environment. This is installed in `/srv/ftp`.

11.1.5 Example Environment for HTTP Server

Apache is the standard web server in SUSE LINUX. Together with the installation of Apache, some example documents are made available in /srv/www. To set up your own web server, include your own DocumentRoot in /etc/httpd/httpd.conf and store your files (documents, picture files) accordingly.

11.2 Hints on Special Software Packages

11.2.1 Package bash and /etc/profile

1. /etc/profile
2. ~/.profile
3. /etc/bash.bashrc
4. ~/.bashrc

Users can make personal entries in ~/.profile or in ~/.bashrc. To ensure the correct processing of these files, it is necessary to copy the basic settings from /etc/skel/.profile or /etc/skel/.bashrc respectively into the home directory of the user. It is recommended to copy the settings from /etc/skel following an update. Execute the following shell commands to prevent the loss of personal adjustments:

```
mv ~/.bashrc ~/.bashrc.old
cp /etc/skel/.bashrc ~/.bashrc
mv ~/.profile ~/.profile.old
cp /etc/skel/.profile ~/.profile
```

The personal adjustments then need to be copied back from the files *.old.

11.2.2 cron Package

The cron tables are now located in /var/cron/tabs. /etc/crontab serves as a system-wide cron table. Enter the name of the user who should run the command directly after the time table (see File 11.1, here root is entered). Package-specific tables, located in /etc/cron.d, have the same format. See man cron.

Example 11.1: *Example of an Entry in /etc/crontab*

```
1-59/5 * * * * root test -x /usr/sbin/atrun && /usr/sbin/atrun
```

/etc/crontab cannot be processed with crontab -e. It must be loaded directly into an editor, modified, then saved.

A number of packages install shell scripts to the directories /etc/cron.hourly, /etc/cron.daily, /etc/cron.weekly, and /etc/cron.monthly, whose instructions are controlled by /usr/lib/cron/run-crons. /usr/lib/cron/run-crons is run every fifteen minutes from the main table (/etc/crontab). This guarantees that processes that may have been neglected can be run at the proper time.

The daily system maintenance jobs have been distributed to various scripts for reasons of clarity. Apart from aaa_base, /etc/cron.daily contains, for instance, the components backup-rpmdb, clean-tmp, or clean-vi.

11.2.3 Log Files: the Package logrotate

There are a number of system services (*daemons*), which, along with the kernel itself, regularly record the system status and specific events to log files. This way, the administrator can regularly check the status of the system at a certain point in time, recognize errors or faulty functions, and troubleshoot them with pinpoint precision. These log files are normally stored in /var/log as specified by FHS and grow on a daily basis. The logrotate package helps control the growth of these files.

Changing to logrotate

The old settings listed below are adopted when updating from a version older than SUSE LINUX 8.0:

- Entries from /etc/logfile not associated with a particular package are moved to /etc/logrotate.d/aaa_base.
- The variable MAX_DAYS_FOR_LOG_FILES from the former rc.config file is mapped as dateext and maxage in the configuration file. Refer to man logrotate.

Configuration

Configure logrotate with the file /etc/logrotate.conf. In particular, the include specification primarily configures the additional files to read. SUSE LINUX ensures that individual packages install files in /etc/logrotate.d (e.g., syslog or yast).

Example 11.2: *Example for /etc/logrotate.conf*

```
# see "man logrotate" for details
# rotate log files weekly
weekly

# keep 4 weeks worth of backlogs
rotate 4

# create new (empty) log files after rotating old ones
create

# uncomment this if you want your log files compressed
#compress

# RPM packages drop log rotation information into this directory
include /etc/logrotate.d

# no packages own lastlog or wtmp - we'll rotate them here
#/var/log/wtmp {
#    monthly
#    create 0664 root utmp
#    rotate 1
#}

# system-specific logs may be also be configured here.
```

logrotate is controlled through cron and it is called daily by /etc/cron.daily/logrotate.

Note

The `create` option reads all settings made by the administrator in `/etc/permissions*`. Ensure that no conflicts arise from any personal modifications.

Note

11.2.4 Man Pages

For some GNU applications (such as tar) the man pages are no longer maintained. For these commands, use the `--help` option to get a quick overview or the info pages, which provide more in-depth instructions. info is GNU's hypertext system. Read an introduction to this system by entering `info info`. Info pages can be viewed either via Emacs, by entering `emacs -f info`, or directly in a console with `info`. You can also use tkinfo, xinfo, or the SUSE help system to view info pages in a convenient way.

11.2.5 The Command ulimit

With the `ulimit` (*user limits*) command, it is possible to set limits for the use of system resources and to have these displayed. `ulimit` is especially useful for limiting the memory available for applications. With this, an application can be prevented from using too much memory on its own, which could bring the system to a standstill.

`ulimit` can be used with various options. To limit memory usage, use the options listed in Table 11.1.

***Table 11.1:** ulimit: Setting Resources for the User*

`-m`	maximum size of physical memory
`-v`	maximum size of virtual memory
`-s`	maximum size of the stack
`-c`	maximum size of the core files
`-a`	display of limits set

System-wide settings can be made in /etc/profile. There, creating core files must be enabled, needed by programmers for *debugging*. A normal user cannot increase the values specified in /etc/profile by the system administrator, but he can make special entries in his own~/.bashrc.

***Example 11.3:** ulimit: Settings in /.bashrc*

```
# Limits of physical memory:
ulimit -m 98304

# Limits of virtual memory:
ulimit -v 98304
```

Details of memory must be specified in KB. For more detailed information, see man bash.

Note

Not all shells support ulimit directives. PAM (for instance, pam_limits) offers comprehensive adjustment possibilities if you depend on encompassing settings for these restrictions.

Note

11.2.6 The free Command

The free command is somewhat misleading if your goal is to find out how much RAM is currently being used. The relevant information can be found in /proc/meminfo. These days, users, who have access to a modern operating system such as Linux, should not really need to worry much about memory. The concept of *available RAM* dates back to before the days of unified memory management. The slogan *free memory is bad memory* applies well to Linux. As a result, Linux has always made the effort to balance out caches without actually allowing free or unused memory.

Basically, the kernel does not have direct knowledge of any applications or user data. Instead, it manages applications and user data in a *page cache*. If memory runs short, parts of it will be either written to the swap partition or to files, from which they can initially be read with the help of the mmap command (see man mmap).

Furthermore, the kernel also contains other caches, such as the *slab cache*, where the caches used for network access are stored. This may explain differences between the counters in /proc/meminfo. Most, but not all of them, can be accessed via /proc/slabinfo.

11.2.7 The File /etc/resolv.conf

Domain name resolution is handled through the file `/etc/resolv.conf`. Refer to Section 13.6 on page 293 about this.

This file is updated by the script `/sbin/modify_resolvconf` exclusively, with no other program having permission to modify `/etc/resolv.conf` directly. Enforcing this rule is the only way to guarantee that the system's network configuration and the relevant files are kept in a consistent state.

11.2.8 Settings for GNU Emacs

GNU Emacs is a complex work environment. More information is available at `http://www.gnu.org/software/emacs/`. The following sections cover the configuration files processed when GNU Emacs is started.

On start-up, Emacs reads several files containing the settings of the user, system administrator, and distributor for customization or preconfiguration. The initialization file `~/.emacs` is installed to the home directories of the individual users from `/etc/skel`. `.emacs`, in turn, reads the file `/etc/skel/.gnu-emacs`. If a user wants to customize the program, the `.gnu-emacs` should be copied to the home directory and the desired settings should be specified there:

```
cp /etc/skel/.gnu-emacs ~/.gnu-emacs
```

`.gnu-emacs` defines the file `~/.gnu-emacs-custom` as `custom-file`. If users make settings with the `customize` options, these are saved to `~/.gnu-emacs-custom`.

With SUSE LINUX, the `emacs` package installs the file `site-start.el` in the directory `/usr/share/emacs/site-lisp`. The file `site-start.el` is loaded *before* the initialization file `~/.emacs`. Among other things, `site-start.el` ensures that special configuration files distributed with Emacs add-on packages (such as `psgml`) are loaded automatically. Configuration files of this type are located in `/usr/share/emacs/site-lisp`, too, and always begin with `suse-start-`. The local system administrator can specify system-wide settings in `default.el`.

More information about these files is available in the Emacs info file under `Init File`: `info:/emacs/InitFile`. Information about how to disable loading these files (if necessary) is also provided at this location.

The components of Emacs are split in several packages:

- The base package `emacs`.
- Usually, `emacs-x11` should be installed. This package contains the program *with* X11 support.
- `emacs-nox` contains the program *without* X11 support.
- `emacs-info`: online documentation in info format.
- `emacs-el` contains the uncompiled library files in Emacs Lisp. These are not required at run-time.
- Numerous add-on packages that can be installed if needed: `emacs-auctex` (for LaTeX), `psgml` (for SGML and XML), `gnuserv` (for client and server operation), and others.

11.3 Booting with the Initial Ramdisk

As soon as the Linux kernel has been booted and the root file system (/) mounted, programs can be run and further kernel modules can be integrated to provide additional functions. To mount the root file system, certain conditions must be met. The kernel needs the corresponding drivers to access the device on which the root file system is located (especially SCSI drivers). The kernel must also contain the code needed to read the file system (`ext2`, `reiserfs`, `romfs`, etc.). It is also conceivable that the root file system is already encrypted. In this case, a password is needed to mount the file system.

For the problem of SCSI drivers, a number of different solutions are possible. The kernel could contain all imaginable drivers, but this might be a problem because different drivers could conflict with each other. Also, the kernel would become very large because of this. Another possibility is to provide different kernels, each one containing just one or a few SCSI drivers. This method has the problem that a large number of different kernels are required, a problem then increased by the differently optimized kernels (Athlon optimization, SMP). The idea of loading the SCSI driver as a module leads to the general problem resolved by the concept of an *initial ramdisk*: running user space programs even before the root file system is mounted.

11.3.1 Concept of the Initial Ramdisk

The *initial ramdisk* (also called *initdisk* or *initrd*) solves precisely the problems described above. The Linux kernel provides an option of having a small file system loaded to a RAM disk and running programs there before the actual root file system is mounted. The loading of `initrd` is handled by the boot loader (GRUB, LILO, etc.). Boot loaders only need BIOS routines to load data from the boot medium. If the boot loader is able to load the kernel, it can also load the initial ramdisk. Special drivers are not required.

11.3.2 The Order of the Booting Process with initrd

The boot loader loads the kernel and the `initrd` to memory and starts the kernel. The boot loader informs the kernel that an `initrd` exists and where it is located in memory. If the `initrd` was compressed (which is typically the case), the kernel decompresses the `initrd` and mounts it as a temporary root file system. A program called linuxrc is then started. This program can now do all the things necessary to mount the proper root file system.

As soon as linuxrc finishes, the temporary `initrd` is unmounted and the boot process continues as normal with the mount of the proper root file system. Mounting the `initrd` and running linuxrc can be seen as a short interlude during a normal boot process.

The kernel tries to remount `initrd` to the `/initrd` immediately after the actual root partition is booted. If this fails because the mount point `/initrd` does not exist, for example, the kernel will attempt to unmount `initrd`. If this does not work, the system is fully functional, but the memory taken up by `initrd` cannot be unlocked, so will no longer be available.

linuxrc

The only requirements for the program linuxrc in the `initrd` are: it must have the special name `linuxrc`, it must be located in the root directory of the `initrd`, and it needs to be executable by the kernel. This means that linuxrc may be dynamically linked. In this case, the shared libraries in `/lib` must be completely available in `initrd`. linuxrc can also be a shell script. For this to work, a shell must exist in `/bin`. In short, `initrd` must contain a minimal Linux system that allows the program linuxrc to be run. When SUSE LINUX is installed, a statically-linked linuxrc is used to keep `initrd` as small as possible. linuxrc is run with `root` permissions.

The Real Root File System

As soon as linuxrc terminates, `initrd` is unmounted and discarded, the boot process carries on as normal, and the kernel mounts the real file system. What is mounted as the root file system can be influenced by linuxrc. It just needs to mount the `/proc` file system and write the value of the real root file system in numerical form to `/proc/sys/kernel/real-root-dev`.

11.3.3 Boot Loaders

Most boot loaders, including GRUB, LILO, and syslinux, can handle `initrd`. Give individual boot loaders instructions for accessing `initrd` as follows:

GRUB Enter the following line in `/boot/grub/menu.lst`:

```
initrd (hd0,0)/initrd
```

As the loading address of the initrd is written to the loaded kernel image, the `initrd` command must follow the `kernel` command.

LILO Enter the following line in `/etc/lilo.conf`:

```
initrd=/boot/initrd
```

syslinux Enter the following line in `syslinux.cfg`:

```
append initrd=initrd
```

Further parameters can be appended to the line.

11.3.4 Using initrd in SUSE

Installing the System

The `initrd` has already been used for some time for the installation: the user can load modules and make the entries necessary for installation. linuxrc then starts YaST, which carries out the installation. When YaST has finished, it tells linuxrc where the root file system of the newly installed system is located. linuxrc writes this value to `/proc` and reboots the system. Then YaST starts again and installs the remaining packages in the system being installed.

Booting the Installed System

In the past, YaST offered more than forty kernels for installing in the system. The main difference between the kernels was that each of them contained a specific SCSI driver. This was necessary to be able to mount the root file system after booting. Further drivers could then be loaded afterwards as modules. As optimized kernels are now available, this concept is no longer feasible — by now, over one hundred kernel images would be needed.

This is why an `initrd` is used now even to start the system normally. The way it is used is similar to the method for installation. The linuxrc used here, however, is simply a shell script with the task of loading a given module. Typically, this is just one single module — the very SCSI driver needed to access the root file system.

Creating an initrd

An `initrd` is created by means of the script `mkinitrd` (previously `mk_initrd`). In SUSE LINUX, the modules to load are specified by the variable `INITRD_MODULES` in `/etc/sysconfig/kernel`. After installation, this variable is automatically set to the correct value (the installation linuxrc saves which modules were loaded). The modules are loaded in exactly the order in which they appear in `INITRD_MODULES`. This is especially important if several SCSI drivers are used, because otherwise the names of the hard disks would change. Strictly speaking, it would be sufficient just to load those drivers needed to access the root file system. However, all SCSI drivers needed for installation are loaded by means of `initrd` because later loading could be problematic.

Note

As the `initrd` is loaded by the boot loader in the same way as the kernel itself (in its `map` file, LILO records the location of the files), the boot loader LILO must be updated every time the `initrd` is modified. This is not necessary for GRUB.

Note

11.3.5 Possible Difficulties — Custom Kernels

A custom kernel can often lead to the following problem: out of habit, the SCSI driver is hard-linked to the kernel, but the existing `initrd` remains unchanged. When you boot, the following occurs: The kernel already contains the SCSI driver, so the hardware is detected. `initrd`, however, now tries to load the driver as a module. With some SCSI drivers, especially with `aic7xxx`, this leads to the system locking. Strictly speaking, this is a kernel error. An already existing driver should not be allowed to be loaded again as a module. The problem is already known from another context, however (serial drivers).

There are several solutions to the problem. Configure the driver as a module (then it will be correctly loaded in the `initrd`. Alternatively, remove the entry for `initrd` from the file `/etc/grub/menu.lst` or `/etc/lilo.conf`, depending on your boot loader. An equivalent to the latter solution is to remove the variable `INITRD_MODULES` then run `mkinitrd`, which then realizes that no `initrd` is needed.

11.3.6 Prospects

It is quite possible in the future that an `initrd` will be used for many more and much more sophisticated things than loading modules needed to access `/`.

- Root file system on software RAID (linuxrc sets up the `md` devices)
- Root file system on LVM
- Root file system is encrypted (linuxrc queries the password)
- Root file system on a SCSI hard disk on a PCMCIA adapter

For more information, see `/usr/src/linux/Documentation/ramdisk.txt`, `/usr/src/linux/Documentation/initrd.txt`, and the man page for initrd.

11.4 linuxrc

linuxrc is a program that is started in the start-up stage of the kernel prior to the actual boot process. This allows you to boot a small modularized kernel and to load the few drivers that are really needed as modules. linuxrc assists in loading relevant drivers manually. However, the automatic hardware detection performed by YaST is usually quite reliable. The use of linuxrc is not limited to the installation; you can also use it as a boot tool for installed system and even for an independent RAM disk–based rescue system. Refer to Section 11.5 on page 238 for more details.

11.4.1 Main Menu

After selecting the language and keyboard, you will be taken to the main menu of linuxrc (see Figure 1.2 on page 11). Normally, linuxrc is used to start Linux. Go to 'Start Installation or System'. Depending on the hardware and the installation procedure, you may be able to access this item directly. Refer to Section 1.1 on page 8 for more information.

11.4.2 Settings / Preferences

Specify your settings for 'Language', 'Screen' (color or monochrome display), 'Keyboard Layout', and 'Debug (experts)'.

11.4.3 System Information

You can check some system information in 'System Information', shown in Figure 11.1 on the facing page. For example, check the used interrupts, I/O ports used, main memory, and recognized PCI devices as detected by Linux.

The next lines show how a hard disk and a CD-ROM connected to an (E)IDE controller announce their start. In this case, you do not need to load additional modules:

```
hda: ST32140A, 2015MB w/128kB Cache, LBA, CHS=1023/64/63
hdb: CD-ROM CDR-S1G, ATAPI CD-ROM drive
Partition check:
 hda: hda1 hda2 hda3 < hda5 >
```

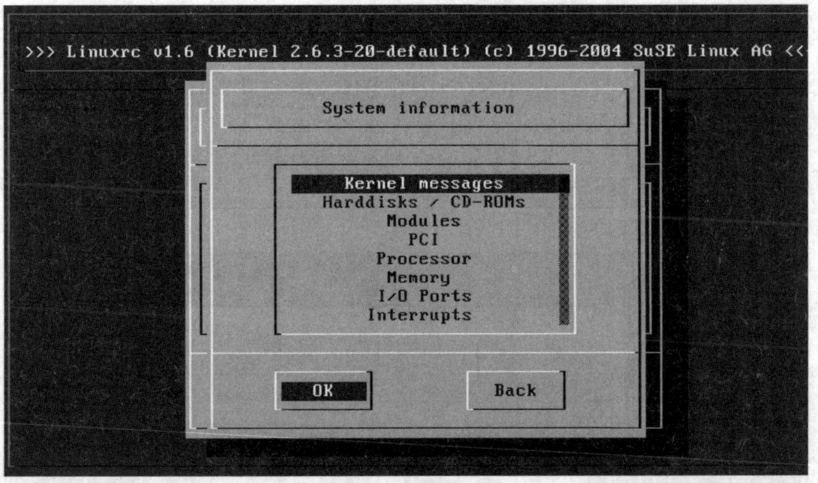

Figure 11.1: System Information

If you booted a kernel that already had a SCSI driver compiled, you do not need this SCSI driver as a module as well. Announcements when loading SCSI adapters and connected devices resemble:

```
scsi: 1 host.
Started kswapd v 1.4.2.2
scsi0: target 0 accepting period 100ns offset 8 10.00MHz FAST SCSI-II
scsi0: setting target 0 to period 100ns offset 8 10.00MHz FAST SCSI-II
  Vendor: QUANTUM   Model: VP32210            Rev: 81H8
  Type:   Direct-Access                      ANSI SCSI revision: 02
Detected scsi disk sda at scsi0, channel 0, id 0, lun 0
scsi0: target 2 accepting period 236ns offset 8 4.23MHz synchronous SCSI
scsi0: setting target 2 to period 248ns offset 8 4.03MHz synchronous SCSI
  Vendor: TOSHIBA   Model: CD-ROM XM-3401TA  Rev: 0283
  Type:   CD-ROM                             ANSI SCSI revision: 02
scsi: detected 1 SCSI disk total.
SCSI device sda:hdwr sector=512 bytes.Sectors=4308352 [2103 MB] [2.1 GB]
Partition check:
 sda: sda1 sda2 sda3 sda4 < sda5 sda6 sda7 sda8 >
```

11.4.4 Loading Modules

Select the modules (drivers) needed. linuxrc offers the available drivers in a list. The name of the respective module is displayed to the left and a brief description of the hardware supported by the driver is displayed to the right. For some components, there several drivers or new alpha drivers are offered.

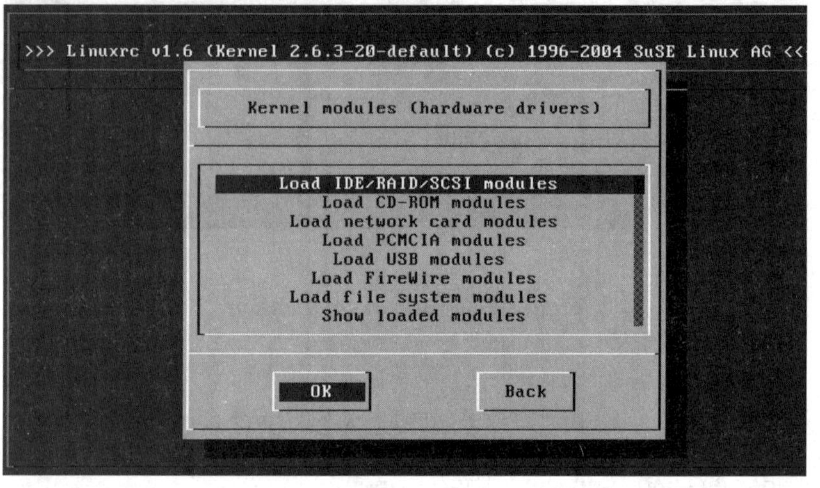

Figure 11.2: Loading Modules

11.4.5 Entering Parameters

Locate a suitable driver for your hardware and press (Enter). This opens a dialog box in which to enter additional parameters for this module. Multiple parameters for one module must be separated by blank spaces.

In many cases, it is not necessary to specify the hardware in detail, as most drivers find their components automatically. Only network cards and older CD-ROM drives with proprietary controller cards may require parameters. If unsure, try pressing (Enter).

For some modules, the detection and initialization of the hardware can take some time. Switch to virtual console 4 ((Alt) + (F4)) to watch the kernel messages while loading. SCSI drivers especially take some time, as they wait until all attached devices respond.

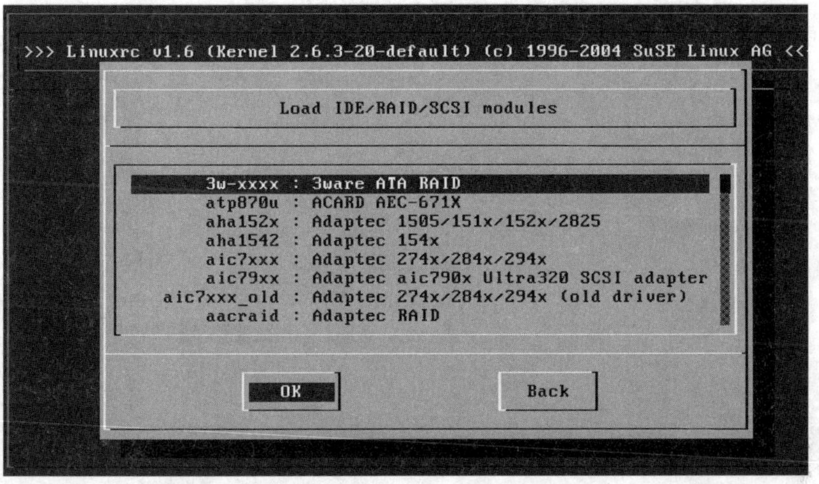

Figure 11.3: Selecting SCSI Drivers

If the module is loaded successfully, linuxrc displays the kernel messages, allowing you to verify that everything worked smoothly. In the event of a problem, the messages may indicate the reason.

11.4.6 Start Installation / System

Once you have set up hardware support via modules, proceed to 'Start Installation or System'. From this menu, a number of procedures can be started: 'Start Installation' (an update is also started from this item), 'Boot Installed System' (the root partition must be known), 'Start Rescue System', and 'Eject CD'.

'Start Live CD' is only available if you booted a *LiveEval CD*. Download ISO images from the FTP server (live-eval-<VERSION>) at ftp://ftp.suse.com/pub/suse/i386/

Note

'Start Live CD' is very useful for testing the compatibility of a computer or laptop without installing the system on the hard disk.

Note

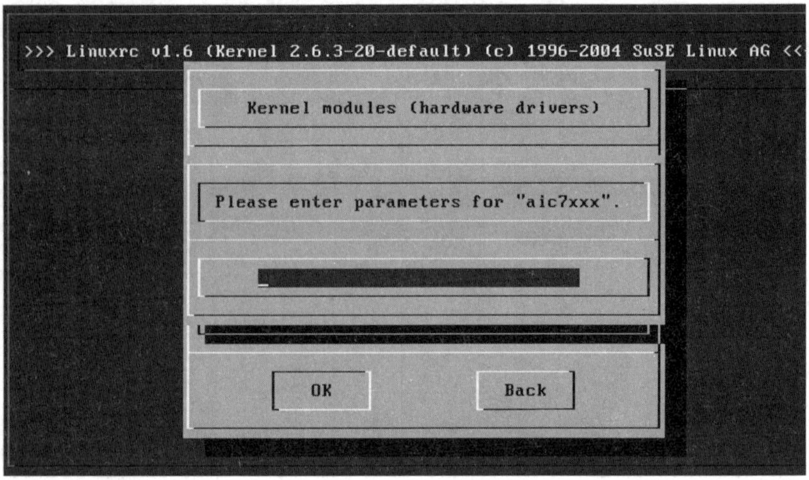

Figure 11.4: Entering Parameters for a Module

For the installation or the rescue system, choose the desired source media. Refer to Figure 11.5 on the next page.

11.4.7 Passing Parameters to linuxrc

If linuxrc does not run in the manual mode, it looks for an info file on a floppy disk or in the `initrd` in `/info`. Subsequently, linuxrc loads the parameters at the kernel prompt. The default values can be edited in the file `/linuxrc.config`. However, the recommended way is to implement changes in the info file.

An info file consists of keywords and values in the format `key: value`. These pairs of keys and values can also be entered in this form at the kernel prompt. A list of possible keys is available in the file `/usr/share/doc/packages/linuxrc/linuxrc.html`. The following list shows some of the most important keys with example values:

- Install: URL (nfs, ftp, hd, etc.)
- HostIP: 10.10.0.2
- Proxy: 10.10.0.1

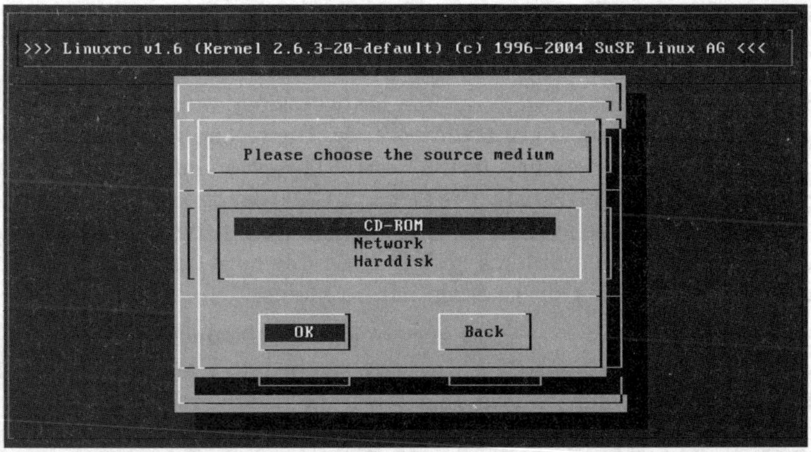

Figure 11.5: Selection of Source Media in linuxrc

- Netdevice: eth0
- Textmode: 0 | 1
- AutoYast: ftp://autoyastfile
- VNC: 0 | 1
- VNCPassword: password
- UseSSH: 0 | 1
- SSHPassword: password
- ForceInsmod: 0 | 1 (use the option `-f` when running `insmod`)
- Insmod: module parameters
- AddSwap: 0 | 3 | dev/hda5

  If the value is 0, `swap` is not requested. If the value is positive, the partition with this number is activated. Alternatively, specify the name of the partition.

11.5 The SUSE Rescue System

SUSE LINUX contains a rescue system for accessing your Linux partitions *from the outside* in the event of an emergency. The rescue system can be loaded from CD, the network, or the SUSE FTP server. Furthermore, there is a bootable SUSE LINUX CD (the *LiveEval CD*) that can be used as a rescue system. The rescue system includes several help programs with which you can remedy large problems with inaccessible hard disks, misconfigured configuration files, or other similar problems.

Another component of the rescue system is Parted, which is used for resizing partitions. This program can be launched from within the rescue system, if you do not want to use the resizer integrated in YaST. Information about Parted can be found at `http://www.gnu.org/software/parted/`.

11.5.1 Starting the Rescue System

The rescue system is launched from CD (or DVD). The CD-ROM or DVD drive must be bootable. If necessary, change the boot sequence in the BIOS setup.

Proceed as follows to start the rescue system:

1. Insert the first SUSE LINUX CD or DVD in the respective drive and turn on your system.
2. Allow the system to boot or select 'Manual Installation' to enter special boot parameters under 'boot options'.
3. In linuxrc, select the correct language and keyboard layout.
4. Load the kernel modules required for your system. Load *all* modules you need for the rescue system. Due to limited space, the rescue system itself contains only very few modules.
5. Select 'Start Installation or System' in the main menu.
6. Select 'Start Rescue System' (see Figure 1.3 on page 12) and specify the desired source medium (Figure 11.6 on the next page).

   'CD-ROM': Uses the rescue system on the CD-ROM.

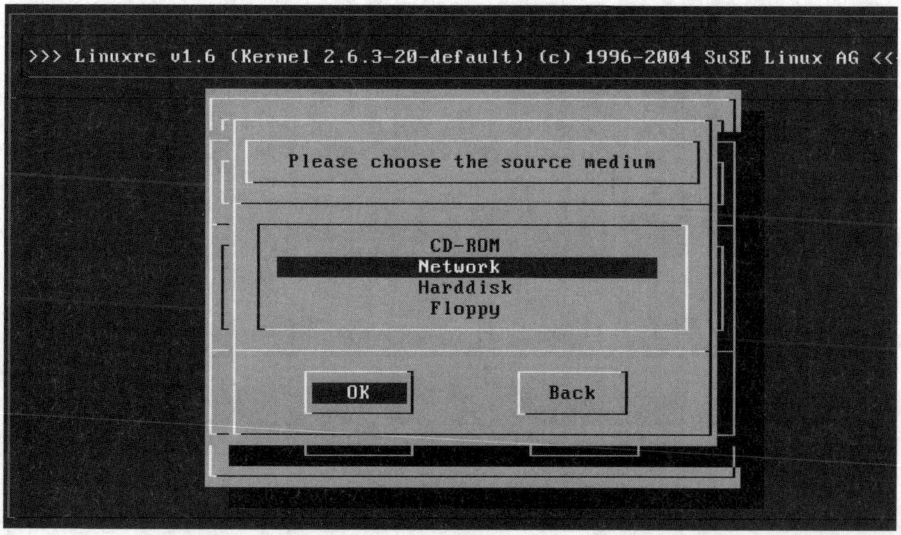

Figure 11.6: Source Medium for the Rescue System

'Network': Starts the rescue system over a network connection. The kernel module for the network card must be loaded first (see Section 1.3.2 on page 15). A submenu offers protocols such as NFS, FTP, and SMB (see Figure 11.7 on the next page).

'Hard Disk': If you previously copied a rescue system to a hard disk to which you have access, its location can be specified here. Subsequently, this rescue system will be loaded.

Regardless of the medium chosen, the rescue system will be decompressed, loaded onto a RAM floppy disk as a new root file system, mounted, and started. Now it is ready for use.

11.5.2 Working with the Rescue System

Under Alt + F1 to Alt + F3, the rescue system provides at least three virtual consoles. You can log in as `root` without a password. Press Alt + F10 to enter the system console displaying the kernel and syslog messages.

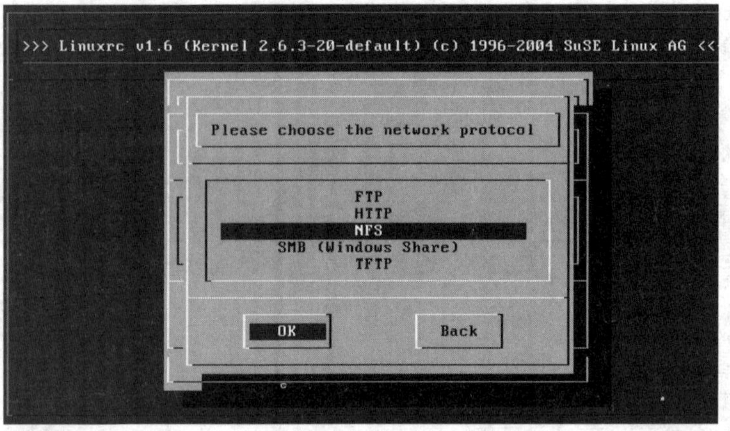

Figure 11.7: *Network Protocols*

A shell and many other useful utilities, such as the mount program, can be found in the `/bin` directory. The `sbin` directory contains important file and network utilities for reviewing and repairing the file system (e.g., e2fsck). This directory also contains the most important binaries for system maintenance, such as fdisk, mkfs, mkswap, mount, mount, init, and shutdown, as well as ifconfig, route, and netstat for maintaining the network. The directory `/usr/bin` contains the vi editor, grep, find, less, and telnet.

Accessing Your Normal System

To mount your SUSE LINUX system using the rescue system, use the mount point `/mnt`. You can also use or create another directory. The following example demonstrates the procedure for a system with the `/etc/fstab` details shown in File 11.4.

Example 11.4: *Example /etc/fstab*

```
/dev/sdb5    swap   swap   defaults  0  0
/dev/sdb3    /      ext2   defaults  1  1
/dev/sdb6    /usr   ext2   defaults  1  2
```

Caution

Pay attention to the order of steps outlined in the following section for mounting the various devices.

Caution

To access your entire system, mount it step by step in the `/mnt` directory using the following commands:

```
mount /dev/sdb3 /mnt
mount /dev/sdb6 /mnt/usr
```

Now, you can access your entire system and, for example, correct mistakes in configuration files, such as `/etc/fstab`, `/etc/passwd`, and `/etc/inittab`. The configuration files are now located in the `/mnt/etc` directory instead of in `/etc`.

Before you recover lost partitions with the fdisk program by simply setting them up again, you should *first* make a printout of `/etc/fstab` and the output of `fdisk -l`.

Repairing File Systems

Damaged file systems are tricky problems for the rescue system. Generally, file systems cannot be repaired on a running system. If you encounter serious problems, you may not even be able to mount your root file system and the system boot may end with `kernel panic`. In this case, the only way is to repair the system from the *outside* using a rescue system.

The SUSE LINUX rescue system contains the utilities e2fsck and dumpe2fs (for diagnosis). These should remedy most problems. In an emergency, man pages often are not available. For this reason, they are included in this manual in Appendix C on page 499.

If mounting a file system fails due to an *invalid* superblock, the e2fsck program would probably fail, too. If this were the case, your superblock may be corrupted, too. There are copies of the superblock located every 8192 blocks (8193, 16385, etc.). If your superblock is corrupted, try one of the copies instead. This is accomplished by entering the command `e2fsck -f -b 8193 /dev/damaged_partition`. The `-f` option forces the file system check and overrides e2fsck's error so that, since the superblock copy is intact, everything is fine.

11.6 Virtual Consoles

Linux is a multiuser and multitasking system. The advantages of these features can be appreciated, even on a stand-alone PC system. In text mode, there are six virtual consoles available. Switch between them using Alt-F1 to Alt-F6. The seventh console is reserved for X11. More or fewer consoles can be assigned by modifying the file `/etc/inittab`.

To switch to a console from X11 without leaving X11, use Ctrl-Alt-F1 to Ctrl-Alt-F6. The key Alt-F7 then returns to X11.

11.7 Keyboard Mapping

To standardize the keyboard mapping of programs, changes were made to the following files:

```
/etc/inputrc
/usr/X11R6/lib/X11/Xmodmap
/etc/skel/.Xmodmap
/etc/skel/.exrc
/etc/skel/.less
/etc/skel/.lesskey
/etc/csh.cshrc
/etc/termcap
/usr/lib/terminfo/x/xterm
/usr/X11R6/lib/X11/app-defaults/XTerm
/usr/share/emacs/<VERSION>/site-lisp/term/*.el
```

These changes only affect applications that use `terminfo` entries or whose configuration files are changed directly (`vi`, `less`, etc.). Other non-SUSE applications should be adjusted to these defaults.

Under X, the compose key (*multikey*) can be accessed using the key combination Ctrl + Shift (right). Also see the corresponding entry in `/usr/X11R6/lib/X11/Xmodmap`.

Detailed information about the input of Chinese, Japanese, and Korean (CJK) is available at Mike Fabian's page: `http://www.suse.de/~mfabian/suse-cjk/input.html`.

11.8 Local Adjustments — I18N and L10N

SUSE LINUX is, to a very large extent, internationalized and can be modified for local needs in a flexible manner. In other words, internationalization (*I18N*) allows specific localizations (*L10N*). The abbreviations I18N and L10N are derived from the first and last letters of the words and, in between, the number of letters omitted.

Settings are made with `LC_` variables defined in the file `/etc/sysconfig/language`. This refers not only to *native language support*, but also to the categories *Messages* (Language), *Character Set*, *Sort Order*, *Time and Date*, *Numbers*, and *Money*. Each of these categories can be defined directly with its own variable or indirectly with a master variable in the file `language` (see the manual page `man locale`).

1. `RC_LC_MESSAGES`, `RC_LC_CTYPE`, `RC_LC_COLLATE`, `RC_LC_TIME`, `RC_LC_NUMERIC`, `RC_LC_MONETARY`: These variables are passed to the shell without the `RC_` prefix and govern the above categories. The files concerned are listed below. The current setting can be shown with the command `locale`.

2. `RC_LC_ALL`: This variable (if set) overwrites the values of the variables mentioned above.

3. `RC_LANG`: If none of the above variables are set, this is the fallback. By default, SUSE LINUX only sets `RC_LANG`. This makes it easier for users to enter their own values.

4. `ROOT_USES_LANG`: A `yes` or `no` variable. If it is set to `no`, `root` always works in the POSIX environment.

The other variables can be set via the YaST sysconfig editor. The value of such a variable contains the language code, country code, encoding, and modifier. The individual components are connected by special characters:

```
LANG=<language>[[_<COUNTRY>].<Encoding>[@<Modifier>]]
```

11.8.1 Some Examples

You should always set the language and country codes together. Language settings follow the standard ISO 639 (http://www.evertype.com/standards/iso639/iso639-en.html and http://www.loc.gov/standards/iso639-2/). Country codes are listed in ISO 3166, see (http://www.din.de/gremien/nas/nabd/iso3166ma/codlstp1/en_listp1.html). It only makes sense to set values for which usable description files can be found in /usr/lib/locale. Additional description files can be created from the files in /usr/share/i18n using the command localedef. A description file for en_US.UTF-8 (for English and United States) can be created with:

```
localedef -i en_US -f UTF-8 en_US.UTF-8
```

LANG=en_US.UTF-8 This is the default setting if English is selected upon installation. If you selected another language, that language is enabled but still with UTF-8 as the character encoding.

LANG=en_US.ISO-8859-1 This sets the variable to English language, country to United States, and the character set to ISO-8859-1. This character set does not support the Euro sign, but it will be useful sometimes for programs that have not been updated to support UTF-8. The string defining the charset (ISO-8859-1 in our case) will then be evaluated by programs like Emacs.

SuSEconfig reads the variables in /etc/sysconfig/language and writes the necessary changes to /etc/SuSEconfig/profile and /etc/SuSEconfig/csh.cshrc. /etc/SuSEconfig/profile is read or *sourced* by /etc/profile. /etc/SuSEconfig/csh.cshrc is sourced by /etc/csh.cshrc. This makes the settings available system-wide.

Users can override the system defaults by editing their ~/.bashrc accordingly. For instance, if you do not want to use the system-wide en_US for program messages, you could include LC_MESSAGES=es_ES so messages are displayed in Spanish instead.

11.8.2 Settings for Language Support

Files in the category *Messages* are, as a rule, only stored in the corresponding language directory (for instance en) to have a fallback. If you set LANG to en_US and the *message* file in /usr/share/locale/en_US/LC_MESSAGES does not exist, it will fall back to /usr/share/locale/en/LC_MESSAGES.

A fallback chain can also be defined, for example, for Breton -> French or for Galician -> Spanish -> Portuguese:

```
LANGUAGE="br_FR:fr_FR"
```

```
LANGUAGE="gl_ES:es_ES:pt_PT"
```

If desired, use the Norwegian variants *nynorsk* and *bokmål* instead (with additional fallback to no):

```
LANG="nn_NO"
```

```
LANGUAGE="nn_NO:nb_NO:no"
```

or

```
LANG="nb_NO"
```

```
LANGUAGE="nb_NO:nn_NO:no"
```

Note that in Norwegian, LC_TIME is also treated differently.

Possible Problems

The thousands comma is not recognized. LANG is probably set to en, but the description the glibc uses is located in /usr/share/locale/en_US/LC_NUMERIC. LC_NUMERIC, for example, must be set to en_US.

For More Information

- *The GNU C Library Reference Manual*, Chap. "Locales and Internationalization"; included in glibc-info.
- Markus Kuhn, *UTF-8 and Unicode FAQ for Unix/Linux*, currently at http://www.cl.cam.ac.uk/~mgk25/unicode.html.
- *Unicode-Howto*, by Bruno Haible file:/usr/share/doc/howto/en/html/Unicode-HOWTO.html.

The SUSE LINUX Boot Concept

Booting and initializing a UNIX system can challenge even an experienced system administrator. This chapter gives a short overview of the SUSE LINUX boot concept. The new implementation is compatible with the *System Initialization* section of the LSB specification (Version 1.3.x). Refer to Section 11.1.1 on page 220 for more information about LSB.

The message "Uncompressing Linux..." signals that the kernel is taking control of your hardware. It checks and sets your console — more precisely: the BIOS registers of graphics cards and output format — to read BIOS settings and to initialize basic hardware interfaces. Next, your drivers *probe* existing hardware and initialize it accordingly. After checking the partitions and mounting the root file system, the kernel starts init, which *boots* (Unix jargon) the main system with all its programs and configurations. The kernel controls the entire system, including hardware access and the CPU time programs use.

12.1 The init Program

The program init is the process responsible for initializing the system itself in the required way. All other processes are considered child processes of init.

init takes a special role. It is started directly by the kernel and resists signal 9, which normally kills processes. All other programs are either started directly by init or by one of its "child" processes.

init is centrally configured via the `/etc/inittab` file. Here, the *runlevels* are defined (see Section 12.2). It also specifies which services and daemons are available in each of the levels. Depending on the entries in `/etc/inittab`, several scripts are run by init. For reasons of clarity, these scripts all reside in the directory `/etc/init.d/`.

The entire process of starting the system and shutting it down is maintained by init. From this point of view, the kernel can be considered a background process whose task it is to maintain all other processes and to adjust CPU time and hardware access according to requests from other programs.

12.2 Runlevels

In Linux, *runlevels* define how the system is started. After booting, the system starts as defined in `/etc/inittab` in the line `initdefault`. Usually this is `3` or `5` (see Table 12.1 on the facing page). As an alternative, the runlevel can be specified at boot time (at the boot prompt, for instance). Any parameters that are not directly evaluated by the kernel itself are passed to init.

To change runlevels while the system is running, enter init and the corresponding number as an argument. Only the system administrator is allowed to do this. `init 1` (or `shutdown now`) causes the system to change to *single user mode*, which is used for system maintenance and administration. After finishing his work, the administrator can switch back to the normal runlevel by entering `init 3`, which starts all the essential programs and allows regular users to log in and to work with the system. `init 0` (or `shutdown -h now`) causes the system to halt. `init 6` (or `shutdown -r now`) causes it to shut down with a subsequent reboot.

Note

Runlevel 2 with a /usr/ Partition Mounted via NFS

You should not use runlevel 2 if your system mounts the `/usr/` partition via NFS. The `/usr/` directory holds important programs essential for the proper functioning of the system. Because the NFS service is not made available by runlevel 2 (local multiuser mode without remote network), the system would be seriously restricted in many aspects.

Note

Table 12.1: Available Runlevels

Runlevel	Description
0	System halt
S	Single user mode; from the boot prompt, only with US keyboard
1	Single user mode
2	Local multiuser mode without remote network (e.g., NFS)
3	Full multiuser mode with network
4	Not used
5	Full multiuser mode with network and X display manager — KDM (default), GDM, or XDM
6	System reboot

Runlevel 5 is the default runlevel in all SUSE LINUX standard installations. Users are prompted for login directly under a graphical interface.

However, if the default runlevel is `3` and you want to change it to `5`, you first need to configure the X Window System in the required way (see Chapter 4 on page 71). After doing so, check whether the system works in the desired way by entering `init 5`. If everything turns out as expected, you can use YaST to set the default runlevel to `5`.

Caution

Modifying /etc/inittab

If `/etc/inittab` is damaged, the system might not boot properly. Therefore, be extremely careful while editing `/etc/inittab` and always keep a backup of an intact version. To repair damage, try entering `init=/bin/sh` after the kernel name at the boot prompt to boot directly into a shell. After that, replace `/etc/inittab` with your backup version using the `cp` command.

Caution

12.3 Changing Runlevels

Generally, two things happen when you change runlevels. First, *stop scripts* of the current runlevel are launched, closing down some programs essential for the current runlevel. Then *start scripts* of the new runlevel are started. Here, in most cases, a number of programs are started. For example, the following occurs when changing from runlevel 3 to 5:

- The administrator (`root`) tells init to change to a different runlevel by entering `init 5`.
- init now consults its configuration file (`/etc/inittab`) and realizes it should start `/etc/init.d/rc` with the new runlevel as a parameter.
- Now rc calls all the stop scripts of the current runlevel, but only for those where there is no start script in the selected new runlevel. In our example, these are all the scripts that reside in `/etc/init.d/rc3.d/` (old runlevel was 3) and start with a `K`. The number following `K` guarantees a certain order to start, as there are some dependencies to consider.

Note

The names of the stop scripts always begin with `K` for kill. Start scripts begin with `S` for start.

Note

- The last things to start are the start scripts of the new runlevel. These are (in our example) in `/etc/init.d/rc5.d/` and begin with an `S`. The same procedure regarding the order in which they are started is applied here.

When changing into the same runlevel as the current runlevel, init only checks `/etc/inittab` for changes and starts the appropriate steps (e.g., for starting a getty on another interface).

12.4 Init Scripts

Scripts in `/etc/init.d/` are divided into two sections:

- scripts executed directly by init. This only applies while booting and shutting down the system immediately (power failure or a user pressing Ctrl + Alt + Del).
- scripts executed indirectly by init. These are run when changing the runlevel and always call the master script /etc/init.d/rc, which guarantees the correct order of the relevant scripts.

All scripts are located in `/etc/init.d/`. Scripts for changing the runlevel are also found there, but are called through symbolic links from one of the subdirectories (`/etc/init.d/rc0.d/` to `/etc/init.d/rc6.d/`). This is just for clarity reasons and avoids duplicate scripts (e.g., if they are used in several runlevels). Because every script can be executed as both a start and a stop script, these scripts must understand the parameters `start` and `stop`. The scripts understand, in addition, the `restart`, `reload`, `force-reload`, and `status` options. These different options are explained in Table 12.2 on the following page.

Table 12.2: Possible init Script Options

Option	Description
`start`	Start service.
`stop`	Stop service.
`restart`	If the service is running, stop it and then restart it. If it is not running, start it.
`reload`	Reload the configuration without stopping and restarting the service.
`force-reload`	Reload the configuration if the service supports this. Otherwise, do the same as if `restart` had been given.
`status`	Show current status of service.

Links in each runlevel-specific subdirectory make it possible to associate scripts with different runlevels. When installing or uninstalling packages, such links are added and removed with the help of the program insserv (or using `/usr/lib/lsb/install_initd`, which is a script calling this program). See the manual page of insserv for details.

Below is a short introduction to the boot and stop scripts launched first (or last, respectively) as well as an explanation of the maintaining script.

boot Executed while starting the system directly using init. It is independent of the chosen runlevel and is only executed once. Here, the `proc/` and `pts/` file systems are mounted and the blogd (boot logging daemon) is activated. If the system is booted for the first time after an update or an installation, the initial system configuration is started.The blogd daemon is a service started by the boot *and* by the rc scripts before any other one. It is stopped after the actions triggered by the above scripts (running a number of subscripts, for example) are completed. The blogd daemon writes any screen output to the log file `/var/log/boot.msg` — but only if and when `/var` is mounted read-write. Otherwise, blogd buffers all screen data until `/var/` becomes available. Further information about blogd can be obtained with `man blogd`.The script `boot` is also responsible for starting all the scripts in `/etc/init.d/boot.d/` with a name that starts with `S`. There, the file systems are checked and loop devices are configured if needed. The system time is also set. If an error occurs while automatically checking and repairing the file system, the system administrator can intervene after first entering the root password. Last executed is the script boot.local.

boot.local Here, enter additional commands to execute at boot before changing into a runlevel. It can be compared to AUTOEXEC.BAT on DOS systems.

boot.setup This script is executed when changing from *single user mode* to any other runlevel and is responsible for a number of basic settings, namely for the keyboard layout and for initializing the virtual consoles.

halt This script is only executed while changing into runlevel 0 or 6. Here, it is executed either as halt or as reboot. Whether the system shuts down or reboots depends on how halt is called.

rc This script calls the appropriate stop scripts of the current runlevel and the start scripts of the newly selected runlevel.

12.4.1 Adding init Scripts

You can create your own scripts and easily integrate them into the scheme described above. For instructions about the formatting, naming, and organization of your custom scripts, refer to the specifications of the LSB and to the man pages of init, init.d/, and insserv. Additionally consult the man pages of startproc and killproc.

Caution

Creating Your Own init Scripts

Faulty init scripts may freeze your machine. Edit such scripts with great care and, if possible, subject them to heavy testing in the multiuser environment. Some useful information about init scripts can be found in Section 12.2 on page 248.

Caution

- To create a custom init script for a given program or service, use the file /etc/init.d/skeleton as a template. Save a copy of this file under the new name and edit the relevant program and file names, paths, and other details as needed. You may also need to enhance the script with your own parts, so the correct actions are triggered by the init procedure.

- The `INIT INFO` block at the top is a required part of the script and should be edited:

***Example 12.1:** A Minimal INIT INFO Block*

```
### BEGIN INIT INFO
# Provides:          FOO
# Required-Start:    $syslog $remote_fs
# Required-Stop:     $syslog $remote_fs
# Default-Start:     3 5
# Default-Stop:      0 1 2 6
# Description:       Start FOO to allow XY and provide YZ
### END INIT INFO
```

  In the first line of the `INFO` block, after `Provides:`, specify the name of the program or service controlled by this init script. In the `Required-Start:` and `Required-Stop:` lines, specify all services that need to be started or stopped, respectively, before the service itself is started or stopped. This information is used later to generate the numbering of script names, as found in the runlevel directories. Under `Default-Start:` and `Default-Stop:`, specify the runlevels in which the service should automatically be started or stopped. Finally, under `Description:`, provide a short description of the service in question.

- To create the links from `/etc/init.d/` to the corresponding runlevel directories (`/etc/init.d/rc?.d/`), enter the command `insserv <new-script-name>`. The insserv program evaluates the `INIT INFO` header to create the necessary links for start and stop scripts in the runlevel directories (`/etc/init.d/rc?.d/`). The program also takes care of the correct start and stop order for each runlevel by including the necessary numbers in the names of these links. If you prefer a graphical tool to create such links, use the runlevel editor provided by YaST, as described in Section 12.5 on the facing page.

On the other hand, if a script already present in `/etc/init.d/` should be integrated into the existing runlevel scheme, create the links in the runlevel directories right away, either with insserv or by enabling the corresponding service in the runlevel editor of YaST. Your changes are applied during the next reboot — the new service will be started automatically.

12.5 The YaST Runlevel Editor

After starting this YaST module, it displays an overview listing all the available services and the current status of each service — whether they are enabled or not. With the radio buttons, decide whether to use the module in 'Simple Mode' or in 'Expert Mode'. The default 'Simple Mode' should be sufficient for most purposes. The left column shows the name of the service, the center column indicates its current status, and the right column gives a short description. For the selected service, a more detailed description is provided in the lower part of the window. To enable a service, select it in the table then select 'Enable'. The same steps apply to disable a service.

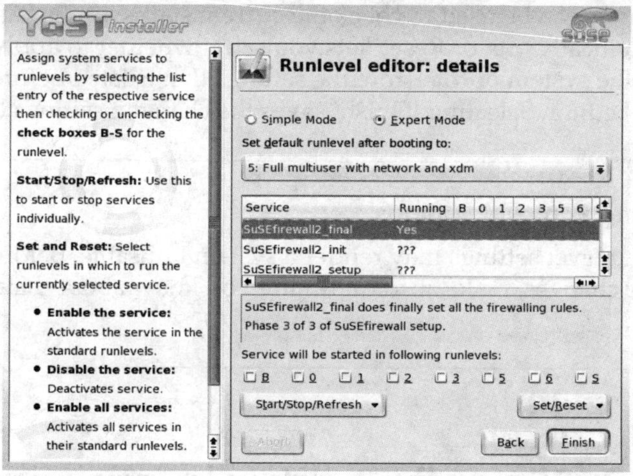

Figure 12.1: YaST: Runlevel Editor

For detailed control over the runlevels in which a service is started or stopped or to change the default runlevel, first select 'Expert Mode'. In this mode, the dialog displays the current default runlevel or "initdefault" (which is the runlevel into which the system boots by default) at the top. Normally, the default runlevel of a SUSE LINUX system is runlevel 5 (full multiuser mode with network and XDM). A suitable alternative might be runlevel 3 (full multiuser mode with network).

This YaST dialog allows the selection of one of the runlevels (as listed in Table 12.1 on page 249) as the new default. Additionally use the table in this window to enable or disable individual services and daemons. The table lists the services and daemons available, tells whether they are currently enabled on your system, and, if so, for which runlevels. After selecting one of the rows with the mouse, click the check boxes representing the runlevels ('B', '0', '1', '2', '3', '5', '6', and 'S') to define the runlevels where the selected service or daemon should be running. Runlevel 4 is initially undefined to allow for the creation of a custom runlevel. Finally, a brief description of the currently selected service or daemon is provided just below the table overview.

With 'Start, Stop, or Refresh', decide whether a service should be activated. 'Refresh status' can be used to check the current status, if this has not been done automatically. 'Set or Reset' lets you select whether to apply your changes to the system or to restore the settings that existed before starting the runlevel editor. Selecting 'Finish' saves the changed settings to disk.

Caution

Changing Runlevel Settings

Faulty runlevel settings may render a system unusable. Before applying your changes, make absolutely sure you know about their consequences.

Caution

12.6 SuSEconfig and /etc/sysconfig

The main configuration of SUSE LINUX can be made with the configuration files in `/etc/sysconfig/`. Former versions of SUSE LINUX relied on `/etc/rc.config` for system configuration, but it became obsolete in previous versions. `/etc/rc.config` is not created at installation time, as all system configuration is controlled by `/etc/sysconfig/`. However, if `/etc/rc.config` exists at the time of a system update, it remains intact.

The individual files in /etc/sysconfig/ are only read by the scripts to which they are relevant. This ensures that network settings, for instance, need to be parsed only by network-related scripts. Apart from that, there are many other system configuration files that are generated according to the settings in /etc/sysconfig/. This task is performed by SuSEconfig. For example, if you change the network configuration, SuSEconfig is likely to make changes to the file /etc/host.conf as well, as this is one of the files relevant for the network configuration.

If you change anything in these files manually, run `SuSEconfig` afterwards to make sure all the necessary changes are made in all the relevant places. If you change the configuration using the YaST sysconfig editor, all changes are applied automatically — YaST automatically starts SuSEconfig to update the configuration files as needed.

This concept enables you to make basic changes to your configuration without needing to reboot the system. Because some changes are rather complex, some programs must be restarted for the changes to take effect. For instance, changes to the network configuration may require a restart of the network programs concerned. This can be achieved by entering the commands `rcnetwork stop` and `rcnetwork start`.

The recommended way to change the system configuration includes the following steps:

- Bring the system into *single user mode* (runlevel 1) with `init 1`.
- Change the configuration files as needed. This can be done using an editor of your choice or with the sysconfig editor of YaST (refer to Section 12.7 on the following page).

Caution

Manual Changes to the System Configuration

If you do *not* use YaST to change the configuration files in /etc/sysconfig/, make sure that empty variable values are represented by two quotation marks (`KEYTABLE=""`) and that values with blanks in them are enclosed in quotation marks. Values consisting of one word only do not need to be quoted.

Caution

- Execute SuSEconfig to make sure that the changes take effect. If you have changed the configuration files with YaST, this is done automatically.

- Bring your system back to the previous runlevel with a command like `init 3` (replace `3` with the previous runlevel).

This procedure is mainly relevant when changing system-wide settings (such as the network configuration). Small changes should not require going into *single user mode*, but you could still do so to make absolutely sure that all the programs concerned are correctly restarted.

Note

To disable the automatic configuration of SuSEconfig, set the variable `ENABLE_SUSECONFIG` in `/etc/sysconfig/suseconfig/` to `no`. Do not disable SuSEconfig if you want to use the SUSE installation support. It is also possible to disable the autoconfiguration partially.

Note

12.7 The YaST sysconfig Editor

The files where the most important SUSE LINUX settings are stored are located in the `/etc/sysconfig/` directory. The sysconfig editor presents the settings options in an easy-to-read manner. The values can be modified and subsequently added to the individual configuration files in this directory. In general, it is not necessary to edit them manually, however, because these files are automatically adjusted when installing a package or configuring a service.

Caution

Modifications of /etc/sysconfig/* files

Do not modify the `/etc/sysconfig/` files if you lack previous experience and knowledge. It could do considerable damage to your system. The files in `/etc/sysconfig/` include a short comment for each variable to explain what effect they actually have.

Caution

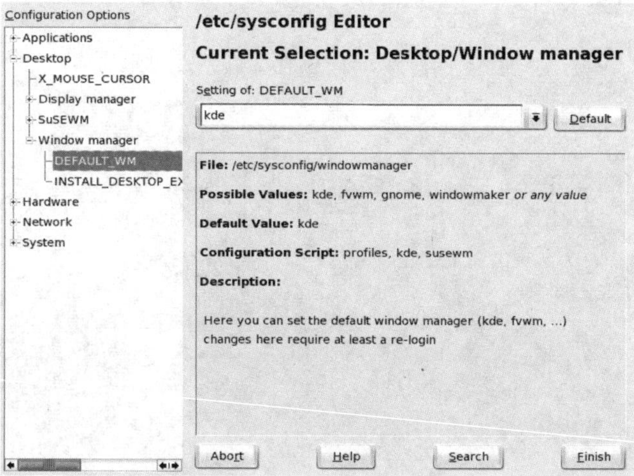

Figure 12.2: *YaST: System Configuration Using the sysconfig Editor*

The YaST sysconfig dialog is split into three parts. The left part of the dialog window shows a tree view of all configurable variables. As soon as you have selected a variable, the right part displays both the current selection and the current setting of this variable. Below, a third window displays a short description of the variable's purpose, possible values, the default value, and the actual configuration file from which this variable originates. The dialog also provides information about which configuration script is executed after changing the variable and which new service is started as a result of the change. YaST asks you to confirm your changes and informs you which scripts will be executed after leaving the dialog by selecting 'Finish'. Also select the services and scripts to skip for now, so they are started later.

Part IV

Network

Linux in the Network

Linux, really a child of the Internet, offers all the necessary networking tools and features for integration into all types of network structures. An introduction into the customary Linux protocol, TCP/IP, follows. The various services and special features of this protocol are discussed. Network access using a network card can be configured with YaST. The central configuration files are discussed and some of the most essential tools described. Only the fundamental mechanisms and the relevant network configuration files are discussed in this chapter.

The configuration of Internet access with PPP via modem, ISDN, or through other means can be completed with YaST. It is described in the *User Guide*.

13.1 TCP/IP — The Protocol Used by Linux

Linux and other Unix operating systems use the TCP/IP protocol. It is not a single network protocol, but a family of network protocols that offer various services. TCP/IP was developed based on an application used for military purposes and was defined in its present form in an RFC in 1981. RFC stands for *Request for Comments*. They are documents that describe various Internet protocols and implementation procedures for the operating system and its applications. Since then, the TCP/IP protocol has been refined, but the basic protocol has remained virtually unchanged.

Note

The RFC documents describe the setup of Internet protocols. To expand your knowledge about any of the protocols, refer to the appropriate RFC document. They are available online at `http://www.ietf.org/rfc.html`.

Note

The services listed in Table 13.1 are provided for the purpose of exchanging data between two Linux machines via TCP/IP. Networks combined by TCP/IP, comprising a world-wide network are also referred to, in their entirety, as "the Internet."

***Table 13.1:** Several Protocols in the TCP/IP Protocol Family*

Protocol	Description
TCP	Transmission Control Protocol: A connection-oriented secure protocol. The data to transmit is first sent by the application as a stream of data then converted by the operating system to the appropriate format. The data arrives at the respective application on the destination host in the original data stream format in which it was initially sent. TCP determines whether any data has been lost during the transmission and that there is no mix-up. TCP is implemented wherever the data sequence matters.

UDP	User Datagram Protocol: A connectionless, insecure protocol. The data to transmit is sent in the form of packets already generated by the application. The order in which the data arrives at the recipient is not guaranteed and data loss is a possibility. UDP is suitable for record-oriented applications. It features a smaller latency period than TCP.
ICMP	Internet Control Message Protocol: Essentially, this is not a protocol for the end user, but a special control protocol that issues error reports and can control the behavior of machines participating in TCP/IP data transfer. In addition, a special echo mode is provided by ICMP that can be viewed using the program `ping`.
IGMP	Internet Group Management Protocol: This protocol controls the machine behavior when implementing IP multicast. The following sections do not contain more information regarding IP multicasting, because of space limitations.

Almost all hardware protocols work on a packet-oriented basis. The data to transmit is packaged in *packets*, as it cannot be sent all at once. This is why TCP/IP only works with small data packets. The maximum size of a TCP/IP packet is approximately 64 kilobytes. The packets are normally quite a bit smaller, as the network software can be a limiting factor. The maximum size of a data packet on an ethernet is about fifteen hundred bytes. The size of a TCP/IP packet is limited to this amount when the data is sent over an ethernet. If more data is transferred, more data packets need to be sent by the operating system.

13.1.1 Layer Model

IP (Internet Protocol) is where the insecure data transfer takes place. TCP (Transmission Control Protocol), to a certain extent, is simply the upper layer for the IP platform serving to guarantee secure data transfer. The IP layer itself is, in turn, supported by the bottom layer, the hardware-dependent protocol, such as ethernet. Professionals refer to this structure as the *layer model*. See Figure 13.1 on the following page.

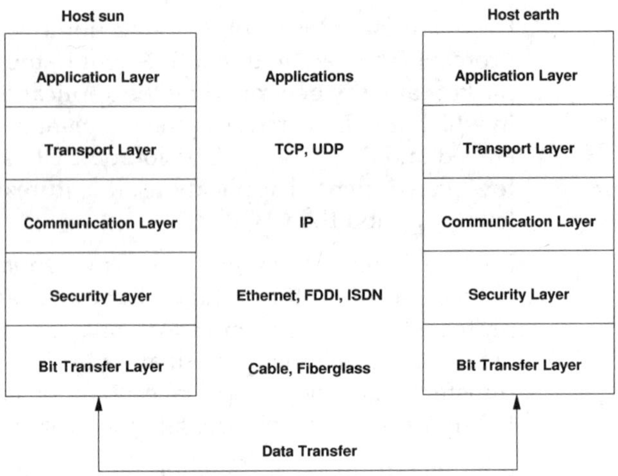

Figure 13.1: *Simplified Layer Model for TCP/IP*

The diagram provides one or two examples for each layer. As you can see, the layers are ordered according to *abstraction levels*. The lowest layer is very close to the hardware. The uppermost layer, however, is almost a complete abstraction from the hardware. Every layer has its own special function. The special functions of each layer are mostly implicit in their description. The bit transfer and security layers represent the physical network used (such as ethernet).

- While layer 1 deals with cable types, signal forms, signal codes, and the like, layer 2 is responsible for accessing procedures (which host may send data?) and error correction. Layer 1 is called the *physical layer*. Layer 2 is called the *data link layer*.
- Layer 3 is the *network layer* and is responsible for remote data transfer. The network layer ensures that the data arrives at the correct remote destination and can be delivered to it.
- Layer 4, the *transport layer*, is responsible for application data. It ensures that data arrives in the correct order and is not lost. While the data link layer is only there to make sure that the data as transmitted is the correct one, the transport layer protects it from being lost.
- Finally, layer 5 is the layer where data is processed by the application itself.

For every layer to serve its designated function, additional information regarding each layer must be saved in the data packet. This takes place in the *header* of the packet. Every layer attaches a small block of data, called the protocol header, to the front of each emerging packet. A sample TCP/IP data packet traveling over an ethernet cable is illustrated in Figure 13.2.

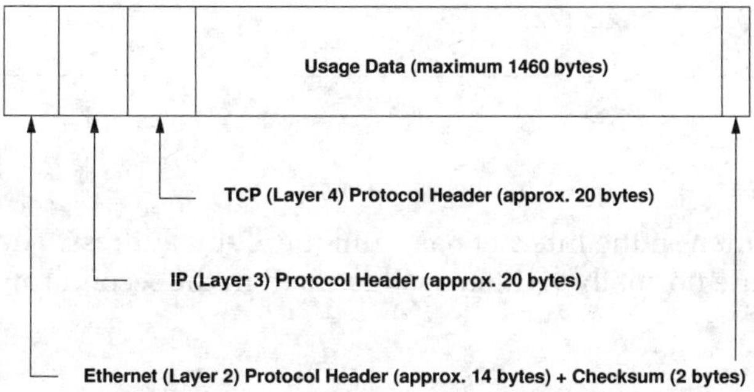

Figure 13.2: *TCP/IP Ethernet Packet*

The proof sum is located at the end of the packet, not at the beginning. This simplifies things for the network hardware. The largest amount of usage data possible in one packet is 1460 bytes in an ethernet network.

When an application sends data over the network, the data passes through each layer, all implemented in the Linux kernel except layer 1 (network card). Each layer is responsible for preparing the data so it can be passed to the next layer below. The lowest layer is ultimately responsible for sending the data. The entire procedure is reversed when data is received. Like the layers of an onion, in each layer the protocol headers are removed from the transported data. Finally, layer 4 is responsible for making the data available for use by the applications at the destination. In this manner, one layer only communicates with the layer directly above or below it. For applications, it is irrelevant whether data is transmitted via a 100 MBit/s FDDI network or via a 56-kbit/s modem line. Likewise, it is irrelevant for the data line which kind of data is being transmitted, as long as packets are in the correct format.

13.1.2 IP Addresses and Routing

Note

The discussion in the following sections is limited to IPv4 networks. For information about IPv6 protocol, the successor to IPv4, refer to Section 13.2 on page 272.

Note

IP Addresses

Every computer on the Internet has a unique 32-bit address. These 32 bits (or 4 bytes) are normally written as illustrated in the second row in Table 13.1.

Example 13.1: *How an IP Address is Written*

```
IP Address (binary):  11000000 10101000 00000000 00010100
IP Address (decimal):      192.      168.        0.      20
```

In decimal form, the four bytes are written in the decimal number system, separated by periods. The IP address is assigned to a host or a network interface. It cannot be used anywhere else in the world. There are certainly exceptions to this rule, but these play a minimal role in the following passages.

The ethernet card itself has its own unique address, the *MAC*, or media access control address. It is 48 bits long, internationally unique, and is programmed into the hardware by the network card vendor. There is, however, an unfortunate disadvantage of vendor-assigned addresses — *MAC* addresses do not make up a hierarchical system, but are instead more or less randomly distributed. Therefore, they cannot be used for addressing remote machines. The *MAC* address still plays an important role in communication between hosts in a local network and is the main component of the protocol header of layer 2.

The points in IP addresses indicate the hierarchical system. Until the 1990s, IP addresses were strictly categorized in classes. However, this system has proven too inflexible so was discontinued. Now, *classless routing* (or CIDR, Classless Inter Domain Routing) is used.

Netmasks and Routing

Netmasks were conceived for the purpose of informing the host with the IP address 192.168.0.0 of the location of the host with the IP address 192.168.0.20. To put it simply, the netmask on a host with an IP address defines what is internal and what is external. Hosts located internally (professionals say, "in the same subnetwork") respond directly. Hosts located externally ("not in the same subnetwork") only respond via a gateway or router. Because every network interface can receive its own IP address, it can get quite complicated.

Before a network packet is sent, the following runs on the computer: the IP address is linked to the netmask via a logical AND and the address of the sending host is likewise connected to the netmask via the logical AND. If there are several network interfaces available, normally all possible sender addresses are verified. The results of the AND links will be compared. If there are no discrepancies in this comparison, the destination, or receiving host, is located in the same subnetwork. Otherwise, it must be accessed via a gateway. The more "1" bits are located in the netmask, the fewer hosts can be accessed directly and the more hosts can be reached via a gateway. Several examples are illustrated in Table 13.2.

Example 13.2: *Linking IP Addresses to the Netmask*

```
IP address (192.168.0.20):   11000000 10101000 00000000 00010100
Netmask    (255.255.255.0):  11111111 11111111 11111111 00000000
---------------------------------------------------------------
Result of the link:          11000000 10101000 00000000 00000000
In the decimal system:            192.      168.        0.       0

IP address (213.95.15.200): 11010101 10111111 00001111 11001000
Netmask    (255.255.255.0): 11111111 11111111 11111111 00000000
---------------------------------------------------------------
Result of the link:          11010101 10111111 00001111 00000000
In the decimal system:            213.       95.       15.       0
```

The netmasks appear, like IP addresses, in decimal form divided by periods. Because the netmask is also a 32-bit value, four number values are written next to each other. Which hosts are gateways or which address domains are accessible over which network interfaces must be entered in the user configuration.

To give another example: all machines connected with the same ethernet cable are usually located in the same subnetwork and are directly accessible. When the ethernet is divided by switches or bridges, these hosts can still be reached.

However, the economical ethernet is not suitable for covering larger distances. You must transfer the IP packets to another hardware (such as FDDI or ISDN). Devices for this transfer are called routers or gateways. A Linux machine can carry out this task. The respective option is referred to as `ip_forwarding`.

If a gateway has been configured, the IP packet is sent to the appropriate gateway. This then attempts to forward the packet in the same manner — from host to host — until it reaches the destination host or the packet's TTL (time to live) has expired.

Table 13.2: *Specific Addresses*

Address Type	Description
Base network address	This is the netmask AND any address in the network, as shown in Table 13.2 on the page before under `Result`. This address cannot be assigned to any hosts.
Broadcast address	This basically says, "Access all hosts in this subnetwork." To generate this, the netmask is inverted in binary form and linked to the base network address with a logical OR. The above example therefore results in 192.168.0.255. This address cannot be assigned to any hosts.
Local host	The address `127.0.0.1` is strictly assigned to the "loopback device" on each host. A connection can be set up to your own machine with this address.

As IP addresses must be unique all over the world, you cannot just come up with your own random addresses. There are three address domains to use to set up a private IP-based network. With these, you cannot set up any connections to the rest of the Internet, unless you apply certain tricks, because these addresses cannot be transmitted over the Internet. These address domains are specified in RFC 1597 and listed in Table 13.3 on the facing page.

Table 13.3: Private IP Address Domains

Network/Netmask	Domain
10.0.0.0/255.0.0.0	10.x.x.x
172.16.0.0/255.240.0.0	172.16.x.x – 172.31.x.x
192.168.0.0/255.255.0.0	192.168.x.x

13.1.3 Domain Name System

DNS assists in assigning an IP address to one or more names and assigning a name to an IP address. In Linux, this conversion is usually carried out by a special type of software known as bind. The machine that takes care of this conversion is called a *name server*. The names make up a hierarchical system in which each name component is separated by dots. The name hierarchy is, however, independent of the IP address hierarchy described above.

Consider a complete name, such as `laurent.suse.de`, written in the format `hostname.domain`. A full name, referred to by experts as a *fully qualified domain name*, or FQDN for short, consists of a host name and a domain name (`suse.de`). The latter also includes the *top level domain* or TLD (`de`).

TLD assignment has become, for historical reasons, quite confusing. Traditionally, three-letter domain names are used in the USA. In the rest of the world, the two-letter ISO national codes are the standard. In addition to that, multiletter TLDs were introduced in 2000 that represent certain spheres of activity (for example, `.info`, `.name`, `.museum`).

In the early days of the Internet (before 1990), the file `/etc/hosts` was used to store the names of all the machines represented over the Internet. This quickly proved to be impractical in the face of the rapidly growing number of computers connected to the Internet. For this reason, a decentralized database was developed to store the host names in a widely distributed manner. This database, similar to the name server, does not have the data pertaining to all hosts in the Internet readily available, but can dispatch requests to other name servers.

The top of the hierarchy is occupied by *root name servers*. These root name servers manage the top level domains and are run by the Network Information Center, or NIC. Each root name server knows about the name servers responsible for a given top level domain. More information about top level domain NICs is available at `http://www.internic.net`.

DNS can do more than just resolve host names. The name server also knows which host is receiving e-mails for an entire domain — the *mail exchanger (MX)*.

For your machine to resolve an IP address, it must know about at least one name server and its IP address. Easily specify such a name server with the help of YaST. If you have a modem dial-up connection, you may not need to configure a name server manually at all. The dial-up protocol provides the name server address as the connection is made. The configuration of name server access with SUSE LINUX is described in Section 13.6 on page 293.

whois

The protocol `whois` is closely related to DNS. With this program, quickly find out who is responsible for any given domain.

13.2 IPv6 — The Next Generation Internet

Due to the emergence of the WWW (World Wide Web), the Internet has experienced explosive growth with an increasing number of computers communicating via TCP/IP in the last ten years. Since Tim Berners-Lee at CERN (`http://public.web.cern.ch`) invented the WWW in 1990, the number of Internet hosts has grown from a few thousand to about 100 million.

As mentioned, an IP address consists of only 32 bits. Also, quite a few IP addresses are lost — they cannot be used due to the way in which networks are organized. The number of addresses available in your subnet is the number of bits squared minus two. A subnetwork has, for example, two, six, or fourteen addresses available. To connect 128 hosts to the Internet, for instance, you need a subnetwork with 256 IP addresses, from which only 254 are usable, because two IP addresses are needed for the structure of the subnetwork itself: the broadcast and the base network address.

Under the current IPv4 protocol, DHCP or NAT (network address translation) are the typical mechanisms used to circumvent the potential address shortage. Combined with the convention to keep private and public address spaces separate, these methods can certainly mitigate the shortage. The problem with them lies in their configuration, which is quite a chore to set up and a burden to maintain. To set up a host in an IPv4 network, you need to find out about quite a number of address items, such as the host's own IP address, the subnetmask, the gateway address, and maybe a name server address. In fact, all these items need to be known, meaning they cannot be derived from somewhere else.

With IPv6, both the address shortage and the complicated configuration should be a thing of the past. The following sections tell more about the improvements and benefits brought by IPv6 and about the transition from the old protocol to the new one.

13.2.1 Advantages of IPv6

The most important and most visible improvement brought by the new protocol is the enormous expansion of the available address space. An IPv6 address is made up of 128 bit values instead of the traditional 32 bits. This provides for as many as several quadrillion IP addresses.

However, IPv6 addresses are not only different from their predecessors with regard to their length. They also have a different internal structure that may contain more specific information about the systems and the networks to which they belong. More details about this are found in Section 13.2.2 on the following page.

The following is a list of some other advantages of the new protocol:

Autoconfiguration IPv6 makes the network "plug and play" capable, which means that a newly set up system integrates into the (local) network without any manual configuration. The new host uses its autoconfig mechanism to derive its own address from the information made available by the neighboring routers, relying on a protocol called the *neighbor discovery* (ND) protocol. This method does not require any intervention on the administrator's part and there is no need to maintain a central server for address allocation — an additional advantage over IPv4, where automatic address allocation requires a DHCP server.

Mobility IPv6 makes it possible to assign several addresses to one network interface at the same time. This allows users to access several networks easily, something that could be compared with the international roaming services offered by mobile phone companies: when you take your mobile phone abroad, the phone automatically logs in to a foreign service as soon as it enters the corresponding area, so you can be reached under the same number everywhere and are able to place an outgoing call just like in your home area.

Secure Communication With IPv4, network security is an add-on function. IPv6 includes IPSec as one of its core features, allowing systems to communicate over a secure tunnel to avoid eavesdropping by outsiders on the Internet.

Backward Compatibility Realistically, it will be impossible to switch the entire Internet from IPv4 to IPv6 in one fell swoop. Therefore, it is crucial that both protocols are able to coexist not only on the Internet, but also on one system. This is ensured by compatible addresses on the one hand (IPv4 addresses can easily be translated into IPv6 addresses) and through the use of a number of tunnels on the other (see Section 13.2.3 on page 279). Also, systems can rely on a *dual stack IP* technique to support both protocols at the same time, meaning that they have two network stacks that are completely separate, such that there is no interference between the two protocol versions.

Custom Tailored Services through Multicasting
With IPv4, some services, such as SMB, need to broadcast their packets to all hosts in the local network. IPv6 allows a much more fine-grained approach by enabling servers to address hosts through *multicasting* — by addressing a number of hosts as parts of a group (which is different from addressing all hosts through *broadcasting* or each host individually through *unicasting*). Which hosts are addressed as a group may depend on the concrete application. There are some predefined groups to address all name servers (the *all name servers multicast group*), for instance, or all routers (the *all routers multicast group*).

13.2.2 The IPv6 Address System

As mentioned, the current IP protocol is lacking in two important aspects: on the one hand, there is an increasing shortage of IP addresses; on the other hand, configuring the network and maintaining the routing tables is becoming a more and more complex and burdensome task. IPv6 solves the first problem by expanding the address space to 128 bits. The second one is countered by introducing a hierarchical address structure, combined with sophisticated techniques to allocate network addresses, as well as *multihoming* (the ability to allocate several addresses to one device, giving access to several networks).

When dealing with IPv6, it is useful to know about three different types of addresses:

Unicast Addresses of this type are associated with exactly one network interface. Packets with such an address are delivered to only one destination. Accordingly, unicast addresses are used to transfer packets to individual hosts on the local network or the Internet.

Multicast Addresses of this type relate to a group of network interfaces. Packets with such an address are delivered to all destinations that belong to the group. Multicast addresses are mainly used by certain network services to communicate with certain groups of hosts in a well-directed manner.

Anycast Addresses of this type are related to a group of interfaces. Packets with such an address are delivered to the member of the group that is closest to the sender, according to the principles of the underlying routing protocol. Anycast addresses are used to make it easier for hosts to find out about servers offering certain services in the given network area. All servers of the same type have the same anycast address. Whenever a host requests a service, it receives a reply from the server with the closest location, as determined by the routing protocol. If this server should fail for some reason, the protocol automatically selects the second closest server, then the third one, and so forth.

Structure of an IPv6 Address

An IPv6 address is made up of eight four-digit fields, each of them representing sixteen bits, written in hexadecimal notation. They are also separated by colons (`:`). Any leading zero bytes within a given field may be dropped, but zeros within the field or at its end may not. Another convention is that more than four consecutive zero bytes may be collapsed into a double colon. However, only one such `::` is allowed per address. This kind of shorthand notation is shown in Output 13.3, where all three lines represent the same address.

***Example 13.3:** Sample IPv6 Address*

```
fe80 : 0000 : 0000 : 0000 : 0000 : 10 : 1000 : 1a4
fe80 :    0 :    0 :    0 :    0 : 10 : 1000 : 1a4
fe80 :                           : 10 : 1000 : 1a4
```

Each part of an IPv6 address has a defined function. The first bytes form the prefix and specify the type of address. The center part is the network portion of the address, but it may be unused. The end of the address forms the host part. With IPv6, the netmask is defined by indicating the length of the prefix after a slash at the end of the address. An address as shown in Output 13.4 contains the information that the first 64 bits form the network part of the address and the last 64 form its host part. In other words, the `64` means that the netmask is filled with 64 1-bit values from the left. Just like with IPv4, the IP address is combined with AND with the values from the netmask to determine whether the host is located in the same subnetwork or in another one.

Example 13.4: *IPv6 Address Specifying the Prefix Length*

```
fe80::10:1000:1a4/64
```

IPv6 knows about several predefined types of prefixes, some of which are shown in Table 13.4.

Table 13.4: *Various IPv6 Prefixes*

Prefix (hex)	Definition
`00`	IPv4 addresses and IPv4 over IPv6 compatibility addresses. These are used to maintain compatibility with IPv4. Their use still requires a router able to translate IPv6 packets into IPv4 packets. Several special addresses (such as the one for the loopback device) have this prefix as well.
`2` or `3` as the first digit	Aggregatable global unicast addresses. As is the case with IPv4, an interface can be assigned to form part of a certain subnetwork. Currently, there are the following address spaces: `2001::/16` (production quality address space) and `2002::/16` (6to4 address space).
`fe80::/10`	Link-local addresses. Addresses with this prefix are not supposed to be routed and should therefore only be reachable from within the same subnetwork.

fec0::/10	Site-local addresses. These may be routed, but only within the network of the organization to which they belong. In effect, they are the IPv6 equivalent of the current private network address space (e.g., 10.x.x.x).
ff	These are multicast addresses.

A unicast address consists of three basic components:

Public Topology The first part (which also contains one of the prefixes mentioned above) is used to route packets through the public Internet. It includes information about the company or institution that provides the Internet access.

Site Topology The second part contains routing information about the subnetwork to which the packet shall be delivered.

Interface ID The third part identifies the interface to which the packet shall be delivered. This also allows for the MAC to form part of the address. Given that the MAC is a globally unique, fixed identifier coded into the device by the hardware maker, the configuration procedure is substantially simplified. In fact, the first 64 address bits are consolidated to form the `EUI-64` token, with the last 48 bits taken from the MAC, and the remaining 24 bits containing special information about the token type. This also makes it possible to assign an `EUI-64` token to interfaces that do not have a MAC, such as those based on PPP or ISDN.

On top of this basic structure, IPv6 distinguishes between five different types of unicast addresses:

`::` (unspecified) This address is used by the host as its source address when the interface is initialized for the first time — when the address cannot yet be determined by other means.

`::1` (loopback) The address of the loopback device.

IPv4 compatible addresses The IPv6 address is formed by the IPv4 address and a prefix consisting of 96 zero bits. This type of compatibility address is used for tunneling (see Section 13.2.3 on the next page) to allow IPv4 and IPv6 hosts to communicate with others operating in a pure IPv4 environment.

IPv4 addresses mapped to IPv6 This type of address specifies a pure IPv4 address in IPv6 notation.

Local addresses There are two address types for local use:

link-local This type of address can only be used in the local subnetwork. Packets with a source or target address of this type are not supposed to be routed to the Internet or other subnetworks. These addresses contain a special prefix (`fe80::/10`) and the interface ID of the network card, with the middle part consisting of null bytes. Addresses of this type are used during autoconfiguration to communicate with other hosts belonging to the same subnetwork.

site-local Packets with this type of address may be routed to other subnetworks, but not to the wider Internet — they must remain inside the organization's own network. Such addresses are used for intranets and are an equivalent of the private address space as defined by IPv4. They contain a special prefix (`fec0::/10`), the interface ID, and a sixteen bit field specifying the subnetwork ID. Again, the rest is filled with null bytes.

As a completely new feature introduced with IPv6, each network interface normally gets several IP addresses, with the advantage that several networks can be accessed through the same interface. One of these networks can be configured in completely automatic fashion, using the MAC and a known prefix, with the result that all hosts on the local network can be reached as soon as IPv6 is enabled (using the link-local address). With the MAC forming part of it, any IP address used in the world is unique. The only variable parts of the address are those specifying the *site topology* and the *public topology*, depending on the actual network in which the host is currently operating.

For a host to go back and forth between different networks, it needs at least two addresses. One of them, the *home address*, not only contains the interface ID but also an identifier of the home network to which it normally belongs (and the corresponding prefix). The home address is a static address and, as such, it does not normally change. Still, all packets destined to the mobile host can be delivered to it, no matter whether it operates in the home network or somewhere outside. This is made possible by the completely new features introduced with IPv6, such as *stateless autoconfiguration* and *neighbor discovery*. In addition to its home address, a mobile host gets one or more further addresses that belong to the foreign networks where it is roaming. These are called *care-of* addresses. The home network has a facility that forwards any packets destined to the host when it is roaming outside. In an IPv6 environment, this task is performed by the *home agent*, which takes all packets destined to the home address and relays them through a tunnel. On the other hand, those packets destined to the care-of address are directly transferred to the mobile host without any special detours.

13.2.3 IPv4 versus IPv6 — Moving between the Two Worlds

It is unlikely that all hosts connected to the Internet will switch from IPv4 to IPv6 overnight. A rather more likely scenario is that both protocols will need to coexist for some time to come. The coexistence on one system is guaranteed where there is a *dual stack* implementation of both protocols. That still leaves the question how an IPv6 enabled host is supposed to communicate with an IPv4 host and how IPv6 packets should be transported by the current networks, which are predominantly IPv4 based.

The first problem can be solved with compatibility addresses (see Section 13.2.2 on page 275), the second one by introducing a number of different tunneling techniques. IPv6 hosts that are more or less isolated in the (worldwide) IPv4 network can communicate through a specially wrapped channel — IPv6 packets are encapsulated as IPv4 packets to move them across an IPv4 network. Such a connection between two IPv4 hosts is called a *tunnel*. To achieve this, packets must include the IPv6 destination address (or the corresponding prefix) as well as the IPv4 address of the remote host at the receiving end of the tunnel. A basic tunnel can be configured *manually* according to an agreement between the hosts' administrators. This is also called *static tunneling*.

However, the configuration and maintenance of static tunnels is often too labor-intensive to use them for daily communication needs. Therefore, IPv6 provides for three different methods of *dynamic tunneling*:

6over4 IPv6 packets are automatically encapsulated as IPv4 packets and sent over an IPv4 network capable of multicasting. IPv6 is tricked into seeing the whole network (Internet) as a huge local area network (LAN). This makes it possible to determine the receiving end of the IPv4 tunnel automatically. However, this method does not scale very well and it is also hampered by the fact that IP multicasting is far from widespread on the Internet. Therefore, it only provides a solution for smaller corporate or institutional networks where multicasting can be enabled. The specifications for this method are laid down in RFC 2529.

6to4 With this method, IPv4 addresses are automatically generated from IPv6 addresses, enabling isolated IPv6 hosts to communicate over an IPv4 network. However, a number of problems have been reported regarding the communication between those isolated IPv6 hosts and the Internet. The method is described in RFC 3056.

IPv6 Tunnel Broker This method relies on special servers that provide dedicated tunnels for IPv6 hosts. It is described in RFC 3053.

Note

The 6bone Initiative

In the heart of the "old-time" Internet, there is already a globally distributed network of IPv6 subnets that are connected through tunnels. This is the *6bone* network (`www.6bone.net`), an IPv6 test environment that may be used by programmers and Internet providers who want to develop and offer IPv6-based services to gain the experience necessary to implement the new protocol. More information can be found on the project's Internet site.

Note

13.2.4 For More Information

The above overview does not cover the topic of IPv6 comprehensively. For a more in-depth look at the new protocol, refer to the following online documentation and books:

`http://www.ngnet.it/e/cosa-ipv6.php`
: An article series providing a well-written introduction to the basics of IPv6. A good primer on the topic.

`http://www.bieringer.de/linux/IPv6/`
: Here, find the Linux IPv6-HOWTO and many links related to the topic.

`http://www.6bone.net/` Visit this site if you want to join a tunneled IPv6 network.

`http://www.ipv6.org/` The starting point for everything about IPv6.

RFC 2640 The fundamental RFC about IPv6.

IPv6 Essentials A book describing all the important aspects of the topic. Silvia Hagen: *IPv6 Essentials*. O'Reilly & Associates, 2002 (ISBN 0-596-00125-8).

13.3 Manual Network Configuration

Manual configuration of the network software should always be the last alternative. Using YaST is recommended. All network interfaces are activated with the script `/sbin/ifup`. To halt the interface, use `ifdown`. To check its status, use `ifstatus`.

If you only use internal network cards, simply configure the interfaces by means of their names. With the commands `ifup eth0`, `ifstatus eth0`, and `ifdown eth0`, start, check, or stop the interface `eth0`. The respective configuration files are stored in `/etc/sysconfig/network/ifcfg-eth0`. `eth0` is the name of the interface and the name of the configuration.

Alternatively, configure the network in relation to the hardware address (MAC address) of a network card. In this case, use a hardware-based configuration file named in the format ifcfg-<hardwareaddresswithoutcolon>. Use lowercase characters in the hardware address, as displayed by the command ip link (ifconfig shows uppercase letters). If ifup finds a configuration file matching the hardware address, a possibly existing file ifcfg-eth0 will be ignored.

Things are a little more complicated with hotplug network cards. If you do not use one of those cards, proceed directly to Section 13.3.1.

Hotplug network cards are assigned the interface name arbitrarily, so the configuration for one of those cards cannot be stored under the name of the interface. Instead, a name is used that contains the kind of hardware and the connection point. In the following, this name is referred to as the hardware description. ifup must be started with two arguments — the hardware description and the current interface name. ifup then determines the configuration that best fits the hardware description.

For example, consider a laptop with two PCMCIA slots, a PCMCIA ethernet network card, and an internal network card configured as eth0. If the internal card is in slot 0, its hardware description is eth-pcmcia-0. The cardmgr or the hotplug network script runs the command ifup eth-pcmcia-0 eth1. ifup searches /etc/sysconfig/network/ for the file ifcfg-eth-pcmcia-0. If this file does not exist, it consecutively searches for ifcfg-eth-pcmcia, ifcfg-pcmcia-0, ifcfg-pcmcia, ifcfg-eth1, and ifcfg-eth. The first of these files found by ifup is used for the configuration. To generate a network configuration valid for all PCMCIA network cards in all slots, the configuration file must be named ifcfg-pcmcia. This file would be used for the ethernet card in slot 0 (eth-pcmcia-0) as well as for a token ring card in slot 1 (tr-pcmcia-1).

A configuration based on the hardware address is treated with higher priority. This option was only omitted in the example for the sake of clarity.

YaST lists the configurations for hotplug cards and accordingly writes the settings to ifcfg-eth-pcmcia-<number>. To use such a configuration file for all slots, ifcfg-eth-pcmcia is linked to this file. Keep this in mind if you sometimes configure the network with and sometimes without YaST.

13.3.1 Configuration Files

This section provides an overview of the network configuration files and explains their purpose and the format used.

/etc/sysconfig/network/ifcfg-*

These files contain data specific to a network interface. They may be named after the network interface (`ifcfg-eth2`), the hardware address of a network card (`ifcfg-000086386be3`), or the hardware description (`ifcfg-usb`). If network aliases are used, the respective files are named `ifcfg-eth2:1` or `ifcfg-usb:1`. The script `ifup` gets the interface name and, if necessary, the hardware description as arguments then searches for the best matching configuration file.

The configuration files contain the IP address (BOOTPROTO="static", IPADDR="10.10.11.214") or the direction to use DHCP (BOOT-PROTO="dhcp"). The IP address should already contain the netmask (IPADDR="10.10.11.214/16"). Refer to `man ifup` for the complete list of variables. In addition, all the variables in the files `dhcp`, `wireless`, and `config` can be used in the `ifcfg-*` files, if a general setting should only be used for one interface. By using the variables `POST_UP_SCRIPT` and `PRE_DOWN_SCRIPT`, individual scripts can be run after starting or before stopping the interface.

/etc/sysconfig/network/config, dhcp, wireless

The file `config` contains general settings for the behavior of `ifup`, `ifdown`, and `ifstatus`. `dhcp` contains settings for DHCP and `wireless` for wireless lan cards. The variables in all three configuration files are commented and can also be used in `ifcfg-*` files, where they are treated with higher priority.

/etc/resolv.conf

The domain to which the host belongs is specified in this file (keyword `search`). Also listed is the status of the name server address (keyword `nameserver`) to access. Multiple domain names can be specified. When resolving a name that is not fully qualified, an attempt is made to generate one by attaching the individual `search` entries. Use multiple name servers by entering several lines, each beginning with `nameserver`. Comments are preceded by # signs.

Example 13.5: */etc/resolv.conf*

```
# Our domain
search example.com
#
# We use sun (192.168.0.20) as nameserver
nameserver 192.168.0.20
```

An example of /etc/resolv.conf is shown in File 13.5 on the preceding page. YaST enters the specified name server here. Some services, like pppd (wvdial), ipppd (isdn), dhcp (dhcpcd and dhclient), pcmcia, and hotplug, modify the file /etc/resolv.conf by means of the script modify_resolvconf.

If the file /etc/resolv.conf has been temporarily modified by this script, it contains a predefined comment giving information about the service by which it has been modified, the location where the original file has been backed up, and how to turn off the automatic modification mechanism. If /etc/resolv.conf is modified several times, the file includes modifications in a nested form. These can be reverted in a clean way even if this reversal takes place in an order different from the order in which modifications where introduced. Services that may need this flexibility include isdn, pcmcia, and hotplug.

If it happens that a service was not terminated in a normal, clean way, modify_resolvconf can be used to restore the original file. Also, on system boot, a check is performed to see whether there is an uncleaned, modified resolv.conf (e.g., after a system crash), in which case the original (unmodified) resolv.conf is restored.

YaST uses the command modify_resolvconf check to find out whether resolv.conf has been modified and will subsequently warn the user that changes will be lost after restoring the file. Apart from this, YaST will not rely on modify_resolvconf, which means that the impact of changing resolv.conf through YaST is the same as that of any manual change. In both cases, changes have a permanent effect. Modifications requested by the above-mentioned services are only temporary.

/etc/hosts

In this file (see File 13.6), IP addresses are assigned to host names. If no name server is implemented, all hosts to which an IP connection will be set up must be listed here. For each host, a line consisting of the IP address, the fully qualified host name, and the host name (e.g., earth) is entered into the file. The IP address must be at the beginning of the line, the entries divided by blanks and tabs. Comments are always preceded by the # sign.

Example 13.6: */etc/hosts*

```
127.0.0.1 localhost
192.168.0.20 sun.example.com sun
192.168.0.0 earth.example.com earth
```

/etc/networks

Here, network names are converted to network addresses. The format is similar to that of the `hosts` file, except the network names precede the addresses (see File 13.7).

Example 13.7: `/etc/networks`

```
loopback      127.0.0.0
localnet      192.168.0.0
```

/etc/host.conf

Name resolution — the translation of host and network names via the *resolver* library — is controlled by this file. This file is only used for programs linked to the libc4 or the libc5. For current glibc programs, refer to the settings in `/etc/nsswitch.conf`. A parameter must always stand alone in its own line. Comments are preceded by a # sign. Table 13.5 shows the parameters available. An example for `/etc/host.conf` is shown in File 13.8 on the following page.

Table 13.5: *Parameters for /etc/host.conf*

order *hosts, bind*	Specifies in which order the services are accessed for the name resolution. Available arguments are (separated by blank spaces or commas): *hosts*: Searches the `/etc/hosts` file *bind*: Accesses a name server *nis*: Via NIS
multi *on/off*	Defines if a host entered in `/etc/hosts` can have multiple IP addresses.
nospoof *on* spoofalert *on/off*	These parameters influence the name server *spoofing*, but, apart from that, do not exert any influence on the network configuration.
`trim domainname`	The specified domain name is separated from the host name after host name resolution (as long as the host name includes the domain name). This option is useful if only names from the local domain are in the `/etc/hosts` file, but should still be recognized with the attached domain names.

Example 13.8: `/etc/host.conf`

```
# We have named running
order hosts bind
# Allow multiple addrs
multi on
```

/etc/nsswitch.conf

The introduction of the GNU C Library 2.0 was accompanied by the introduction of the "Name Service Switch" (NSS). Refer to `man 5 nsswitch.conf` and *The GNU C Library Reference Manual* for more details.

The order for queries is defined in the file `/etc/nsswitch.conf`. An example of `nsswitch.conf` is shown in File 13.9. Comments are introduced by # signs. In this example, the entry under the `hosts` database means that a request is sent to `/etc/hosts` (`files`) via DNS (see Section 13.6 on page 293).

Example 13.9: `/etc/nsswitch.conf`

```
passwd:     compat
group:      compat

hosts:      files dns
networks:   files dns

services:   db files
protocols:  db files

netgroup:   files
automount:  files nis
```

The "databases" available over NSS are listed in Table 13.6 on the next page. In addition, `automount`, `bootparams`, `netmasks`, and `publickey` are expected in the near future. The configuration options for NSS databases are listed in Table 13.7 on the facing page.

Table 13.6: Databases Available via /etc/nsswitch.conf

aliases	Mail aliases implemented by sendmail; see man 5 aliases.
ethers	Ethernet addresses.
group	For user groups, used by getgrent. See also the man page for group.
hosts	For host names and IP addresses, used by gethostbyname and similar functions.
netgroup	Valid host and user lists in the network for the purpose of controlling access permissions; see man 5 netgroup.
networks	Network names and addresses, used by getnetent.
passwd	User passwords, used by getpwent; see man 5 passwd.
protocols	Network protocols, used by getprotoent; see man 5 protocols.
rpc	Remote procedure call names and addresses, used by getrpcbyname and similar functions.
services	Network services, used by getservent.
shadow	Shadow passwords of users, used by getspnam; see man 5 shadow.

Table 13.7: Configuration Options for NSS Databases

files	directly access files, for example, to /etc/aliases
db	access via a database
nis	NIS, see also Section 13.8 on page 320
nisplus	
dns	can only be used as an extension for hosts and networks
compat	can only be used as an extension for passwd, shadow, and group

/etc/nscd.conf

This file is used to configure nscd (Name Service Cache Daemon). See `man 8 nscd` and `man 5 nscd.conf`). By default, the system entries of `passwd` and `groups` are cached by nscd. `hosts` is not cached by default, because the mechanism in nscd to cache hosts causes the local system to be unable to trust forward and reverse lookup checks. Instead of asking nscd to cache names, set up a caching DNS server.

If the caching for `passwd` is activated, it usually takes about fifteen seconds until a newly added local user is recognized. This waiting time can be reduced by restarting nscd with the command `rcnscd restart`.

/etc/HOSTNAME

Here is the host name without the domain name attached. This file is read by several scripts while the machine is booting. It may only contain one line in which the host name is set.

13.3.2 Start-Up Scripts

Apart from the configuration files described above, there are also various scripts that load the network programs while the machine is booting. These are started as soon as the system is switched to one of the *multiuser runlevels* (see also Table 13.8).

Table 13.8: *Some Start-Up Scripts for Network Programs*

`/etc/init.d/network`	This script handles the configuration of the network hardware and software when the system is booted.
`/etc/init.d/inetd`	Starts xinetd. xinetd can be used to make server services available on the system. For example, it can start vsftpd whenever an FTP connection is initiated.
`/etc/init.d/portmap`	Starts the portmapper needed for the RPC server, such as an NFS server.
`/etc/init.d/nfsserver`	Starts the NFS server.
`/etc/init.d/sendmail`	Controls the sendmail process.
`/etc/init.d/ypserv`	Starts the NIS server.
`/etc/init.d/ypbind`	Starts the NIS client.

13.4 Network Integration

Currently TCP/IP is the standard network protocol by which all modern operating systems can communicate. Nevertheless, Linux also supports other network protocols, such as the IPX protocol (formerly) used by Novell Netware or the Appletalk protocol used by Macintosh machines. This chapter merely focuses on the integration of a Linux host in a TCP/IP network. To integrate arcnet, token ring, or FDDI network cards, refer to the kernel source documentation in `/usr/src/linux/Documentation` (package `kernel-source`).

13.4.1 Requirements

The machine must have a supported network card. Normally, the network card is detected during the installation and a suitable driver is loaded. To see if your card has been integrated correctly with the appropriate driver, enter the command `ifstatus eth0`. The output should show the network device `eth0`.

If the kernel support for the network card is implemented as a module, which is done by default for the SUSE kernel, the name of the module must be entered as an alias in `/etc/modules.conf`. For example, the entry for the first ethernet card could be `alias eth0 tulip`. This is done automatically when the driver support for the network card is loaded in linuxrc during the first installation. This task can also be done after installation with YaST.

If you are using a hotplug network card (e.g., PCMCIA or USB), the drivers are autodetected when the card is plugged in. No configuration is necessary.

13.4.2 Configuration with YaST

To configure the network card with YaST, start the Control Center and select 'Network Devices' -> 'Network Card Configuration'. With 'Add', configure a new network card. With 'Delete', remove it from the configuration. With 'Edit', modify the network card configuration.

Activate 'Advanced Settings' → 'Hardware Details' to modify the hardware data for an already configured network card with 'Edit'. This opens the dialog for changing the settings of the network card, shown in Figure 13.3 on the next page.

Normally, the correct driver for your network card is configured during installation and is activated. Therefore, manual hardware configuration is only needed if multiple network cards are used or if the network hardware is not automatically recognized. In this case, select 'Add' to specify a new driver module.

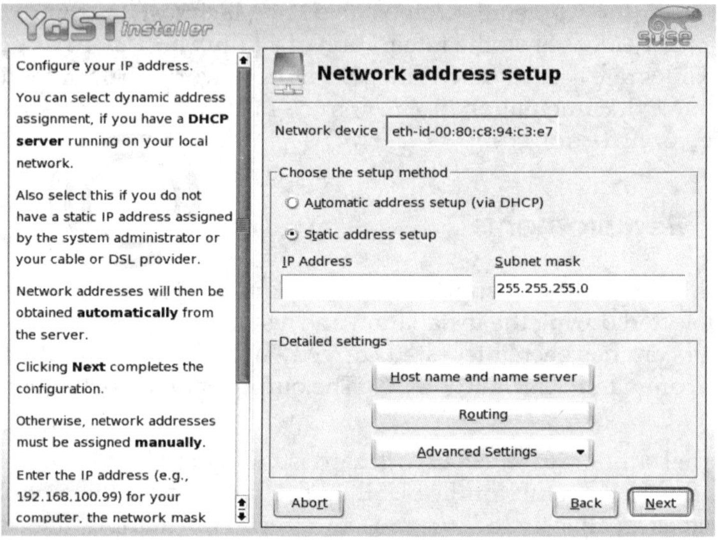

Figure 13.3: Configuring the Hardware Parameters

In this dialog, set the network card type and, for an ISA card, the interrupt to implement and the I/O port. For some network drivers, also specify special parameters, such as the interface to use or whether it uses an `RJ-45` or a `BNC` connection. For this, refer to the driver module documentation. To use PCMCIA or USB, activate the respective check boxes.

After entering the hardware parameters, configure additional network interface data. Select 'Interface' in the 'Network Base Configuration' to activate the network card and assign it an IP address. Select the card number then click 'Edit'. A new dialog appears in which to specify the IP address and other IP network data. Find information about assigning addresses to your own network in Section 13.1 on page 264 and Table 13.3 on page 271. Otherwise, enter the address assigned by your network administrator in the designated fields.

Configure a name server under 'Host Name and Name Server' so the name resolution functions as described in Section 13.6 on page 293. Via 'Routing', set up the routing. Select 'Configuration for Experts' to make advanced settings.

If you are using wireless LAN cards, activate 'Wireless Device'. Important settings, such as the operation mode, network names, and the key for encrypted data transfer, can be made in a special dialog.

With that, the network configuration is complete. YaST starts SuSEconfig and transfers the settings to the corresponding files (see Section 13.3 on page 281). For the changes to take effect, the relevant programs must be reconfigured and the required daemons must be restarted. Do this by entering `rcnetwork restart`.

13.4.3 Hotplug and PCMCIA

Hotplug network cards, like PCMCIA or USB devices, are managed in a somewhat special way. Normal network cards are fixed components assigned a permanent device name, such as `eth0`. By contrast, PCMCIA cards are assigned a free device name dynamically on an as-needed basis. To avoid conflicts with fixed network cards, hotplug and PCMCIA services are loaded after the network has been started.

PCMCIA-related configuration and start scripts are located in the directory `/etc/sysconfig/pcmcia`. The scripts are executed as soon as cardmgr, the PCMCIA device manager, detects a newly inserted PCMCIA card — which is why PCMCIA services do not need to be started before the network during boot.

13.4.4 Configuring IPv6

To configure IPv6, you will not normally need to make any changes on the individual workstations. However, IPv6 support must be loaded. To do this, enter `modprobe ipv6` as `root`.

Because of the autoconfiguration concept of IPv6, the network card is assigned an address in the *link-local* network. Normally, no routing table management takes place on a workstation. The network routers can be queried by the workstation, using the *router advertisement protocol*, for what prefix and gateways should be implemented. The radvd program can be used to set up an IPv6 router. This program informs the workstations which prefix to use for the IPv6 addresses and which routers. Alternatively, use zebra for automatic configuration of both addresses and routing.

Consult the manual page of ifup (`man ifup`) to get information about how to set up various types of tunnels using the `/etc/sysconfig/network` files.

13.5 Routing in SUSE LINUX

The routing table is set up in SUSE LINUX via the configuration files `/etc/sysconfig/network/routes` and `/etc/sysconfig/network/ifroute-*`. All the static routes required by the various system tasks can be entered in the `/etc/sysconfig/network/routes` file: routes to a host, routes to a host via a gateway, and routes to a network. For each interface that needs individual routing, define an additional configuration file: `/etc/sysconfig/network/ifroute-*`. Replace `*` with the name of the interface. The entries in the routing configuration files look like this:

```
DESTINATION           GATEWAY NETMASK   INTERFACE [ TYPE ] [ OPTIONS ]
DESTINATION           GATEWAY PREFIXLEN INTERFACE [ TYPE ] [ OPTIONS ]
DESTINATION/PREFIXLEN GATEWAY -         INTERFACE [ TYPE ] [ OPTIONS ]
```

To omit GATEWAY, NETMASK, PREFIXLEN, or INTERFACE, write - instead. The entries TYPE and OPTIONS may just be omitted.

- The route's destination is in the first column. This column may contain the IP address of a network or host or, in the case of *reachable* name servers, the fully qualified network or host name.
- The second column contains the default gateway or a gateway through which a host or a network can be accessed.
- The third column contains the netmask for networks or hosts behind a gateway. The mask is `255.255.255.255`, for example, for a host behind a gateway.
- The last column is only relevant for networks connected to the local host such as loopback, ethernet, ISDN, PPP, and dummy device. The device name must be entered here.

The following scripts in the directory `/etc/sysconfig/network/scripts/` assist with the handling of routes:

ifup-route for setting up a route

ifdown-route for disabling a route

ifstatus-route for checking the status of the routes

13.6 DNS — Domain Name System

DNS (domain name system) is needed to resolve the domain and host names into IP addresses. In this way, the IP address 192.168.0.0 is assigned to the host name `earth`, for example. Before setting up your own name server, read the general information about DNS in Section 13.1.3 on page 271. The configuration examples below are only valid for BIND 9, which is the new default DNS server with SUSE LINUX.

13.6.1 Starting the Name Server BIND

On a SUSE LINUX system, the name server BIND (short for *Berkeley Internet Name Domain*) comes preconfigured so it can be started right after installation without any problem. If you already have a functioning Internet connection and have entered `127.0.0.1` as the name server address for `localhost` in `/etc/resolv.conf`, you normally already have a working name resolution without needing to know the DNS of the provider. BIND carries out the name resolution via the root name server, a notably slower process. Normally, the DNS of the provider should be entered with its IP address in the configuration file `/etc/named.conf` under `forwarders` to ensure effective and secure name resolution. If this works so far, the name server runs as a pure *caching-only* name server. Only when you configure its own zones will it become a proper DNS. A simple example of this is included in the documentation as `/usr/share/doc/packages/bind/sample-config`.

However, do not set up any official domains until assigned one by the responsible institution. Even if you have your own domain and it is managed by the provider, you are better off not to use it, as BIND would otherwise not forward any more requests for this domain. The provider's web server, for example, would not be accessible for this domain.

To start the name server, enter the command `rcnamed start` as `root`. If "done" appears to the right in green, named, as the name server process is called, has been started successfully. Test the name server immediately on the local system with the `host` or `dig` programs, which should return `localhost` as the default server with the address `127.0.0.1`. If this is not the case, `/etc/resolv.conf` probably contains an incorrect name server entry or the file does not exist at all. For the first test, enter `host 127.0.0.1`, which should always work. If you get an error message, use `rcnamed status` to see whether the server is actually running. If the name server does not start or behaves in an unexpected way, you can usually find the cause in the log file `/var/log/messages`.

To use the name server of the provider or one already running on your network as the forwarder, enter the corresponding IP address or addresses in the `options` section under `forwarders`. The addresses included in File 13.10 are just examples. Change these entries according to your own setup.

***Example 13.10:** Forwarding Options in named.conf*

```
options {
        directory "/var/lib/named";
        forwarders { 10.11.12.13; 10.11.12.14; };
        listen-on { 127.0.0.1; 192.168.0.99; };
        allow-query { 127/8; 192.168.0/24; };
        notify no;
        };
```

The `options` entry is followed by entries for the zone, for `localhost`, `0.0.127.in-addr.arpa`, and the `type hint` entry under ".", which should always be present. The corresponding files do not need to be modified and should work as is. Also make sure that each entry is closed with a ";" and that the curly braces are in the correct places. After changing the configuration file `/etc/named.conf` or the zone files, tell BIND to reread them with the command `rcnamed reload`. You can achieve the same by stopping and restarting the name server with the command `rcnamed restart`. The server can also be stopped at any time by entering the command `rcnamed stop`.

13.6.2 The Configuration File /etc/named.conf

All the settings for the BIND name server itself are stored in the file `/etc/named.conf`. However, the zone data for the domains to handle, consisting of the host names, IP addresses, and so on, are stored in separate files in the `/var/lib/named` directory. The details of this are described further below.

The `/etc/named.conf` is roughly divided into two areas. One is the `options` section for general settings and the other consists of `zone` entries for the individual domains. A `logging` section as well as `acl` (access control list) entries are optional. Comment lines begin with a "#" sign or "//". A minimalistic `/etc/named.conf` looks like File 13.11 on the facing page.

Example 13.11: A Basic /etc/named.conf

```
options {
        directory "/var/lib/named";
        forwarders { 10.0.0.1; };
        notify no;
};

zone "localhost" in {
       type master;
       file "localhost.zone";
};

zone "0.0.127.in-addr.arpa" in {
        type master;
        file "127.0.0.zone";
};

zone "." in {
        type hint;
        file "root.hint";
};
```

13.6.3 Important Configuration Options

directory "/var/lib/named"; specifies the directory where BIND can find the files containing the zone data.

forwarders 10.0.0.1;; specifies the name servers (mostly of the provider) to which DNS requests should forwarded if they cannot be resolved directly.

forward first; causes DNS requests to be forwarded before an attempt is made to resolve them via the root name servers. Instead of `forward first`, `forward only` can be written to have all requests forwarded and none sent to the root name servers. This makes sense for firewall configurations.

listen-on port 53 127.0.0.1; 192.168.0.1;; tells BIND to which network interface and port to listen. The `port 53` specification can be left out, as 53 is the default port. If this entry is completely omitted, BIND accepts requests on all interfaces.

listen-on-v6 port 53 any; ; tells BIND on which port it should listen for IPv6 client requests. The only alternative to `any` is `none`. As far as IPv6 is concerned, the server only accepts a wild card address.

query-source address * port 53; This entry is necessary if a firewall is blocking outgoing DNS requests. This tells BIND to post requests externally from port 53 and not from any of the high ports above 1024.

query-source-v6 address * port 53; tells BIND which port to use for IPv6 queries.

allow-query 127.0.0.1; 192.168.1/24;;
defines the networks from which clients can post DNS requests. The `/24` at the end is an abbreviated expression for the netmask, in this case, `255.255.255.0`.

allow-transfer ! *;; controls which hosts can request zone transfers. In the example, such requests are completely denied with `! *`. Without this entry, zone transfers can be requested from anywhere without restrictions.

statistics-interval 0; In the absence of this entry, BIND generates several lines of statistical information per hour in `/var/log/messages`. Specify 0 to completely suppress such statistics or specify an interval in minutes.

cleaning-interval 720; This option defines at which time intervals BIND clears its cache. This triggers an entry in `/var/log/messages` each time it occurs. The time specification is in minutes. The default is 60 minutes.

interface-interval 0; BIND regularly searches the network interfaces for new or nonexisting interfaces. If this value is set to `0`, this is not done and BIND only listens at the interfaces detected at start-up. Otherwise, the interval can be defined in minutes. The default is 60 minutes.

notify no; `no` prevents other name servers from being informed when changes are made to the zone data or when the name server is restarted.

13.6.4 The Configuration Section Logging

What, how, and where logging takes place can be extensively configured in BIND. Normally, the default settings should be sufficient. File 13.12 on the next page represents the simplest form of such an entry and completely suppresses any logging.

Example 13.12: Entry to Disable Logging

```
logging {
        category default { null; };
};
```

13.6.5 Zone Entry Structure

Example 13.13: Zone Entry for my-domain.de

```
zone "my-domain.de" in {
      type master;
      file "my-domain.zone";
      notify no;
};
```

After `zone`, the name of the domain to administer is specified, `my-domain.de`, followed by `in` and a block of relevant options enclosed in curly braces, as shown in File 13.13. To define a *slave zone*, the `type` is simply switched to `slave` and a name server is specified that administers this zone as `master` (which, in turn, may be a slave of another master), as shown in File 13.14.

Example 13.14: Zone Entry for other-domain.de

```
zone "other-domain.de" in {
      type slave;
      file "slave/other-domain.zone";
      masters { 10.0.0.1; };
};
```

The zone options:

type master; By specifying `master`, tell BIND that the zone is handled by the local name server. This assumes that a zone file has been created in the correct format.

type slave; This zone is transferred from another name server. Must be used together with `masters`.

type hint; The zone `.` of the `hint` type is used to set the root name servers. This zone definition can be left as is.

file `my-domain.zone` or file "slave/other-domain.zone";
This entry specifies the file where zone data for the domain is located. This file is not required for a slave, as this data is fetched from another name server. To differentiate master and slave files, the directory `slave` is specified for the slave files.

masters 10.0.0.1;; This entry is only needed for slave zones. It specifies from which name server the zone file should be transferred.

allow-update ! *;; This option controls external write access, which would allow clients to make a DNS entry — something not normally desirable for security reasons. Without this entry, zone updates are not allowed at all. The above entry achieves the same because `! *` effectively bans any such activity.

13.6.6 Structure of Zone Files

Two types of zone files are needed. One serves to assign IP addresses to host names and the other does the reverse — supplies a host name for an IP address.

The `.` has an important meaning in the zone files. If host names are given without ending with a `.`, the zone is appended. Thus, complete host names specified with a complete domain must end with a `.` so the domain is not added to it again. A missing period or one in the wrong place is probably the most frequent cause of name server configuration errors.

The first case to consider is the zone file `world.zone`, responsible for the domain `world.cosmos`, shown in File 13.15.

Example 13.15: *File /var/lib/named/world.zone*

```
$TTL 2D
world.cosmos. IN SOA      gateway  root.world.cosmos. (
            2003072441  ; serial
            1D          ; refresh
            2H          ; retry
            1W          ; expiry
            2D )        ; minimum

            IN NS       gateway
            IN MX       10 sun

```

```
12 gateway       IN A          192.168.0.1
13               IN A          192.168.1.1
14 sun           IN A          192.168.0.2
15 moon          IN A          192.168.0.3
16 earth         IN A          192.168.1.2
17 mars          IN A          192.168.1.3
18 www           IN CNAME      moon
```

Line 1: `$TTL` defines the default time to live that should apply to all the entries in this file. In this example, entries are valid for a period of two days (`2 D`).

Line 2: This is where the SOA control record begins:

- The name of the domain to administer is `world.cosmos` in the first position. This ends with a `.`, because otherwise the zone would be appended a second time. Alternatively, a `@` can be entered here, in which case the zone would be extracted from the corresponding entry in `/etc/named.conf`.
- After `IN SOA` is the name of the name server in charge as master for this zone. The name is expanded from `gateway` to `gateway.world.cosmos`, because it does not end with a `.`.
- An e-mail address of the person in charge of this name server will follow. Because the `@` sign already has a special meaning, `.` is entered here instead, so for `root@world.cosmos` the entry must read `root.world.cosmos.`. Again the `.` sign must be included at the end to prevent the zone from being added.
- The `(` is used to include all lines up to `)` into the SOA record.

Line 3: The `serial number` is an arbitrary number that is increased each time this file is changed. It is needed to inform the secondary name servers (slave servers) of changes. For this, a ten-digit number of the date and run number, written as YYYYMMDDNN, has become the customary format.

Line 4: The `refresh rate` specifies the time interval at which the secondary name servers verify the zone `serial number`. In this case, one day.

Line 5: The `retry rate` specifies the time interval at which a secondary name server, in case of error, attempts to contact the primary server again. Here, two hours.

Line 6: The `expiration time` specifies the time frame after which a secondary name server discards the cached data if it has not regained contact to the primary server. Here, it is a week.

Line 7: The last entry in the SOA record specifies the `negative caching TTL` — the time for which results of unresolved DNS queries from other servers may be cached.

Line 9: The `IN NS` specifies the name server responsible for this domain. `gateway` is extended to `gateway.world.cosmos` because it does not end with a `.`. There can be several lines like this — one for the primary and one for each secondary name server. If `notify` is not set to `no` in `/etc/named.conf`, all the name servers listed here will be informed of the changes made to the zone data.

Line 10: The MX record specifies the mail server that accepts, processes, and forwards e-mails for the domain `world.cosmos`. In this example, this is the host `sun.world.cosmos`. The number in front of the host name is the preference value. If there are multiple MX entries, the mail server with the smallest value is taken first and, if mail delivery to this server fails, an attempt will be made with the next higher value.

Lines 12–17: These are the actual address records where one or more IP addresses are assigned to host names. The names are listed here without a `.` because they do not include their domain, so `world.cosmos` is added to all of them. Two IP addresses are assigned to the host `gateway`, because it has two network cards. Wherever the host address is a traditional one (IPv4), the record is marked with an `A`. If the address is an IPv6 address, the entry is marked with `A6`. (The previous token for IPv6 addresses was `AAAA`, which is now obsolete.)

Line 18: The alias `www` can be used to address `mond` (`CNAME` = *canonical name*).

The pseudodomain `in-addr.arpa` is used for the reverse lookup of IP addresses into host names. It is appended to the network part of the address in reverse notation. So `192.168.1` is resolved into `1.168.192.in-addr.arpa`. See File 13.16 on the next page.

Example 13.16: Reverse Lookup

```
1 $TTL 2D
2 1.168.192.in-addr.arpa. IN SOA gateway.world.cosmos. root.world.cosmos. (
3                         2003072441      ; serial
4                         1D              ; refresh
5                         2H              ; retry
6                         1W              ; expiry
7                         2D )            ; minimum
8
9                         IN NS           gateway.world.cosmos.
10
11 1                      IN PTR          gateway.world.cosmos.
12 2                      IN PTR          earth.world.cosmos.
13 3                      IN PTR          mars.world.cosmos.
```

Line 1: $TTL defines the standard TTL that applies to all entries here.

Line 2: The configuration file is supposed to activate reverse lookup for the network `192.168.1.0`. Given that the zone is called `1.168.192.in-addr.arpa`, we would not want to add this to the host names. Therefore, all host names are entered in their complete form — with their domain and with a `.` at the end. The remaining entries correspond to those described for the previous `world.cosmos` example.

Lines 3–7: See the previous example for `world.cosmos`.

Line 9: Again this line specifies the name server responsible for this zone. This time, however, the name is entered in its complete form with the domain and a `.` at the end.

Lines 11–13: These are the pointer records hinting at the IP addresses on the respective hosts. Only the last part of the IP address is entered at the beginning of the line, without the `.` at the end. Appending the zone to this (without the `.in-addr.arpa`) results in the complete IP address in reverse order.

Normally, zone transfers between different versions of BIND should be possible without any problem.

13.6.7 Secure Transactions

Secure transactions can be carried out with the help of transaction signatures (TSIGs) based on shared secret keys (also called TSIG keys). This section describes how to generate and use such keys.

Secure transactions are needed for the communication between different servers and for the dynamic update of zone data. Making the access control dependent on keys is much more secure than merely relying on IP addresses.

A TSIG key can be generated with the following command (for details, see `man dnssec-keygen`):

```
dnssec-keygen -a hmac-md5 -b 128 -n HOST host1-host2
```

This creates two files with names similar to these:

```
Khost1-host2.+157+34265.private Khost1-host2.+157+34265.key
```

The key itself (a string like `ejIkuCyyGJwwuN3xAteKgg==`) is found in both files. To use it for transactions, the second file (`Khost1-host2.+157+34265.key`) must be transferred to the remote host, preferably in a secure way (using `scp`, for instance). On the remote server, the key must be included in the file `/etc/named.conf` to enable a secure communication between `host1` and `host2`:

```
key host1-host2. {
 algorithm hmac-md5;
 secret ";ejIkuCyyGJwwuN3xAteKgg==;
};
```

Caution

Make sure the permissions of `/etc/named.conf` are properly restricted. The default for this file is `0640`, with the owner being `root` and the group `named`. As an alternative, move the keys to an extra file with specially limited permissions, which is then included from `/etc/named.conf`.

Caution

To enable the server `host1` to use the key for `host2` (which has the address `192.168.2.3` in our example), the server's `/etc/named.conf` must include the following rule:

```
server 192.168.2.3 {
  keys { host1-host2. ;};
};
```

Analogous entries must be included in the configuration files of host2.

In addition to any ACLs that are defined for IP addresses and address ranges, add TSIG keys for these to enable transaction security. The corresponding entry could look like this:

```
allow-update { key host1-host2. ;};
```

This topic is discussed in more detail in the *BIND Administrator Reference Manual* under update-policy.

13.6.8 Dynamic Update of Zone Data

The term *dynamic update* refers to operations by which entries in the zone files of a master server are added, changed, or deleted. This mechanism is described in RFC 2136. Dynamic update is configured individually for each zone entry by adding an optional allow-update or update-policy rule. Zones to update dynamically should not be edited by hand.

Transmit the entries to update to the server with the command nsupdate. For the exact syntax of this command, check the manual page for nsupdate(man 8 nsupdate). For security reasons, any such update should be performed using TSIG keys, as described in Section 13.6.7 on page 301.

13.6.9 DNSSEC

DNSSEC, or DNS security, is described in RFC 2535. The tools available for DNSSEC are discussed in the BIND Manual.

A zone considered secure must have one or several zone keys associated with it. These are generated with dnssec-keygen, just like the host keys. Currently the DSA encryption algorithm is used to generate these keys. The public keys generated should be included in the corresponding zone file with an $INCLUDE rule.

All keys generated are packaged into one set, using the command dnssec-makekeyset, which must then be transferred to the parent zone in a secure manner. On the parent, the set is signed with dnssec-signkey. The files generated by this command are then used to sign the zones with dnssec-signzone, which in turn generates the files to include for each zone in /etc/named.conf.

13.6.10 For More Information

For additional information, refer to the *BIND Administrator Reference Manual*, which is installed under `/usr/share/doc/packages/bind/`. Consider additionally consulting the RFCs referenced by the manual and the manual pages included with BIND.

13.7 LDAP — A Directory Service

It is crucial within a networked environment to keep important information structured and quickly available. Data chaos does not only loom when using the Internet. The search for important data in the company network can just as quickly grow disproportionately. "What is the extension number of colleague XY? What is his e-mail address?" This problem is solved by a directory service that, like the common yellow pages, keeps information available in a well-structured, quickly searchable form.

In the ideal case, a central server keeps the data in a directory and distributes it to all clients using a certain protocol. The data is structured in a way that a wide range of applications can access them. That way, it is not necessary for every single calendar tool and e-mail client to keep its own database — a central repository can be accessed instead. This notably reduces the administration effort for the concerned information. The use of an open and standardized protocol like LDAP ensures that as many different client applications as possible can access such information.

A directory in this context is a type of database optimized for quick and effective reading and searching:

- To make numerous (concurrent) reading accesses possible, the writing access is limited to a small number of updates by the administrator. Conventional databases are optimized for accepting the largest possible data volume in a short time.
- Because writing accesses can only be executed in a restricted fashion, a directory service is employed for administering mostly unchanging, static information. Data in a conventional database typically changes very often (*dynamic* data). Phone numbers in a company directory do not change nearly as often as, for instance, the figures administered in accounting.

- When static data is administered, updates of the existing data sets are very rare. When working with dynamic data, especially when data sets like bank accounts or accounting are concerned, the consistency of the data is of primary importance. If an amount should be subtracted from one place to be added to another, both operations must happen concurrently, within a *transaction*, to ensure the balance over the whole data stock. Databases support such transactions. Directories do not. Short-term inconsistencies of the data are quite acceptable in directories.

The design of a directory service like LDAP is not laid out to support complex update or query mechanisms. All applications accessing this service should gain access quickly and easily.

Many directory services have previously existed and still exist both in Unix and outside it. Novell NDS, Microsoft ADS, Banyan's Street Talk, and the OSI standard X.500 are just a few examples. LDAP was originally planned as a lean flavor of the DAP, the Directory Access Protocol, which was developed for accessing X.500. The X.500 standard regulates the hierarchical organization of directory entries.

LDAP is relieved of a few functions of the DAP. Without having to miss the X.500 entry hierarchy you profit from LDAP's cross-platform capabilities and save resources. and can be employed, The use of TCP/IP makes it substantially easier to establish interfaces between a docking application and the LDAP service.

LDAP, meanwhile, has evolved and is increasingly employed as a standalone solution without X.500 support. LDAP supports *referrals* with LDAPv3 (the protocol version in package openldap2), making it possible to realize distributed databases. The usage of SASL (Simple Authentication and Security Layer) is also new.

LDAP is not limited to querying data from X.500 servers, as it was originally planned. There is an open source server slapd, which can store object information in a local database. There is also an extension called slurpd, which is responsible for replicating multiple LDAP servers.

The `openldap2` package consists of:

slapd A stand-alone LDAPv3 server that administers object information in a BerkeleyDB-based database.

slurpd This program enables the replication of modifications to data on the local LDAP server to other LDAP servers installed on the network.

additional tools for system maintenance
slapcat, slapadd, slapindex

13.7.1 LDAP versus NIS

The Unix system administrator traditionally uses the NIS service for name resolution and data distribution in a network. The configuration data contained in the files in `/etc/` and the directories `group/`, `hosts/`, `mail/`, `netgroup/`, `networks/`, `passwd/`, `printcap/`, `protocols/`, `rpc/`, and `services/` are distributed by clients all over the network. These files can be maintained without major effort because they are simple text files. The handling of larger amounts of data, however, becomes increasingly difficult due to nonexistent structuring. NIS is only designed for Unix platforms, which makes its employment as a central data administrator in a heterogeneous network impossible.

Unlike NIS, the LDAP service is not restricted to pure Unix networks. Windows servers (from 2000) support LDAP as a directory service. Novell also offers an LDAP service. Application tasks mentioned above are additionally supported in non-Unix systems.

The LDAP principle can be applied to any data structure that should be centrally administered. A few application examples are:

- Employment as a replacement for the NIS service.
- Mail routing (postfix, sendmail).
- Address books for mail clients like Mozilla, Evolution, and Outlook.
- Administration of zone descriptions for a BIND9 name server.

This list can be extended because LDAP is extensible as opposed to NIS. The clearly-defined hierarchical structure of the data greatly helps the administration of very large amounts of data, because it can be searched better.

13.7.2 Structure of an LDAP Directory Tree

An LDAP directory has a tree structure. All entries (called objects) of the directory have a defined position within this hierarchy. This hierarchy is called the *directory information tree* or, for short, DIT. The complete path to the desired entry, which unambiguously identifies it, is called *distinguished name* or DN. The single nodes along the path to this entry are called *relative distinguished name* or RDN. Objects can generally be assigned to one of two possible types:

container These objects can themselves contain other objects. Such object classes are `root` (the root element of the directory tree, which does not really exist), `c` (country), `ou` (organizational unit), and `dc` (domain component). This model is comparable to the directories (folders) in a file system.

leaf These objects sit at the end of a branch and have no subordinate objects. Examples are `person`, `InetOrgPerson`, or `groupofNames`.

The top of the directory hierarchy has a root element `root`. This can contain `c` (country), `dc` (domain component), or `o` (organization) as subordinate elements. The relations within an LDAP directory tree become more evident in the following example, shown in Figure 13.4.

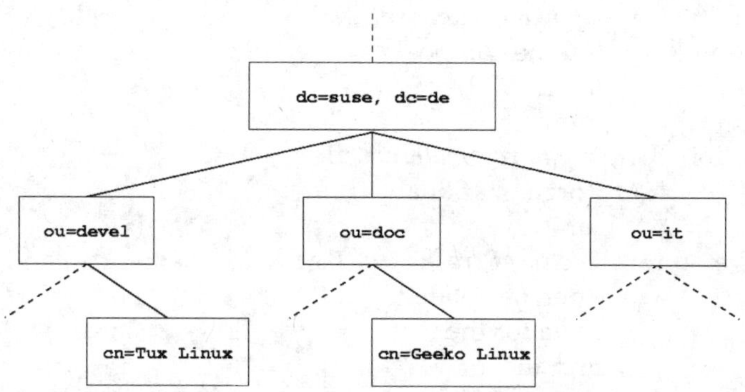

***Figure 13.4:** Structure of an LDAP Directory*

The complete diagram comprises a fictional directory information tree. The entries on three levels are depicted. Each entry corresponds to one box in the picture. The complete, valid *distinguished name* for the fictional SUSE employee `Geeko Linux`, in this case, is `cn=Geeko Linux,ou=doc,dc=suse,dc=de`. It is composed by adding the RDN `cn=Geeko Linux` to the DN of the preceding entry `ou=doc,dc=suse,dc=de`.

The global determination of which types of objects should be stored in the DIT is done following a *scheme*. The type of an object is determined by the *object class*. The object class determines what attributes the concerned object must or can be assigned. A scheme, therefore, must contain definitions of all object classes and attributes used in the desired application scenario. There are a few common schemes (see RFC 2252 and 2256). It is, however, possible to create custom schemes or to use multiple schemes complementing each other if this is required by the environment in which the LDAP server should operate.

Table 13.9 offers a small overview of the object classes from `core.schema` and `inetorgperson.schema` used in the example, including required attributes and valid attribute values.

***Table 13.9:** Commonly Used Object Classes and Attributes*

Object Class	Meaning	Example Entry	Compulsory Attributes
dcObject	*domainComponent* (name components of the domain)	suse	dc
organizationalUnit	*organizationalUnit* (organizational unit)	doc	ou
inetOrgPerson	*inetOrgPerson* (person-related data for the intranet or Internet)	Geeko Linux	sn and cn

Example 13.17 shows an excerpt from a scheme directive with explanations offering some understanding of the new schemes.

***Example 13.17:** Excerpt from schema.core (line numbering for explanatory reasons)*

```
#1 attributetype ( 2.5.4.11 NAME ( 'ou' 'organizationalUnitName' )
#2        DESC 'RFC2256: organizational unit this object belongs to'
#3        SUP name )

...
#4 objectclass ( 2.5.6.5 NAME 'organizationalUnit'
```

```
#5        DESC 'RFC2256: an organizational unit'
#6        SUP top STRUCTURAL
#7        MUST ou
#8        MAY ( userPassword $ searchGuide $ seeAlso $ businessCategory $
              x121Address $ registeredAddress $ destinationIndicator $
              preferredDeliveryMethod $ telexNumber $
              teletexTerminalIdentifier $ telephoneNumber $
              internationaliSDNNumber $ facsimileTelephoneNumber $
              street $ postOfficeBox $ postalCode $ postalAddress
              $ physicalDeliveryOfficeName $ st $ l $ description) )
...
```

The attribute type `organizationalUnitName` and the corresponding object class `organizationalUnit` serve as an example here. Line 1 features the name of the attribute, its unique OID (*object identifier*) (numerical), and the abbreviation of the attribute.

Line 2 gives brief description of the attribute with `DESC`. The corresponding RFC on which the definition is based is also mentioned here. `SUP` in line 3 indicates a superordinate attribute type to which this attribute belongs.

The definition of the object class `organizationalUnit` begins in line 4, like in the definition of the attribute, with an OID and the name of the object class. Line 5 features a brief description of the object class. Line 6 with its entry `SUP top` indicates that this object class is not subordinate to another object class. Line 7, starting with `MUST`, lists all attribute types that *must* be used in conjunction with an object of the type `organizationalUnit`. Line 8 starting with `MAY` lists all attribute types that are allowed to be used in conjunction with this object class.

A very good introduction in the use of schemes can be found in the documentation of OpenLDAP. When installed, find it in `/usr/share/doc/packages/openldap2/admin-guide/index.html`.

13.7.3 Server Configuration with slapd.conf

Your installed system contains a complete configuration file for your LDAP server at `/etc/openldap/slapd.conf`. The single entries are briefly described here and necessary adjustments are explained. Entries prefixed with a hash prefix (#) are inactive. This comment character must be removed to activate them.

Global Directives in slapd.conf

Example 13.18: slapd.conf: Include Directive for Schemes

```
include /etc/openldap/schema/core.schema
include /etc/openldap/schema/inetorgperson.schema
```

This first directive in `slapd.conf`, shown in Example 13.18, specifies the scheme by which the LDAP directory is organized. The entry `core.schema` is compulsory. Additionally required schemes are appended to this directive (`inetorgperson.schema` has been added here as an example). More available schemes can be found in the directory `/etc/openldap/schema`. For replacing NIS with an analogous LDAP service, include the two schemes `rfc2307.schema` and `cosine.schema`. Information can be found in the included OpenLDAP documentation.

Example 13.19: slapd.conf: pidfile and argsfile

```
pidfile /var/run/slapd.pid
argsfile /var/run/slapd.args
```

These two files contain the PID (process ID) and some of the arguments with which the slapd process is started. There is no need for modifications here.

Example 13.20: slapd.conf: Access Control

```
# Sample Access Control
#       Allow read access of root DSE
#       Allow self write access
#       Allow authenticated users read access
#       Allow anonymous users to authenticate
#
access to dn="" by * read
access to *
       by self write
       by users read
       by anonymous auth
#
# if no access controls are present, the default is:
#       Allow read by all
#
# rootdn can always write!
```

Example 13.20 on the preceding page is the excerpt from `slapd.conf` that regulates the access permissions for the LDAP directory on the server. The settings made here in the global section of `slapd.conf` are valid as long as no custom access rules are declared in the database-specific section. These would overwrite the global declarations. As presented here, all users have read access to the directory, but only the administrator (`rootdn`) can write into this directory. Access control regulation in LDAP is a highly complex process. The following tips can help:

- Every access rule has the following structure:

```
access to <what> by <who> <access>
```

- ⟨*what*⟩ is a placeholder for the object or attribute to which access is granted. Individual directory branches can explicitly be protected with separate rules. It is also possible to process whole regions of the directory tree with one rule by using regular expressions. slapd evaluates all rules in the order in which they are listed in the configuration file. More general rules should be listed after more specific ones — the first rule slapd regards as valid is evaluated and all following entries are ignored.

- ⟨*who*⟩ determines who should be granted access to the areas determined with ⟨*what*⟩. Regular expressions may be used. slapd again aborts the evaluation of `who` after the first match so more specific rules should be listed before the more general ones. The entries shown in Table 13.10 are possible.

***Table 13.10:** User Groups and Their Access Grants*

Tag	Scope
`*`	all users without exception
`anonymous`	not authenticated ("anonymous") users
`users`	authenticated users
`self`	users connected with the target object
`dn=<regex>`	all users matching the regular expression

- ⟨*access*⟩ specifies the type of access. It is distinguished from the options listed below in Table 13.11 on the next page.

Table 13.11: Types of Access

Tag	Scope of Access
`none`	no access
`auth`	for contacting the server
`compare`	to objects for comparison access
`search`	for the employment of search filters
`read`	read access
`write`	write access

slapd compares the access right requested by the client with those granted in `slapd.conf`. The client is granted access if the rules allow a higher or equal right than the requested one. If the client requests higher rights than those declared in the rules, it is denied access.

Example 13.21 shows a simple example for a simple access control that can be arbitrarily developed using regular expressions.

***Example 13.21:** slapd.conf: Example for Access Control*

```
access to  dn.regex="ou=([^,]+),dc=suse,dc=de"
by cn=administrator,ou=$1,dc=suse,dc=de write
by user read
by * none
```

This rule declares that only its respective administrator has write access to an individual `ou` entry. All other authenticated users have read access and the rest of the world has no access.

Note

Establishing Access Rules

If there is no `access to` rule or no matching `by who` directive, access is denied. Only explicitly declared access rights are granted. If no rules are declared at all, the default principle is write access for the administrator and read access for the rest of the world.

Note

Find detailed information and an example configuration for LDAP access rights in the online documentation of the installed openldap2 package.

Apart from the possibility to administer access permissions with the central server configuration file (`slapd.conf`), there is ACI, access control information. ACI allows storage of the access information for individual objects within the LDAP tree. This type of access control is not yet common and is still considered experimental by the developers. Refer to `http://www.openldap.org/faq/data/cache/758.html` for information.

Database-Specific Directives in slapd.conf

Example 13.22: slapd.conf: Database-Specific Directives

```
database ldbm
suffix  "dc=suse,dc=de"
rootdn "cn=admin,dc=suse,dc=de"
# Cleartext passwords, especially for the rootdn, should
# be avoided.  See slappasswd(8) and slapd.conf(5) for details.
# Use of strong authentication encouraged. rootpw secret
# The database directory MUST exist prior to running slapd AND
# should only be accessible by the slapd/tools. Mode 700 recommended.
directory /var/lib/ldap
# Indices to maintain
index   objectClass    eq
```

The type of database, LDBM in this case, is determined in the first line of this section (see Example 13.22). The second line determines, with `suffix`, for which portion of the LDAP tree this server should be responsible. The following `rootdn` determines who owns administrator rights to this server. The user declared here does not need to have an LDAP entry or exist as regular user. The administrator password is set with `rootpw`. Instead of using `secret` here, it is possible to enter the hash of the administrator password created by slappasswd. The `directory` directive indicates the directory (in the file system) where the database directories are stored on the server. The last directive, `index objectClass eq`, results in the maintenance of an index over all object classes. Attributes for which users search most often can be added here according to experience. Custom `Access` rules defined here for the database are used instead of the global `Access` rules.

Starting and Stopping the Servers

Once the LDAP server is fully configured and all desired entries have been made according to the pattern described below in Section 13.7.4, start the LDAP server as `root` by entering `rcldap start`. To stop the server manually, enter the command `rcldap stop`. Request the status of the running LDAP server with `rcldap status`.

The YaST runlevel editor, described in Section 12.5 on page 255, can be used to have the server started and stopped automatically on boot and halt of the system. It is also possible to create the corresponding links to the starting and stopping scripts with the `insserv` command from a command prompt as described in Section 12.4.1 on page 253.

13.7.4 Data Handling in the LDAP Directory

OpenLDAP offers a series of tools for the administration of data in the LDAP directory. The four most important tools for adding to, deleting from, searching through, and modifying the data stock are briefly explained below.

Inserting Data into an LDAP Directory

Once the configuration of your LDAP server in `/etc/openldap/lsapd.conf` is correct and ready to go, meaning that it features appropriate entries for `suffix`, `directory`, `rootdn`, `rootpw`, and `index`, proceed to entering records. OpenLDAP offers the `ldapadd` command for this task. If possible, add the objects to the database in bundles for practical reasons. LDAP is able to process the LDIF format (LDAP Data Interchange Format) to accomplish this. An LDIF file is a simple text file that can contain an arbitrary number of pairs of attribute and value. Refer to the schema files declared in `slapd.conf` for the available object classes and attributes. The LDIF file for creating a rough framework for the example in Figure 13.4 on page 307 would look like that in File 13.23.

***Example 13.23:** Example for an LDIF File*

```
# The SuSE Organization
dn: dc=suse,dc=de
objectClass: dcObject
objectClass: organization
o: SuSE AG
dc: suse
```

```
# The organizational unit development (devel)
dn: ou=devel,dc=suse,dc=de
objectClass: organizationalUnit
ou: devel

# The organizational unit documentation (doc)
dn: ou=doc,dc=suse,dc=de
objectClass: organizationalUnit
ou: doc

# The organizational unit internal IT (it)
dn: ou=it,dc=suse,dc=de
objectClass: organizationalUnit
ou: it
```

Note

Encoding of LDIF Files

LDAP works with UTF-8 (Unicode). Umlauts therefore must be encoded correctly. Use an editor that supports UTF-8 (such as Kate or recent versions of Emacs). Otherwise, it would be necessary to avoid umlauts and other special characters or to use recode to recode the input to UTF-8.

Note

The file is saved with the `.ldif` suffix and is passed to the server with the following command:

```
ldapadd -x -D <dn of the administrator> -W -f <file>.ldif
```

The first option `-x` switches off the authentication with SASL in this case. The `-D` switch declares the user that calls the operation. The valid DN of the administrator is entered here just like it has been configured in `slapd.conf`. In the current example, this would be `cn=admin,dc=suse,dc=de`. The switch `-W` circumvents entering the password on the command line (in clear text) and activates a separate password requesting prompt. This password was previously determined in `slapd.conf` with `rootpw`. The `-f` switch passes the file name. See the details of running `ldapadd` in Example 13.24 on the next page.

Example 13.24: ldapadd with example.ldif

```
ldapadd -x -D cn=admin,dc=suse,dc=de -W -f example.ldif

Enter LDAP password:
adding new entry "dc=suse,dc=de"
adding new entry "ou=devel,dc=suse,dc=de"
adding new entry "ou=doc,dc=suse,dc=de"
adding new entry "ou=it,dc=suse,dc=de"
```

The user data of the individual colleagues can be prepared in separate LDIF files. The following example, shown in Example 13.25, adds the colleague `Tux` to the new LDAP directory.

Example 13.25: LDIF Data for Tux

```
# coworker Tux
dn: cn=Tux Linux,ou=devel,dc=suse,dc=de
objectClass: inetOrgPerson
cn: Tux Linux
givenName: Tux
sn: Linux
mail: tux@suse.de
uid: tux
telephoneNumber: +49 1234 567-8
```

An LDIF file can contain an arbitrary number of objects. It is possible to pass entire directory branches to the server at once or only parts of it as shown in the example of individual objects. If it is necessary to modify some data relatively often, a fine subdivision of single objects is recommended.

Modifying Data in the LDAP Directory

The tool `ldapmodify` is provided for modifying the data stock. The easiest way to do this is to modify the corresponding LDIF file then pass this modified file to the LDAP server. To change the telephone number of colleague Tux from `+49 1234 567-8` to `+49 1234 567-10`, the LDIF file must be edited like in Example 13.26 on the next page.

Example 13.26: Modified LDIF File tux.ldif

```
# coworker Tux
dn: cn=Tux Linux,ou=devel,dc=suse,dc=de
changetype: modify
replace: telephoneNumber
telephoneNumber: +49 1234 567-10
```

Import the modified file into the LDAP directory with the following command:

```
ldapmodify -x -D cn=admin,dc=suse,dc=de -W -f tux.ldif
```

Alternatively, pass the attributes to change directly to `ldapmodify`. The procedure for this is described below:

- Start `ldapmodify` and enter your password:

  ```
  ldapmodify -x -D cn=admin,dc=suse,dc=de -W

  Enter LDAP password:
  ```

- Enter the changes while carefully complying with the syntax in the order it is presented below:

  ```
  dn: cn=Tux Linux,ou=devel,dc=suse,dc=de
  changetype: modify
  replace: telephoneNumber
  telephoneNumber: +49 1234 567-10
  ```

Read detailed information about `ldapmodify` and its syntax in its corresponding man page.

Searching or Reading Data from an LDAP Directory

OpenLDAP provides, with `ldapsearch`, a command line tool for searching data within an LDAP directory and reading data from it. A simple query would have the following syntax:

```
ldapsearch -x -b dc=suse,dc=de "(objectClass=*)"
```

The option -b determines the search base — the section of the tree within which the search should be performed. In the current case, this is `dc=suse,dc=de`. To perform a more finely-grained search in specific subsections of the LDAP directory (for instance, only within the `devel` department), pass this section to ldapsearch with `-b`. The `-x` switch requests the activation of simple authentication. `(objectClass=*)` declares that all objects contained in the directory should be read. This command option can be used after the creation of a new directory tree to verify that all entries have been recorded correctly and the server responds as desired. More information about the use of `ldapsearch` can be found in the corresponding man page (`man ldapsearch`).

Deleting Data from an LDAP Directory

Delete unwanted entries with `ldapdelete`. The syntax is similar to that of the commands described above. To delete, for example, the complete entry for `Tux Linux`, issue the following command:

```
ldapdelete -x -D cn=admin,dc=suse,dc=de -W cn=Tux \
Linux,ou=devel,dc=suse,dc=de
```

13.7.5 For More Information

More complex subjects, like SASL configuration or establishment of a replicating LDAP server that distributes the workload among multiple slaves, were intentionally not included in this chapter. Detailed information about both subjects can be found in the *OpenLDAP 2.1 Administrator's Guide* (see below for references).

The web site of the OpenLDAP project offers exhaustive documentation for beginning and advanced LDAP users:

OpenLDAP Faq-O-Matic A very rich question and answer collection concerning installation, configuration, and employment of OpenLDAP. `http://www.openldap.org/faq/data/cache/1.html`.

Quick Start Guide Brief step-by-step instructions for installing your first LDAP server.`http://www.openldap.org/doc/admin21/quickstart.html` or on an installed system in `/usr/share/doc/packages/openldap2/admin-guide/quickstart.html`

OpenLDAP 2.1 Administrator's Guide
A detailed introduction to all important aspects of LDAP

configuration, including access controls and encryption. http://www.openldap.org/doc/admin21/ or on an installed system in /usr/share/doc/packages/openldap2/admin-guide/index.html

The following redbooks from IBM exist regarding the subject of LDAP:

Understanding LDAP A detailed general introduction to the basic principles of LDAP: http://www.redbooks.ibm.com/redbooks/pdfs/sg244986.pdf.

LDAP Implementation Cookbook
The target audience consists of administrators of *IBM SecureWay Directory*. However, important general information about LDAP is also contained here: http://www.redbooks.ibm.com/redbooks/pdfs/sg245110.pdf.

Printed literature about LDAP:

- Howes, Smith, and Good: *Understanding and Deploying LDAP Directory Services*. Addison-Wesley, 2. Aufl., 2003. (ISBN 0-672-32316-8)
- Hodges: *LDAP System Administration*. O'Reilly & Associates, 2003. (ISBN 1-56592-491-6)

The ultimate reference material for the subject of LDAP is the corresponding RFCs (request for comments), 2251 to 2256.

13.8 NIS — Network Information Service

As soon as multiple UNIX systems in a network want to access common resources, it becomes important that all user and group identities are the same for all machines in that network. The network should be transparent to the user: whatever machine a user uses, he will always find himself in exactly the same environment. This is made possible by means of NIS and NFS services. NFS distributes file systems over a network and is discussed in Section 13.9 on page 325.

NIS (Network Information Service) can be described as a database-like service that provides access to the contents of `/etc/passwd`, `/etc/shadow`, and `/etc/group` across networks. NIS can also be used for other purposes (to make available the contents of files like `/etc/hosts` or `/etc/services`, for instance), but this is beyond the scope of this introduction. People often refer to NIS under the term of "YP", which simply stands for the idea of the network's "yellow pages".

13.8.1 NIS Master and Slave Servers

For the configuration, select 'NIS Server' from the YaST module 'Network Services'. If no NIS server existed so far in your network, activate 'Install and set up a Master NIS Server' in the next screen. If you already have a NIS server (a *master*), you can add a NIS slave server (for example, if you want to configure a new subnetwork). First, the configuration of the master server is described.

If some needed packages are missing, insert the respective CD or DVD as requested to install the packages automatically. Enter the domain name at the top of the configuration dialog, which is shown in Figure 13.5 on the next page. With the check box below, define whether the host should also be a NIS client, enabling users to log in and access data from the NIS server.

To configure additional NIS servers (*slave servers*) in your network afterwards, activate 'Active Slave NIS Server Exists' now. Select 'Fast Map Distribution' to set fast transfer of the database entries from the master to the slave server.

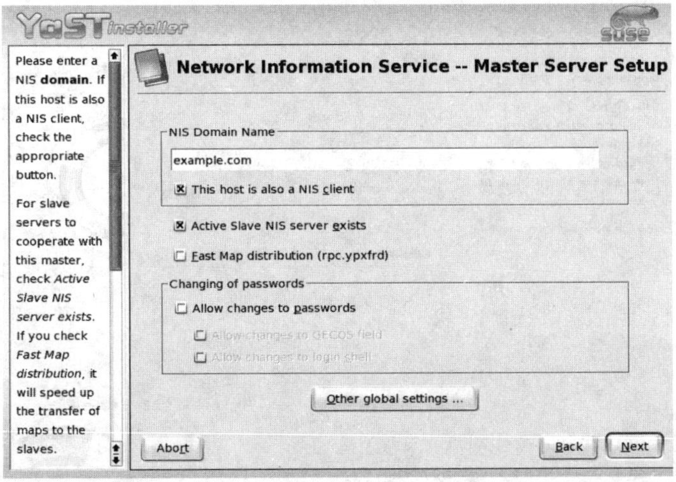

Figure 13.5: YaST: NIS Server Configuration Tool

To allow users in your network (both local users and those managed through the NIS server) to change their passwords on the NIS server (with the command `yppasswd`), activate the corresponding option. This makes 'Allow Changes to GECOS Field' and 'Allow Changes to Login Shell' available. "GECOS" means that the users can also change their names and address settings with the command `ypchfn`. "SHELL" allows users to change their default shell with the command `ypchsh`, for example, to switch from bash to sh.

By clicking 'Other Global Settings...', access a screen, shown in Figure 13.6 on the following page, in which to change the source directory of the NIS server (`/etc/` by default). In addition, passwords and groups can be merged here. The setting should be 'Yes' so the files (`/etc/passwd`, `/etc/shadow`, and `/etc/group`) can be synchronized. Also determine the smallest user and group ID. Press 'OK' to confirm your settings and return to the previous screen. Then click 'Next'.

If you previously enabled 'Active Slave NIS Server Exists', enter the host names used as slaves and click 'Next'. If you do not use slave servers, the slave configuration is skipped and you continue directly to the dialog for the database configuration. Here, specify the *maps*, the partial databases to transfer from the NIS server to the client. The default settings are usually adequate, so normally they should be left unchanged.

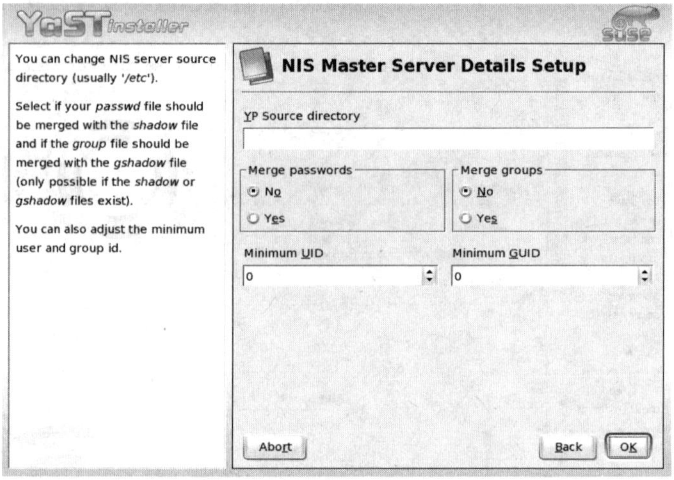

Figure 13.6: *YaST: Changing the Directory and Synchronizing Files for a NIS Server*

'Next' continues to the last dialog, shown in Figure 13.7 on the next page. Specify from which networks requests can be sent to the NIS server. Normally, this is your internal network. In this case, there should be the following two entries:

```
255.0.0.0       127.0.0.0
0.0.0.0         0.0.0.0
```

The first one enables connections from your own host, which is the NIS server. The second one allows all hosts with access to the same network to send requests to the server.

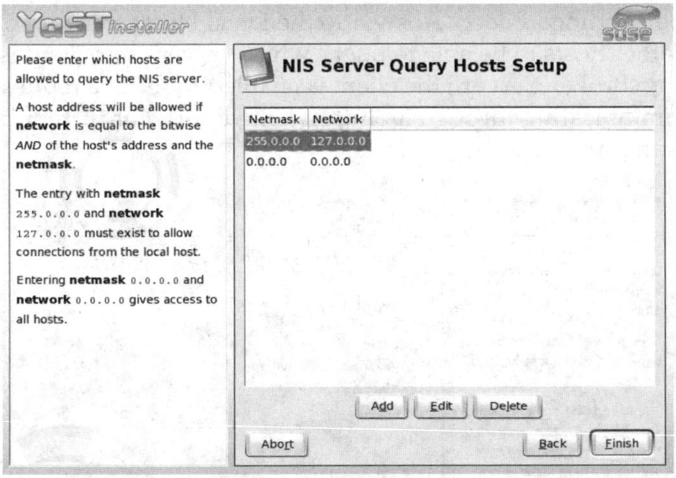

Figure 13.7: YaST: Setting Request Permissions for a NIS Server

13.8.2 The NIS Client Module of YaST

This module facilitates the configuration of the NIS client. After choosing to use NIS and, depending on the circumstances, the automounter, this dialog opens. Select whether the host has a fixed IP address or receives one issued by DHCP. DHCP also provides the NIS domain and the NIS server. For further information about DHCP, see Section 13.10 on page 329. If a static IP address is used, specify the NIS domain and the NIS server manually (see Figure 13.8 on the next page). The button 'Find' makes YaST search for an active NIS server in your network.

In addition, you can specify multiple domains with one default domain. Use 'Add' to specify multiple servers including the broadcast function for the individual domains.

In the expert settings, check 'Answer to the Local Host Only', if you do not want other hosts to be able to query which server your client is using. By checking 'Broken Server', the client is enabled to receive replies from a server communicating through an unprivileged port. For further information, see `man ypbind`.

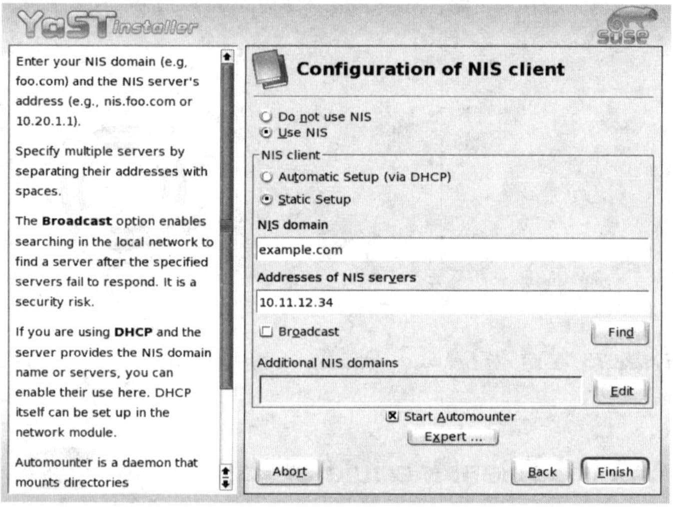

Figure 13.8: *Setting Domain and Address of NIS Server*

13.9 NFS — Shared File Systems

As mentioned in Section 13.8 on page 320, NFS (together with NIS) makes a network transparent to the user. With NFS, it is possible to distribute file systems over the network. It does not matter at which terminal a user is logged in. He will always find himself in the same environment.

As with NIS, NFS is an asymmetric service. There are NFS servers and NFS clients. A machine can be both — it can supply file systems over the network (export) and mount file systems from other hosts (import). Generally, these are servers with a very large hard disk capacity, whose file systems are mounted by other clients.

13.9.1 Importing File Systems with YaST

Any user authorized to do so can mount NFS directories from an NFS server into his own file tree. This can be achieved most easily using the YaST module 'NFS Client'. Just enter the host name of the NFS server, the directory to import, and the mount point at which to mount this directory locally. All this is done after clicking 'Add' in the first dialog (Figure 13.9).

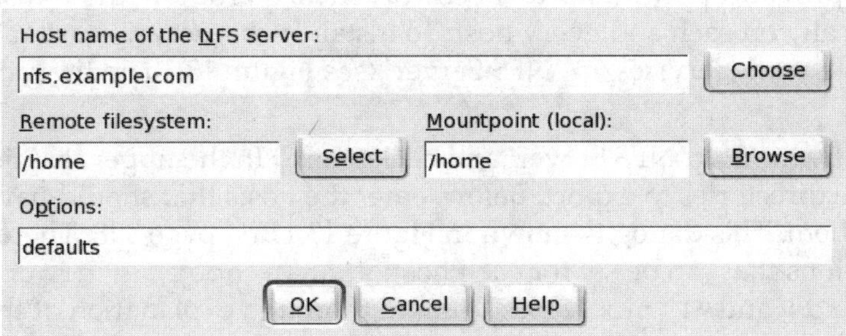

Figure 13.9: NFS Client Configuration with YaST

13.9.2 Importing File Systems Manually

File systems can easily be imported manually from an NFS server. The only prerequisite is a running RPC port mapper, which can be started by entering the command `rcportmap start` as `root`. Once this prerequisite is met, remote file systems exported on the respective machines can be mounted in the file system just like local hard disks using the command `mount` with the following syntax:

```
mount host:remote-path local-path
```

If user directories from the machine sun, for example, should be imported, the following command can be used:

```
mount sun:/home /home
```

13.9.3 Exporting File Systems with YaST

With YaST, turn a host in your network into an NFS server — a server that exports directories and files to all hosts granted access to it. This could be done to provide applications to all coworkers of a group without installing them locally on each and every host. To install such a server, start YaST and select 'Network Services' -> 'NFS Server' (see Figure 13.10 on the facing page).

Next, activate 'Start NFS Server' and click 'Next'. In the upper text field, enter the directories to export. Below, enter the hosts that should have access to them. This dialog is shown in Figure 13.11 on page 328. There are four options that can be set for each host: `single host`, `netgroups`, `wildcards`, and `IP networks`. A more thorough explanation of these options is provided by `man exports`. 'Exit' completes the configuration.

13.9.4 Exporting File Systems Manually

If you do not want to use YaST, make sure the following systems run on the NFS server:

- RPC portmapper (portmap)
- RPC mount daemon (rpc.mountd)
- RPC NFS daemon (rpc.nfsd)

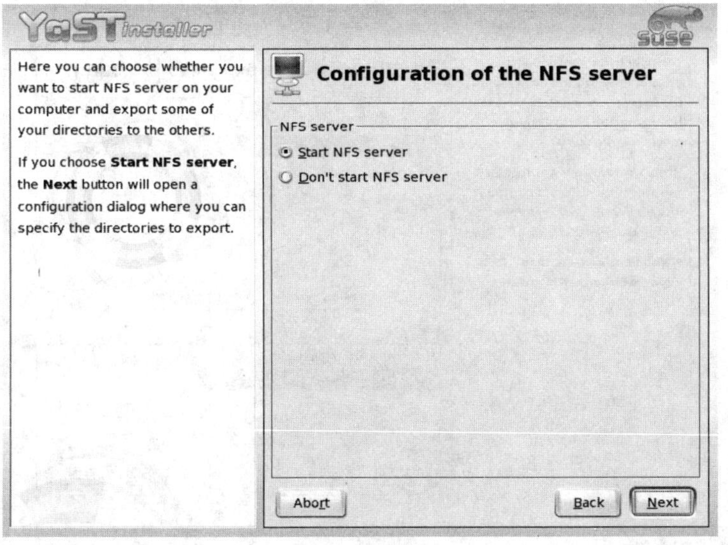

Figure 13.10: *NFS Server Configuration Tool*

For these services to be started by the scripts `/etc/init.d/portmap` and `/etc/init.d/nfsserver` when the system is booted, enter the commands `insserv /etc/init.d/nfsserver` and `insserv /etc/init.d/portmap`. Also define which file systems should be exported to which host in the configuration file `/etc/exports`.

For each directory to export, one line is needed to set which machines may access that directory with what permissions. All subdirectories of this directory are automatically exported as well. Authorized machines are usually specified with their full names (including domain name), but it is possible to use wild cards like `*` or `?` (which expand the same way as in the Bash shell). If no machine is specified here, any machine is allowed to import this file system with the given permissions.

Set permissions for the file system to export in brackets after the machine name. The most important options are:

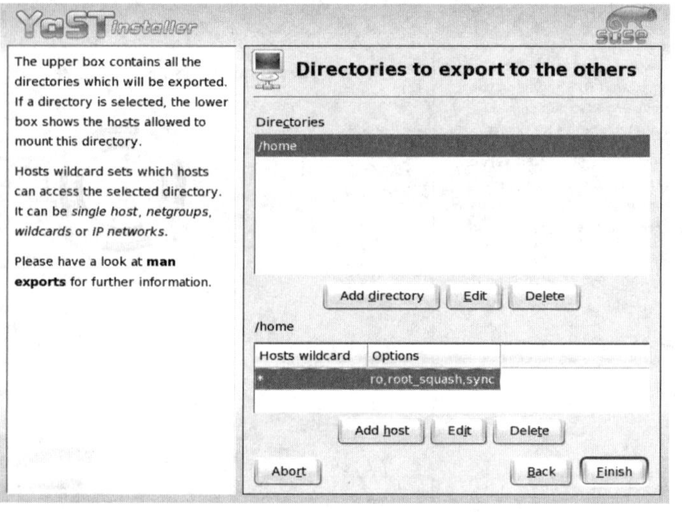

Figure 13.11: *Configuring an NFS Server with YaST*

Table 13.12: *Permissions for Exported File System*

option	meaning
ro	File system is exported with read-only permission (default).
rw	File system is exported with read-write permission.
root_squash	This makes sure the user `root` of the given machine does not have `root` permissions on this file system. This is achieved by assigning user ID `65534` to users with user ID `0` (`root`). This user ID should be set to `nobody` (which is the default).
no_root_squash	Does not assign user ID `0` to user ID `65534`, keeping the `root` permissions valid.
link_relative	Converts absolute links (those beginning with `/`) to a sequence of `../`. This is only useful if the entire file system of a machine is mounted (default).
link_absolute	Symbolic links remain untouched.

map_identity	User IDs are exactly the same on both client and server (default).
map_daemon	Client and server do not have matching user IDs. This tells nfsd to create a conversion table for user IDs. The **ugidd** daemon is required for this to work.

Your `exports` file might look like File 13.27.

Example 13.27: /etc/exports

```
#
# /etc/exports
#
/home             sun(rw)    venus(rw)
/usr/X11          sun(ro)    venus(ro)
/usr/lib/texmf    sun(ro)    venus(rw)
/                 earth(ro,root_squash)
/home/ftp         (ro)
# End of exports
```

`/etc/exports` is read by mountd and nfsd. If you change anything in this file, restart mountd and nfsd for your changes to take effect. This can easily be done with `rcnfsserver restart`.

13.10 DHCP

13.10.1 The DHCP Protocol

The purpose of the *Dynamic Host Configuration Protocol* is to assign network settings centrally from a server rather than configuring them locally on each and every workstation. A client configured to use DHCP does not have control over its own static address. It is enabled to configure itself completely and automatically according to directions from the server.

One way to use DHCP is to identify each client using the hardware address of its network card (which is fixed in most cases) then supply that client with identical settings each time it connects to the server. DHCP can also be configured so the server assigns addresses to each interested host dynamically from an address pool set up for that purpose. In the latter case, the DHCP server will try to assign the same address to the client each time it receives a request from it (even over longer periods). This, of course, will not work if there are more client hosts in the network than network addresses available.

With these possibilities, DHCP can make life easier for system administrators in two ways. Any changes (even bigger ones) related to addresses and the network configuration in general can be implemented centrally by editing the server's configuration file. This is much more convenient than reconfiguring lots of client machines. Also it is much easier to integrate machines, particularly new machines, into the network, as they can be given an IP address from the pool. Retrieving the appropriate network settings from a DHCP server can be especially useful in the case of laptops regularly used in different networks.

A DHCP server not only supplies the IP address and the netmask, but also the host name, domain name, gateway, and name server addresses to be used by the client. In addition to that, DHCP allows for a number of other parameters to be configured in a centralized way, for example, a time server from which clients may poll the current time or even a print server.

The following section gives an overview of DHCP without describing the service in every detail. In particular, we want to show how to use the DHCP server dhcpd in your own network to easily manage its entire setup from one central point.

13.10.2 DHCP Software Packages

Both a DHCP server and DHCP clients are available for SUSE LINUX. The DHCP server available is dhcpd (published by the Internet Software Consortium). On the client side, choose between two different DHCP client programs: dhclient (also from ISC) and the DHCP client daemon in the `dhcpcd` package.

SUSE LINUX installs dhcpcd by default. The program is very easy to handle and will be launched automatically on each system boot to watch for a DHCP server. It does not need a configuration file to do its job and should work out of the box in most standard setups. For more complex situations, use the ISC dhclient, which is controlled by means of the configuration file `/etc/dhclient.conf`.

13.10.3 The DHCP Server dhcpd

The core of any DHCP system is the dynamic host configuration protocol daemon. This server *leases* addresses and watches how they are used, according to the settings as defined in the configuration file `/etc/dhcpd.conf`. By changing the parameters and values in this file, a system administrator can influence the program's behavior in numerous ways. Look at a basic sample `/etc/dhcpd.conf` file:

***Example 13.28:** The Configuration File /etc/dhcpd.conf*

```
default-lease-time 600;         # 10 minutes
max-lease-time 7200;            # 2  hours

option domain-name "kosmos.all";
option domain-name-servers 192.168.1.1, 192.168.1.2;
option broadcast-address 192.168.1.255;
option routers 192.168.1.254;
option subnet-mask 255.255.255.0;

subnet 192.168.1.0 netmask 255.255.255.0
 {
  range 192.168.1.10 192.168.1.20;
  range 192.168.1.100 192.168.1.200;
 }
```

This simple configuration file should be sufficient to get the DHCP server to assign IP addresses in the network. Make sure a semicolon is inserted at the end of each line, because otherwise dhcpd will not be started.

The above sample file can be divided into three sections. The first one defines how many seconds an IP address is leased to a requesting host by default (`default-lease-time`) before it should apply for renewal. The section also includes a statement of the maximum period for which a machine may keep an IP address assigned by the DHCP server without applying for renewal (`max-lease-time`).

In the second part, some basic network parameters are defined on a global level:

- The line `option domain-name` defines the default domain of your network.

- With the entry `option domain-name-servers`, specify up to three values for the DNS servers used to resolve IP addresses into host names (and vice versa). Ideally, configure a name server on your machine or somewhere else in your network before setting up DHCP. That name server should also define a host name for each dynamic address and vice versa. To learn how to configure your own name server, read Section 13.6 on page 293.
- The line `option broadcast-address` defines the broadcast address to be used by the requesting host.
- With `option routers`, tell the server where to send data packets that cannot be delivered to a host on the local network (according to the source and target host address and the subnet mask provided). In most cases, especially in smaller networks, this router is identical to the Internet gateway.
- With `option subnet-mask`, specify the netmask assigned to clients.

The last section of the file is there to define a network, including a subnet mask. To finish, specify the address range that the DHCP daemon should use to assign IP addresses to interested clients. In our example, clients may be given any address between `192.168.1.10` and `192.168.1.20` as well as `192.168.1.100` and `192.168.1.200`.

After editing these few lines, you should be able to activate the DHCP daemon with the command `rcdhcpd start`. It will be ready for use immediately. You can also use the command `rcdhcpd check-syntax` to perform a brief syntax check. If you encounter any unexpected problems with your configuration — the server aborts with an error or does not return "done" on start — you should be able to find out what has gone wrong by looking for information either in the main system log `/var/log/messages` or on console 10 (Ctrl + Alt + F10).

On a default SUSE LINUX system, the DHCP daemon is started in a chroot environment for security reasons. The configuration files must be copied to the chroot environment so the daemon can find them. Normally, there is no need to worry about this because the command `rcdhcpd start` automatically copies the files.

13.10.4 Hosts with Fixed IP Addresses

As mentioned above, DHCP can also be used to assign a predefined, static address to a specific host for each request. As might be expected, addresses assigned explicitly always take priority over addresses from the pool of dynamic addresses. Furthermore, a static address never expires in the way a dynamic address would, for example, if there were not enough addresses available so the server needed to redistribute them among hosts.

To identify a host configured with a *static* address, dhcpd uses the hardware address, which is a globally unique, fixed numerical code consisting of six octet pairs for the identification of all network devices (for example `00:00:45:12:EE:F4`). If the respective lines, like the ones in File 13.29, are added to the configuration file of File 13.28 on page 331, the DHCP daemon will assign the same set of data to the corresponding host under all circumstances.

***Example 13.29:** Additions to the Configuration File*

```
host earth {
hardware ethernet 00:00:45:12:EE:F4;
fixed-address 192.168.1.21;
}
```

The structure of this entry is almost self-explanatory: The name of the respective host (`host` <host name>) is entered in the first line and the MAC address in the second line. On Linux hosts, this address can be determined with the command `ifstatus` followed by the network device (for example `eth0`). If necessary, activate the network card first: `ifup eth0`. The output should contain something like

```
link/ether 00:00:45:12:EE:F4
```

In the above example, a host with a network card having the MAC address `00:00:45:12:EE:F4` is assigned the IP address `192.168.1.21` and the host name earth automatically. The type of hardware to enter is `ethernet` in nearly all cases, although `token-ring`, which is often found on IBM systems, is also supported.

13.10.5 The SUSE LINUX Version

To improve security, the SUSE version of the ISC's DHCP server comes with the non-root/chroot patch by Ari Edelkind applied. This enables dhcpd to:

- run with the permissions of `nobody`
- run in a chroot environment (`/var/lib/dhcp/`)

To make this possible, the configuration file `/etc/dhcpd.conf` needs to be located in `/var/lib/dhcp/etc/`. The corresponding init script automatically copies the file to this directory upon starting.

The server's behavior with regard to this feature can be controlled through the configuration file `/etc/sysconfig/dhcpd`. To continue running dhcpd without the chroot environment, set the variable `DHCPD_RUN_CHROOTED` in `/etc/sysconfig/dhcpd` to "no".

To enable dhcpd to resolve host names even from within the chroot environment, some other configuration files need to be copied as well, namely:

- /etc/localtime
- /etc/host.conf
- /etc/hosts
- /etc/resolv.conf

These files are copied to `/var/lib/dhcp/etc/` when starting the init script. These copies must be taken into account for any changes that they require, if they are dynamically modified by scripts like `/etc/ppp/ip-up`. However, there should be no need to worry about this if the configuration file only specifies IP addresses (instead of host names).

If your configuration includes additional files that should be copied into the chroot environment, specify these under the variable `DHCPD_CONF_INCLUDE_FILES` in the file `etc/sysconfig/dhcpd`. To make sure the DHCP logging facility keeps working even after a restart of the syslog daemon, it is necessary to add the option `"-a /var/lib/dhcp/dev/log"` under `SYSLOGD_PARAMS` in the file `/etc/sysconfig/syslog`.

13.10.6 For More Information

For more information, the page of the *Internet Software Consortium* on the subject (http://www.isc.org/products/DHCP/) is a good source to read about the details of DHCP, including about version 3 of the protocol, currently in beta testing. Apart from that, you can always rely on the man pages for further help. Try man dhcpd, man dhcpd.conf, man dhcpd.leases, and man dhcp-options. Also, several books about DHCP have been published over the years that take an in-depth look at the topic.

With dhcpd, it is even possible to offer a file to a requesting host, as defined with the parameter filename, and for this file to contain a bootable Linux kernel. This allows you to build client hosts that do not need a hard disk — they are enabled to load both their operating system and their network data over the network (*diskless clients*), which could be an interesting option for both cost and security reasons.

13.11 Time Synchronization with xntp

Keeping track of the exact current time is an important aspect in many processes in a computer system. Computers have a built-in clock for this. Unfortunately, this clock often does not meet the requirements of some applications, like databases. This problem is usually solved by repeatedly correcting the time of the local computer by hand or over a network. A computer clock should, at best, never be set back and the amount it gets set forward should not exceed a certain time interval. It is relatively simple to occasionally correct the time kept by the computer clock with ntpdate. This, however, results in a sudden jump in time that may not be tolerated by all applications.

An interesting approach to solving this problem is offered by xntp. xntp continuously corrects the local computer clock by following statistically gathered correction data. It also constantly corrects the local time by querying time servers in the network. The third correction method offers accessing local time normals, like radio-controlled clocks.

13.11.1 Configuration in a Network

The default setting of xntp in SUSE LINUX is that of only respecting the local computer clock as a time reference. The most simple possibility to access a time server in the network is the declaration of *server* parameters. For example, if a time server is available with the name `ntp.example.com`, add this server to the file `/etc/ntp.conf` in the format `server ntp.example.com`.

Enter additional time servers by inserting additional lines with the keyword *server*. After xntpd has been started with the command `rcxntpd start`, the application waits for one hour until the time has stabilized before creating the *drift file* for the correction of the local computer clock. The *drift file* offers the long-term advantage of predicting, right after booting the computer, by how much the hardware clock will be off over time. The correction becomes immediately effective, which ensures a high stability of the computer time.

The name of the time server in your network does not need to be known if it is also available by broadcast. This can be reflected in the configuration file `/etc/ntp.conf` with the parameter `broadcastclient`. However, some authentication mechanisms should be activated in this case to prevent a faulty time server in the network from changing the time on your computer.

Any xntpd in the network can also commonly be accessed as a time server. To run xntpd with broadcasts, activate the broadcast option:

```
broadcast 192.168.0.255
```

Adjust the broadcast address to your specific case. It should, however, be ensured that the time server really serves the correct time. Time normals are well-suited for this.

13.11.2 Establishing a Local Time Normal

The program package xntp also contains drivers that allow connection to local time normals. A list of supported clocks is provided in the package xntp-doc in the file `/usr/share/doc/packages/xntp-doc/html/refclock.htm`. Each driver has been assigned a number. The actual configuration in xntp is done over pseudo-IPs. The clocks are registered in the file `/etc/ntp.conf` as if they were time servers available over the network.

These clocks are assigned special IP addresses that follow the pattern 127.127.t.u. The value t is assigned from the previously mentioned file with the reference clocks. The value u is the device number that only then deviates from 0 if more than one clock of the same type is connected to the computer. For example, a "Type 8 Generic Reference Driver (PARSE)" clock has the pseudo-IP address 127.127.8.0.

The various drivers usually have special parameters that describe the configuration in more detail. The file /usr/share/doc/packages/xntp-doc/html/refclock.htm provides links to the corresponding driver page describing these parameters. It is, for instance, necessary to provide an additional mode that specifies the clock more accurately. The module "Conrad DCF77 receiver module", for example, has mode 5. The keyword prefer must be specified to make xntp accept this clock as a reference. The complete server entry for a *Conrad DCF77 receiver module* therefore is:

```
server 127.127.8.0 mode 5 prefer
```

Other clocks follow the same pattern. Find xntp documentation in the directory /usr/share/doc/packages/xntp-doc/html after the installation of the package xntp-doc.

The Apache Web Server

With a share of more than sixty percent, Apache is the world's most widely-used web server (source: `http://www.netcraft.com`). For web applications, Apache is often combined with Linux, the database MySQL, and the programming languages PHP and Perl. This combination is commonly referred to as *LAMP*.

14.1 Basics

14.1.1 Web Server

A web server issues `HTML` pages requested by a client. These pages can be stored in a directory (passive or static pages) or generated in response to a query (active contents).

14.1.2 HTTP

The clients are usually web browsers, like Konqueror or Mozilla. Communication between the browser and the web server takes place by way of the *H*yper*T*ext *T*ransfer *P*rotocol (HTTP). The current version, HTTP 1.1, is documented in RFC 2068 and in the update RFC 2616. These RFCs are available at `http://www.w3.org`.

14.1.3 URLs

Clients use URLs, such as `http://www.suse.com/index_us.html`, to request pages from the server. A URL consists of:

- A protocol. Frequently-used protocols:
  - ▷ `http://` HTTP protocol
  - ▷ `https://` Secure, encrypted version of HTTP
  - ▷ `ftp://` file transfer protocol for uploading and downloading files
- A domain, in this example, `www.suse.com`. The domain can be subdivided in two parts. The first part (`www`) points to a computer. The second part (`suse.com`) is the actual domain. Together, they are referred to as FQDN (fully qualified domain name).
- A resource, in this example, `index_us.html`. This part specifies the full path to the resource. The resource can be a file, as in this example. However, it can also be a CGI script, a Java server page, or some other resource.

The responsible Internet mechanism (such as the domain name system, DNS) conveys the query to the domain, directing it to one or several computers hosting the resource. Apache then delivers the actual resource (in this example, the page `index_us.html`) from its file directory. In this case, the file is located in the top level of the directory. However, resources can also be located in subdirectories, as in `http://www.suse.com/us/business/services/support/index.html`.

The file path is relative to the `DocumentRoot`, which can be changed in the configuration file. Section 14.7.2 on page 347 describes how this is done.

14.1.4 Automatic Display of a Default Page

If no default page is specified, Apache automatically appends one of the common names to the URL. The most frequently-used name for such pages is `index.html`. This function, together with the actual page names to be used by the server, can be configured as described in Section 14.7.2 on page 348. In our example, `http://www.suse.com` is sufficient to prompt the server to deliver the page `http://www.suse.com/index_us.html`.

14.2 Setting up the HTTP Server with YaST

Apache 2 can easily be set up with the help of YaST, but some knowledge about the subject is needed to set up a web server this way. After selecting 'Network Services' -> 'HTTP Server' in the YaST control center, you may be prompted for the installation of some packages that are still missing. As soon as everything is installed, YaST displays the configuration dialog.

In this dialog, first enable the HTTP service itself, which requires setting the following three options: 'Server Name', 'Server Administrator E-Mail', and 'Listen on'. The last option is already set to the default of port 80. You can then use 'Add' to set further options. Selecting 'Edit' enables changing the value of the highlighted option. Selecting 'Delete' allows removing it completely.

With 'Advanced', view the logs ('Show Access Log' and 'Show Error Log') or specify the 'Server Modules' to load. The latter opens a dialog in which to enable or disable modules by selecting 'Toggle Status' and add modules by selecting 'Add Module'.

14.3 Apache Modules

By means of modules, Apache can be expanded with a wide range of functions. For example, Apache can execute CGI scripts in diverse programming languages by means of modules. Apart from Perl and PHP, additional scripting languages, such as Python or Ruby, are also available. Furthermore, there are modules for secure data transmission (Secure Sockets Layer, SSL), user authentication, expanded logging, and other functions.

By means of custom modules, Apache can be adapted to all kinds of requirements and preferences. This requires a certain amount of know-how. For further information, refer to Section 14.13.4 on page 363.

When Apache processes a query, several "handlers" can be specified for handling the query (by means of directives in the configuration file). These handlers can be part of Apache or a module invoked for processing the query. Thus, this procedure can be arranged in a very flexible way. It is also possible to use your own custom modules with Apache to influence the way in which requests are processed.

The modularization in Apache 2 has reached an advanced level, where almost everything except some minor tasks is handled by means of modules. In Apache 2, even HTTP is processed by way of modules. Accordingly, Apache 2 does not necessarily need to be a web server. It can also be used for completely different purposes with other modules. For example, there is a proof-of-concept mail server (POP3) module based on Apache.

Apache supports a number of useful features, some of which are described below.

Virtual Hosts Support for virtual hosts means that a single instance of Apache and a single machine can be used for several web sites. For the users, the web server appears as several independent web servers. The virtual hosts can be configured on different IP addresses or on the basis of names. Thus, you can save the acquisition costs and administration workload for additional machines.

Flexible URL Rewriting Apache offers a number of possibilities for manipulating and rewriting URLs. Check the Apache documentation for details.

Content Negotiation Apache can deliver a page that is adapted to the capabilities of the client (browser). For example, simple versions without frames can be delivered for older browsers or browsers that only operate in text mode, such as Lynx. In this way, the notorious

JavaScript incompatibility of various browsers can be circumvented by delivering a special page version for every browser (provided you are prepared to adapt the JavaScript code for each individual browser).

Flexible Error Handling You can react in a flexible way and provide a suitable response in the event of an error, such as nonexistent pages. The response can even be generated actively, for example, with CGI.

14.4 New Features of Apache 2

The following is a list of the main new features of Apache 2. For detailed information about version 2.0 of the Apache HTTP server, refer to `http://httpd.apache.org/docs-2.0/en/`.

- Multiple queries may be processed as threads or processes. The process management has been relocated to a separate module, called the multiprocessing module (MPM). Depending on the MPM, Apache 2 responds to queries in different ways, with different effects on the performance and the use of modules. Details are provided below.
- The innards of Apache have been thoroughly revised. Apache now uses a new, special base library (Apache Portable Runtime, APR) as the interface to system functions and for the memory management. Moreover, important and widespread modules, such as mod_gzip (successor: mod_deflate) and mod_ssl, which have a profound impact on the processing of requests, are now integrated more fully in Apache.
- Apache 2 supports the Internet protocol IPv6.
- A new mechanism now enables manufacturers of modules to specify the desired loading sequence for modules. Thus, users are no longer required to do this themselves. The order in which modules are executed is often significant. Previously, it was determined by means of the loading sequence. For example, a module that only gives authenticated users access to certain resources must be run first to prevent the pages from being displayed to users who do not have any access permissions.
- Queries to and replies from Apache can be processed with filters.

- Support for files that are larger than 2 GB (large file support, LFS) on 32-bit systems.
- Some of the newer modules are only available for Apache 2.
- Multilanguage error responses.

14.5 Threads

A thread is a "lighter" form of a process. The advantage of a thread over a process is its lower resource consumption. Therefore, the use of threads instead of processes increases the performance. The disadvantage is that applications executed in a thread environment must be thread-safe. This means that:

- Functions (or the methods in object-oriented applications) must be reentrant — a function with the same input always returns the same result, even if other threads concurrently execute the same function. Accordingly, functions must be programmed in such a way that they can be executed simultaneously by severals threads.
- The access to resources (usually variables) must be arranged in such a way that concurrent threads do not conflict.

Apache 2 handles queries as separate processes or in a mixed mode combining processes and threads. The MPM *prefork* is responsible for the execution as process. The MPM *worker* prompts the execution as thread. Select the MPM to use during the installation (see Section 14.6). The third mode — *perchild* — is not yet fully mature and is therefore not available for installation in SUSE LINUX.

14.6 Installation

14.6.1 Package Selection in YaST

For a basic installation, it is sufficient to select the Apache package `apache2`. Additionally, you may install one of the MPM (multiprocessing module) packages, such as `apache2-prefork` or `apache2-worker`. When choosing an MPM, remember that the thread-based worker MPM cannot be used with `mod_php4`, as some of the libraries of `mod_php4` are not yet thread-safe.

14.6.2 Activating Apache

After installation, Apache will not be started automatically. To start Apache, activate it in the runlevel editor. To start it permanently when the system is booted, check runlevels 3 and 5 in the runlevel editor. To test whether Apache is running, go to `http://localhost/` in a browser. If Apache is active, you will see an example page, provided `apache2-example-pages` is installed.

14.6.3 Modules for Active Contents

To use active contents with the help of modules, install the modules for the respective programming languages. These are `apache2-mod_perl` for Perl, `mod_php4` for PHP, and `mod_python` for Python. The use of these modules is covered in Section 14.9.5 on page 354.

14.6.4 Other Recommended Packages

Additionally, you should install the extensive documentation provided in `apache2-doc`. An alias (Section 14.7 on the next page explains what an alias is) is available for the documentation, enabling you to access it with the URL `http://localhost/manual` following the installation.

To develop modules for Apache or compile third-party modules, install `apache2-devel` and the needed development tools. These include the `apxs` tools, which are described in Section 14.6.5.

14.6.5 Installation of Modules with apxs

`apxs2` is an important tool for module developers. This program enables the compilation and installation of modules from source code with a single command (including the required changes to the configuration files). Furthermore, you can also install modules available as object files (extension `.o`) or static libraries (extension `.a`). When installing from sources, `apxs2` creates a dynamic shared object (DSO), which is directly used by Apache as a module.

The installation of a module from source code can be performed with a command like `apxs2 -c -i -a mod_foo.c`. Other options of `apxs2` are described in its man page.

apxs2 is available in several versions: apxs2, apxs2-prefork, and apxs2-worker. apxs2 installs modules so they can be used for all MPMs. The other two programs install modules so they can only be used for the respective MPMs (prefork or worker). apxs2 installs modules in /usr/lib/apache2/ and apxs2-prefork installs modules in /usr/lib/apache2-prefork/.

The option -a should not be used with Apache 2, as this would cause the changes to be written directly to /etc/apache2/httpd.conf. Rather, modules should be activated by means of the entry APACHE_MODULES in /etc/sysconfig/apache2 as described in Section 14.7.1.

14.7 Configuration

Following the installation of Apache, additional changes are only necessary if you have special needs or preferences. Apache can be configured either with SuSEconfig or by directly editing the file /etc/apache2/httpd.conf.

14.7.1 Configuration with SuSEconfig

The settings made in /etc/sysconfig/apache2 are applied to the Apache configuration files by SuSEconfig. The offered configuration options should be sufficient for most scenarios. Each variable found in the file is provided with a comment to explain its effect.

Custom Configuration Files

Instead of performing changes directly in the configuration file /etc/apache2/httpd.conf, you can designate your own configuration file (such as httpd.conf.local) with the help of the variable APACHE_CONF_INCLUDE_FILES. Consequently, the file will be interpreted by the main configuration file. In this way, changes to the configuration will be retained even if the file /etc/apache2/httpd.conf is overwritten during a new installation.

Modules

Modules installed with YaST can be activated by including the name of the module in the list specified under the variable APACHE_MODULES. This variable is defined in the file /etc/sysconfig/apache2.

Flags

APACHE_SERVER_FLAGS can be used to specify flags that activate or deactivate certain sections of the configuration file. If a section in the configuration file is enclosed in

```
<IfDefine someflag>
.
.
.
</IfDefine>
```

it will only be activated if the respective flag is set in ACTIVE_SERVER_-FLAGS: ACTIVE_SERVER_FLAGS = ... someflag ... . In this way, extensive sections of the configuration file can easily be activated or deactivated for test purposes.

14.7.2 Manual Configuration

You can edit the configuration file /etc/apache2/httpd.conf to enable features that are not available through the settings defined in /etc/sysconfig/apache2. The following sections describe some of the parameters that can be set. They are listed below in the order in which they appear in the file.

DocumentRoot

One basic setting is the DocumentRoot — the directory under which Apache expects web pages the server should deliver. For the default virtual host, it is set to /srv/www/htdocs. Normally, this setting does not need to be changed.

Timeout

Specifies the waiting period after which the server reports a time-out for a request.

MaxClients

The maximum number of clients Apache can handle concurrently. The default setting is 150, but this value may be too small for a heavily frequented web site.

LoadModule

The `LoadModule` directives specify the modules to load. In the case of Apache 2, the loading sequence is determined by the modules themselves (see Section 14.4 on page 343). These directives also specify the file containing the module.

Port

Specifies the port on which Apache listens for queries. Usually, this is port 80, the default port for HTTP. Normally, this setting should not be changed. One reason for letting Apache listen to another port may be the test of a new version of a web site. In this way, the operational version of the web site continues to be accessible via default port 80.

Another reason may be that you merely want to make pages available on the intranet, as they contain information that is not intended for the public. For this purpose, set the port to a value like `8080` and block external access to this port by means of the firewall. In this way, the server can be protected against external access.

Directory

This directive can be used to set the access permissions and other permissions for a directory. A directive of this kind also exists for the `DocumentRoot`. The directory name specified here must be changed whenever the `DocumentRoot` is changed.

DirectoryIndex

Here, determine for which files Apache should search to complete a URL lacking a file specification. The default setting is `index.html`. For example, if the client requests the URL `http://www.xyz.com/foo/bar` and the directory `foo/bar` containing a file called `index.html` exists under the `DocumentRoot`, Apache returns this page to the client.

AllowOverride

Every directory from which Apache delivers documents may contain a file that can override the global access permissions and other settings for this directory. These settings are applied recursively to the current directory and its subdirectories until they are overridden by another such file in a subdirectory. Accordingly, settings specified in such a file are applied globally if it is located in the `DocumentRoot`. Such files normally have the name `.htaccess`, but this can be changed as described in Section 14.7.2.

Use `AllowOverride` to determine if the settings specified in local files may override the global settings. Possible values are `None`, `All`, and any combination of `Options`, `FileInfo`, `AuthConfig`, and `Limit`. The meanings of these values are described in detail in the Apache documentation. The (safe) default setting is `None`.

Order

This option determines the order in which the settings for `Allow` and `Deny` access permissions are applied. The default setting is:

```
Order allow,deny
```

Accordingly, the access permissions for allowed accesses are applied first, followed by the access permissions for denied accesses. The underlying approach is based on one of the following:

allow all allow every access and define exceptions

deny all deny every access and define exceptions

Example for `deny all`:

```
Order deny,allow
Deny from all
Allow from example.com
Allow from 10.1.0.0/255.255.0.0
```

AccessFileName

Here, set the name for the files that can override the global access permissions and other settings for directories delivered by Apache (see Section 14.7.2 on the facing page). The default setting is `.htaccess`.

ErrorLog

Specifies the name of the file in which Apache logs error messages. The default setting is `/var/log/httpd/errorlog`. Error messages for virtual hosts (see Section 14.10 on page 358) are also logged in this file, unless a special log file was specified in the `VirtualHost` section of the configuration file.

LogLevel

Error messages are classified according to various severity levels. This setting specifies the severity level from which error messages are logged. Setting it to a level causes error messages of this and higher severity levels to be logged. The default setting is `warn`.

Alias

Using an alias, specify a shortcut for a directory that enables direct access to this directory. For example, the alias `/manual/` enables access to the directory `/srv/www/htdocs/manual` even if the `DocumentRoot` is set to a directory other than `/srv/www/htdocs` (the alias will make no difference at all if the `DocumentRoot` is set to that directory). With this alias, `http://localhost/manual` enables direct access to the respective directory. To define the permissions for the new target directory as specified with an `Alias` directive, you may want to specify a `Directory` directive for it (see Section 14.7.2 on page 348)

ScriptAlias

This directive is similar to `Alias`. In addition, it indicates that the files in the target directory should be treated as CGI scripts.

Server-Side Includes

Server-side includes can be activated by searching all executable files for SSIs. This can be done with the following instruction:

```
<IfModule mod_include.c>
XBitHack on </IfModule>
```

To search a file for SSIs, use the command `chmod +x` ⟨*filename*⟩ to make the file executable. Alternatively, explicitly specify the file type to search for SSIs. This can be done with the following instruction:

```
AddType text/html .shtml
AddHandler server-parsed .shtml
```

It is *not* advisable to simply state `.html`, as this will cause Apache to search all pages for SSIs (even those that definitely do not contain any), which greatly impedes the performance. In SUSE LINUX, these two directives are already included in the configuration files, so normally no changes are necessary.

UserDir

With the help of the module `mod_userdir` and the directive `UserDir`, specify a directory in a user's home directory from which files may be published through Apache. This can be configured in SuSEconfig by setting the variable `HTTPD_SEC_PUBLIC_HTML` accordingly. To enable the publishing of files, the variable must be set to `yes`. This results in the following entry in the file `/etc/httpd/suse_public_html.conf` (which is interpreted by `/etc/apache2/httpd.conf`).

```
<IfModule mod_userdir.c>
UserDir public_html
</IfModule>
```

14.8 Using Apache

To display static web pages with Apache, simply place your files in the correct directory. In SUSE LINUX, the correct directory is `/srv/www/htdocs`. A few small example pages may already be installed there. Use these pages to check if Apache was installed correctly and is currently active. Subsequently, you can simply overwrite or uninstall these pages. Custom CGI scripts are installed in `/srv/www/cgi-bin`.

During operation, Apache writes log messages to the file `/var/log/httpd/access_log` or `/var/log/apache2/access_log`. These messages show which resources were requested and delivered at what time and with which method (`GET`, `POST`, etc.). Error messages are logged to `/var/log/apache2`.

14.9 Active Contents

Apache provides several possibilities for the delivery of active contents. Active contents are HTML pages that are generated on the basis of variable input data from the client, such as search engines that respond to the input of one or several search strings (possibly interlinked with logical operators like AND or OR) by returning a list of pages containing these search strings.

Apache offers three ways of generating active contents:

Server Side Includes (SSI) These are directives that are embedded in an HTML page by means of special comments. Apache interprets the content of the comments and delivers the result as part of the HTML page.

Common Gateway Interface (CGI)
These are programs that are located in certain directories. Apache forwards the parameters transmitted by the client to these programs and returns the output of the programs. This kind of programming is quite easy, especially since existing command-line programs can be designed in such a way that they accept input from Apache and return their output to Apache.

Module Apache offers interfaces for executing any modules within the scope of request processing. Apache gives these programs access to important information, such as the request or the HTTP headers. Programs can take part in the generation of active contents as well as in other functions (such as authentication). The programming of such modules requires some expertise. The advantages of this approach are high performance and possibilities that exceed those of SSI and CGI.

While CGI scripts are executed directly by Apache (under the user ID of their owner), modules are controlled by a persistent interpreter that is embedded in Apache. In this way, separate processes do not need to be started and terminated for every request (this would result in a considerable overhead for the process management, memory management, etc.). Rather, the script is handled by the interpreter running under the ID of the web server.

However, this approach has a catch. Compared to modules, CGI scripts are relatively tolerant of careless programming. With CGI scripts, errors, such as a failure to release resources and memory, do not have a lasting effect, because the programs are terminated after the request has been processed. This results in the clearance of memory that was not released by the program due to a programming error. With modules, the effects of programming errors accumulate, as the interpreter is persistent. If the server is not restarted and the interpreter runs for several months, the failure to release resources, such as database connections, can be quite disturbing.

14.9.1 Server Side Includes: SSI

Server-side includes are directives that are embedded in special comments and executed by Apache. The result is embedded in the output. For example, the current date can be printed with `<!--#echo var="DATE_LOCAL" -->`. The # at the end of the opening comment mark `<!––` shows Apache that this is an SSI directive and not a simple comment.

SSIs can be activated in several ways. The easiest approach is to search all executable files for SSIs. Another approach is to specify certain file types to search for SSIs. Both settings are explained in Section 14.7.2 on page 350.

14.9.2 Common Gateway Interface: CGI

CGI is the abbreviation for *Common Gateway Interface*. With CGI, the server does not simply deliver a static HTML page, but executes a program that generates the page. This enables the generation of pages representing the result of a calculation, such as the result of the search in a database. By means of arguments passed to the executed program, the program can return an individual response page for every request.

The main advantage of CGI is that this technology is quite simple. The program merely must exist in a specific directory to be executed by the web server just like a command-line program. The server sends the program output on the standard output channel (`stdout`) to the client.

14.9.3 GET and POST

Input parameters can be passed to the server with `GET` or `POST`. Depending on which method is used, the server passes the parameters to the script in various ways. With `POST`, the server passes the parameters to the program on the standard input channel (`stdin`). The program would receive its input in the same way when started from a console.

With `GET`, the server uses the environment variable `QUERY_STRING` to pass the parameters to the program. An environment variable is a variable made available globally by the system (such as the variable `PATH`, which contains a list of paths the system searches for executable commands when the user enters a command).

14.9.4 Languages for CGI

Theoretically, CGI programs can be written in any programming language. Usually, scripting languages (interpreted languages), such as Perl or PHP, are used for this purpose. If speed is critical, C or C++ may be more suitable.

In the simplest case, Apache looks for these programs in a specific directory (`cgi-bin`). This directory can be set in the configuration file, described in Section 14.7 on page 346).

If necessary, additional directories can be specified. In this case, Apache searches these directories for executable programs. However, this represents a security risk, as any user will be able to let Apache execute programs (some of which may be malicious). If executable programs are restricted to `cgi-bin`, the administrator can easily see who places which scripts and programs in this directory and check them for any malicious intent.

14.9.5 Generating Active Contents with Modules

A variety of modules is available for use with Apache. The term "module" is used in two different senses. First, there are modules that can be integrated in Apache for the purpose of handling specific functions, such as modules for embedding programming languages. These modules are introduced below.

Second, in connection with programming languages, modules refer to an independent group of functions, classes, and variables. These modules are integrated in a program to provide a certain functionality, such as the CGI modules available for all scripting languages. These modules facilitate the programming of CGI applications by providing various functions, such as methods for reading the request parameters and for the HTML output.

14.9.6 mod_perl

Perl is a popular, proven scripting language. There are numerous modules and libraries for Perl, including a library for expanding the Apache configuration file. The home page for Perl is `http://www.perl.com/`. A range of libraries for Perl is available in the Comprehensive Perl Archive Network (CPAN) at `http://www.cpan.org/`.

Setting up mod_perl

To set up mod_perl in SUSE LINUX, simply install the respective package (see Section 14.6 on page 344). Following the installation, the Apache configuration file will include the necessary entries (see /etc/apache2/mod_perl-startup.pl). Information about mod_perl is available at http://perl.apache.org/.

mod_perl versus CGI

In the simplest case, run a previous CGI script as a mod_perl script by requesting it with a different URL. The configuration file contains aliases that point to the same directory and execute any scripts it contains either via CGI or via mod_perl. All these entries already exist in the configuration file. The alias entry for CGI is as follows:

```
ScriptAlias /cgi-bin/ "/srv/www/cgi-bin/"
```

The entries for mod_perl are as follows:

```
<IfModule mod_perl.c>
# Provide two aliases to the same cgi-bin directory,
# to see the effects of the 2 different mod_perl modes.
# for Apache::Registry Mode
ScriptAlias /perl/          "/srv/www/cgi-bin/"
# for Apache::Perlrun Mode
ScriptAlias /cgi-perl/      "/srv/www/cgi-bin/"
</IfModule>
```

The following entries are also needed for mod_perl. These entries already exist in the configuration file.

```
#
# If mod_perl is activated, load configuration information
#
<IfModule mod_perl.c>
Perlrequire /usr/include/apache/modules/perl/startup.perl
PerlModule Apache::Registry

#
# set Apache::Registry Mode for /perl Alias
#
<Location /perl>
SetHandler  perl-script
PerlHandler Apache::Registry
Options ExecCGI
PerlSendHeader On
```

```
</Location>

#
# set Apache::PerlRun Mode for /cgi-perl Alias
#
<Location /cgi-perl>
SetHandler  perl-script
PerlHandler Apache::PerlRun
Options ExecCGI
PerlSendHeader On
</Location>

</IfModule>
```

These entries create aliases for the `Apache::Registry` and `Apache::PerlRun` modes. The difference between these two modes is as follows:

Apache::Registry All scripts are compiled and kept in a cache. Every script is applied as the content of a subroutine. Although this is good for performance, there is a disadvantage: the scripts must be programmed extremely carefully, as the variables and subroutines persist between the requests. This means that you must reset the variables to enable their use for the next request. If, for example, the credit card number of a customer is stored in a variable in an online banking script, this number could appear again when the next customer uses the application and requests the same script.

Apache::PerlRun The scripts are recompiled for every request. Variables and subroutines disappear from the namespace between the requests (the namespace is the entirety of all variable names and routine names that are defined at a given time during the existence of a script). Therefore, `Apache::PerlRun` does not necessitate painstaking programming, as all variables are reinitialized when the script is started and no values are kept from previous requests. For this reason, `Apache::PerlRun` is slower than `Apache::Registry` but still a lot faster than CGI (in spite of some similarities to CGI), because no separate process is started for the interpreter.

14.9.7 mod_php4

PHP is a programming language that was especially developed for use with web servers. In contrast to other languages whose commands are stored in separate files (scripts), the PHP commands are embedded in an HTML page (similar to SSI). The PHP interpreter processes the PHP commands and embeds the processing result in the HTML page.

The home page for PHP is `http://www.php.net/`. For PHP to work, install `mod_php4-core` and, in addition, `apache2-mod_php4` for Apache 2.

14.9.8 mod_python

Python is an object-oriented programming language with a very clear and legible syntax. An unusual but convenient feature is that the program structure depends on the indentation. Blocks are not defined with braces (as in C and Perl) or other demarcation elements (such as `begin` and `end`), but by their level of indentation. The package to install is `apache2-mod_python`.

More information about this language is available at `http://www.python.org/`. For more information about `mod_python`, visit the URL `http://www.modpython.org/`.

14.9.9 mod_ruby

Ruby is a relatively new, object-oriented high-level programming language that resembles certain aspects of Perl and Python and is ideal for scripts. Like Python, it has a clean, transparent syntax. On the other hand, Python has adopted abbreviations, such as `$.r` for the number of the last line read in the input file — a feature that is welcomed by some programmers and abhorred by others. The basic concept of Ruby closely resembles Smalltalk.

The home page of Ruby is `http://www.ruby-lang.org/`. An Apache module is available for Ruby. The home page is `http://www.modruby.net/`.

14.10 Virtual Hosts

Using virtual hosts, host several domains with a single web server. In this way, save the costs and administration workload for separate servers for each domain. One of the first web servers that offered this feature, Apache offers several possibilities for virtual hosts:

- Name-based virtual hosts
- IP-based virtual hosts
- Operation of multiple instances of Apache on one machine

14.10.1 Name-Based Virtual Hosts

With name-based virtual hosts, one instance of Apache hosts several domains. You do not need to set up multiple IPs for a machine. This is the easiest, preferred alternative. Reasons against the use of name-based virtual hosts are covered in the Apache documentation.

Configure it directly by way of the configuration file (`/etc/apache2/httpd.conf`). To activate name-based virtual hosts, a suitable directive must be specified: `NameVirtualHost *.*` is sufficient to prompt Apache to accept all incoming requests. Subsequently, the individual hosts must be configured:

```
<VirtualHost *>
    ServerName www.mycompany.com
    DocumentRoot /srv/www/htdocs/mycompany.com
    ServerAdmin webmaster@mycompany.com
    ErrorLog /var/log/httpd/www.my.company.com-error_log
    CustomLog /var/log/httpd/www.mycompany.com-access_log common
</VirtualHost>

<VirtualHost *>
    ServerName www.myothercompany.com
    DocumentRoot /srv/www/htdocs/myothercompany.com
    ServerAdmin webmaster@myothercompany.com
    ErrorLog /var/log/httpd/www.myothercompany.com-error_log
    CustomLog /var/log/httpd/www.myothercompany.com-access_log common
</VirtualHost>
```

In the case of Apache 2, however, the paths of log files as shown in the above example (and in any examples further below) should be changed from /var/log/httpd to /var/log/apache2. A VirtualHost entry also must be configured for the domain originally hosted on the server (www.mycompany.com). So in this example, the original domain and one additional domain (www.myothercompany.com) are hosted on the same server.

Just as in NameVirtualHost, a * is used in the VirtualHost directives. Apache uses the host field in the HTTP header to connect the request with the virtual host. The request is forwarded to the virtual host whose ServerName matches the host name specified in this field.

For the directives ErrorLog and CustomLog, the log files do not need to contain the domain name. Here, use a name of your choice.

ServerAdmin designates the e-mail address of the responsible person that can be contacted if problems arise. In the event of errors, Apache gives this address in the error messages it sends to the client.

14.10.2 IP-Based Virtual Hosts

This alternative requires the setup of multiple IPs for a machine. In this case, one instance of Apache hosts several domains, each of which is assigned a different IP. The following example shows how Apache can be configured to host the original IP (192.168.1.10) plus two additional domains on additional IPs (192.168.1.20 and 192.168.1.21). This particular example only works on an intranet, as IPs ranging from 192.168.0.0 to 192.168.255.0 are not routed on the Internet.

Configuring IP Aliasing

For Apache to host multiple IPs, the underlying machine must accept requests for multiple IPs. This is called multi-IP hosting. For this purpose, IP aliasing must be activated in the kernel. This is the default setting in SUSE LINUX.

Once the kernel has been configured for IP aliasing, the commands ifconfig and route can be used to set up additional IPs on the host. These commands must be executed as root. For the following example, it is assumed that the host already has its own IP (such as 192.168.1.10), which is assigned to the network device eth0.

Enter the command ifconfig to find out the IP of the host. Further IPs can be added with commands such as the following:

```
/sbin/ifconfig eth0:0 192.168.1.20
/sbin/ifconfig eth0:1 192.168.1.21
```

All these IPs will be assigned to the same physical network device (eth0).

Virtual Hosts with IPs

Once IP aliasing has been set up on the system or the host has been configured with several network cards, Apache can be configured. Specify a separate `VirtualHost` block for every virtual server:

```
<VirtualHost 192.168.1.20>
    ServerName www.myothercompany.com
    DocumentRoot /srv/www/htdocs/myothercompany.com
    ServerAdmin webmaster@myothercompany.com
    ErrorLog /var/log/httpd/www.myothercompany.com-error_log
    CustomLog /var/log/httpd/www.myothercompany.com-access_log common
</VirtualHost>

<VirtualHost 192.168.1.21>
    ServerName www.anothercompany.com
    DocumentRoot /srv/www/htdocs/anothercompany.com
    ServerAdmin webmaster@anothercompany.com
    ErrorLog /var/log/httpd/www.anothercompany.com-error_log
    CustomLog /var/log/httpd/www.anothercompany.com-access_log common
</VirtualHost>
```

`VirtualHost` directives are only specified for the additional domains. The original domain (`www.mycompany.com`) is configured through its own settings (under `DocumentRoot`, etc.) outside the `VirtualHost` blocks.

14.10.3 Multiple Instances of Apache

With the above methods for providing virtual hosts, administrators of one domain can read the data of other domains. To segregate the individual domains, start several instances of Apache, each with its own settings for `User`, `Group`, and other directives in the configuration file.

In the configuration file, use the `Listen` directive to specify the IP handled by the respective Apache instance. For the above example, the directive for the first Apache instance would be as follows:

```
Listen 192.168.1.10:80
```

For the other two instances:

```
Listen 192.168.1.20:80
Listen 192.168.1.21:80
```

14.11 Security

14.11.1 Minimizing the Risk

If you do not need a web server on a machine, deactivate Apache in the runlevel editor, uninstall it, or refrain from installing it in the first place. To minimize the risk, deactivate all unneeded servers. This especially applies to hosts used as firewalls. If possible, do not run any servers on these hosts.

14.11.2 Access Permissions

DocumentRoot Should Belong to root

By default, the `DocumentRoot` directory (`/srv/www/htdocs`) and the CGI directory belong to the user `root`. You should not change this setting. If the directories were writable for all, any user could place files into them. These files might then be executed by Apache with the permissions of user `wwwrun`. Also, Apache should not have any write permissions for the data and scripts it delivers. Therefore, these should not belong to the user `wwwrun`, but to another user (such as `root`).

To enable users to place files in the document directory of Apache, do not make it writable for all. Instead, create a subdirectory that is writable for all (such as `/srv/www/htdocs/miscellaneous`).

Publishing Documents from Home Directories

Another possibility to make sure that users can publish their files in the network is to specify a subdirectory in users' home directories in the configuration file. Users can then place any files for web presentations in this directory (for instance, `~/public_html`). By default, this is activated in SUSE LINUX. See Section 14.7.2 on page 351 for details.

These web pages can be accessed by specifying the user in the URL. The URL contains the element `~username` as a shortcut for the respective directory in the user's home directory. For example, enter `http://localhost/~tux` in a browser to list the files in the directory `public_html` in the home directory of the user tux.

14.11.3 Staying Updated

If you operate a web server and especially if this web server is publicly accessible, stay informed about bugs and potential vulnerable spots. Sources for exploits and fixes are listed in Section 14.13.3 on page 363.

14.12 Troubleshooting

If problems appear, for example, Apache does not display a page or does not display it correctly, the following procedures can help find the problems.

- First, take a look at the error log and check if the messages it contains reveal the error. The general error log is located in `/var/log/httpd/error_log` or `/var/log/apache2/error_log`.

  A proven approach is to track the log files in a console to see how the server reacts to an access. This can be done by entering `tail -f /var/log/apache2/*_log` in a `root` console.

- Check the online bug database at `http://bugs.apache.org/`.

- Read the relevant mailing lists and newsgroups. The mailing list for users is available at `http://httpd.apache.org/userslist.html`. Recommended newsgroups are `comp.infosystems.www.servers.unix` and related groups.

- If none of these possibilities provide any solution and you are sure that you have detected a bug in Apache, report it at `http://www.suse.de/feedback/`.

14.13 For More Information

14.13.1 Apache

Apache is shipped with detailed documentation. The installation of this documentation is described in Section 14.6 on page 344. Following the installation, access the documentation at `http://localhost/manual`. The latest documentation is available from the Apache home page at `http://httpd.apache.org`.

14.13.2 CGI

More information about CGI is available at the following pages:

- `http://apache.perl.org/`

- http://perl.apache.org/
- http://www.modperl.com/
- http://www.modperlcookbook.org/
- http://www.fastcgi.com/
- http://www.boutell.com/cgic/

14.13.3 Security

The latest patches for the SUSE packages are made available at http://www.suse.com/us/security/. Visit this URL at regular intervals. Here, you can also sign up for the SUSE mailing list for security announcements.

The Apache team promotes an open information policy with regard to bugs in Apache. The latest bug reports and possible vulnerable spots are published at http://httpd.apache.org/security_report.html.

If you detect a security bug (check the mentioned pages to make sure it has not already been discovered), report it to security@suse.de or to security@apache.org.

Other sources for information about security issues of Apache (and other Internet programs):

- http://www.cert.org/
- http://www.vnunet.com/
- http://www.securityfocus.com/

14.13.4 Additional Sources

If you experience difficulties, take a look at the SUSE Support Database at http://sdb.suse.de/en/. An online newspaper focusing on Apache is available at http://www.apacheweek.com/.

The history of Apache is provided at http://httpd.apache.org/ABOUT_APACHE.html. This page also explains why the server is actually called Apache.

File Synchronization

Today, many people use several computers — one computer at home, one or several computers at the workplace, and possibly a laptop or PDA on the road. Many files are needed on all these computers. You may want to be able work with all computers and modify the files and subsequently have the latest version of the data available on all computers.

15.1 Data Synchronization Software

Data synchronization is no problem for computers that are permanently linked by means of a fast network. In this case, use a network file system like NFS and store the files on a server, enabling all hosts to access the same data via the network. This approach is impossible if the network connection is poor or not permanent. When you are on the road with a laptop, you need to keep copies of all needed files on the local hard disk. However, it is then necessary to synchronize modified files. When you modify a file on one computer, make sure a copy of the file is updated on all other computers. For occasional copies, this can be done manually with scp or rsync. However, if many files are involved, the procedure can be complicated and requires great care to avoid errors, such as overwriting a new file with an old file.

Caution

Risk of Data Loss

Before you start managing your data with a synchronization system, you should be well acquainted with the program used and test its functionality. A backup is indispensable for important files.

Caution

The time-consuming and error-prone task of manually synchronizing data can be avoided by using one of the programs that employ various methods to automate this job. The following summaries are merely intended to convey a general understanding of how these programs work and how they can be used. If you plan to use them, read the program documentation.

15.1.1 InterMezzo

The idea of InterMezzo is the implementation of a file system that exchanges files via the network like NFS, but stores local copies on the individual computers, thus ensuring that the files are available even when the network connection is down. The local copies can be edited. All changes are noted in a special log file. When the connection is restored, these changes are automatically forwarded and the files are synchronized. More information about InterMezzo is available in `/usr/share/doc/packages/InterMezzo/InterMezzo-HOWTO.html`, if the package is installed.

15.1.2 Unison

Unison is not a network file system. Rather, the files are simply saved and edited locally. The program Unison can be executed manually to synchronize files. When the synchronization is performed for the first time, a database is created on the two hosts, containing check sums, time stamps, and permissions of the selected files. The next time it is executed, Unison can recognize which files were changed and propose the transmission from or to the other host. Usually all suggestions can be accepted.

15.1.3 CVS

CVS, which is mostly used for managing program source versions, offers the possibility to keep copies of the files on multiple computers. Accordingly, it is also suitable for our purpose.

CVS maintains a central repository on the server, in which not only the files but also changes to files are saved. Changes that are performed locally are committed to the repository and can be retrieved from other computers by means of an update. Both procedures must be initiated by the user.

CVS is very resilient to errors in the event that changes occur on several computers. The changes are merged and, if changes took place in the same lines, a conflict is reported. When a conflict occurs, the database remains in a consistent state. The conflict is only visible for resolution on the client host.

15.1.4 mailsync

In contrast to the synchronization tools covered in the previous sections, mailsync merely serves the purpose of synchronizing e-mails between mailboxes. The procedure can be applied to local mailbox files as well as to mailboxes on an IMAP server.

Based on the message ID contained in the e-mail header, the individual messages are either synchronized or deleted. Synchronization is possible between individual mailboxes and between mailbox hierarchies.

15.2 Determining Factors for Selecting a Program

15.2.1 Client-Server versus Peer-to-Peer

Two different models are commonly used for distributing data. In the first model, all clients synchronize their files with a central server. The server must be accessible by all clients at least from time to time. This model is used by CVS and InterMezzo.

The other possibility is to let equal hosts synchronize their data among each other. This is the approach Unison uses.

15.2.2 Portability

InterMezzo is a solution that only supports Linux systems at present. In the past, the support was limited to 32-bit little endian architectures (ix86). Due to the migration from the perl-based lento to InterSync, this limitation no longer applies. Nevertheless, caution is needed when synchronizing between different architectures, as this feature has not yet been tested thoroughly. CVS and Unison are also available for many other operating systems, including various Unix and Windows systems.

15.2.3 Interactive versus Automatic

In InterMezzo, the data synchronization normally occurs automatically in the background as soon as a network connection can be established with the server. Manual intervention is only required when conflicts arise.

In CVS and Unison, the data synchronization is started manually by the user. This enables more control over the data to synchronize and easier conflict handling. On the other hand, if the synchronization intervals are too long, conflicts are more likely to occur.

15.2.4 Speed

Due to their interactive character, Unison and CVS appear to be slower than InterMezzo, which operates in the background. Usually CVS is somewhat faster than Unison.

15.2.5 Conflicts: Incidence and Solution

Conflicts do not occur often in CVS, even if several people work on one large program project. This is because the documents are merged on the basis of individual lines. When a conflict occurs, only one client is affected. Usually conflicts can easily be resolved in CVS.

Unison reports conflicts, allowing the affected files to be excluded from the synchronization. However, changes cannot be merged as easy as in CVS.

Due to the noninteractive character of InterMezzo, conflicts cannot simply be resolved interactively. When conflicts occur, InterSync terminates with an alert message. In this case, the system administrator must intervene and possibly transfer files manually (using rsync or scp) to restore a consistent state.

15.2.6 Selecting and Adding Files

InterMezzo synchronizes the entire file system. Newly added files in the file system automatically appear on the other computers.

Configured in the simplest way possible, Unison synchronizes an entire directory tree. New files appearing in the tree are automatically included in the synchronization.

In CVS, new directories and files must be added explicitly using the command `cvs add`. Thus, the user has more control over the files to synchronize. On the other hand, new files are often overlooked, especially if the question marks in the output of `cvs update` are ignored because of the number of files.

15.2.7 History

An additional feature of CVS is that old file versions can be reconstructed. A brief editing remark can be inserted for each change and the development of the files can easily be traced later based on the content and the remarks. This is a valuable aid for theses and program texts.

15.2.8 Data Volume and Hard Disk Requirements

An adequate amount of free space for all distributed data is required on the hard disks of all involved hosts. CVS requires additional space for the repository on the server. The file history is also stored on the server, requiring even more space. When files in text format are changed, only the modified lines need to be saved. Binary files require additional space amounting to the size of the file every time the file is changed.

15.2.9 GUI

Unison offers a graphical user interface that displays the synchronization procedures Unison wants to perform. Accept the proposal or exclude individual files from the synchronization. In text mode, you can interactively confirm the individual procedures.

Experienced users normally control CVS from the command line. However, graphical user interfaces are available for Linux, such as cervisia, and for other operating systems, like wincvs. Many development tools (such as kdevelop) and text editors (such as emacs) provide CVS support. The resolution of conflicts is often much easier with these front-ends.

InterMezzo does not offer that much comfort. On the other hand, normally it does not require any interaction and should simply do its job in the background once it is configured.

15.2.10 User Friendliness

The configuration of InterMezzo is relatively difficult and should only be performed by a system administrator who has some experience with Linux. `root` privileges are required for the configuration. Unison is easy to use and is also suitable for newcomers.

CVS is more difficult to use. Users should understand the interaction between the repository and local data. Changes to the data should first be merged locally with the repository. This is done with the command `cvs update`. Then the data must be sent back to the repository with the command `cvs commit`. Once this procedure has been grasped, newcomers are also able to use CVS with ease.

15.2.11 Security against Attacks

During transmission, the data should be protected against interception and manipulation. Both Unison and CVS can easily be used via ssh (Secure Shell), providing security against attacks of this kind. Use of CVS or Unison via rsh (Remote Shell) should be avoided and access by way of the CVS *pserver* mechanism in insecure networks is not advisable either.

In InterMezzo, the data synchronization is performed via http. This protocol can easily be intercepted or altered. To increase the level of security, SSL can be used, but this makes the configuration a little bit more difficult. InterMezzo should only be used without SSL in secure, trustworthy networks.

15.2.12 Protection against Data Loss

CVS looks back on a long record of deployment by developers for the management of program projects and is extremely stable. As the development history is saved, CVS even provides protection against certain user errors, such as the unintentional deletion of a file.

Unison is still relatively new, but boasts a high level of stability. However, it is more sensitive to user errors. Once the synchronization of the deletion of a file has been confirmed, there is no way to restore the file.

Currently, InterMezzo is still in alpha stage. As the files are stored in a separate file system, the probability of a major data loss is relatively low. However, something could go wrong with the file synchronization itself, leaving behind wrecked files. The resilience to user errors is also limited: when a file is deleted locally, the same step is performed on all synchronized hosts. For this reason, backups are strongly recommended.

Table 15.1: Features of the File Synchronization Tools -- = very poor, - = poor or not available, o = medium, + = good, ++ = excellent, x = available

	InterMezzo	**unison**	**CVS**	**mailsync**
C-S/equal	C-S	equal	C-S	equal
Portability	Linux(i386)	Lin,Un*x,Win	Lin,Un*x,Win	Lin,Un*x
Interactivity	-	x	x	-
Speed	++	-	o	+
Conflicts	-	o	++	+
File selection	File system	Directory	Selection	Mailbox
History	-	-	x	-
Hard Disk Space	o	o	--	+
GUI	-	+	o	-
Difficulty	-	+	o	o
Attacks	-	+(ssh)	+(ssh)	+(SSL)
Data Loss	o	+	++	+

15.3 Introduction to InterMezzo

15.3.1 Architecture

InterMezzo uses a special file system type. The files are stored locally on the hard disks of the individual hosts. One of the file systems available in Linux is used for this purpose, preferably `ext3` or one of the other journaling file systems. Following the preparation of the partition, the file system is mounted with the type `intermezzo`. The kernel loads a module with InterMezzo support and all changes performed in this file system are written to a log file.

Following these preliminary steps, InterSync can be started. This program starts a web server, such as Apache, other hosts can access to exchange data. When configuring a client, the name of the server must be specified in InterSync. This server will be contacted. A freely selectable designation for the file system — the "fileset" — is used to identify the file system.

InterSync is the next generation of the older InterMezzo system, which used a perl daemon called lento for the file synchronization. The documentation of InterSync still refers to this older system occasionally. However, this system has been replaced by InterSync. Unfortunately, the module included in standard kernels still supports lento and does not work with InterSync. A newer module is available in the SUSE kernel. For custom kernels, the kernel module should be built with `km_intersync`.

The configuration of InterMezzo requires system administrator permissions. As indicated above, the configuration of InterMezzo is relatively difficult and should therefore be performed by an experienced system administrator. The configuration described below does not provide any protective mechanisms. Thus, others can easily intercept and manipulate the data synchronized with InterMezzo. For this reason, the configuration should only take place in a trustworthy environment, such as a wired private network protected by a firewall.

15.3.2 Configuring an InterMezzo Server

One of the hosts, preferably one having a good network connection, is assigned the role of the server. The entire data synchronization traffic traverses this server.

A separate file system must be set up for the data storage. If you do not have a spare partition and do not use LVM, the easiest way is to set up the file system in the form of a *loop device*, which enables the use of a file in the local file system as a separate file system.

In the following example, an InterMezzo/ext3 file system with a size of 256 MB is set up in the root directory. The file set is assigned the designation `fset0`.

```
dd if=/dev/zero of=/izo0 bs=1024 count=262144
mkizofs -r fset0 /izo0  # The warning can be ignored
```

This file system is mounted to `/var/cache/intermezzo`.

```
mount -t intermezzo -ofileset=fset0,loop /izo /var/cache/intermezzo
```

To do this automatically when the system is booted, an entry must be made in the file `/etc/fstab`. Now InterSync can be configured by customizing `/etc/sysconfig/intersync`. The following is entered in this file:

```
INTERSYNC_CLIENT_OPTS="--fset=fset0"
INTERSYNC_CACHE=/var/cache/intermezzo
INTERSYNC_PROXY=""
```

Now InterSync can be started with `/etc/init.d/intersync start`. To do this automatically when the system is booted, the service can be entered in the list of services to start with `insserv intersync`.

15.3.3 Configuring InterMezzo Clients

The configuration of the clients (one server can serve multiple clients) is virtually the same as that of the server. The only difference is that the name of the server must be specified in the variable `INTERSYNC_CLIENT_OPTS` when configuring `/etc/sysconfig/intersync`:

```
INTERSYNC_CLIENT_OPTS="--fset=fset0 --server=sun.example.com"
```

sun.example.com must be replaced with the network name of the server. If possible, the file systems on all computers should have the same size.

15.3.4 Troubleshooting

As soon as a client is started, changes to files located in the directory `/var/cache/intermezzo/` should also be visible on the server and all other clients. If this is not the case, this is usually because no connection can be established to the server or due to a configuration error, such as a wrong "fileset" designation. To find the error, analyze the log messages in the system log `/var/log/messages`. The web server started logs its data to `/var/intermezzo-X/`. The log file of the kernel, which records changes to the file system, is located in `/var/cache/intermezzo/.intermezzo/fset0/kml` and can be viewed with `kmlprint`.

When a conflict occurs, normally one of the `InterSync` processes is aborted. If the file synchronization is no longer performed, look for indications in the log file and use `/etc/init.d/intersync status` to check if the synchronization service is still active.

If necessary, refer to the package documentation:

```
/usr/share/doc/packages/intersync/
http://www.inter-mezzo.org/
```

15.4 Introduction to Unison

15.4.1 Uses

Unison is an excellent solution for synchronizing and transferring entire directory trees. The synchronization is performed in both directions and can be controlled by means of an intuitive graphical front-end. A console version can also be used. The synchronization can be automated so interaction with the user is not required, but experience is necessary.

15.4.2 Requirements

Unison must be installed on the client as well as on the server. In this context, the term *server* refers to a second, remote host (unlike CVS, explained in Section 15.1.3 on page 367).

In the following section, Unison is used together with ssh. An ssh client must be installed on the client and an ssh server must be installed on the server.

15.4.3 Using Unison

The approach used by Unison is the association of two directories (*roots*) with each other. This association is symbolic — it is not an online connection. In this example, the directory layout is as follows:

Client:	`/home/tux/dir1`
Server:	`/home/geeko/dir2`

You want to synchronize these two directories. The user is known as tux on the client and as `geeko` on the server. The first thing to do is to test if the client-server communication works:

```
unison -testserver /home/tux/dir1 ssh://geeko@server//homes/geeko/dir2
```

The most frequently encountered problems are:

- The Unison versions used on the client and server are not compatible.

- The server does not allow SSH connections.
- Neither of the two specified paths exists.

If everything works, omit the option `-testserver`.

During the first synchronization, Unison does not yet know the relationship between the two directories and submits suggestions for the transfer direction of the individual files and directories. The arrows in the 'Action' column indicate the transfer direction. A question mark means that Unison is not able to make a suggestion regarding the transfer direction, as both versions were changed or are new.

The arrow keys can be used to set the transfer direction for the individual entries. If the transfer directions are correct for all displayed entries, simply click "Go".

The characteristics of Unison (e.g., whether to perform the synchronization automatically in clear cases) can be controlled by means of command-line parameters specified when the program is started. The complete list of all parameters can be viewed with `unison --help`.

For each pair, a synchronization log is maintained in the user directory `~/.unison`. Configuration sets such as `~/.unison/example.prefs` can also be stored in this directory:

To start the synchronization, specify this file as the command-line parameter as in `unison example.prefs`.

15.4.4 More Information

The official documentation of Unison is extremely useful. For this reason, this section merely provides a brief introduction. The complete manual is available at `http://www.cis.upenn.edu/~bcpierce/unison/` and in the SUSE `unison`.

15.5 Introduction to CVS

15.5.1 Uses

CVS is suitable for synchronization purposes if individual files are edited frequently and are stored in a loose file format, such as ASCII text or program source text. The use of CVS for synchronizing data in other formats, such as JPEG files, is possible, but leads to large amounts of data, as all variants of a file are stored permanently on the CVS server. Furthermore, in such cases most of the capabilities of CVS cannot be used.

The use of CVS for synchronizing files is only possible if all workstations can access the same server. In contrast, with the program Unison the data can be passed by host A through the hosts B and C to the server S.

15.5.2 Configuring a CVS Server

The *server* is the place where all valid files are located, including the latest versions of all files. Any stationary workstation can be used as a server. If possible, the data of the CVS repository should be included in regular backups.

When configuring a CVS server, it might be a good idea to grant the user access to the server via ssh. If the user is known to the server as tux and the CVS software is installed on the server as well as on the client (e.g., notebook), the following environment variables must be set on the client side:

```
CVS_RSH=ssh CVS_ROOT=tux@server:/serverdir
```

The command `cvsinit` can be used to initialize the CVS server from the client side. This needs to be done only once.

Finally, the synchronization must be assigned a name. Select or create a directory on the client that will exclusively contain files to manage with CVS (the directory can also be empty). The name of the directory will also be the name of the synchronization. In our example, we use a directory called `synchome`. Change to this directory and enter the following command to set the synchronization name to `synchome`:

```
cvs import synchome tux wilber
```

Many CVS commands require a comment. For this purpose, CVS starts an editor (the editor defined in the environment variable `$EDITOR` or vi if no editor was defined). The editor call can be circumvented by entering the comment in advance on the command line, such as in the following example:

```
cvs import -m 'this is a test' synchome tux wilber
```

15.5.3 Using CVS

From now on, the synchronization repository can be "checked out" from all hosts:

```
cvs co synchome
```

This creates a new subdirectory `synchome` on the client. To commit your changes to the server, change to the directory `synchome` (or one of its subdirectories) and enter `cvs commit`.

By default, all files (including subdirectories) are committed to the server. To commit only individual files or directories, specify them as in `cvs commit file1 directory1`. New files and directories must be added to the repository before they are committed to the server with a command like `cvs add file1 directory1`. Subsequently, the newly added files and directories can be committed: `cvs commit file1 directory1`.

If you change to another workstation, "check out" the synchronization repository, provided this has not been done during an earlier session at the same workstation (see above).

The synchronization with the server is started with the command `cvs update`. You can also update individual files or directories as in `cvs update file1 directory1`. If you first want to see the difference from the versions stored on the server, use the command `cvs diff` or `cvs diff file1 directory1`. Use `cvs -nq update` to see which files would be affected by an update.

Here are some of the status symbols displayed during an update:

U The local version was updated.

M The local version was modified. If there were changes on the server, it was possible to merge the differences in the local copy.

P The local version was patched with the version on the server.

C The local file conflicts with current version in the repository.

? This file does not exist in CVS.

The status `M` indicates a locally modified file. Either commit the local copy to the server or remove the local file and run the update again. In this case, the missing file is retrieved from the server. If you commit a locally modified file and the file was changed and commited before in the same line, you might get a conflict indicated with `C`.

In this case look at conflict marks (»> and «<) in the file and decide between the two versions. As this can be a rather unpleasant job, you might decide to abandon your changes, delete the local file, and enter `cvs up` to retrieve the current version from the server.

15.5.4 More Information

This section merely offers a brief introduction to the many possibilities of CVS. Extensive documentation is available at the following URLs:

```
http://www.cvshome.org/
http://www.gnu.org/manual/
```

15.6 Introduction to mailsync

15.6.1 Uses

mailsync is mainly suitable for the following three tasks:

- Synchronization of locally stored e-mails with mails stored on a server
- Migration of mailboxes to a different format or to a different server
- Integrity check of a mailbox or search for duplicates

15.6.2 Configuration and Use

mailsync distinguishes between the mailbox itself (the *store*) and the connection between two mailboxes (the *channel*. The definitions of the stores and channels are stored in `~/.mailsync`. The following paragraphs explain a number of store examples.

A simple definition might appear as follows:

```
store saved-messages {
   pat Mail/saved-messages
prefix  Mail/
}
```

`Mail/` is a subdirectory of the user's home directory that contains e-mail folders, including the folder `saved-messages`. If mailsync is started with `mailsync -m saved-messages` an index of all messages is listed in `saved-messages`. If the following definition is made

```
store localdir {
pat     Mail/*
prefix  Mail/
}
```

the command `mailsync -m localdir` causes all messages stored under `Mail/` to be listed. In contrast, the command `mailsync localdir` lists the folder names. The specifications of a store on an IMAP server appear as follows:

```
store imapinbox {
server {mail.edu.harvard.com/user=gulliver}
ref     {mail.edu.harvard.com}
pat     INBOX
}
```

The above example merely addresses the main folder on the IMAP server. A store for the subfolders would appear as follows:

```
store imapdir {
server {mail.edu.harvard.com/user=gulliver}
ref {mail.edu.harvard.com}
pat INBOX.*
prefix  INBOX.
}
```

If the IMAP server supports encrypted connections, the server specification should be changed to

```
server {mail.edu.harvard.com/ssl/user=gulliver}
```

or, if the server certificate is not known, to

```
server {mail.edu.harvard.com/ssl/novalidate-cert/user=gulliver}
```

The prefix is explained later.

Now the folders under `Mail/` should be connected to the subdirectories on the IMAP server:

```
channel folder localdir imapdir {
msinfo .mailsync.info
}
```

mailsync uses the `msinfo` file to keep track of the messages that have already been synchronized.

The command `mailsync folder` does the following:

- The mailbox pattern is expanded on both sides
- The prefix is removed from the resulting folder names
- The folders are synchronized in pairs (or created if they do not exist)

Accordingly, the folder `INBOX.sent-mail` on the IMAP server is synchronized with the local folder `Mail/sent-mail` (provided the definitions explained above exist). The synchronization between the individual folder is performed as follows:

- If a message already exists on both sides, nothing happens.
- If the message is missing on one side and is new (not listed in the `msinfo` file), it is transmitted there.
- If the message merely exists on one side and is old (already listed in the `msinfo` file), it is deleted there (because the message that had obviously existed on the other side was deleted).

To know in advance which messages will be transmitted and which will be deleted during a synchronization, start mailsync with a channel *and* a store with `mailsync folder localdir`. This command produces a list of all messages that are new on the local host as well as a list of all messages that would be deleted on the IMAP side during a synchronization. Similarly, the command `mailsync folder imapdir` produces a list of all messages that are new on the IMAP side and a list of all messages that would be deleted on the local host during a synchronization.

15.6.3 Possible Problems

In the event of a data loss, the safest method is to delete the relevant channel log file `msinfo`. Accordingly, all messages that only exist on one side are viewed as new and are therefore transmitted during the next synchronization.

Only messages with a message ID are included in the synchronization. Messages lacking a message ID are simply ignored, which means they are neither transmitted nor deleted. A missing message ID is usually caused by faulty programs when sending or writing a message.

On certain IMAP servers, the main folder is addressed with `INBOX` and subfolders are addressed with a randomly selected name (in contrast to INBOX and INBOX.name). Therefore, for such IMAP servers, it is not possible to specify a pattern exclusively for the subfolders.

After the successful transmission of messages to an IMAP server, the mailbox drivers (c-client) used by mailsync set a special status flag. For this reason, some e-mail programs, like mutt, are not able to recognize these messages as new. The setting of this special status flag can be disabled with the option `-n`.

15.6.4 More Information

The `README` in `/usr/share/doc/packages/mailsync/`, which is included in `mailsync`, provides additional information. In this connection, RFC 2076 "Common Internet Message Headers" is of special interest.

Heterogenous Networks

In addition to connecting to other Linux systems, Linux is also able to connect to Windows and Macintosh computers and communicate over Novell networks. This chapter shows the requirements for and configuration of heterogenous networks.

16.1 Samba

16.1.1 Introduction to Samba

With the program Samba, convert a UNIX machine into a file and print server for DOS, Windows, and OS/2 machines. The Samba Project is run by the Samba Team and was originally developed by the Australian Andrew Tridgell.

Samba has now become a fully-fledged and rather complex product. This section presents an overview of its basic functionality. Samba offers plenty of online documentation. Enter `apropos samba` at the command line to display some manual pages or just browse the `/usr/share/doc/packages/samba` directory if Samba is installed for more online documentation and examples. A commented example configuration (`smb.conf.SuSE`) can be found in the `examples` subdirectory.

Beginning from version 9.1, the SUSE LINUX `samba` package provides version 3 of the Samba suite, which brings some important added features:

- Support for Active Directory
- Much improved Unicode support
- The internal authentication mechanisms have been completely revised
- Improved support for the Windows 200x/XP printing system
- Servers can be set up as member servers in Active Directory domains
- Adoption of an NT4 domain, enabling the migration from the latter to a Samba domain.

Samba uses the SMB protocol (Server Message Block) that is based on the NetBIOS services. Due to pressure from IBM, Microsoft released the protocol so other software manufacturers could establish connections to a Microsoft domain network. With Samba, the SMB protocol works on top of the TCP/IP protocol, so the TCP/IP protocol must be installed on all clients.

> **Note**
>
> **Migration to Samba3**
>
> There are some special points to take into account when migrating from Samba 2.x to Samba 3. A discussion of this topic is included in the Samba HOWTO Collection, where an entire chapter is dedicated to it. After installing the `samba-doc` package, find the HOWTO in `/usr/share/doc/packages/samba/Samba-HOWTO-Collection.pdf`.
>
> **Note**

NetBIOS

NetBIOS is a software interface (API) designed for communication between machines. Here, a name service is provided. It enables machines connected to the net to reserve names for themselves. After reservation, these machines can be addressed by name. There is no central process that checks names. Any machine on the network can reserve as many names as it wants, if the names are not already in use. The NetBIOS interface can now be implemented for different network architectures. An implementation that works relatively closely with network hardware is called NetBEUI, but this is often referred to as NetBIOS. Network protocols implemented with NetBIOS are IPX from Novell™ (NetBIOS via TCP/IP) and TCP/IP.

The NetBIOS names sent via TCP/IP have nothing in common with the names used in `/etc/hosts` or those defined by DNS. NetBIOS uses its own, completely independent naming convention. However, it is recommended to use names that correspond to DNS host names to make administration easier. This is the default used by Samba.

Clients

All common operating systems, such as Mac OS X, Windows, and OS/2, support the SMB protocol. The TCP/IP protocol must be installed on all computers. Samba provides a client for the different UNIX flavors. For Linux, there is a file-system kernel module for SMB that allows the integration of SMB resources on the Linux system level.

SMB servers provide hardware space to their clients by means of shares. A share includes a directory and its subdirectories on the server. It is exported by means of a name and can be accessed by its name. The share name can be set to any name — it does not have to be the name of the export directory. A printer is also assigned a name. Clients can access the printer by its name.

16.1.2 Installing and Configuring the Server

If you intend to use Samba as a server, install `samba`. The services required for Samba can be started with `rcnmb start && rcsmb start` and stopped with `rcsmb stop && rcnmb stop`.

The main configuration file of Samba is `/etc/samba/smb.conf`. This file can be divided into two logical parts. The `[global]` section contains the central and global settings. The `[share]` sections contain the individual file and printer shares. By means of this approach, details regarding the shares can be set differently or globally in the `[global]` section, which enhances the structural transparency of the configuration file.

The global Section

The following parameters of the `[global]` section need some adjustment to match the requirements of your network setup so other machines can access your Samba server via SMB in a Windows environment.

workgroup = TUX-NET This line assigns the Samba server to a workgroup. Replace `TUX-NET` with an appropriate workgroup of your networking environment. Your Samba server appears under its DNS name unless this name has been assigned to any other machine in the net. If the DNS name is not available, set the server name using `netbiosname=MYNAME`. See `mansmb.conf` for more details about this parameter.

os level = 2 This parameter triggers whether your Samba server tries to become LMB (Local Master Browser) for its work group. Choose a very low value to spare the existing Windows network from any disturbances caused by a misconfigured Samba server. More information about this important topic can be found in the files `BROWSING.txt` and `BROWSING-Config.txt` under the `textdocs` subdirectory of the package documentation. If no other SMB server is present in your network (such as a Windows NT or 2000 server) and you want the Samba server to keep a list of all systems present in the local environment, set the `os level` to a higher value (for example, `65`). Your Samba server is then chosen as LMB for your local network. When changing this setting, consider carefully how this could affect an existing Windows network environment. A misconfigured Samba server can cause serious problems when trying to become LMB for its workgroup. Contact your administrator and subject your configuration to some heavy testing either in an isolated network or at a noncritical time of day.

wins support and wins server To integrate your Samba server into an existing Windows network with an active WINS server, enable the `wins server` option and set its value to the IP address of that WINS server. If your Windows machines are connected to separate subnets and should still be aware of each other, you need to set up a WINS server. To turn a Samba server into such a WINS server, set the option `wins support = Yes`. Make sure that only one Samba server of the network has this setting enabled. The options `wins server` and `wins support` must never be enabled at the same time in your `smb.conf` file.

Shares

The following examples illustrate how a CD-ROM drive and the user directories (`homes`) are made available to the SMB clients.

[cdrom] To avoid having the CD-ROM drive accidentally made available, these lines are deactivated with comment marks (semicolons in this case). Remove the semicolons in the first column to share the CD-ROM drive with Samba.

Example 16.1: *A CD-ROM Share*

```
;[cdrom]
;        comment = Linux CD-ROM
;        path = /media/cdrom
;        locking = No
```

`[cdrom]` and `comment` The entry `[cdrom]` is the name of the share that can be seen by all SMB clients on the net. An additional `comment` can be added to further describe the share.

`path = /media/cdrom` `path` exports the directory `/media/cdrom`.

By means of a very restrictive default configuration, this kind of share is only made available to the users present on this system. If this share should be made available to everybody, add a line `guest ok = yes` to the configuration. This setting gives read permissions to anyone on the network. It is recommended to handle this parameter with great care. This applies even more to the use of this parameter in the `[global]` section.

[homes] The `[home]` share is of special importance here. If the user has a valid account and password for the Linux file server and his own home directory, he can be connected to it.

***Example 16.2:** homes Share*

```
[homes]
        comment = Home Directories
        valid users = %S
        browseable = No
        read only = No
        create mask = 0640
        directory mask = 0750
```

[homes] As long as there is no other share using the share name of the user connecting to the SMB server, a share is dynamically generated using the `[homes]` share directives. The resulting name of the share is identical to the user name.

valid users = %S `%S` is replaced by the concrete name of the share as soon as a connection has been successfully established. For a `[homes]` share, this is always identical to the user's name. As a consequence, access rights to a user's share are restricted exclusively to the user.

browseable = No This setting enables the share to be invisible in the network environment.

read only = No By default, Samba prohibits write access to any exported share by means of the `read only = Yes` parameter. To make a share writable, set the value `read only = No`, which is synonymous with `writeable = Yes`.

create mask = 0640 Systems that are not based on MS Windows NT do not understand the concept of UNIX permissions, so they cannot assign permissions when creating a file. The parameter `create mask` defines the access permissions assigned to newly created files. This only applies to writable shares. In effect, this setting means the owner has read and write permissions and the members of the owner's primary group have read permissions. `valid users = %S` prevents read access even if the group has read permissions. Therefore, if you want the group to have read or write access, the line `valid users = %S` must be deactivated.

Security Levels

The SMB protocol comes from the DOS and Windows world and directly takes into consideration the problem of security. Each share access can be protected with a password. SMB has three possible ways of checking the permissions:

Share Level Security (security = share):
A password is firmly assigned to a share. Everyone who knows this password has access to that share.

User Level Security (security = user):
This variation introduces the concept of the user to SMB. Each user must register with the server with his own password. After registering, the server can grant access to individual exported shares dependent on user names.

Server Level Security (security = server):
To its clients, Samba pretends to be working in User Level Mode. However, it passes all password queries to another User Level Mode Server, which takes care of authentication. This setting expects an additional parameter (`password server =`).

The distinction between share, user, and server level security applies to the entire server. It is not possible to offer individual shares of a server configuration with share level security and others with user level security. However, you can run a separate Samba server for each configured IP address on a system.

More information about this subject can be found in the Samba HOWTO Collection. For multiple servers on one system, pay attention to the options `interfaces` and `bind interfaces only`.

Note

For simple administration tasks with the Samba server, there is also the program swat. It provides a simple web interface with which to configure the Samba server conveniently. In a web browser, open `http://localhost:901` and log in as user `root`. However, swat must also be activated in the files `/etc/xinetd.d/samba` and `/etc/services`. To do so in `/etc/xinetd.d/samba`, edit the `disable` line so it reads: `disable = no`. More information about swat is provided in the man page.

Note

16.1.3 Samba as Login Server

In networks where predominantly Windows clients are found, it is often preferable that users may only register with a valid account and password. This can be brought about with the help of a Samba server. In a Windows-based network, this task is handled by a Windows NT server configured as a primary domain controller (PDC). The entries that must be made in the `[global]` section of `smb.conf` are shown in File 16.3.

Example 16.3: *Global Section in smb.conf*

```
[global]
  workgroup = TUX-NET
  domain logons = Yes
  domain master = Yes
```

If encrypted passwords are used for verification purposes — this is the default setting with well-maintained MS Windows 9x installations, MS Windows NT 4.0 from service pack 3, and all later products — the Samba server must be able to handle these. The entry `encrypt passwords = yes` in the `[global]` section enables this (with Samba version 3 this is now the default). In addition, it is necessary to prepare user accounts and passwords in an encryption format that conforms with Windows. This is done with the command `smbpasswd -a name`. Create the domain account for the computers, required by the Windows NT domain concept, with the following commands:

Example 16.4: *Setting up a Machine Account*

```
useradd hostname\$
smbpasswd -a -m hostname
```

With the `useradd` command, a dollar sign is added. The command `smbpasswd` inserts this automatically when the parameter `-m` is used. The commented configuration example (`/usr/share/doc/packages/Samba/examples/smb.conf.SuSE`) contains settings that automate this task.

Example 16.5: Automated Setup of a Machine Account

```
add machine script = /usr/sbin/useradd -g machines \
                -c "NT Machine Account" -d \
                /dev/null -s /bin/false %m
```

To make sure that Samba can execute this script correctly, choose a Samba user with the required administrator permissions. To do so, select one user and add it to the `ntadmin` group. After that, all users belonging to this Linux group can be assigned `Domain Admin` status with the command:

```
net groupmap add ntgroup="Domain Admins" unixgroup=ntadmin
```

More information about this topic is provided in Chapter 12 of the Samba HOWTO Collection, found in: `/usr/share/doc/packages/samba/Samba-HOWTO-Collection.pdf`.

16.1.4 Installing Clients

Clients can only access the Samba server via TCP/IP. NetBEUI and NetBIOS via IPX cannot be used with Samba.

Windows 9x and ME

Windows 9x and ME already have built-in support for TCP/IP. However, this is not installed as the default. To add TCP/IP, go to 'Control Panel' -> 'System' and choose 'Add' -> 'Protocols' -> 'TCP/IP from Microsoft'. After rebooting your Windows machine, find the Samba server by double-clicking the desktop icon for the network environment.

Note

To use a printer on the Samba server, install the standard or Apple-PostScript printer driver from the corresponding Windows version. It is best to link this to the Linux printer queue, which accepts Postscript as an input format.

Note

16.1.5 Optimization

`socket options` is one possible optimization provided with the sample configuration that ships with your Samba version. Its default configuration refers to a local ethernet network. For additional information about `socket options`, refer to the section *socket options* in the manual pages of `smb.conf` and to the manual page of `socket(7)`. Further information is provided in the `Samba performance tuning` chapter of the Samba HOWTO Collection.

The standard configuration in `/etc/samba/smb.conf` is designed to provide useful settings based on the default settings of the Samba team. However, a ready-to-use configuration is not possible, especially in view of the network configuration and the workgroup name. The commented sample configuration `examples/smb.conf.SuSE` contains information that is helpful for the adaption to local requirements.

Note

The Samba HOWTO Collection provided by the Samba team includes a section about troubleshooting. In addition to that, Part V of the document provides a step-by-step guide to checking your configuration.

Note

16.2 Netatalk

With `Netatalk`, obtain a high-performance file and print server for MacOS clients. With it, access data on a Linux machine from a Macintosh or print to a connected printer. `Netatalk` is a suite of Unix programs that run on kernel-based DDP (Datagram Delivery Protocol) and implement the AppleTalk protocol family (ADSP, ATP, ASP, RTMP, NBP, ZIP, AEP, and PAP).

AppleTalk is, in effect, an equivalent to the more familiar protocol TCP (Transmission Control Protocol). It has counterparts to many TCP/IP-based services, including services for resolving host names and time synchronization. For example, the command `aecho` (AEP, AppleTalk Echo Protocol) is used instead of `ping` (ICMP ECHO_REQUEST, Internet Control Message Protocol).

The three daemons described below are normally started on the server:

- atalkd ("AppleTalk Network Manager"), which corresponds to the program ip

- afpd ("AppleTalk Filing Protocol daemon"), which provides an interface for Macintosh clients to Unix file systems.
- papd ("Printer Access Protocol daemon"), which makes printers available in the (AppleTalk) network.

Server directories can be exported with Netatalk at the same time as with Samba for Windows clients (see Section 16.1.1 on page 385) and via NFS (see Section 13.9 on page 325), which is very useful in heterogeneous network environments. This centralizes the management of data backup and user permissions on the Linux server.

There are a number of limitations when working with `Netatalk`:

- Due to Macintosh client restrictions, the user passwords on the server cannot be longer than eight characters.
- Macintosh clients cannot access Unix files with names longer than 31 characters.
- File names may not contain colons (`:`) because they serve as path name separators in MacOS.

16.2.1 Configuring the File Server

In the default configuration, `Netatalk` is already fully functional as a file server for home directories of the Linux system. To use the extended features, define some settings in the configuration files. These are located in the `/etc/netatalk/` directory.

All configuration files are pure text files. Text that follows a hash mark # (comments) and empty lines can be disregarded. The various services (printing, Appletalk broadcast, Appletalk via TCP/IP, time server) can be activated through the file `/etc/netatalk/netatalk.conf`:

```
ATALKD_RUN=yes
PAPD_RUN=yes
AFPD_RUN=yes
TIMELORD_RUN=no
```

Configuring the Network — atalkd.conf

Define, in `/etc/netatalk/atalkd.conf`, over which interfaces services are provided. This is usually `eth0`. In the example file that comes with `Netatalk`, this is the case. Enter additional interfaces to use several network cards at the same time. When the server is started, it searches the network for existing zones and servers and modifies the corresponding lines by entering the set AppleTalk network addresses. You will then find a line such as

```
eth0 -phase 2 -net 0-65534 -addr 65280.57
```

at the end of the file. For more complex configurations, refer to examples in the configuration file. Find documentation about additional options in the manual page of afpd.

Defining File Servers — afpd.conf

The `afpd.conf` file contains definitions for how your file server appears on MacOS machines as an item under the 'Chooser' dialog. As is the case with the other configuration files, these also contain detailed comments explaining the wide variety of options.

If you do not change anything here, the default server is simply started and displayed with the host name in the 'Chooser'. Therefore, you do not necessarily need to enter anything. However, you can give additional file servers a variety of names and options here, for example, to provide a specific guest server on which everybody can save files as "guest".

```
"Guest server" -uamlist uams_guest.so
```

Define a server that denies guests access, but which is only accessible for users who already exist in the Linux system with:

```
"Font server" -uamlist uams_clrtxt.so,uams_dhx.so
```

This behavior is controlled by the option `uamlist` followed by a list of authentication modules to use separated by commas. If you do not provide this option, all procedures are active by default.

An AppleShare server not only provides its services by default via AppleTalk, but also via TCP/IP (*encapsulated*). The default port is 548. Assign dedicated ports to additional AppleShare servers (on the same machine) if these should also run via TCP. The availability of the service via TCP/IP enables access to the server even over non-AppleTalk networks, such as the Internet. In this case, the syntax would read:

```
"Font server" -uamlist uams_clrtxt.so,uams_dhx.so -port 12000
```

The AppleShare server, set to the port 12000, then appears in the network with the name `Font server` and does not allow guest access. In this way, it is also accessible via TCP/IP routers.

The file `AppleVolumes.default` (described in detail below) defines which directories located on the server are made available by each AppleShare server as network *volumes*. By using the `-defaultvol` option for a given AppleShare server, specify another file that defines different directories. The corresponding command (read as one line) is:

```
"Guest server" -uamlist uams_guest.so -defaultvol
/etc/netatalk/AppleVolumes.guest
```

Further options are explained in the `afpd.conf` file itself.

Directories and Access Permissions — AppleVolumes.default

Here, define directories to export. The access permissions are defined with the customary Unix user and group permissions. This is configured in the `AppleVolumes.default` file. Along with `AppleVolumes.default`, additional files can be created, such as `AppleVolumes.guest`, used by some servers (by giving the option `-defaultvol` in the `afpd.conf` file. See the previous section).

Note

Here, the syntax has partially changed. Take this into consideration if you are updating this version from a previous one. For example, it is now `allow:` instead of `access=` (a typical symptom would be if, instead of the drive descriptions, you were to see a display of the drive options on the Mac clients in the 'Chooser'). Because the new files are created with the `.rpmnew` endings during an update, it is possible that your previous settings may no longer function as a result of the modified syntax. Create backups of your configuration files, copy your old configuration into the new files, then rename these files to the proper names. This way, benefit from the current comments contained in the configuration files, which provide a detailed explanation of the options.

Note

The example shown here:

```
/usr/local/psfonts "PostScript Fonts"
```

indicates that the Linux directory `/usr/local/psfonts`, located in the root directory, is available as an AppleShare volume with the name "PostScript Fonts".

Options are separated by a space and attached to the end of a line. A very useful option is the access restriction:

```
/usr/local/psfonts "PostScript Fonts" allow:User1,@group0
```

This restricts access to the volume "PostScript Fonts" to the user "User1" and all members of the group "group0". The users and groups entered here must be known to the Linux system. Likewise, explicitly deny users access with `deny:User2`. These restrictions only apply to access via AppleTalk and not to the normal access rights users have if they can log in to the server itself.

Netatalk maps the customary Resource Fork of MacOS files to `.AppleDouble/` directories in the Linux file system. Using the `noadouble` option, set these directories to be created only when they are actually needed. The syntax is:

```
/usr/local/guests "Guests" options:noadouble
```

Additional options and features can be found in the explanations included in the file itself.

The tilde (~) in this configuration file stands for the home directory for each and every user on the server. This way, every user can easily access his home directory without each one being defined explicitly here. The example file installed already includes a tilde, which is why `Netatalk` makes the home directory available by default as long as you do not modify anything in this file.

afpd also searches for a file `Applevolumes` or `.Applevolumes` in the home directory of a user logged in to the system. Entries in this file supplement the entries in the server files `AppleVolumes.system` and `AppleVolumes.default` to enable individual type and creator file settings and to access specific directories. These entries are extensions and do not allow access for the user for whom access permission is denied from the server side.

The `netatalk.pamd` file is used, via PAM (pluggable authentication modules), for authentication purposes. Using PAM is, however, irrelevant in this context.

File Specifications — AppleVolumes.system

In the `AppleVolumes.System` file, define which customary MacOS type and creator specifications are assigned to certain file endings. An entire series of default values are already predefined. If a file is displayed by a generic white icon, there is not yet an entry for it in this file. If you encounter a problem with a text file belonging to another system, which cannot be opened properly in MacOS or vice versa, check the entries there.

16.2.2 Configuring the Print Server

Make a laserwriter service available by configuring the `papd.conf` file. The printer must be already functioning locally with `lpd`, so configure a printer as described in Chapter 5 on page 87. If you can print a text file locally using the command `lpr file.txt`, the first step has been successfully completed.

You do not necessarily need to enter anything in `papd.conf` if a local printer is configured in Linux, because print jobs can simply be forwarded to the print daemon lpd without additional settings. The printer registers itself in the AppleTalk network as Laserwriter. You can, however, extend your printer entries as follows:

```
Printer_Reception:pr=lp:pd=/etc/netatalk/kyocera.ppd
```

This causes the printer named `Printer_Reception` to appear as a 'Chooser' item. The corresponding printer description file is usually provided by the vendor. Otherwise, refer to the file `Laserwriter` located in the 'System Extensions' folder. However, when using this file you often cannot use all of the printer's features.

16.2.3 Starting the Server

The server can be started at system boot time via its init script or manually with `rcatalk start`. The init script is located at `/etc/init.d/netatalk`. The actual starting of the server takes place in the background. It takes about a minute until the AppleTalk interfaces are set up and responsive. Check for the status as shown in the following (all servers are running if `OK` is reported three times):

```
rcatalk status

Checking for service atalk:OKOKOK
```

From a Mac running MacOS, check for AppleTalk activation, choose 'File-sharing', then double-click 'AppleShare'. The names of the servers should then appear in the window. Double-click a server and log in. It should then be possible to access a shared volume.

The procedure is a bit different for AppleShare servers configured to use TCP only (and no DDP). To connect, press 'Server IP address' and enter the respective IP address. If necessary, append the port number, separated by a colon (`:`).

16.2.4 Additional Information

To take full advantage of all the options `Netatalk` offers, read the corresponding manual pages. Find them by entering the command `rpm -qd netatalk`. The `/etc/netatalk/netatalk.conf` file is not used in our `Netatalk`version, so disregard it. Helpful URLs:

- `http://netatalk.sourceforge.net/`
- `http://www.umich.edu/~rsug/netatalk/`
- `http://www.anders.com/projects/netatalk/`

16.3 NetWare Emulation with MARSNWE

The NetWare emulator MARSNWE can easily replace the file and print services of a Novell NetWare 2.2 or 3.11 server. It can also be be used in this manner as an IPX router. However, it does not offer the features of newer NetWare versions, such as NDS (NetWare Directory Services). Workstations running DOS or Windows already configured to access a NetWare 2.2, 3.11, or 3.12 server can use the Linux server with the NetWare emulator MARSNWE as a server without changing the configuration much. Server administration can be done under Linux.

16.3.1 Starting the NetWare Emulator MARSNWE

On a SUSE LINUX system, MARSNWE comes preconfigured for initial testing, so you can start it right after installation. The required IPX kernel support is available as a loadable kernel module and is automatically loaded by the start script. The IPX interface is automatically set up by MARSNWE. At this point, the network number and the protocol to use are both read from the extensively commented configuration file `/etc/nwserv.conf`.

Start MARSNWE with the command `rcnwe start`. The `done` message to the right of the screen in green indicates that MARSNWE has been successfully started. Use `rcnwe status` to check whether the NetWare emulator is running. Halt it with `rcnwe stop`.

16.3.2 The Configuration File /etc/nwserv.conf

The configuration options are grouped in numbered sections — every configuration line starts with the number of the corresponding section. Only sections 1 to 22 are relevant for our purposes and among these there are some which are not used. The following sections should be sufficient to cover most configuration scenarios:

1 NetWare Volumes

2 Server Name

4 IPX Network

13 User Names

21 Printers

After modifying the configuration, MARSNWE must be restarted with the command `rcnwe restart`.

The configuration options in detail are:

Volumes (Section 1):

```
1     SYS     /usr/local/nwe/SYS/     kt       711 600
```

Here, the volumes to export are defined. Every line begins with the section number (here 1), followed by the volume name and the server directory path. In addition, specify various options, represented by specific letters, and a umask for the generation of both directories and files. If a umask is not specified, the default value from Section 9 is used. The volume for SYS is already entered. To avoid problems with uppercase and lowercase letters in the file names, it is recommended to use the `k` option, so all the file names are converted to lowercase letters.

Server Name (Section 2):

```
2     MARS
```

This setting is optional. The host name is used by default.

Internal Network Number (Section 3):

```
3     auto
```

The internal network number is generated from the network card's MAC address if `auto` is specified here. This setting is usually retained.

IPX Configuration (Section 4):

```
4     0x0      *        AUTO              1
4     0x22     eth0     ethernet_ii       1
```

This sets the NetWare network number as well as the network interface to which it should be bound with which protocol. The first example sets up everything automatically. The second binds the network number `0x22` to the network card `eth0` with the frame type `Ethernet-II`. If you have several network cards and enter all these with different network numbers, IPX is routed among them.

Create Mode (Section 9):

```
9     0751     0640
```

Sets the default permission with which directories and files are created.

GID and GID with minimal permissions (Section 10, 11):

```
10    65534
11    65534
```

Group ID and user ID for users not logged in. Here `nogroup` and `nobody`.

Supervisor Login (Section 12):

```
12    SUPERVISOR        root
```

The supervisor is mapped to user `root`.

User Logins (Section 13):

```
13    LINUX             linux
```

Specifies how NetWare user names are mapped to Linux user names. A fixed password can optionally be entered here.

Automatic User Mapping (Section 15):

```
15    0         top-secret
```

If `1` is specified here instead of `0`, Linux logins are automatically made available as NetWare logins. In this case, the password is "top-secret".

Printer Queues (Section 21):

```
21    LP        -         lpr -
```

The first parameter `LP` is the name of the NetWare printer. Second, the name of the spool directory can be given. The print command is listed last.

Print Server (Section 22):

```
22    PS_NWE  LP_PS    1
```

Define printers here that are accessed over the pserver by `ncpfs`.

16.3.3 Access to and Administration of NetWare Servers

`ncpfs` is a collection of small programs that can be used to administer a NetWare 2.2 or 3.11 server from Linux, mount NetWare volumes, and manage printers. To access a newer NetWare server (version 4 or higher), enable the bindery emulation and IPX on it.

The following programs are available. Refer to the manual pages for their functions:

nwmsg	ncopy	ncpmount	ncpumount
nprint	nsend	nwauth	nwbocreate
nwbols	nwboprops	nwborm	nwbpadd
nwbpcreate	nwbprm	nwbpset	nwbpvalues
nwdir	nwdpvalues	nwfsctrl	nwfsinfo
nwfstime	nwgrant	nwpasswd	nwpurge
nwrevoke	nwrights	nwsfind	nwtrustee
nwtrustee2	nwuserlist	nwvolinfo	pqlist
pqrm	pqstat	pserver	slist

As one essential command of this suite, `ncpmount` can be used to mount volumes of a NetWare server from a Linux host. The `ncpumount` command, on the other hand, unmounts them. In addition, `ncpfs` contains tools to configure the IPX protocol and IPX routing:

```
ipx_cmd
ipx_configure
ipx_interface
ipx_internal_net
ipx_route
```

With `ipx_configure` and `ipx_interface`, configure the the network card's IPX. If you already have MARSNWE running, however, it takes care of this configuration automatically.

16.3.4 IPX Router with ipxrip

Another package for converting Linux into an IPX router is `ipxrip`. Usually, it is not needed, because an IPX router can be configured with `MARSNWE` or the tools from `ncpfs`.

Internet

The Internet has become the number one platform for network communications worldwide. As true network system, Linux can handle a broad range of Internet related tasks — both as a server and as a client system. This chapter discusses some of the topics relevant to the Internet: the configuration of the smpppd (the SUSE Meta PPP Daemon), the manual configuration of ADSL access, and the configuration of the Squid proxy.

17.1 The smpppd as Dial-up Assistant

17.1.1 Program Components for the Internet Dial-Up

Most home users do not have a dedicated line connecting them to the Internet. Rather, they use dial-up connections. Depending on the dial-up method (ISDN or DSL), the connection is controlled by the ipppd or the pppd. Basically, all that needs to be done to go online is to start these programs correctly.

If you have a flat-rate connection that does not generate any additional costs for the dial-up connection, simply start the respective daemon. Control the dial-up connection with a KDE applet or a command-line interface. If the Internet gateway is not the host you are using, you might want to control the dial-up connection by way of a network host.

This is where smpppd is involved. It provides a uniform interface for auxiliary programs and acts in two directions: first, it programs the required pppd or ipppd and controls its dial-up properties. Second, it makes various providers available to the user programs and transmits information about the current status of the connection. As smpppd can also be controlled by way of the network, it is suitable for controlling dial-up connections to the Internet from a workstation in a private subnetwork.

17.1.2 Configuring smpppd

The connections provided by smpppd are automatically configured by YaST. The actual dial-up programs kinternet and cinternet are also preconfigured. Manual settings are only required to configure additional features of smpppd, such as remote control.

The configuration file of smpppd is `/etc/smpppd.conf`. By default, it does not enable remote control. The most important options of this configuration file are as follows:

open-inet-socket = `<yes|no>` To control smpppd via the network, this option must be set to `yes`. The port on which the smpppd listens is `3185`. If this parameter is set to `yes`, the parameters `bind-address`, `host-range`, and `password` should also be set accordingly.

bind-address = `<ip>` If a host has several IP addresses, this parameter can be used to determine by which IP address smpppd should accept connections.

host-range = `<min ip> <max ip>`
The parameter `host-range` can be used to define a network range. Hosts whose IP addresses are within this range are granted access to smpppd. All hosts not within this range are denied access.

password = `<password>` By assigning a password, limit the clients to authorized hosts. As this is a plain-text password, you should not overrate the security it provides. If no password is assigned, all clients are entitled to access smpppd.

More information about smpppd is available in `man 8 smpppd` and `man 5 smpppd.conf`.

17.1.3 Configuring kinternet and cinternet for Remote Use

The programs kinternet and cinternet can be used locally as well as for controlling a remote smpppd. cinternet is the the command-line counterpart of the graphical kinternet. To prepare these utilities for use with a remote smpppd, edit the configuration file `/etc/smpppd-c.conf` manually or using kinternet. This file only uses three options:

server = `<server>` Here, specify the host on which smpppd runs. If this host is the same as the default gateway of the host, it is sufficient to set the `gateway-fallback` to `yes`.

gateway-fallback = `<yes|no>` If no server was specified and there is no local smpppd, this option, which is enabled by default, causes a search for an smpppd on the default gateway.

password = `<password>` Insert the password selected for smpppd.

If the smpppd is active, you can now try to access it. This can be done with the command `cinternet --verbose --interface-list`. If you experience difficulties at this point, refer to `man 5 smpppd-c.conf` and `man 8 cinternet`

17.2 Configuring an ADSL or T-DSL Connection

17.2.1 Default Configuration

Currently, SUSE LINUX supports DSL connections that work with the point-to-point over ethernet protocol (PPPoE) used by most major providers. If you are not sure what protocol is used for your DSL connections, ask your provider. If you have a single-user workstation with a graphical interface, the DSL connection should be set up with the YaST modules ADSL or T-DSL.

1. The `ppp` and `smpppd` packages must be installed. It is best to use YaST for this purpose.
2. Configure your network card with YaST. Do not activate `dhcp`, but set a fixed IP address instead, such as `192.168.2.22`.
3. The parameters set with the DSL module of YaST are saved in the file `/etc/sysconfig/network/providers/provider0`. In addition, there are configuration files for the smpppd (SUSE meta ppp daemon) and its front-ends kinternet and cinternet. For information, refer to `man smpppd`.
4. If necessary, start the network with the command `rcnetwork start` and smpppd with the command `rcsmpppd start`.
5. On a system without a graphical user interface, use the commands `cinternet --start` and `cinternet -stop` to establish or terminate a connection. On a graphical user interface, this can be done with kinternet. This program is started automatically in KDE if you used YaST to set up DSL. Click the gear icon in the control panel. Select 'Communication/Internet' → 'Internet Tools' → 'kinternet'. A plug icon then appears in the control panel. You can now start the connection with a simple click on the icon and terminate the connection later with another click.

17.2.2 DSL Connection by Dial-on-Demand

Dial-on-demand means that the connection is automatically set up when the user goes online, for example, when visiting a web site in a browser or when sending an e-mail. After a certain amount of idle time when no data is sent or received, the connection is automatically be dropped. Because the dial-up connection via PPPoE, the protocol for ADSL, is very fast, it seems as if it were a dedicated line to the Internet.

Using dial-on-demand, however, really only makes sense if you have a flat-rate connection. If you use it but are charged for time online, make sure there are no interval processes, such as a cronjob, periodically establishing a connection. This could get quite expensive.

Although a permanent online connection would also be possible using a DSL flat-rate connection, there are certain advantages to having a connection that only exists for a short amount of time when needed:

- Most providers drop the connection after a certain period of time.
- A permanent connection can be considered as a drain on resources (e.g., IP addresses).
- Being online permanently is a security risk, because hackers may be able to comb the system systematically for vulnerable areas. A system that is only accessible over the Internet when necessary and is always changing IP addresses is significantly more difficult to attack.

Dial-on-demand can be enabled using YaST (also refer to the *User Guide*). Alternatively, set it up manually:

Set the parameter `DEMAND=yes` in the `/etc/sysconfig/network/providers/provider0` file then define an idle time via the variable `IDLETIME=60`. This way, an unused connection is dropped after sixty seconds.

To set up a DSL gateway for private networks, refer to the following article from our support portal:
`http://portal.suse.de/sdb/en/2002/07/masq80.html`

17.3 Proxy Server: Squid

Squid is a widely-used proxy cache for Linux and UNIX platforms. The chapter discusses its configuration, the settings required to get it running, how to configure the system to do transparent proxying, how to gather statistics about the cache's use with the help of programs like Calamaris and cachemgr, and how to filter web contents with squidGuard.

17.3.1 Squid as Proxy Cache

Squid acts as a proxy cache. It behaves like an agent that receives requests from clients, in this case web browsers, and passes them to the specified server. When the requested objects arrive at the agent, it stores a copy in a disk cache.

The main advantage of this becomes obvious as soon as different clients request the same objects: these are served directly from the disk cache, much faster than obtaining them from the Internet. At the same time, this results in less network traffic and thus saves bandwidth.

Note

Squid covers a wide range of features, including distributing the load over intercommunicating hierarchies of proxy servers, defining strict access control lists for all clients accessing the proxy, and (with the help of other applications) allowing or denying access to specific web pages. It also can also produce data about web usage patterns, for example, statistics about the most-visited web sites.

Note

Squid is not a generic proxy. It proxies normally only HTTP connections. It does also support the protocols FTP, Gopher, SSL, and WAIS, but it does not support other Internet protocols, such as Real Audio, news, or video conferencing. Because Squid only supports the UDP protocol to provide communication between different caches, many other multimedia programs are not supported.

17.3.2 Some Facts about Proxy Caches

Squid and Security

It is also possible to use Squid together with a firewall to secure internal networks from the outside using a proxy cache. The firewall denies all clients access to external services except Squid. All web connections must be established by way of the proxy.

If the firewall configuration includes a DMZ, the proxy should operate within this zone. In this case, it is important that all computers in the DMZ send their log files to hosts inside the secure network. The possibility of implementing a *transparent* proxy is covered in Section 17.3.6 on page 418.

Multiple Caches

Several proxies can be configured in such a way that objects can be exchanged between them, reducing the total system load and increasing the chances of finding an object already existing in the local network. It is also possible to configure cache hierarchies, so a cache is able to forward object requests to sibling caches or to a parent cache — causing it to get objects from another cache in the local network or directly from the source.

Choosing the appropriate topology for the cache hierarchy is very important, because is not desirable to increase the overall traffic on the network. For a very large network, it would make sense to configure a proxy server for every subnetwork and connect them to a parent proxy, which in turn is connected to the proxy cache of the ISP.

All this communication is handled by ICP (Internet Cache Protocol) running on top of the UDP protocol. Data transfers between caches are handled using HTTP (Hyper Text Transmission Protocol) based on TCP.

To find the most appropriate server from which to get the objects, one cache sends an ICP request to all sibling proxies. These answer the requests via ICP responses with a HIT code if the object was detected or a MISS if it was not. If multiple HIT responses were found, the proxy server decides from which server to download, depending on factors such as which cache sent the fastest answer or which one is closer. If no satisfactory responses are received, the request is sent to the parent cache.

Note

To avoid duplication of objects in different caches in the network, other ICP protocols are used, such as CARP (Cache Array Routing Protocol) or HTCP (HyperText Cache Protocol). The more objects maintained in the network, the greater the possibility of finding the desired one.

Note

Caching Internet Objects

Not all objects available in the network are static. There are a lot of dynamically generated CGI pages, visitor counters, and encrypted SSL content documents. Objects like this are not cached because they change each time they are accessed.

The question remains as to how long all the other objects stored in the cache should stay there. To determine this, all objects in the cache are assigned one of various possible states.

Web and proxy servers find out the status of an object by adding headers to these objects, such as "Last modified" or "Expires" and the corresponding date. Other headers specifying that objects must not be cached are used as well.

Objects in the cache are normally replaced, due to a lack of free hard disk space, using algorithms such as LRU (Last Recently Used). Basically this means that the proxy expunges the objects that have not been requested for the longest time.

17.3.3 System Requirements

The most important thing is to determine the maximum load the system must bear. It is, therefore, important to pay more attention to the load peaks, because these might be more than four times the day's average. When in doubt, it would be better to overestimate the system's requirements, because having Squid working close to the limit of its capabilities could lead to a severe loss in the quality of the service. The following sections point to the system factors in order of significance.

Hard Disks

Speed plays an important role in the caching process, so this factor deserves special attention. For hard disks, this parameter is described as *random seek time*, measured in milliseconds. Because the data blocks that Squid reads from or writes to the hard disk will tend to be rather small, the seek time of the hard disk is more important than its data throughput. For the purposes of a proxy, hard disks with high rotation speeds are probably the better choice, because they allow the read-write head to be positioned in the required spot much quicker. Fast SCSI hard disks nowadays have a seek time of under 4 milliseconds.

One possibility to speed up the system is to use a number of disks concurrently or to employ striping RAID arrays.

Size of the Disk Cache

In a small cache, the probability of a HIT (finding the requested object already located there) is small, because the cache is easily filled so the less requested objects are replaced by newer ones. On the other hand, if, for example, `1 GB` is available for the cache and the users only surf `10 MB` a day, it would take more than one hundred days to fill the cache.

The easiest way to determine the needed cache size is to consider the maximum transfer rate of the connection. With a `1 Mbit/s` connection, the maximum transfer rate is `125 KB/s`. If all this traffic ends up in the cache, in one hour it would add up to `450 MB` and, assuming that all this traffic is generated in only eight working hours, it would reach `3.6 GB` in one day. Because the connection is normally not used to its upper volume limit, it can be assumed that the total data volume handled by the cache is approximately `2 GB`. This is why `2 GB` of disk space is required in the example for `Squid` to keep one day's worth of browsed data cached.

RAM

The amount of memory required by Squid directly correlates to the number of objects in the cache. Squid also stores cache object references and frequently requested objects in the main memory to speed up retrieval of this data. Random access memory is much faster than a hard disk.

In addition to that, there is other data that Squid needs to keep in memory, such as a table with all the IP addresses handled, an exact domain name cache, the most frequently requested objects, access control lists, buffers, and more.

It is very important to have sufficient memory for the Squid process, because system performance is dramatically reduced if it must be swapped to disk. The cachemgr.cgi tool can be used for the cache memory management. This tool is introduced in Section 17.3.7 on page 421.

CPU

Squid is not a program that requires intensive CPU usage. The load of the processor is only increased while the contents of the cache are loaded or checked. Using a multiprocessor machine does not increase the performance of the system. To increase efficiency, it is better to buy faster disks or add more memory.

17.3.4 Starting Squid

Squid is already preconfigured in SUSE LINUX, so you can start it easily right after installation. A prerequisite for a smooth start is an already configured network, at least one name server, and Internet access. Problems can arise if a dial-up connection is used with a dynamic DNS configuration. In cases such as this, at least the name server should be clearly entered, because Squid does not start if it does not detect a DNS server in `/etc/resolv.conf`.

To start Squid, enter `rcsquid start` at the command line as `root`. For the initial start-up, the directory structure must first be defined in `/var/squid/cache`. This is done by the start script `/etc/init.d/squid` automatically and can take a few seconds or even minutes. If `done` appears to the right in green, Squid has been successfully loaded. Test Squid's functionality on the local system by entering `localhost` and `Port 3128` as proxy in the browser.

To allow all users to access Squid and, through it, the Internet, change the entry in the configuration file `/etc/squid/squid.conf` from `http_access deny all` to `http_access allow all`. However, in doing so, consider that Squid is made completely accessible to anyone by this action. Therefore, define ACLs that control access to the proxy. More information about this is available in Section 17.3.5 on page 416.

If you have made changes in the configuration file `/etc/squid/squid.conf`, tell Squid to load the changed file by entering `rcsquid reload`. Alternatively, do a complete restart of Squid with `rcsquid restart`.

Another important command is `rcsquid status`, which allows you to determine whether the proxy is running. Finally, the command `rcsquid stop` causes Squid to shut down. This can take a while, because Squid waits up to half a minute (`shutdown_lifetime` option in `/etc/squid/squid.conf`) before dropping the connections to the clients and writing its data to the disk.

Caution

Terminating Squid

Terminating Squid with `kill` or `killall` can lead to the destruction of the cache, which then must be fully removed to restart Squid.

Caution

If Squid dies after a short period of time even though it was started successfully, check whether there is a faulty name server entry or whether the

/etc/resolv.conf file is missing. The cause of a start failure is logged by Squid in the /var/squid/logs/cache.log file. If Squid should be loaded automatically when the system boots, use the YaST runlevel editor to activate Squid for the desired runlevels.

An uninstall of Squid does not remove the cache or the log files. To remove these, delete the /var/cache/squid directory manually.

Local DNS Server

Setting up a local DNS server, such as BIND9, makes sense even if the server does not manage its own domain. It then simply acts as a caching-only DNS and is also able to resolve DNS requests via the root name servers without requiring any special configuration. If you enter the local DNS server in the /etc/resolv.conf file with the IP address 127.0.0.1 for localhost, Squid should always find a valid name server when it starts. For this to work, it is sufficient just to start the BIND server after installing the corresponding package. The name server of the provider should be entered in the configuration file /etc/named.conf under forwarders along with its IP address. However, if you have a firewall running, you need to make sure that DNS requests can pass it.

17.3.5 The Configuration File /etc/squid/squid.conf

All Squid proxy server settings are made in the /etc/squid/squid.conf file. To start Squid for the first time, no changes are necessary in this file, but external clients are initially denied access. The proxy must be made available for the localhost, usually with 3128 as port. The options are extensive and therefore provided with ample documentation and examples in the preinstalled /etc/squid/squid.conf file. Nearly all entries begin with a # sign (the lines are commented) and the relevant specifications can be found at the end of the line. The given values almost always correlate with the default values, so removing the comment signs without changing any of the parameters actually has little effect in most cases. It is better to leave the sample as it is and reinsert the options along with the modified parameters in the line below. In this way, easily interpret the default values and the changes.

Note

Update from Version 2.4 to Version 2.5

Following an update of Squid from version 2.4 to version 2.5, the cache of Squid must be deleted, as the directory structure was changed.

Note

If you have updated from an earlier Squid version, it is recommended to edit the new `/etc/squid/squid.conf` and only apply the changes made in the previous file. If you try to implement the old `squid.conf`, run a risk that the configuration will no longer function, because options are sometimes modified and new changes added.

General Configuration Options (Selection)

http_port 3128 This is the port on which Squid listens for client requests. The default port is `3128`, but `8080` is also common. If desired, specify several port numbers separated by blank spaces.

cache_peer <hostname> <type> <proxy-port> <icp-port> Here, for example, enter a parent proxy to use the proxy of your ISP. As *<hostname>*, enter the name and IP address of the proxy to use and, as *<type>*, *parent*. For *<proxy-port»*, enter the port number that is also set by the operator of the parent for use in the browser, usually `8080`. Set the *<icp-port>* to `7` or `0` if the ICP port of the parent is not known and its use is irrelevant to the provider. In addition, *default* and *no-query* should be specified after the port numbers to prohibit the use of the ICP protocol. Squid then behaves like a normal browser as far as the provider's proxy is concerned.

cache_mem 8 MB This entry defines the amount of memory Squid can use for the caches. The default is `8 MB`.

cache_dir ufs /var/cache/squid/ 100 16 256 The entry *cache_dir* defines the directory where all the objects are stored on disk. The numbers at the end indicate the maximum disk space in `MB` to use and the number of directories in the first and second level. The *ufs* parameter should be left alone. The default is `100 MB` occupied disk space in the `/var/cache/squid` directory and creation of sixteen subdirectories inside it, each containing 256 more subdirectories. When specifying the disk space to use, leave sufficient reserve disk space. Values from a minimum of fifty to a maximum of eighty percent of the available disk space make the most sense here. The last two numbers for the directories should only be increased with caution, because too many directories can also lead to performance problems. If you have several disks that share the cache, enter several *cache_dir* lines.

cache_access_log /var/log/squid/access.log
path for log messages

cache_log /var/log/squid/cache.log
path for log messages

cache_store_log /var/log/squid/store.log
path for log messages

These three entries specify the paths where Squid logs all its actions. Normally, nothing is changed here. If Squid is experiencing a heavy usage burden, it might make sense to distribute the cache and the log files over several disks.

emulate_httpd_log off If the entry is set to *on*, obtain readable log files. Some evaluation programs cannot interpret this, however.

client_netmask 255.255.255.255 With this entry, mask the logged IP addresses in the log files to hide the clients' identity. The last digit of the IP address is set to zero if you enter `255.255.255.0` here.

ftp_user Squid@ With this, set the password Squid should use for the anonymous FTP login. It can make sense to specify a valid e-mail address here, because some FTP servers can check these for validity.

cache_mgr webmaster An e-mail address to which Squid sends a message if it unexpectedly crashes. The default is *webmaster*.

logfile_rotate 0 If you run `squid -k rotate`, `Squid` can rotate secured log files. The files are numbered in this process and, after reaching the specified value, the oldest file is overwritten. The value here is usually `0` because archiving and deleting log files in SUSE LINUX is carried out by a cronjob found in the configuration file `/etc/logrotate/squid`.

append_domain <domain> With *append_domain*, specify which domain to append automatically when none is given. Usually, your own domain is entered here, so entering *www* in the browser accesses your own web server.

forwarded_for on If you set the entry to *off*, Squid removes the IP address and the system name of the client from the HTTP requests.

negative_ttl 5 minutes; negative_dns_ttl 5 minutes
Normally, you do not need to change these values. If you have a dial-up connection, however, the Internet may, at times, not be accessible. Squid will make a note of the failed requests then refuse to issue new ones, although the Internet connection has been reestablished. In a case such as this, change the *minutes* to *seconds* then, after clicking *Reload* in the browser, the dial-up process should be reengaged after a few seconds.

never_direct allow <acl_name> To prevent Squid from taking requests directly from the Internet, use the above command to force connection to another proxy. This must have previously been entered in *cache_peer*. If *all* is specified as the *<acl_name>*, force all requests to be forwarded directly to the *parent*. This might be necessary, for example, if you are using a provider that strictly stipulates the use of its proxies or denies its firewall direct Internet access.

Options for Access Controls

Squid provides an intelligent system that controls access to the proxy. By implementing ACLs, it can be configured easily and comprehensively. This involves lists with rules that are processed sequentially. ACLs must be defined before they can be used. Some default ACLs, such as *all* and *localhost*, already exist. However, the mere definition of an ACL does not mean that it is actually applied. This only happens in conjunction with *http_access* rules.

acl <acl_name> <type> <data> An ACL requires at least three specifications to define it. The name *<acl_name>* can be chosen arbitrarily. For *<type>*, select from a variety of different options, which can be found in the *ACCESS CONTROLS* section in the `/etc/squid/squid.conf` file. The specification for *<data>* depends on the individual ACL type and can also be read from a file, for example, via host names, IP addresses, or URLs. The following are some simple examples:

```
acl mysurfers srcdomain .my-domain.com
acl teachers src 192.168.1.0/255.255.255.0
acl students src 192.168.7.0-192.168.9.0/255.255.255.0
acl lunch time MTWHF 12:00-15:00
```

http_access allow <acl_name> *http_access* defines who is allowed to use the proxy and who can access what on the Internet. For this, ACLs must be given. *localhost* and *all* have already been defined above, which can deny or allow access via *deny* or *allow*. A list containing any number of *http_access* entries can be created, processed from top to bottom, and, depending on which occurs first, access is allowed or denied to the respective URL. The last entry should always be *http_-access deny all*. In the following example, the *localhost* has free access to everything while all other hosts are denied access completely.

```
http_access allow localhost
http_access deny all
```

In another example using these rules, the group `teachers` always has access to the Internet. The group `students` only gets access Monday to Friday during lunch time.

```
http_access deny localhost
http_access allow teachers
http_access allow students lunch time
http_access deny all
```

The list with the *http_access* entries should only be entered, for the sake of readability, at the designated position in the `/etc/squid/squid.conf` file. That is, between the text

```
# INSERT YOUR OWN RULE(S) HERE TO ALLOW ACCESS FROM YOUR
# CLIENTS
```

and the last

```
http_access deny all
```

redirect_program /usr/bin/squidGuard
With this option, specify a redirector such as squidGuard, which allows blocking unwanted URLs. Internet access can be individually controlled for various user groups with the help of proxy authentication and the appropriate ACLs. squidGuard is a package in and of itself that can be separately installed and configured.

authenticate_program /usr/sbin/pam_auth
If users must be authenticated on the proxy, a corresponding program, such as pam_auth, can be set here. When accessing pam_-auth for the first time, the user sees a login window in which to enter the user name and password. In addition, an ACL is still required, so only clients with a valid login can use the Internet:

```
acl password proxy_auth REQUIRED

http_access allow password
http_access deny all
```

The *REQUIRED* after *proxy_auth* can be replaced with a list of permitted user names or with the path to such a list.

ident_lookup_access allow <acl_name>
With this, have an ident request run for all ACL-defined clients to find each user's identity. If you apply *all* to the *<acl_name>*, this is valid for all clients. Also, an ident daemon must be running on all clients. For Linux, install the pidentd package for this purpose. For `Windows`, there is free software available to download from the Internet. To ensure that only clients with a successful ident lookup are permitted, a corresponding ACL also needs to be defined here:

```
acl identhosts ident REQUIRED

http_access allow identhosts
http_access deny all
```

Here, too, replace *REQUIRED* with a list of permitted user names. Using *ident* can slow down the access time quite a bit, because ident lookups are repeated for each request.

17.3.6 Transparent Proxy Configuration

The usual way of working with proxy servers is the following: the web browser sends requests to a certain port in the proxy server and the proxy provides these required objects, whether they are in its cache or not. When working in a real network, several situations may arise:

- For security reasons, it is recommended that all clients use a proxy to surf the Internet.
- All clients must use a proxy whether they are aware of it or not.
- The proxy in a network is moved, but the existing clients should retain their old configuration.

In all these cases, a transparent proxy may be used. The principle is very easy: the proxy intercepts and answers the requests of the web browser, so the web browser receives the requested pages without knowing from where they are coming. This entire process is done transparently, hence the name.

Configuration Options in /etc/squid/squid.conf

The options to activate in the /etc/squid/squid.conf file to get the transparent proxy up and running are:

- httpd_accel_host virtual
- httpd_accel_port 80 # the port number where the actual HTTP server is located
- httpd_accel_with_proxy on
- httpd_accel_uses_host_header on

Firewall Configuration with SUSEfirewall2

Now redirect all incoming requests via the firewall with help of a port forwarding rule to the Squid port. To do this, use the SUSE-provided tool SESEfirewall2. Its configuration file can be found in /etc/sysconfig/SuSEfirewall2. The configuration file consists of well-documented entries. Even to set only a transparent proxy, you must configure some firewall options. In our example:

- Device pointing to the Internet: FW_DEV_EXT="eth1"
- Device pointing to the network: FW_DEV_INT="eth0"

Set ports and services (see /etc/exports) on the firewall permitted access from untrusted networks such as the Internet. In this example, only web services are offered to the outside:

```
FW_SERVICES_EXT_TCP="www"
```

Define ports or services (see /etc/exports) on the firewall permitted access from the secure network, both TCP and UDP services:

```
FW_SERVICES_INT_TCP="domain www 3128"
FW_SERVICES_INT_UDP="domain"
```

This allows accessing web services and Squid (whose default port is 3128).

The service "domain" stands for DNS. This service is commonly used. Otherwise, simply take it out of the above entries and set the following option to no:

```
FW_SERVICE_DNS="yes"
```

The most important option is number 15:

Example 17.1: Firewall Configuration: Option 15

```
#
# 15.)
# Which accesses to services should be redirected to a local port
# on the firewall machine?
#
# This can be used to force all internal users to surf via your
# Squid proxy, or transparently redirect incoming web traffic to
# a secure web server.
#
# Choice: leave empty or use the following explained syntax of
# redirecting rules, separated with spaces.
# A redirecting rule consists of 1) source IP/net,
# 2) destination IP/net, 3) original destination port and
# 4) local port to redirect the traffic to, separated by a colon,
# e.g. "10.0.0.0/8,0/0,80,3128 0/0,172.20.1.1,80,8080"
#
```

The comments above show the syntax to follow. First, enter the IP address and the netmask of the internal networks accessing the proxy firewall. Second, enter the IP address and the netmask to which these clients send their requests. In the case of web browsers, specify the networks `0/0`, a wild card that means "to everywhere." After that, enter the original port to which these requests are sent and, finally, the port to which all these requests are redirected. As Squid supports more protocols than HTTP, redirect requests from other ports to the proxy, such as FTP (port 21), HTTPS, or SSL (port 443). The example uses the default port 3128. If there are more networks or services to add, they only need to be separated by a single blank character in the corresponding entry.

```
FW_REDIRECT_TCP="192.168.0.0/16,0/0,80,3128 192.168.0.0/16,0/0,21,3128"
FW_REDIRECT_UDP="192.168.0.0/16,0/0,80,3128 192.168.0.0/16,0/0,21,3128"
```

To start the firewall and the new configuration with it, change an entry in the `/etc/sysconfig/SuSEfirewall2` file. The entry `START_FW` must be set to `"yes"`.

Start Squid as shown in Section 17.3.4 on page 412. To check if everything is working properly, check the Squid logs in `/var/log/squid/access.log`.

To verify that all ports are correctly configured, perform a port scan on the machine from any computer outside your network. Only the web services port (80) should be open. To scan the ports with nmap, the command syntax is `nmap -O IP_address`.

17.3.7 Squid and Other Programs

In the following, see how other applications interact with Squid. cachemgr.cgi enables the system administrator to check the amount of memory needed for caching objects. squidGuard filters web pages. Calamaris is a report generator for Squid.

cachemgr.cgi

The cache manager (cachemgr.cgi) is a CGI utility for displaying statistics about the memory usage of a running Squid process. It is also a more convenient way to manage the cache and view statistics without logging the server.

Setup

First, a running web server on your system is required. To check if Apache is already running, as `root` enter the command `rcapache status`. If a message like this appears:

```
Checking for service httpd: OK
Server uptime: 1 day 18 hours 29 minutes 39 seconds
```

Apache is running on your machine. Otherwise, enter `rcapache start` to start Apache with the SUSE LINUX default settings.

The last step to set it up is to copy the file `cachemgr.cgi` to the Apache directory `cgi-bin`:

```
cp /usr/share/doc/packages/squid/scripts/cachemgr.cgi /srv/www/cgi-bin/
```

Cache Manager ACLs in /etc/squid/squid.conf

There are some default settings in the original file required for the cache manager:

```
acl manager proto cache_object
acl localhost src 127.0.0.1/255.255.255.255
```

With the following rules:

```
http_access allow manager localhost
http_access deny manager
```

the first ACL is the most important, as the cache manager tries to communicate with Squid over the cache_object protocol.

The following rules assume that the web server and Squid are running on the same machine. If the communication between the cache manager and Squid originates at the web server on another computer, include an extra ACL as in File 17.2.

Example 17.2: *Access Rules*

```
acl manager proto cache_object
acl localhost src 127.0.0.1/255.255.255.255
acl webserver src 192.168.1.7/255.255.255.255 # webserver IP
```

Then add the rules as in File 17.3.

Example 17.3: *Access Rules*

```
http_access allow manager localhost
http_access allow manager webserver
http_access deny manager
```

Configure a password for the manager for access to more options, like closing the cache remotely or viewing more information about the cache. For this, configure the entry `cachemgr_passwd` with a password for the manager and the list of options to view. This list appears as a part of the entry comments in `/etc/squid/squid.conf`.

Restart Squid every time the configuration file is changed. This can easily be done with `rcsquid reload`.

Viewing the Statistics

Go to the corresponding web site `http://webserver.example.org/cgi-bin/cachemgr.cgi`. Press 'continue' and browse through the different statistics. More details for each entry shown by the cache manager is in the Squid FAQ at `http://www.squid-cache.org/Doc/FAQ/FAQ-9.html`.

squidGuard

This section is not intended to go through an extensive configuration of squidGuard, only to introduce it and give some advice for using it. For more in-depth configuration issues, refer to the squidGuard web site at `http://www.squidguard.org`.

squidGuard is a free (GPL), flexible, and fast filter, redirector, and access controller plug-in for Squid. It lets you define multiple access rules with different restrictions for different user groups on a Squid cache. squidGuard uses Squid's standard redirector interface.

squidGuard can be used for the following:

- limit the web access for some users to a list of accepted or well-known web servers or URLs
- block access to some listed or blacklisted web servers or URLs for some users
- block access to URLs matching a list of regular expressions or words for some users
- redirect blocked URLs to an "intelligent" CGI-based info page
- redirect unregistered users to a registration form
- redirect banners to an empty GIF
- have different access rules based on time of day, day of the week, date, etc.
- have different rules for different user groups

Neither squidGuard or "Squid" can be used to:

- Edit, filter, or censor text inside documents
- Edit, filter, or censor HTML-embedded script languages, such as JavaScript or VBscript

Using squidGuard

Install squidGuard. Edit a minimal configuration file /etc/squidguard.conf. There are plenty of configuration examples in http://www.squidguard.org/config/. Experiment later with more complicated configuration settings.

Next, create a dummy "access denied" page or a more or less intelligent CGI page to redirect Squid if the client requests a blacklisted web site. Using Apache is strongly recommended.

Now, tell Squid to use squidGuard. Use the following entry in the /etc/squid.conf file:

```
redirect_program /usr/bin/squidGuard
```

There is another option called redirect_children configuring how many different "redirect" (in this case squidGuard) processes are running on the machine. squidGuard is fast enough to cope with lots of requests (squidGuard is quite fast: 100,000 requests within 10 seconds on a 500MHz Pentium with 5900 domains, 7880 URLs, total 13780). Therefore, it is not recommended to set more than four processes, because this may lead to an unnecessary increase of memory for the allocation of these processes.

```
redirect_children 4
```

Last, have Squid read its new configuration by running rcsquid reload. Now, test your settings with a browser.

Cache Report Generation with Calamaris

Calamaris is a Perl script used to generate reports of cache activity in ASCII or HTML format. It works with native Squid access log files. The Calamaris home page is located at http://Calamaris.Cord.de/. The use of the program is quite easy.

Log in as root then enter cat access.log.files | calamaris [options] > reportfile It is important when piping more than one log file that the log files are chronologically ordered with older files first. These are some options of the program:

-a output of all available reports

-w an HTML report

-l a message or logo in the header of the report

More information about the various options can be found in the program's manual page with `man calamaris`.

A typical example is:

```
cat access.log.2 access.log.1 access.log | calamaris -a -w \
> /usr/local/httpd/htdocs/Squid/squidreport.html
```

This puts the report in the directory of the web server. Apache is required to view the reports.

Another powerful cache report generator tool is SARG (Squid Analysis Report Generator). More information about this can be found in the relevant Internet pages at `http://web.onda.com.br/orso/`.

More Information about Squid

Visit the home page of Squid at `http://www.squid-cache.org/`. Here, find the Squid User Guide and a very extensive collection of FAQs on Squid.

There is a Mini-Howto regarding transparent proxies in `howtoen` under `/usr/share/doc/howto/en/txt/TransparentProxy.gz`. In addition, mailing lists are available for Squid at `squid-users@squid-cache.org`. The archive for this is located at: `http://www.squid-cache.org/mail-archive/squid-users/`.

Security in the Network

Masquerading, firewall, and Kerberos constitute the basis for a secure network, enabling control of the data traffic. The secure shell (SSH) allows users to log in to remote hosts by way of an encrypted connection. The information in this chapter gives basic instructions for securing a network and working securely in the network with these tools.

18.1 Masquerading and Firewalls

Because of its outstanding network capabilities, Linux is frequently used as a router operating system for dial-up or dedicated lines. *Router*, in this case, refers to a host with multiple network interfaces that transmits any packets not destined for one of its own network interfaces to another host communicating with it. This router is often called a *gateway*. The packet filtering mechanism provided by the Linux kernel allows precise control over which packets of the overall traffic are transferred.

In general, defining the exact rules for a packet filter requires at least some experience on the part of the administrator. For the less experienced user, SUSE LINUX includes a separate package, `SUSEfirewall2`, intended to make it easier to set up these rules.

`SUSEfirewall2` is highly configurable, making it also a good choice for a more complex packet filtering setup. With this packet filter solution, a Linux machine can be used as a router with masquerading to link a local network through a dial-up or dedicated connection where only one IP address is visible to the outside world. Masquerading is accomplished by implementing rules for packet filtering.

Caution

This chapter only describes standard procedures that should work well in most situations. Although every effort has been made to provide accurate and complete information, no guarantee is included. SUSE cannot be held responsible for the success or failure of your security measures. We do appreciate your criticism and comments. Although you might not receive a direct answer from us, rest assured that suggestions for improvement are taken seriously.

Caution

18.1.1 Masquerading Basics

Masquerading is the Linux-specific form of NAT (Network Address Translation). The basic principle is a simple one: Your router has more than one network interface, typically a network card and a separate interface to the Internet (such as an ISDN interface). While this interface links with the outside world, the remaining ones are used to connect this router with the other hosts in your network. For example, the dial-up is conducted via

ISDN and the network interface is ippp0. Several hosts in your local network are connected to the network card of your Linux router, in this example, eth0. Hosts in the network should be configured to send packets destined outside the local network to this gateway.

Note

When configuring your network, make sure that both the broadcast address and the network mask are the same for all the hosts.

Note

When one of the hosts sends a packet destined for an Internet address, this packet is sent to the network's default router. The router needs to be configured before it can forward such packets. However, SUSE LINUX does not enable this with a default installation for security reasons. Therefore, set the variable IP_FORWARD, defined in the file /etc/sysconfig/sysctl, to IP_FORWARD=yes. The forwarding mechanism is enabled after rebooting or after issuing the command echo 1 > /proc/sys/net/ipv4/ip_forward.

The target host can only see your router, but knows nothing about the host in your internal network from which the packets originated. This internal host is disguised behind the router, which is why the technique is called masquerading. Because of the address translation, the router is the first destination of any packets coming back in reply. Now the router must identify these incoming packets and translate their target address, so packets can be forwarded back to the correct host in the local network.

The identification of packets belonging to a connection, as handled by a masquerading router, is done with the help of a table, which is maintained by the kernel of your router as long as the connection exists. root can study this table with the iptables command. Read the man page of this command for detailed instructions. Masqueraded connections are identified not only by their source and target addresses, but also by the port numbers used and the protocols involved. This makes it possible for a router to keep open many different connections for each internal host simultaneously.

With the routing of inbound traffic depending on the masquerading table, there is no way to open a connection to an internal host from the outside. For such a connection, there would be no entry in the table. In addition, any established connection is assigned a status entry in the table, so the entry cannot be used by another connection. As a consequence of all this, you might experience some problems with a number of applications, such as ICQ, cucme, IRC (DCC, CTCP), Quake, and FTP (in PORT mode). Netscape, the standard FTP program, and many others use the PASV mode. This passive mode is much less problematic as far as packet filtering and masquerading is concerned.

18.1.2 Firewalling Basics

Firewall is probably the most widely used term to describe a mechanism to control the data traffic between two networks and to provide and manage the link between networks. There are various types of firewalls, which mostly differ in regard to the abstract level on which traffic is analyzed and controlled. Strictly speaking, the mechanism described in this section is called a *packet filter*. Like any other type of firewall, a packet filter alone does not guarantee full protection from all security risks. A packet filter implements a set of rules related to protocols, ports, and IP addresses to decide whether data may pass. This blocks any packets that, according to the address or destination, are not supposed to reach your network. Packets sent to the telnet service of your hosts on port 23, for example, should be blocked, while you might want people to have access to your web server and therefore enable the corresponding port. A packet filter does not scan the contents of any packets as long as they have legitimate addresses (e.g., directed to your web server). Thus, packets could attack your CGI server, but the packet filter would let them through.

A more effective, but more complex mechanism is the combination of several types of systems, such as a packet filter interacting with an application gateway or proxy. In this case, the packet filter rejects any packets destined to disabled ports. Only packets directed to the application gateway are accepted. This gateway or proxy pretends to be the actual client of the server. In a sense, such a proxy could be considered a masquerading host on the protocol level used by the application. One example for such a proxy is `Squid`, an HTTP proxy server. To use `Squid`, the browser must be configured to communicate via the proxy. Any HTTP pages requested will be served from the proxy cache and pages not found in the cache are fetched from the Internet by the proxy. As another example, the SUSE proxy suite (`proxy-suite`) provides a proxy for the FTP protocol.

The following section focuses on the packet filter that comes with SUSE LINUX. For more information and links, read the Firewall HOWTO included in `howto`. If this package is installed, read the HOWTO with `less /usr/share/doc/howto/en/txt/Firewall-HOWTO.gz`.

18.1.3 SuSEfirewall2

The configuration of SuSEfirewall2 requires a certain degree of experience and understanding. The documentation of SuSEfirewall2 is available in /usr/share/doc/packages/SuSEfirewall2.

The configuration can be performed with YaST (see Section 18.1.3 on page 433) or manually in the file /etc/sysconfig/SuSEfirewall2, which is well commented.

Manual Configuration

The following paragraphs provide step-by-step instructions for a successful configuration. For each configuration item, find a note specifying whether it is relevant for firewalling or for masquerading. Aspects related to the DMZ (*demilitarized zone*) are not covered here. If your requirements are strictly limited to masquerading, only fill out items marked "masquerading".

- First, use the YaST runlevel editor to enable SuSEfirewall2 in your runlevel (3 or 5 most likely). It sets the symlinks for the SuSEfirewall2_* scripts in the /etc/init.d/rc?.d/ directories.
- FW_DEV_WORLD (firewall, masquerading): The device linked to the Internet, such as eth0 or, in the case of ISDN, ippp0.
- FW_DEV_INT (firewall, masquerading): The device linked to the internal, private network. Leave this blank if there is no internal network and the firewall is supposed to protect only the one host.
- FW_ROUTE (firewall, masquerading): If you need the masquerading function, enter yes here. Your internal hosts will not be visible to the outside, because their private network addresses (for instance 192.168.x.x) are ignored by Internet routers.

  For a firewall without masquerading, only set this to yes to allow access to the internal network. Your internal hosts need to use officially registered IPs in this case. Normally, however, you should *not* allow access to your internal network from the outside.
- FW_MASQUERADE (masquerading): Set this to yes if you need the masquerading function. It is more secure to have a proxy server between the hosts of the internal network and the Internet.

- `FW_MASQ_NETS` (masquerading): Specify the hosts or networks to masquerade, leaving a space between the individual entries. For example, `FW_MASQ_NETS`="192.168.0.0/24 192.168.10.1"
- `FW_PROTECT_FROM_INTERNAL` (firewall): Set this to `yes` to protect your firewall host from attacks originating in your internal network. Services will only be available to the internal network if explicitly enabled. See also `FW_SERVICES_INTERNAL_TCP` and `FW_SERVICES_INTERNAL_UDP`.
- `FW_AUTOPROTECT_GLOBAL_SERVICES` (firewall): This should normally be `yes`.
- `FW_SERVICES_EXTERNAL_TCP` (firewall): Enter the services that should be available, for example, `www smtp ftp domain 443`. Leave this blank for a workstation at home that should not offer any services.
- `FW_SERVICES_EXTERNAL_UDP` (firewall): Leave this blank if you do not run a name service that should be made available to the outside. Otherwise, enter the ports to use.
- `FW_SERVICES_INTERNAL_TCP` (firewall): This defines the services available to the internal network. The notation is the same as for external TCP services, but, in this case, refers to the internal network.
- `FW_SERVICES_INTERNAL_UDP` (firewall): See above.
- `FW_TRUSTED_NETS` (firewall): Specify the hosts you *really* trust ("trusted hosts"). Note, however, that these also need to be protected from attacks.

  "`172.20.0.0/16 172.30.4.2`" means that all hosts with an IP address beginning with `172.20.x.x` and the host with the IP address `172.30.4.2` are allowed to pass information through the firewall.
- `FW_SERVICES_TRUSTED_TCP` (firewall): Here, specify the port addresses that may be used by the trusted hosts. For example, to grant them access to all services, enter `1:65535`. Usually, it is sufficient to enter the port address of `ssh` to allow this as the only service.
- `FW_SERVICES_TRUSTED_UDP` (firewall): Just like above, but for UDP ports.
- `FW_ALLOW_INCOMING_HIGHPORTS_TCP` (firewall): Set this to `ftp-data` if you intend to use normal (active) FTP services.

- FW_ALLOW_INCOMING_HIGHPORTS_UDP (firewall): Set this to dns to use the name servers registered in /etc/resolv.conf. If you enter yes here, all high ports will be enabled.
- FW_SERVICE_DNS (firewall): Enter yes if you run a name server that should be available to external hosts. At the same time, enable port 53 under FW_TCP_SERVICES_*.
- FW_SERVICE_DHCLIENT (firewall): Enter yes here if you use dhclient to assign your IP address.
- FW_LOG_* (firewall): Specify the firewall's logging activity. For normal operation, it is sufficient to set FW_LOG_DENY_CRIT to yes.
- FW_STOP_KEEP_ROUTING_STATE (firewall): Insert yes if you have configured your dial-up procedure to work automatically via diald or ISDN (dial-on-demand).

Now that you have configured the firewall, do not forget to test your setup (for example, with telnet from an external host). Have a look at /var/log/messages, where you should see something like:

```
Mar 15 13:21:38 linux kernel: SFW2-INext-DROP-DEFLT IN=eth0
OUT= MAC=00:80:c8:94:c3:e7:00:a0:c9:4d:27:56:08:00 SRC=192.168.10.0
DST=192.168.10.1 LEN=60 TOS=0x10 PREC=0x00 TTL=64 ID=15330 DF PROTO=TCP
SPT=48091 DPT=23 WINDOW=5840 RES=0x00 SYN URGP=0
OPT (020405B40402080A061AFEBC0000000001030300)
```

Configuration with YaST

The YaST dialogs for the graphical configuration can be accessed from the YaST Control Center. Select 'System and Users' -> 'Firewall'. The configuration is divided in four sections:

Basic Settings Specify the interfaces to protect. To protect an individual host to which no internal network is connected, just specify the interface facing the Internet. If an internal network is connected to your system, the interface facing the network must also be specified. Exit this dialog with 'Next'.

Services You only need this option to use your system to offer services accessible from the Internet (web server, mail server, etc.). Activate the respective check boxes or use 'Expert...' to enable services by way of their port numbers (listed in /etc/services). If you are not going to use your host as a server, press 'Next' to exit this dialog without making any changes.

Features Here, select the main features of your firewall:

- 'Allow traceroute' assists in checking the routing to your firewall.
- 'Forward Traffic and Do Masquerading' protects hosts in the internal network against the Internet — all Internet services appear to be used by your firewall, while the internal hosts remain invisible.
- 'Protect All Running Services' indicates that network access to TCP and UDP services of the firewall is denied entirely. This does not affect the services explicitly made available in the preceding step.
- 'Protect from Internal Network' Only the released firewall services are available for *internal* hosts. As it is not possible to make services available here, deactivate this option to grant access from the internal network.

Upon completion of the feature configuration, exit this dialog with 'Next'.

Logging Determine the scope of logging for your firewall. Before you activate the 'Logging options', consider that these log files produce a great amount of output. The configuration of the logging function is the final step of the firewall configuration. Exit the dialog with 'Next' and confirm the following message to activate the firewall.

18.2 SSH — Secure Shell, the Safe Alternative

With more and more computers installed in networked environments, it often becomes necessary to access hosts from a remote location. This normally means that a user sends login and password strings for authentication purposes. As long as these strings are transmitted as plain text, they could be intercepted and misused to gain access to that user account without the authorized user even knowing about it. Apart from the fact that this would open all the user's files to an attacker, the illegal account could be used to obtain administrator or `root` access or to penetrate other systems. In the past, remote connections were established with telnet, which offers no guards against eavesdropping in the form of encryption or other security mechanisms. There are other unprotected communication channels, like the traditional FTP protocol and some remote copying programs.

The SSH suite provides the necessary protection by encrypting the authentication strings (usually a login name and a password) and all the other data exchanged between the hosts. With SSH, the data flow could still be recorded by a third party, but the contents are encrypted and cannot be reverted to plain text unless the encryption key is known. So SSH enables secure communications over insecure networks such as the Internet. The SSH flavor that comes with SUSE LINUX is OpenSSH.

18.2.1 The OpenSSH Package

SUSE LINUX installs the package OpenSSH by default. The programs ssh, scp, and sftp are then available as alternatives to telnet, rlogin, rsh, rcp, and ftp.

18.2.2 The ssh Program

Using the ssh program, it is possible to log in to remote systems and work interactively. It replaces both telnet and rlogin. The slogin program is just a symbolic link pointing to ssh. For example, you can log in to the host sun with the command `ssh sun`. The host then prompts for the password on sun.

After successful authentication, you can work on the remote command line or use interactive applications, such as YaST. If the local user name is different from the remote user name, you can log in using a different login name with `ssh -l augustine sun` or `ssh augustine@sun`.

Furthermore, ssh offers the possibility to run commands on remote systems, as known from rsh. In the following example, run the command `uptime` on the host sun and create a directory with the name `tmp/`. The program output is displayed on the local terminal of the host earth.

```
ssh otherplanet "uptime; mkdir tmp"
tux@otherplanet's password:
1:21pm  up  2:17,  9 users,  load average: 0.15, 0.04, 0.02
```

Quotation marks are necessary here to send both instructions with one command. It is only by doing this that the second command is likewise executed on sun.

18.2.3 scp — Secure Copy

scp copies files to a remote machine. It is a secure and encrypted substitute for rcp. For example, `scp MyLetter.tex sun:` copies the file `MyLetter.tex` from the host earth to the host sun. If the user name on earth is different from the user name on sun, specify the latter using the `username@host` format. There is no `-l` option for this command.

After the correct password is entered, scp starts the data transfer and shows a growing row of asterisks to simulate a progress bar. In addition, the program displays the estimated time of arrival to the right of the progress bar. All output can be suppressed by giving the option `-q`.

scp also provides a recursive copying feature for entire directories. The command `scp -r src/ sun:backup/` copies the entire contents of the directory `src/` including all subdirectories to the `backup/` directory on the host sun. If this subdirectory does not exist yet, it is created automatically.

The option `-p` tells scp to leave the time stamp of files unchanged. `-C` compresses the data transfer. This minimizes the data volume to transfer, but creates a heavier burden on the processor.

18.2.4 sftp — Secure File Transfer

The sftp program can be used instead of scp for secure file transfer. During an sftp session, you can use many of the familiar commands as known from ftp. The sftp program may be a better choice than scp, especially when transferring data for which the file names are unknown beforehand.

18.2.5 The SSH Daemon (sshd) — Server-Side

To work with the SSH client programs ssh and scp, a server, the SSH daemon, must be running in the background, listening for connections on `TCP/IP port 22`.

The daemon generates three key pairs when starting for the first time. Each key pair consist of a private and a public key. Therefore, this procedure is referred to as public key–based. To guarantee the security of the communication via SSH, access to the private key files must be restricted to the system administrator. The file permissions are set accordingly by the default installation. The private keys are only required locally by the SSH daemon and must not be given to anyone else. The public key components (recognizable by the name extension .pub) are sent to the client requesting the connection. They are readable for all users.

A connection is initiated by the SSH client. The waiting SSH daemon and the requesting SSH client exchange identification data to compare the protocol and software versions and to prevent connections through the wrong port. Because a child process of the original SSH daemon replies to the request, several SSH connections can be made simultaneously.

For the communication between SSH server and SSH client, OpenSSH supports versions 1 and 2 of the SSH protocol. A newly installed SUSE LINUX system defaults to version 2. If you want to keep using version 1 after an update, follow the instructions in `/usr/share/doc/packages/openssh/README.SuSE`. This document also describes how an SSH 1 environment can be transformed into a working SSH 2 environment with just a few steps.

When using version 1 of SSH, the server sends its public host key, as well as a server key, which is regenerated by the SSH daemon every hour. Both allow the SSH client to encrypt a freely chosen session key, which is sent over to the SSH server. The SSH client also tells the server which encryption method (cipher) to use.

Version 2 of the SSH protocol does not require a server key. Both sides use an algorithm according to Diffie-Helman instead to exchange their keys.

The private host and server keys are absolutely required to decrypt the session key and cannot be derived from the public parts. Only the SSH daemon contacted can decrypt the session key using its private keys (see `man /usr/share/doc/packages/openssh/RFC.nroff`). This initial connection phase can be watched closely by turning on the verbose debugging option `-v` of the SSH client.

Version 2 of the SSH protocol is used by default. Override this to use version 1 of the protocol with the `-1` switch. The client stores all public host keys in `~/.ssh/known_hosts` after its first contact with a remote host. This prevents any man-in-the-middle attacks — attempts by foreign SSH servers to use spoofed names and IP addresses. Such attacks are detected either by a host key that is not included in `~/.ssh/known_hosts` or by the server's inability to decrypt the session key in the absence of an appropriate private counterpart.

It is recommended to backup the private and public keys stored in /etc/ssh/ in a secure, external location. In this way, key modifications can be detected and the old ones can be used again after a reinstallation. This spares users any unsettling warnings. If it is verified that, despite the warning, it is indeed the correct SSH server, the existing entry regarding this system must be removed from ~/.ssh/known_hosts.

18.2.6 SSH Authentication Mechanisms

Now the actual authentication takes place, which, in its simplest form, consists of entering a password as mentioned above. The goal of SSH was to introduce a secure software that is also easy to use. As it is meant to replace rsh and rlogin, SSH must also be able to provide an authentication method appropriate for daily use. SSH accomplishes this by way of another key pair, which is generated by the user. The SSH package provides a helper program for this: ssh-keygen. After entering ssh-keygen -t rsa or ssh-keygen -t dsa, the key pair is generated and you are prompted for the base file name in which to store the keys:

```
Enter file in which to save the key (/home/tux/.ssh/id_rsa):
```

Confirm the default setting and answer the request for a passphrase. Even if the software suggests an empty passphrase, a text from ten to thirty characters is recommended for the procedure described here. Do not use short and simple words or phrases. Confirm by repeating the passphrase. Subsequently, you will see where the private and public keys are stored, in this example, the files id_rsa and id_rsa.pub.

```
Enter same passphrase again:
Your identification has been saved in /home/tux/.ssh/id_rsa
Your public key has been saved in /home/tux/.ssh/id_rsa.pub.
The key fingerprint is:
79:c1:79:b2:e1:c8:20:c1:89:0f:99:94:a8:4e:da:e8 tux@sun
```

Use ssh-keygen -p -t rsa or ssh-keygen -p -t dsa to change your old passphrase. Copy the public key component (id_rsa.pub in the example) to the remote machine and save it to ~/.ssh/authorized_keys. You will be asked to authenticate yourself with your passphrase the next time you establish a connection. If this does not occur, verify the location and contents of these files.

In the long run, this procedure is more troublesome than giving your password each time. Therefore, the SSH package provides another tool, ssh-agent, which retains the private keys for the duration of an X session. The entire X session is started as a child process of ssh-agent. The easiest way to do this is to set the variable `usessh` at the beginning of the `.xsession` file to `yes` and log in via a display manager, such as KDM or XDM. Alternatively, enter `ssh-agent startx`.

Now you can use `ssh` or `scp` as usual. If you have distributed your public key as described above, you are no longer prompted for your password. Take care of terminating your X session or locking it with a password protection application, such as xlock.

All the relevant changes that resulted from the introduction of version 2 of the SSH protocol are also documented in the file `/usr/share/doc/packages/openssh/README.SuSE`.

18.2.7 X, Authentication, and Other Forwarding Mechanisms

Beyond the previously described security-related improvements, SSH also simplifies the use of remote X applications. If you run `ssh` with the option `-X`, the DISPLAY variable is automatically be set on the remote machine and all X output is exported to the remote machine over the existing SSH connection. At the same time, X applications started remotely and locally viewed with this method cannot be intercepted by unauthorized individuals.

By adding the option `-A`, the ssh-agent authentication mechanism is carried over to the next machine. This way, you can work from different machines without having to enter a password, but only if you have distributed your public key to the destination hosts and properly saved it there.

Both mechanisms are deactivated in the default settings, but can be permanently activated at any time in the system-wide configuration file `/etc/ssh/sshd_config` or the user's `~/.ssh/config`.

ssh can also be used to redirect TCP/IP connections. In the examples below, SSH is told to redirect the SMTP and the POP3 port, respectively:

```
ssh -L 25:sun:25 earth
```

With this command, any connection directed to *earth Port 25* (SMTP) is redirected to the SMTP port on sun via an encrypted channel. This is especially useful for those using SMTP servers without SMTP-AUTH or POP-before-SMTP features. From any arbitrary location connected to a network, e-mail can be transferred to the "home" mail server for delivery. Similarly, all POP3 requests (port 110) on earth can be forwarded to the POP3 port of sun with this command:

```
ssh -L 110:sun:110 earth
```

Both commands must be executed as `root`, because the connection is made to privileged local ports. E-mail is sent and retrieved by normal users in an existing SSH connection. The SMTP and POP3 host must be set to `localhost` for this to work. Additional information can be found in the manual pages for each of the programs described above and also in the files under `/usr/share/doc/packages/openssh`.

18.3 Network Authentication — Kerberos

An open network provides no means to ensure that a workstation can identify its users properly except the usual password mechanisms. In common installations, the user must enter the password each time a service inside the network is accessed. Kerberos provides an authentication method with which a user must register once and is then trusted in the complete network for the rest of the session. To have a secure network, the following requirements must be met:

- Have all users prove their identity for each desired service and make sure no one can take the identity of someone else.
- Make sure each network server also proves its identity. If you do not, an attacker might be able to impersonate the server and obtain sensitive information transmitted to the server. This concept is called *mutual authentication*, because the client authenticates to the server and vice versa.

Kerberos helps you meet the above requirements by providing strongly encrypted authentication. The following shows how this is achieved. Only the basic principles of Kerberos are discussed here. For detailed technical instruction, refer to the documentation provided with your implementation of Kerberos.

Note

The original Kerberos was designed at the MIT. Besides the MIT Kerberos, several other implementations of Kerberos exist. SUSE LINUX ships with a free implementation of Kerberos 5, the Heimdal Kerberos 5 from KTH. Because the following text covers features common to all versions, the program itself is referred to as Kerberos as long as no Heimdal-specific information is presented.

Note

18.3.1 Kerberos Terminology

The following glossary defines some Kerberos terminology.

credential Users or clients need to present some kind of credentials that authorize them to request services. Kerberos knows two kinds of credentials — tickets and authenticators.

ticket A ticket is a per-server credential used by a client to authenticate at a server from which it is requesting a service. It contains the name of the server, the client's name, the client's Internet address, a time stamp, a lifetime, and a random session key. All this data is encrypted using the server's key.

authenticator Combined with the ticket, an authenticator is used to prove that the client presenting a ticket is really the one it claims to be. An authenticator is built of the client's name, the workstation's IP address, and the current workstation's time all encrypted with the session key only known to the client and the server from which it is requesting a service. An authenticator can only be used once, unlike a ticket. A client can build an authenticator itself.

principal A Kerberos principal is a unique entity (a user or service) to which it can assign a ticket. A principal consists of the following components:

- **primary** — the first part of the principal, which can be the same as your user name in the case of a user.
- **instance** — some optional information characterizing the primary. This string is separated from the primary by a `/`.
- **realm** — this specifies your Kerberos realm. Normally, your realm is your domain name in uppercase letters.

mutual authentication Kerberos ensures that both client and server can be sure of each others identity. They share a (session) key, which they can use to communicate securely.

session key Session keys are temporary private keys generated by Kerberos. They are known to the client and used to encrypt the communication between the client and the server for which it requested and received a ticket.

replay Almost all messages sent in a network can be eavesdropped, stolen, and resent. In the Kerberos context, this would be most dangerous if an attacker manages to obtain your request for a service containing your ticket and authenticator. He could then try to resend it (*replay*) to impersonate you. However, Kerberos implements several mechanisms to deal with that problem.

server or service *Service* is used to refer to a specific action to perform. The process behind this action is referred to as a *server*.

18.3.2 How Kerberos Works

Kerberos is often called a third party trusted authentication service, which means all its clients trust Kerberos's judgment of another client's identity. Kerberos keeps a database of all its users and their private keys.

To ensure Kerberos is worth all the trust put in it, run both the authentication and ticket-granting server on a dedicated machine. Make sure only the administrator can access this machine physically and over the network. Reduce the (networking) services run on it to the absolute minimum — do not even run sshd.

First contact Your first contact with Kerberos is quite similar to any login procedure at a normal networking system. Enter your user name. This piece of information and the name of the ticket-granting service are sent to the authentication server (Kerberos). If the authentication server knows about your existence, it will generate a (random) session key for further use between your client and the ticket-granting server. Now the authentication server prepares a ticket for the ticket-granting server. The ticket contains the following information — all encrypted with a session key only the authentication server and the ticket-granting server know:

- the names both of the client and the ticket-granting server

- the current time
- a lifetime assigned to this ticket
- the client's IP address
- the newly-generated session key

This ticket is then sent back to the client together with the session key, again in encrypted form, but this time the private key of the client is used. This private key is only known to Kerberos and the client, because it is derived from your user password. Now that the client has received this response, you are prompted for your password. This password is converted into the key that can decrypt the package sent by the authentication server. The package is "unwrapped" and password and key are erased from the workstation's memory. As long as the lifetime given to the ticket used to obtain other tickets does not expire, your workstation can prove your identity.

Requesting a service To request a service from any server in the network, the client application needs to prove its identity to the server. Therefore, the application generates an authenticator. An authenticator consists of the following components:

- the client's principal
- the client's IP address
- the current time
- a checksum (chosen by the client)

All this information is encrypted using the session key that the client has already received for this special server. The authenticator and the ticket for the server are sent to the server. The server uses its copy of the session key to decrypt the authenticator, which gives him all information needed about the client requesting its service to compare it to that contained in the ticket. The server checks if the ticket and the authenticator originate from the same client.Without any security measures implemented on the server side, this stage of the process would be an ideal target for replay attacks. Someone could try to resend a request stolen off the net some time before. To prevent this, the server will not accept any request with a time stamp and ticket received previously. In addition to that, a request with a time stamp differing too much from the time the request is received can be ignored.

Mutual authentication Kerberos authentication can be used in both directions. It is not only a question of the client being the one it claims to be. The server should also be able to authenticate itself to the client requesting its service. Therefore, it sends some kind of authenticator itself. It adds one to the checksum it received in the client's authenticator and encrypts it with the session key, which is shared between it and the client. The client takes this response as a proof of the server's authenticity and they both start cooperating.

Ticket-granting — getting into contact with all servers
Tickets are designed to be used for one server at a time. This implies that you have to get a new ticket each time you request another service. Kerberos implements a mechanism to obtain tickets for individual servers. This service is called the "ticket-granting service". The ticket-granting service is a service just like any other service mentioned before, so uses the same access protocols that have already been outlined. Any time an application needs a ticket that has not already been requested, it contacts the ticket-granting server. This request consists of the following components:

- the requested principal
- the ticket-granting ticket
- an authenticator

Like any other server, the ticket-granting server now checks the ticket-granting ticket and the authenticator. If they are considered valid, the ticket-granting server builds a new session key to be used between the original client and the new server. Then the ticket for the new server is built, containing the following information:

- the client's principal
- the server's principal
- the current time
- the client's IP address
- the newly-generated session key

The new ticket is assigned a lifetime, which is the lesser of the remaining lifetime of the ticket-granting ticket and the default for the service. The client receives this ticket and the session key, which are sent by the ticket-granting service, but this time the answer is encrypted with the session key that came with the original ticket-granting ticket. The client can decrypt the response without requiring the user's password when a new service is contacted. Kerberos can thus acquire ticket after ticket for the client without bothering the user more than once at login time.

Compatibility to Windows 2000 Windows 2000 contains a Microsoft implementation of Kerberos 5. As SUSE LINUX makes use of the Heimdal implementation of Kerberos 5, find useful information and guidance in the Heimdal documentation. See Section 18.3.4 on the next page.

18.3.3 Users' View of Kerberos

Ideally, a user's one and only contact with Kerberos happens during login at his workstation. The login process includes obtaining a ticket-granting ticket. At logout, a user's Kerberos tickets are automatically destroyed, which hinders anyone else from impersonating this user when not logged in. The automatic destruction of tickets can lead to a somewhat awkward situation when a user's login session lasts longer than the maximum lifespan given to the ticket-granting ticket (a reasonable setting is ten hours). However, the user can get a new ticket-granting ticket by running kinit. Enter the password again and Kerberos obtains access to desired services without additional authentication. Those interested in a list of all the tickets silently acquired for them by Kerberos should run klist.

Here is a short list of some applications that use Kerberos authentication. These applications can be found under `/usr/lib/heimdal/bin`. They all have the full functionality of their common UNIX and Linux brothers plus the additional bonus of transparent authentication managed by Kerberos:

- telnet, telnetd
- rlogin
- rsh, rcp, rshd
- popper, push
- ftp, ftpd
- su

- imapd
- pine

You no longer have to type your password for using these applications because Kerberos has already proven your identity. ssh, if compiled with Kerberos support, can even forward all the tickets acquired for one workstation to another one. If you use ssh to log in to another workstation, ssh makes sure the encrypted contents of the tickets are adjusted to the new situation. Simply copying tickets between workstations is not sufficient as the ticket contains workstation-specific information (the IP address). XDM and KDM offer Kerberos support, too. Read more about the Kerberos network applications in the *Kerberos V5 UNIX User's Guide* at `http://web.mit.edu/kerberos/www/krb5-1.3/krb5-1.3/doc/krb5-user.html`.

18.3.4 For More Information

SUSE LINUX contains a free implementation of Kerberos called Heimdal. Its documentation is installed along with the package `heimdal` under `/usr/share/doc/packages/heimdal/doc/heimdal.info`. It is also available at the project's home page at `http://www.pdc.kth.se/heimdal/`.

The official site of the MIT Kerberos is `http://web.mit.edu/kerberos/www/`. There, find links to any other relevant resource concerning Kerberos. A "classical" dialog pointing out the principles of Kerberos is available at `http://web.mit.edu/kerberos/www/dialogue.html`. It is a less technical but still a comprehensive read.

The paper at `ftp://athena-dist.mit.edu/pub/kerberos/doc/usenix.PS` gives quite an extensive insight to the basic principles of Kerberos without being too difficult to read. It also provides a lot of opportunities for further investigation and reading about Kerberos.

These links provide a short introduction to Kerberos and answer many questions regarding Kerberos installation, configuration, and administration:

`http://web.mit.edu/kerberos/www/krb5-1.3/krb5-1.3/doc/krb5-user.html`,

`http://web.mit.edu/kerberos/www/krb5-1.3/krb5-1.3/doc/krb5-install.html`,

`http://web.mit.edu/kerberos/www/krb5-1.3/krb5-1.3/doc/krb5-admin.html`.

The official Kerberos FAQ is available at `http://www.nrl.navy.mil/CCS/people/kenh/kerberos-faq.html`. The book *Kerberos — A Network Authentication System* by Brian Tung (ISBN 0-201-37924-4) offers extensive information.

18.4 Installing and Administering Kerberos

This section covers the installation of the Heimdal Kerberos implementation as well as some aspects of administration. This section assumes you are familiar with the basic concepts of Kerberos (see also Section 18.3 on page 440).

18.4.1 Choosing the Kerberos Realms

The domain of a Kerberos installation is called a realm and is identified by a name, such as `FOOBAR.COM` or simply `ACCOUNTING`. Kerberos is case-sensitive, so `foobar.com` is actually a different realm than `FOOBAR.COM`. Use the case you prefer. It is common practice, however, to use uppercase realm names.

It is also a good idea to use your DNS domain name (or a subdomain, such as `ACCOUNTING.FOOBAR.COM`). As shown below, your life as an administrator can be much easier if you configure your Kerberos clients to locate the KDC and other Kerberos services via DNS. To do so, it is helpful if your realm name is a subdomain of your DNS domain name.

Unlike the DNS name space, Kerberos is not hierarchical. You cannot set up a realm named `FOOBAR.COM`, have two "subrealms" named `DEVELOPMENT` and `ACCOUNTING` underneath it, and expect the two subordinate realms to somehow inherit principals from `FOOBAR.COM`. Instead, you would have three separate realms for which you would have to configure crossrealm authentication for users from one realm to interact with servers or other users from another realm.

For the sake of simplicity, assume you are setting up just one realm for your entire organization. Setting up crossrealm authentication is described in [15], for instance. For the remainder of this section, the realm name `SAMPLE.COM` is used in all examples.

18.4.2 Setting up the KDC Hardware

The first thing required to use Kerberos is a machine that will act as the key distribution center, or KDC for short. This machine holds the entire Kerberos user database with passwords and all information.

The KDC is the most important part of your security infrastructure — if someone breaks into it, all user accounts and all of your infrastructure protected by Kerberos is compromised. An attacker with access to the Kerberos database can impersonate any principal in the database. Tighten security for this machine as much as possible:

- Put the server machine into a physically secured location, such as a locked server room to which only a very few people have access.
- Do not run any network applications on it except the KDC. This includes servers and clients — for instance, the KDC should not import any file systems via NFS or use DHCP to retrieve its network configuration.
- It is probably a good approach to install a minimal system first then check the list of installed packages and remove any unneeded packages. This includes servers, such as inetd, portmap, and cups, as well as anything X11-based. Even installing an SSH server should be considered a potential security risk.
- No graphical login is provided on this machine as an X server is a potential security risk. Kerberos provides its own administration interface.
- Configure `/etc/nsswitch.conf` to use only local files for user and group lookup. Change the lines for `passwd` and `group` to look like this:

  ```
  passwd:         files
  group:          files
  ```

  Edit the `passwd`, `group`, `shadow`, and `gshadow` files in `/etc/` and remove the lines that start with a + character (these are for NIS lookups).

  Also consider disabling DNS lookups, because there is a potential risk involved. If there is a security bug in the DNS resolver library, an attacker might be able to trick the KDC into performing a DNS query that triggers this bug. To disable DNS lookups, simply remove `/etc/resolv.conf`.

- Disable all user accounts except root's account by editing /etc/shadow and replacing the hashed passwords with * or ! characters.

18.4.3 Clock Synchronization

To use Kerberos successfully, make sure all system clocks within your organization are synchronized within a certain range. This is important because Kerberos protects against replayed credentials. An attacker might be able to observe Kerberos credentials on the network and reuse them to attack the server. Kerberos employs several defenses to prevent this. One of them is that it puts time stamps into its tickets. A server receiving a ticket with a time stamp that differs from the current time rejects the ticket.

Kerberos allows a certain leeway when comparing time stamps. However, computer clocks can be very inaccurate in keeping time — it is not unheard of for PC clocks to lose or gain half an hour over the course of a week. For this reason, configure all hosts on the network to synchronize their clocks with a central time source.

A simple way to do so is by installing an NTP time server on one machine and having all clients synchronize their clocks with this server. Do this either by running an NTP daemon in client mode on all these machines or by running ntpdate once a day from all clients (this solution will probably work for a small number of clients only). The KDC itself needs to be synchronized to the common time source as well. Because running an NTP daemon on this machine would be a security risk, it is probably a good idea to do this by running ntpdate via a cron entry. NTP configuration itself is beyond the scope of this section. For more information, refer to the NTP documentation included in your installed system under /usr/share/doc/packages/xntp-doc/.

It is also possible to adjust the maximum deviation Kerberos allows when checking time stamps. This value (called "clock skew") can be set via the krb5.conf file as described in Section 18.4.6 on page 454.

18.4.4 Log Configuration

By default, the Kerberos daemons running on the KDC host log information to the syslog daemon. To keep an eye on what your KDC is doing, process these log files regularly, scanning for unusual events or potential problems. Either do this by running a log scanner script on the KDC host itself or by copying these files from the KDC to another host with rsync.

Forwarding all log output via syslogd's log forwarding mechanisms is not recommended, because information traverses the network unencrypted.

18.4.5 Installing the KDC

This section covers the initial installation of the KDC, including creation of an administrative principal.

Installing the RPMs

Before you can start, install the Kerberos software. On the KDC, install the packages `heimdal`, `heimdal-lib`, and `heimdal-tools` with `rpm -ivh heimdal-*.rpm heimdal-lib-*.rpm heimdal-tools*.rpm`.

Setting the Master Key

Your next step is to initialize the database where Kerberos keeps all information about principals. First, set the database master key, which is used to protect the database from accidental disclosure, in particular when it is backed up to a tape. The master key is derived from a pass phrase and is stored in a file called the stash file. This is so you do not need to type in the password every time the KDC is restarted. Make sure you choose a good pass phrase, such as a sentence from a book opened to a random page.

When you make tape backups of the Kerberos database (`/var/heimdal/heimdal.db`), do not back up the stash file (which is in `/var/heimdal/m-key`). Otherwise, everyone able to read the tape could also decrypt the database. Therefore, it is also a good idea to keep a copy of the pass phrase in a safe or some other secure location, because you will need it when restoring your database from backup tape after a crash.

To set the master key, run kstash without arguments and enter the pass phrase twice:

```
kstash

Master key:<enter pass phrase>
Verifying password - Master key:<enter pass phrase again>
```

Creating the Realm

Finally, create entries for your realm in the Kerberos database. Run `kadmin` with the -l option as shown. This option tells kadmin to access the database locally. By default, it tries to contact the Kerberos admin service over the network. At this stage, this will not work because it is not running yet.

Now, tell kadmin to initialize your realm. It will ask you a number of questions in return. It is best to accept the default settings offered by kadmin initially:

```
kadmin -l

kadmin> init SAMPLE.COM
Realm max ticket life [unlimited]: <press return>
Realm max renewable ticket life [unlimited]: <press return>
```

To verify that it did anything, use the list command:

```
kadmin> list *
default@SAMPLE.COM
kadmin/admin@SAMPLE.COM
kadmin/hprop@SAMPLE.COM
kadmin/changepw@SAMPLE.COM
krbtgt/SAMPLE.COM@SAMPLE.COM
changepw/kerberos@SAMPLE.COM
```

This shows that there are now a number of principals in the database. All of these are for internal use by Kerberos.

Creating a Principal

Next, create two Kerberos principals for yourself: one normal principal for your everyday work and one for administrative tasks relating to Kerberos. Assuming your login name is `newbie`, proceed as follows:

```
kadmin -l

kadmin> add newbie
Max ticket life [1 day]: <press return>
Max renewable life [1 week]: <press return>
Principal expiration time [never]: <press return>
Password expiration time [never]: <press return>
Attributes []: <press return>
newbie@SAMPLE.COM's Password: <type password here>
Verifying password: <re-type password here>
```

Accepting the defaults by pressing (Enter) is okay. Choose a good password, however.

Next, create another principal named `newbie/admin` by typing `add newbie/admin` at the `kadmin` prompt. The `admin` suffixed to your user name is a "role". Later, use this role when administering the Kerberos database. A user can have several roles for different purposes. Roles are basically completely different accounts with similar names.

Starting the KDC

Start the KDC daemons. This includes kdc itself (the daemon handling user authentication and ticket requests), kadmind (the server performing remote administration), and kpasswddd (handling user's password change requests). To start the daemon manually, enter `rckdc start`. Also make sure KDC is started by default when the server machine is rebooted with the command `insserv kdc`.

18.4.6 Configuring Kerberos Clients

When configuring Kerberos, there are basically two approaches you can take — static configuration via the `/etc/krb5.conf` file or dynamic configuration via DNS. With DNS configuration, Kerberos applications try to locate the KDC services via DNS records. With static configuration, add the host names of your KDC server to `krb5.conf` (and update the file whenever you move the KDC or reconfigure your realm in other ways).

DNS-based configuration is generally a lot more flexible and the amount of configuration work per machine is a lot less. However, it requires that your realm name is either the same as your DNS domain or a subdomain of it. Configuring Kerberos via DNS also creates a minor security issue — an attacker can seriously disrupt your infrastructure through your DNS (by shooting down the name server, by spoofing DNS records, etc). However, this amounts to a denial of service at most. A similar scenario applies to the static configuration case unless you enter IP addresses in `krb5.conf` instead of host names.

Static Configuration

One way to configure Kerberos is to edit the configuration file `/etc/krb5.conf`. The file installed by default contains various sample entries. Erase all of these entries before starting. `krb5.conf` is made up of several sections, each introduced by the section name included in brackets like `[this]`.

To configure your Kerberos clients, add the following stanza to `krb5.conf` (where `kdc.sample.com` is the host name of the KDC):

```
[libdefaults]
        default_realm = SAMPLE.COM

[realms]
        SAMPLE.COM = {
```

```
                kdc = kdc.sample.com
                kpasswd_server = kdc.sample.com
                admin_server = kdc.sample.com
        }
```

The `default_realm` line sets the default realm for Kerberos applications. If you have several realms, just add another statement to the `[realms]` section.

Also add a statement to this file that tells applications how to map host names to a realm. For instance, when connecting to a remote host, the Kerberos library needs to know in which realm this host is located. This must be configured in the `[domain_realms]` section:

```
[domain_realm]
        .sample.com = SAMPLE.COM
        www.foobar.com = SAMPLE.COM
```

This tells the library that all hosts in the `sample.com` DNS domains are in the `SAMPLE.COM` Kerberos realm. In addition, one external host named `www.foobar.com` should also be considered a member of the `SAMPLE.COM` realm.

DNS-Based Configuration

DNS-based Kerberos configuration makes heavy use of SRV records (see *(RFC2052) A DNS RR for specifying the location of services* at `http://www.ietf.org`). These records are not supported in earlier implementations of the BIND name server. At least BIND version 8 is required for this.

The name of an SRV record, as far as Kerberos is concerned, is always in the format `_service._proto.realm`, where realm is the Kerberos realm. Domain names in DNS are case insensitive, so case-sensitive Kerberos realms would break when using this configuration method. `_service` is a service name (different names are used when trying to contact the KDC or the password service, for example). `_proto` can be either `_udp` or `_tcp`, but not all services support both protocols.

The data portion of SRV resource records consists of a priority value, a weight, a port number, and a host name. The priority defines the order in which hosts should be tried (lower values indicate a higher priority). The weight is there to support some sort of load balancing among servers of equal priority. You will probably never need any of this, so it is okay to set these to zero.

Heimdal Kerberos currently looks up the following names when looking for services:

_kerberos This defines the location of the KDC daemon (the authentication and ticket granting server). Typical records look like this:

```
_kerberos._udp.SAMPLE.COM.  IN  SRV    0 0 88 kdc.sample.com.
_kerberos._tcp.SAMPLE.COM.  IN  SRV    0 0 88 kdc.sample.com.
```

_kpasswd This describes the location of the password changing server. Typical records look like this:

```
_kpasswd._udp.SAMPLE.COM.   IN  SRV    0 0 464 kdc.sample.com.
```

Because kpasswdd does not support TCP, there should be no `_tcp` record.

_kerberos-adm This describes the location of the remote administration service. Typical records look like this:

```
_kerberos-adm._tcp.SAMPLE.COM. IN  SRV    0 0 749 kdc.sample.com.
```

Because kadmind does not support UDP, there should be no `_udp` record.

As with the static configuration file, there is a mechanism to inform clients that a specific host is in the `SAMPLE.COM` realm, even if it is not part of the sample.com DNS domain. This can be done by attaching a TXT record to `_keberos.hostname`, as shown here:

```
_keberos.www.foobar.com.  IN TXT "SAMPLE.COM"
```

Adjusting the Clock Skew

The *clock skew* is the tolerance for accepting tickets with time stamps that do not exactly match the host's system clock. Usually, the clock skew is set to 300 seconds, or 5 minutes. This means a ticket can have a time stamp somewhere between 5 minutes ago and 5 minutes in the future from the server's point of view.

When using NTP to synchronize all hosts, you can reduce this value to about one minute. The clock skew value can be set in `/etc/krb5.conf` like this:

```
[libdefaults]
        clockskew = 120
```

18.4.7 Remote Kerberos Administration

To be able to add and remove principals from the Kerberos database without accessing the KDC's console directly, tell the Kerberos administration server which principals are allowed to do what. Do this by editing the file `/var/heimdal/kadmind.acl` (ACL is an abbreviation for access control list). The ACL file allows you to specify privileges with a fine degree of control. For details, refer to the manual page with `man 8 kadmind`.

Right now, just grant yourself the privilege to do anything you want with the database by putting the following line into the file:

```
newbie/admin                all
```

Replace the user name `newbie` with your own. Restart the KDC for the change to take effect.

Using kadmin for Remote Administration

You should now be able to perform Kerberos administration tasks remotely using the kadmin tool. First, obtain a ticket for your admin role and use that ticket when connecting to the kadmin server:

```
kinit newbie/admin

newbie/admin@SAMPLE.COM's Password: <enter password>
/usr/sbin/kadmin
kadmin> privs
change-password, list, delete, modify, add, get
```

Using the privs command, verify which privileges you have. The list shown above is the full set of privileges.

As an example, modify the principal `newbie`:

```
kadmin> mod newbie

Max ticket life [1 day]:2 days
Max renewable life [1 week]:
Principal expiration time [never]:2005-01-01
Password expiration time [never]:
Attributes []:
```

This changes the maximum ticket life time to two days and sets the expiration date for the account to January 1, 2005..

Basic kadmin Commands

Here is a brief list of kadmin commands. For more information, refer to the manual page of `kadmin`.

add `principal` add a new principal

modify `principal` edit various attributes of a principal, such as maximum ticket life time and account expiration date

delete `principal` remove a principal from the database

rename `principal newname` renames a principal to `newname`

list `pattern` list all principals matching the given pattern. Patterns work much like the shell globbing patterns: `list newbie*` would list `newbie` and `newbie/admin` in our example.

get `principal` display detailed information about the principal

passwd `principal` changes a principal's password

At all stages, help is available by typing ? and Enter. This even works in prompt environments generated by `modify` and `add`.

The `init` command used when initially creating the realm (as well as a few others) is not available in remote mode. To create a new realm, go to the KDC's console and use kadmin in local mode (using the `-l` command line option). The same is true for dumping and restoring the KDC database using the `dump`, `load`, and `merge` commands.

18.4.8 Creating Kerberos Host Principals

In addition to making sure every machine on your network knows which Kerberos realm it is in and what KDC to contact, create a *host principal* for it. So far, only user credentials have been discussed. However, Keberos-compatible services usually need to authenticate themselves to the client user, too. Therefore, special host principals must be present in the Kerberos database for each host in the realm.

The naming convention for host principals is `host/>hostname<@<REALM>`, where `hostname` is the host's fully qualified host name. Host principals are similar to user principals, but have significant differences. The main difference between a user principal and a host principal is that the key of the former is protected by a password

— when a user obtains a ticket-granting ticket from the KDC, he needs to type his password so Kerberos can decrypt the ticket. Obviously, it would be quite inconvenient for the system administrator if he had to obtain new tickets for the SSH daemon every eight hours or so.

Instead, the key required to decrypt the initial ticket for the host principal is extracted by the administrator from the KDC once and stored in a local file called the *keytab*. Services such the SSH daemon read this key and use it to obtain new tickets automatically when needed. The default keytab file resides in `/etc/krb5.keytab`.

To create a host principal for `machine.sample.com`, enter the following commands during your kadmin session:

```
kinit newbie/admin

newbie/admin@SAMPLE.COM's Password: <type password>
kadmin add -r host/machine.sample.com
Max ticket life [1 day]:
Max renewable life [1 week]:
Principal expiration time [never]:
Password expiration time [never]:
Attributes []:
```

Instead of setting a password for the new principal, the -r flag tells kadmin to generate a random key. This is used here because no user interaction is wanted for this principal. It is a server account for the machine.

Finally, extract the key and store it in the local keytab file `/etc/krb5.keytab`. This file is owned by the superuser, so you must be root to execute the next command:

```
ktutil get host/machine.sample.com
```

When completed, make sure you destroy the admin ticket obtained via kinit above with `kdestroy`.

18.4.9 Enabling PAM Support for Kerberos

SUSE LINUX comes with a PAM module named `pam_krb5`, which supports Kerberos login and password update. This module can be used by applications, such as console login, su, and graphical login applications like KDM, where the user presents a password and would like the authenticating application to obtain an initial Kerberos ticket on his behalf.

The `pam_unix` module, too, supports Kerberos authentication and password updating. To enable Kerberos support in `pam_unix`, edit the file `/etc/security/pam_unix2.conf` so it contains the following lines:

```
auth:        use_krb5 nullok
account:     use_krb5
password:    use_krb5 nullok
session:     none
```

After that, all programs evaluating the entries in this file use Kerberos for user authentication. For a user that does not have a Kerberos principal, pam_unix falls back on the normal password authentication mechanism. For those users who have a principal, it should now be possible to change their Kerberos passwords transparently using the passwd command.

To make fine adjustments to the way in which pam_krb5 is used, edit the file /etc/krb5.conf and add default applications to pam. For details refer to the manual page with man 5 pam_krb5.

The pam_krb5 module was specifically **not** designed for network services that accept Kerberos tickets as part of user authentication. This is an entirely different matter, which is discussed below.

18.4.10 Configuring SSH for Kerberos Authentication

OpenSSH supports Kerberos authentication in both protocol version 1 and 2. In version 1, there are special protocol messages to transmit Kerberos tickets. Version 2 does not use Kerberos directly anymore, but relies on "GSSAPI", the General Security Services API. This is a programming interface that is not specific to Kerberos — it was designed to hide the peculiarities of the underlying authentication system, be it Kerberos, a public-key authentication system like SPKM, or others. The GSSAPI library included in SUSE LINUX supports only Kerberos, however.

To use sshd with Kerberos authentication, edit /etc/ssh/sshd_config and set the following options:

```
# These are for protocol version 1
KerberosAuthentication yes
KerberosTgtPassing yes
# These are for version 2
GSSAPIAuthentication yes
GSSAPIKeyExchange yes
```

Then restart your SSH daemon using rcsshd restart.

To use Kerberos authentication with protocol version 2, enable it on the client-side as well. Do this either in the system-wide configuration file /etc/ssh/ssh_config or on a per-user level by editing ~/.ssh/config. In both cases, add the option GSSAPIAuthentication yes.

You should now be able to connect using Kerberos authentication. Use `klist` to verify you have a valid ticket then connect to the SSH server. To force SSH protocol version 1, specify option `-1` on the command line.

18.4.11 Using LDAP and Kerberos

When using Kerberos, one way to distribute the user information (such as user ID, groups, home directory, etc.) in your local network is to use LDAP. This requires a strong authentication mechanism that prevents packet spoofing and other attacks. One solution is to use Kerberos for LDAP communication, too.

OpenLDAP implements most authentication flavors through SASL, the simple authentication session layer. SASL is basically a network protocol designed for authentication. The SASL implementation used in SUSE LINUX is cyrus-sasl, which supports a number of different authentication flavors. Kerberos authentication is performed through GSSAPI (General Security Services API). By default, the SASL plugin for GSSAPI is not installed. Install it manually with `rpm -ivh cyrus-sasl-gssapi-*.rpm`.

To enable Kerberos binding to the OpenLDAP server, create a principal `ldap/earth.sample.com` and add that to the keytab:

```
kadmin add -r ldap/earth.sample.com

ktutil get ldap/earth.sample.com
```

By default, the LDAP server slapd runs as user and group `ldap`, while the keytab file is readable by `root` only. Therefore, either change the LDAP configuration so the server runs as `root` or make the keytab file readable by group `ldap`.

To run slapd as root, edit `/etc/sysconfig/openldap`. Disable the `OPENLDAP_USER` and `OPENLDAP_GROUP` variables by putting a comment character in front of them.

To make the keytab file readable by group LDAP, execute

```
chgrp ldap /etc/krb5.keytab

chmod 640 /etc/krb5.keytab
```

Neither solution is perfect. However, at the moment it is not possible to configure OpenLDAP to make it use a separate keytab file. Finally, restart the LDAP server using `rcldap restart`.

Using Kerberos Authentication with LDAP

You should now be able to use tools, such as ldapsearch, with Kerberos authentication automatically.

```
ldapsearch -b ou=People,dc=suse,dc=de '(uid=newbie)'

SASL/GSSAPI authentication started
SASL SSF: 56
SASL installing layers
[...]

# newbie, People, suse.de
dn: uid=newbie,ou=People,dc=suse,dc=de
uid: newbie
cn: Olaf Kirch
[...]
```

As you can see, ldapsearch prints a message that it started GSSAPI authentication. The next message is admittedly very cryptic, but it shows that the "Security Strength Factor" (SSF for short) is 56. (The value 56 is somewhat arbitrary. Most likely it was chosen because this is the number of bits in a DES encryption key.) What this tells you is that GSSAPI authentication was successful and that encryption is being used to provide integrity protection and confidentiality of the LDAP connection. If there are several SASL mechanisms that could be used, you can force `ldapsearch` to use GSSAPI by adding `-Y GSSAPI` to the command line options.

In Kerberos, authentication is always mutual. This means that not only have you authenticated yourself to the LDAP server, but also the LDAP server authenticated itself to you. In particular, this means communication is with the desired LDAP server, rather than some bogus service set up by an attacker.

Kerberos Authentication and LDAP Access Control

Now, allow each user to modify the login shell attribute of their LDAP user record. Assuming you have a schema where the LDAP entry of user `joe` is located at `uid=joe, ou=people, dc=suse, dc=de`, set up the following access controls in `/etc/openldap/slapd.conf`:

```
# This is required for things to work _at all_
access to dn.base="" by * read
# Let each user change their login shell
access to dn="*,ou=people,dc=suse,dc=de" attrs=loginShell
       by self write
```

```
# Every user can read everything
access to *
       by users read
```

The second statement gives authenticated users write access to the `loginShell` attribute of their own LDAP entry. The third statement gives all authenticated users read access to the entire LDAP directory.

There is one minor piece of the puzzle missing, which is how the LDAP server can find out that the Kerberos user `joe@SAMPLE.COM` corresponds to the LDAP distinguished name `uid=joe,ou=people,dc=suse,dc=de`. This sort of mapping must be configured manually using the `saslExpr` directive. In our example, add the following to `slapd.conf`:

```
saslRegexp
     uid=(.*),cn=GSSAPI,cn=auth
     uid=$1,ou=people,dc=example,dc=com
```

To understand how this works, you need to know that when SASL authenticates a user, OpenLDAP forms a distinguished name from the name given to it by SASL (such as `joe`) and the name of the SASL flavor (`GSSAPI`). The result would be `uid=joe,cn=GSSAPI,cn=auth`.

If a `saslRegexp` has been configured, it checks the DN formed from the SASL information using the first argument as a regular expression. If this regular expression matches, the name is replaced with the second argument of the `saslRegexp` statement. The placeholder `$1` is replaced with the substring matched by the `(.*)` expression.

More complicated match expressions are possible. If you have a more complicated directory structure or a schema in which the user name is not part of the DN, you can even use search expressions to map the SASL DN to the user DN.

18.5 Security and Confidentiality

18.5.1 Basic Considerations

One of the main characteristics of a Linux or UNIX system is its ability to handle several users at the same time (multiuser) and to allow these users to perform several tasks (multitasking) on the same computer simultaneously. Moreover, the operating system is network transparent. The users often do not know whether the data and applications they are using are provided locally from their machine or made available over the network.

With the multiuser capability, the data of different users must be stored separately. Security and privacy need to be guaranteed. Data security was already an important issue, even before computers could be linked through networks. Just like today, the most important concern was the ability to keep data available in spite of a lost or otherwise damaged data medium, a hard disk in most cases.

This chapter is primarily focused on confidentiality issues and on ways to protect the privacy of users, but it cannot be stressed enough that a comprehensive security concept should always include procedures to have a regularly updated, workable, and tested backup in place. Without this, you could have a very hard time getting your data back — not only in the case of some hardware defect, but also if the suspicion arises that someone has gained unauthorized access and tampered with files.

18.5.2 Local Security and Network Security

There are several ways of accessing data:

- personal communication with people who have the desired information or access to the data on a computer
- directly from the console of a computer (physical access)
- over a serial line
- using a network link

In all these cases, a user should be authenticated before accessing the resources or data in question. A web server might be less restrictive in this respect, but you still would not want it to disclose all your personal data to any surfer.

In the list above, the first case is the one where the highest amount of human interaction is involved, such as when you are contacting a bank employee and are required to prove that you are the person owning that bank account. Then you are asked to provide a signature, a PIN, or a password to prove that you are the person you claim to be. In some cases, it might be possible to elicit some intelligence from an informed person just by mentioning known bits and pieces to win the confidence of that person by using clever rhetoric. The victim could be led to reveal gradually more information, maybe without even becoming aware of it. Among hackers, this is called *social engineering*. You can only guard against this by educating people and by dealing with language and information in a conscious way. Before breaking into computer systems, attackers often try to target receptionists, service people working with the company, or even family members. In many cases, such an attack based on social engineering is only discovered at a much later time.

A person wanting to obtain unauthorized access to your data could also use the traditional way and try to get at your hardware directly. Therefore, the machine should be protected against any tampering so that no one can remove, replace, or cripple its components. This also applies to backups and even any network cable or the power cord. Also secure the boot procedure, because there are some well-known key combinations that might provoke unusual behavior. Protect yourself against this by setting passwords for the BIOS and the boot loader.

Serial terminals connected to serial ports are still used in many places. Unlike network interfaces, they do not rely on a network protocol to communicate with the host. A simple cable or an infrared port is used to send plain characters back and forth between the devices. The cable itself is the weakest point of such a system: with an older printer connected to it, it is easy to record anything that runs over the wires. What can be achieved with a printer can also be accomplished in other ways, depending on the effort that goes into the attack.

Reading a file locally on a host requires other access rules than opening a network connection with a server on a different host. There is a distinction between local security and network security. The line is drawn where data must be put into packets to be sent somewhere else.

Local Security

Local security starts with the physical environment in the location where the computer is running. Set up your machine in a place where security is in line with your expectations and needs. The main goal of local security is to keep users separate from each other, so no user can assume the permissions or the identity of another. This is a general rule to be observed, but it is especially true for the user `root`, who holds the supreme power on the system. `root` can take on the identity of any other local user without being prompted for the password and read any locally stored file.

Passwords

On a Linux system, passwords are, of course, not stored as plain text and the text string entered is not simply matched with the saved pattern. If this were the case, all accounts on your system would be compromised as soon as someone got access to the corresponding file. Instead, the stored password is encrypted and, each time it is entered, is encrypted again and the two encrypted strings are compared. This only provides more security if the encrypted password cannot be reverse-computed into the original text string.

This is actually achieved by a special kind of algorithm, also called *trapdoor algorithm*, because it only works in one direction. An attacker who has obtained the encrypted string is not able to get your password by simply applying the same algorithm again. Instead, it would be necessary to test all the possible character combinations until a combination is found that looks like your password when encrypted. With passwords eight characters long, there are quite a number of possible combinations to calculate.

In the seventies, it was argued that this method would be more secure than others due to the relative slowness of the algorithm used, which took a few seconds to encrypt just one password. In the meantime, however, PCs have become powerful enough to do several hundred thousand or even millions of encryptions per second. Because of this, encrypted passwords should not be visible to regular users (`/etc/shadow` cannot be read by normal users). It is even more important that passwords are not easy to guess, in case the password file becomes visible due to some error. Consequently, it is not really useful to "translate" a password like "tantalise" into "t@nt@1ls3".

Replacing some letters of a word with similar looking numbers is not safe enough. Password cracking programs that use dictionaries to guess words also play with substitutions like that. A better way is to make up a word with no common meaning, something that only makes sense to you personally, like the first letters of the words of a sentence or the title of a book, such as "The Name of the Rose" by Umberto Eco. This would give the following safe password: "TNotRbUE9". In contrast, passwords like "beerbuddy" or "jasmine76" are easily guessed even by someone who has only some casual knowledge about you.

The Boot Procedure

Configure your system so it cannot be booted from a floppy or from CD, either by removing the drives entirely or by setting a BIOS password and configuring the BIOS to allow booting from a hard disk only. Normally, a Linux system is started by a boot loader, allowing you to pass additional options to the booted kernel. This is crucial to your system's security. Not only does the kernel itself run with `root` permissions, but it is also the first authority to grant `root` permissions at system start-up. Prevent others from using such parameters during boot by setting an additional password in `/boot/grub/menu.lst` (see Chapter 6 on page 135).

File Permissions

As a general rule, always work with the most restrictive privileges possible for a given task. For example, it is definitely not necessary to be `root` to read or write e-mail. If the mail program has a bug, this bug could be exploited for an attack that acts with exactly the permissions of the program when it was started. By following the above rule, minimize the possible damage.

The permissions of the more than 200,000 files included in a SUSE distribution are carefully chosen. A system administrator who installs additional software or other files should take great care when doing so, especially when setting the permission bits. Experienced and security-conscious system administrators always use the `-l` option with the command `ls` to get an extensive file list, which allows them to detect any incorrect file permissions immediately. An incorrect file attribute does not only mean that files could be changed or deleted. These modified files could be executed by `root` or, in the case of configuration files, programs could use such files with the permissions of `root`. This significantly increases the possibilities of an attacker. Attacks like this are called cuckoo eggs, because the program (the egg) is executed (hatched) by a different user (bird), just like a cuckoo tricks other birds into hatching its eggs.

A SUSE LINUX system includes the files `permissions`, `permissions.easy`, `permissions.secure`, and `permissions.paranoid`, all in the directory `/etc`. The purpose of these files is to define special permissions, such as world-writable directories or, for files, the setuser ID bit (programs with the setuser ID bit set do not run with the permissions of the user that has launched it, but with the permissions of the file owner, in most cases `root`). An administrator can use the file `/etc/permissions.local` to add his own settings.

To define which of the above files is used by SUSE's configuration programs to set permissions accordingly, select 'Security' in YaST. To learn more about the topic, read the comments in `/etc/permissions` or consult the manual page of `chmod` (`man chmod`).

Buffer Overflows and Format String Bugs

Special care must be taken whenever a program is supposed to process data that can or could be changed by a user, but this is more of an issue for the programmer of an application than for regular users. The programmer must make sure that his application interprets data in the correct way, without writing them into memory areas that are too small to hold them. Also, the program should hand over data in a consistent manner, using the interfaces defined for that purpose.

A *buffer overflow* can happen if the actual size of a memory buffer is not taken into account when writing to that buffer. There are cases where this data (as generated by the user) uses up some more space than what is available in the buffer. As a result, data is written beyond the end of that buffer area, which, under certain circumstances, makes it possible that a program executes program sequences influenced by the user (and not by the programmer), rather than just processing user data. A bug of this kind may have serious consequences, in particular if the program is being executed with special privileges (see Section 18.5.2 on the page before).

Format string bugs work in a slightly different way, but again it is the user input that could lead the program astray. In most cases, these programming errors are exploited with programs executed with special permissions — setuid and setgid programs — which also means that you can protect your data and your system from such bugs by removing the corresponding execution privileges from programs. Again, the best way is to apply a policy of using the lowest possible privileges (see Section 18.5.2 on the preceding page).

Given that buffer overflows and format string bugs are bugs related to the handling of user data, they are not only exploitable if access has been given to a local account. Many of the bugs that have been reported can also be exploited over a network link. Accordingly, buffer overflows and format string bugs should be classified as being relevant for both local and network security.

Viruses

Contrary to what some people say, there are viruses that run on Linux. However, the viruses that are known were released by their authors as a *proof of concept* to prove that the technique works as intended. None of these viruses have been spotted *in the wild* so far.

Viruses cannot survive and spread without a host on which to live. In our case, the host would be a program or an important storage area of the system, such as the master boot record, which needs to be writable for the program code of the virus. Owing to its multiuser capability, Linux can restrict write access to certain files, especially important with system files. Therefore, if you did your normal work with `root` permissions, you would increase the chance of the system being infected by a virus. In contrast, if you follow the principle of using the lowest possible privileges as mentioned above, chances of getting a virus are slim.

Apart from that, you should never rush into executing a program from some Internet site that you do not really know. SUSE's RPM packages carry a cryptographic signature as a digital label that the necessary care was taken to build them. Viruses are a typical sign that the administrator or the user lacks the required security awareness, putting at risk even a system that should be highly secure by its very design.

Viruses should not be confused with worms, which belong to the world of networks entirely. Worms do not need a host to spread.

Network Security

Network security is important for protecting from an attack that is started outside. The typical login procedure requiring a user name and a password for user authentication is still a local security issue. In the particular case of logging in over a network, differentiate between the two security aspects. What happens until the actual authentication is network security and anything that happens afterwards is local security.

X Window System and X11 Authentication

As mentioned at the beginning, network transparency is one of the central characteristics of a UNIX system. X11, the windowing system of UNIX operating systems, can make use of this feature in an impressive way. With X11, it is basically no problem to log in at a remote host and start a graphical program that is then be sent over the network to be displayed on your computer.

When an X client should be displayed remotely using an X server, the latter should protect the resource managed by it (i.e., the display) from unauthorized access. In more concrete terms, certain permissions must be given to the client program. With the X Window System, there are two ways to do this, called host-based access control and cookie-based access control. The former relies on the IP address of the host where the client should run. The program to control this is xhost. xhost enters the IP address of a legitimate client into a tiny database belonging to the X server. However, relying on IP addresses for authentication is not very secure. For example, if there were a second user working on the host sending the client program, that user would have access to the X server as well — just like someone stealing the IP address. Because of these shortcomings, this authentication method is not described in more detail here, but you can learn about it with `man xhost`.

In the case of cookie-based access control, a character string is generated that is only known to the X server and to the legitimate user, just like an ID card of some kind. This cookie (the word goes back not to ordinary cookies, but to Chinese fortune cookies, which contain an epigram) is stored on login in the file `.Xauthority` in the user's home directory and is available to any X client wanting to use the X server to display a window. The file `.Xauthority` can be examined by the user with the tool `xauth`. If you were to rename `.Xauthority` or if you deleted the file from your home directory by accident, you would not be able to open any new windows or X clients. Read more about X Window System security mechanisms in the man page of `Xsecurity` (`man Xsecurity`).

ssh (secure shell) can be used to encrypt a network connection completely and forward it to an X server transparently without the encryption mechanism being perceived by the user. This is also called X forwarding. X forwarding is achieved by simulating an X server on the server side and setting a DISPLAY variable for the shell on the remote host. Further details about ssh can be found in Section 18.2 on page 434.

Caution

If you do not consider the host where you log in to be a secure host, do not use X forwarding. With X forwarding enabled, an attacker could authenticate via your ssh connection to intrude on your X server and sniff your keyboard input, for instance.

Caution

Buffer Overflows and Format String Bugs

As discussed on Section *Buffer Overflows and Format String Bugs*, buffer overflows and format string bugs should be classified as issues concerning both local and network security. As with the local variants of such bugs, buffer overflows in network programs, when successfully exploited, are mostly used to obtain `root` permissions. Even if that is not the case, an attacker could use the bug to gain access to an unprivileged local account to exploit any other vulnerabilities that might exist on the system.

Buffer overflows and format string bugs exploitable over a network link are certainly the most frequent form of remote attacks in general. Exploits for these — programs to exploit these newly-found security holes — are often posted on the security mailing lists. They can be used to target the vulnerability without knowing the details of the code. Over the years, experience has shown that the availability of exploit codes has contributed to more secure operating systems, obviously due to the fact that operating system makers were forced to fix the problems in their software. With free software, anyone has access to the source code (SUSE LINUX comes with all available source codes) and anyone who finds a vulnerability and its exploit code can submit a patch to fix the corresponding bug.

DoS — Denial of Service

The purpose of this kind of attack is to block a server program or even an entire system, something that could be achieved by various means: overloading the server, keeping it busy with garbage packets, or exploiting a remote buffer overflow. Often a DoS attack is done with the sole purpose of making the service disappear. However, once a given service has become unavailable, communications could become vulnerable to *man-in-the-middle attacks* (sniffing, TCP connection hijacking, spoofing) and DNS poisoning.

Man in the Middle: Sniffing, Hijacking, Spoofing

In general, any remote attack performed by an attacker who puts himself between the communicating hosts is called a *man-in-the-middle attack*. What almost all types of man-in-the-middle attacks have in common is that the victim is usually not aware that there is something happening. There are many possible variants, for example, the attacker could pick up a connection request and forward that to the target machine himself. Now the victim has unwittingly established a connection with the wrong host, because the other end is posing as the legitimate destination machine.

The simplest form of a man-in-the-middle attack is called *sniffer* — the attacker is "just" listening to the network traffic passing by. As a more complex attack, the "man in the middle" could try to take over an already established connection (hijacking). To do so, the attacker would need to analyze the packets for some time to be able to predict the TCP sequence numbers belonging to the connection. When the attacker finally seizes the role of the target host, the victims will notice this, because they get an error message saying the connection was terminated due to a failure. The fact that there are protocols not secured against hijacking through encryption, which only perform a simple authentication procedure upon establishing the connection, makes it easier for attackers.

Spoofing is an attack where packets are modified to contain counterfeit source data, mostly the IP address. Most active forms of attack rely on sending out such fake packets — something that, on a Linux machine, can only be done by the superuser (`root`).

Many of the attacks mentioned are carried out in combination with a DoS. If an attacker sees an opportunity to bring down a certain host abruptly, even if only for a short time, it makes it easier for him to push the active attack, because the host will not be able to interfere with the attack for some time.

DNS Poisoning

DNS poisoning means that the attacker corrupts the cache of a DNS server by replying to it with spoofed DNS reply packets, trying to get the server to send certain data to a victim who is requesting information from that server. Many servers maintain a trust relationship with other hosts, based on IP addresses or host names. The attacker needs a good understanding of the actual structure of the trust relationships between hosts to disguise itself as one of the trusted hosts. Usually, the attacker analyzes some packets received from the server to get the necessary information. The attacker often needs to target a well-timed DoS attack at the name server as well. Protect yourself by using encrypted connections that are able to verify the identity of the hosts to which to connect.

Worms

Worms are often confused with viruses, but there is a clear difference between the two. Unlike viruses, worms do not need to infect a host program to live. Rather, they are specialized to spread as quickly as possible on network structures. The worms that appeared in the past, such as Ramen, Lion, or Adore, make use of well-known security holes in server programs like bind8 or lprNG. Protection against worms is relatively easy. Given that some time elapses between the discovery of a security hole and the moment the worm hits your server, there is a good chance that an updated version of the affected program is available on time. That is only useful if the administrator actually installs the security updates on the systems in question.

18.5.3 Some General Security Tips and Tricks

Information: To handle security competently, it is important to keep up with new developments and to stay informed about the latest security issues. One very good way to protect your systems against problems of all kinds is to get and install the updated packages recommended by security announcements as quickly as possible. SUSE security announcements are published on a mailing list to which you can subscribe by following the link `http://www.suse.de/security`. The list `suse-security-announce@suse.de` is a first-hand source of information regarding updated packages and includes members of SUSE's security team among its active contributors.

The mailing list `suse-security@suse.de` is a good place to discuss any security issues of interest. Subscribe to it under the URL as given above for `suse-security-announce@suse.de`.

`bugtraq@securityfocus.com` is one of the best-known security mailing lists worldwide. Reading this list, which receives between 15 and 20 postings per day, is recommended. More information can be found at `http://www.securityfocus.com`.

The following is a list of rules you may find useful in dealing with basic security concerns:

- According to the rule of using the most restrictive set of permissions possible for every job, avoid doing your regular jobs as `root`. This reduces the risk of getting a cuckoo egg or a virus and protects you from your own mistakes.
- If possible, always try to use encrypted connections to work on a remote machine. Using `ssh` (secure shell) to replace `telnet`, `ftp`, `rsh`, and `rlogin` should be standard practice.
- Avoid using authentication methods based on IP addresses alone.
- Try to keep the most important network-related packages up-to-date and subscribe to the corresponding mailing lists to receive announcements on new versions of such programs (bind, sendmail, ssh, etc.). The same should apply to software relevant to local security.
- Change the `/etc/permissions` file to optimize the permissions of files crucial to your system's security. If you remove the setuid bit from a program, it might well be that it cannot do its job anymore in the intended way. On the other hand, consider that, in most cases,

the program will also have ceased to be a potential security risk. You might take a similar approach with world-writable directories and files.

- Disable any network services you do not absolutely require for your server to work properly. This will make your system safer. Open ports, with the socket state LISTEN, can be found with the program netstat. As for the options, it is recommended to use `netstat -ap` or `netstat -anp`. The `-p` option allows you to see which process is occupying a port under which name.

  Compare the netstat results with those of a thorough port scan done from outside your host. An excellent program for this job is nmap, which not only checks out the ports of your machine, but also draws some conclusions as to which services are waiting behind them. However, port scanning may be interpreted as an aggressive act, so do not do this on a host without the explicit approval of the administrator. Finally, remember that it is important not only to scan TCP ports, but also UDP ports (options `-sS` and `-sU`).

- To monitor the integrity of the files of your system in a reliable way, use the program `tripwire`, available on the SUSE LINUX distribution. Encrypt the database created by `tripwire` to prevent someone from tampering with it. Furthermore, keep a backup of this database available outside your machine, stored on an external data medium not connected to it by a network link.

- Take proper care when installing any third-party software. There have been cases where a hacker had built a trojan horse into the tar archive of a security software package, which was fortunately discovered very quickly. If you install a binary package, have no doubts about the site from which you downloaded it.

  SUSE's RPM packages are gpg-signed. The key used by SUSE for signing is:

  ID:9C800ACA 2000-10-19 SUSE Package Signing Key <build@suse.de>

  Key fingerprint = 79C1 79B2 E1C8 20C1 890F 9994 A84E DAE8 9C80 0ACA

  The command `rpm --checksig package.rpm` shows whether the checksum and the signature of an uninstalled package are correct. Find the key on the first CD of the distribution and on most key servers worldwide.

- Check your backups of user and system files regularly. Consider that if you do not test whether the backup will work, it might actually be worthless.
- Check your log files. Whenever possible, write a small script to search for suspicious entries. Admittedly, this is not exactly a trivial task. In the end, only you can know which entries are unusual and which are not.
- Use `tcp_wrapper` to restrict access to the individual services running on your machine, so you have explicit control over which IP addresses can connect to a service. For further information regarding `tcp_wrappers`, consult the manual pages of tcpd and `hosts_access` (`man 8 tcpd`, `man hosts_access`).
- Use SUSEfirewall to enhance the security provided by tcpd (tcp_-wrapper).
- Design your security measures to be redundant: a message seen twice is much better than no message at all.

18.5.4 Using the Central Security Reporting Address

If you discover a security-related problem (please check the available update packages first), write an e-mail to `security@suse.de`. Please include a detailed description of the problem and the version number of the package concerned. SUSE will try to send a reply as soon as possible. You are encouraged to pgp encrypt your e-mail messages. SUSE's pgp key is:

```
ID:3D25D3D9 1999-03-06 SUSE Security Team <security@suse.de>
Key fingerprint = 73 5F 2E 99 DF DB 94 C4 8F 5A A3 AE AF 22 F2 D5
```

This key is also available for download from `http://www.suse.de/security`.

Part V

Appendixes

A

File Systems in Linux

Linux supports a number of different file systems. This chapter presents a brief overview of the most popular Linux file systems, elaborating on their design concept, advantages, and fields of application. Some additional information about LFS ("Large File Support") in Linux is also provided.

Glossary

metadata A file system–internal data structure that assures all the data on disk is properly organized and accessible. Essentially, it is "data about the data." Almost every file system has its own structure of metadata, which is partly why the file systems show different performance characteristics. It is of major importance to maintain metadata intact, because otherwise all data on the file system could become inaccessible.

inode Inodes contain various information about a file, including size, number of links, date and time of creation, modification, and access, as well as pointers to the disk blocks where the file contents are actually stored.

journal In the context of a file system, a journal is an on-disk structure containing a kind of log in which the file system stores what it is about to change in the file system's metadata. *Journaling* greatly reduces the recovery time of a Linux system because it obsoletes the lengthy search process that checks the whole file system at system start-up. Instead, only the journal is replayed.

Major File Systems in Linux

Unlike two or three years ago, choosing a file system for a Linux system is no longer a matter of a few seconds (Ext2 or ReiserFS?). Kernels starting from 2.4 offer a variety of file systems from which to choose. The following is an overview of how those file systems basically work and which advantages they offer.

It is very important to bear in mind that there may be no file system that best suits all kinds of applications. Each file system has its particular strengths and weaknesses, which must be taken into account. Even the most sophisticated file system cannot substitute for a reasonable backup strategy, however.

The terms *data integrity* and *data consistency*, when used in this chapter, do not refer to the consistency of the user space data (the data your application writes to its files). Whether this data is consistent must be controlled by the application itself.

Note

Setting up File Systems

Unless stated otherwise in this chapter, all the steps required to set up or to change partitions and file systems can be performed using the YaST module.

Note

Ext2

The origins of Ext2 go back to the early days of Linux history. Its predecessor, the Extended File System, was implemented in April 1992 and integrated in Linux 0.96c. The Extended File System underwent a number of modifications and, as Ext2, became the most popular Linux file system for years. With the creation of journaling file systems and their astonishingly short recovery times, Ext2 became less important.

A brief summary of Ext2's strengths might help understand why it was — and in some areas still is — the favorite Linux file system of many Linux users.

Solidity Being quite an "old-timer", Ext2 underwent many improvements and was heavily tested. This may be the reason why people often refer to it as *rock-solid*. After a system outage when the file system could not be cleanly unmounted, e2fsck starts to analyze the file system data. Metadata is brought into a consistent state and pending files or data blocks are written to a designated directory (called `lost+found`). In contrast to journaling file systems, e2fsck analyzes the entire file system and not just the recently modified bits of metadata. This takes significantly longer than checking the log data of a journaling file system. Depending on file system size, this procedure can take half an hour or more. Therefore, it is not desirable to choose Ext2 for any server that needs high availability. Yet, as Ext2 does not maintain a journal and uses significantly less memory, it is sometimes faster than other file systems.

Easy Upgradability The code for Ext2 is the strong foundation on which Ext3 could become a highly-acclaimed next-generation file system. Its reliability and solidity were elegantly combined with the advantages of a journaling file system.

Ext3

Ext3 was designed by Stephen Tweedie. In contrast to all other "next-generation" file systems, Ext3 does not follow a completely new design principle. It is based on Ext2. These two file systems are very closely related to each other. An Ext3 file system can be easily built on top of an Ext2 file system. The most important difference between Ext2 and Ext3 is that Ext3 supports journaling. In summary, Ext3 has three major advantages to offer:

Easy and Highly Reliable Upgrades from Ext2
As Ext3 is based on the Ext2 code and shares its on-disk format as well as its metadata format, upgrades from Ext2 to Ext3 are incredibly easy. Unlike transitions to other journaling file systems, such as ReiserFS, JFS, or XFS, which can be quite tedious (making backups of the entire file system and recreating it from scratch), a transition to Ext3 is a matter of minutes. It is also very safe, as the recreation of an entire file system from scratch might not work flawlessly. Considering the number of existing Ext2 systems that await an upgrade to a journaling file system, you can easily figure out why Ext3 might be of some importance to many system administrators. Downgrading from Ext3 to Ext2 is as easy as the upgrade. Just perform a clean unmount of the Ext3 file system and remount it as an Ext2 file system.

Reliability and Performance Other journaling file systems follow the "metadata-only" journaling approach. This means your metadata will always be kept in a consistent state but the same cannot be automatically guaranteed for the file system data itself. Ext3 is designed to take care of both metadata and data. The degree of "care" can be customized. Enabling Ext3 in the `data=journal` mode offers maximum security (i.e., data integrity), but can slow down the system as both metadata and data are journaled. A relatively new approach is to use the `data=ordered` mode, which ensures both data and metadata integrity, but uses journaling only for metadata. The file system driver collects all data blocks that correspond to one metadata update. These blocks are grouped as a "transaction" and will be written to disk before the metadata is updated. As a result, consistency is achieved for metadata and data without sacrificing performance. A third option to use is `data=writeback`, which allows data to be written into the main file system after its metadata has been committed to the journal. This option is often considered the best in performance. It can, however, allow old data to reappear in files after crash and recovery while internal file system integrity is maintained. Unless you specify something else, Ext3 is run with the `data=ordered` default.

Note

Converting an Ext2 File System into an Ext3 File System

Converting from Ext2 to Ext3 involves two separate steps:

Creating the Journal Log in as `root` and run `tune2fs -j`. This creates an Ext3 journal with the default parameters. To decide yourself how large the journal should be and on which device it should reside, run `tune2fs -J` instead, together with the desired journal options `size=` and `device=`. More information about the tune2fs program is available in its manual page (`man 8 tune2fs`).

Specifying the file system type in /etc/fstab
To ensure that the Ext3 file system is recognized as such, edit the file `/etc/fstab`, changing the file system type specified for the corresponding partition from `ext2` to `ext3`. The change takes effect after the next reboot.

Note

ReiserFS

Officially one of the key features of the 2.4 kernel release, ReiserFS has been available as a kernel patch for 2.2.x SUSE kernels since SUSE LINUX version 6.4. ReiserFS was designed by Hans Reiser and the Namesys development team. ReiserFS has proven to be a powerful alternative to the old Ext2. Its key assets are better disk space utilization, better disk access performance, and faster crash recovery. However, there is a minor drawback: ReiserFS pays great care to metadata but not to the data itself. Future generations of ReiserFS will include data journaling (both metadata and actual data are written to the journal) as well as ordered writes.

ReiserFS's strengths, in more detail, are:

Better Disk Space Utilization In ReiserFS, all data is organized in a structure called B^*-balanced tree. The tree structure contributes to better disk space utilization as small files can be stored directly in the B^* tree leaf nodes instead of being stored elsewhere and just maintaining a pointer to the actual disk location. In addition to that, storage is not allocated in chunks of 1 or 4 kB, but in portions of the exact size needed. Another benefit lies in the dynamic allocation of inodes. This keeps the file system more flexible than traditional file systems, like Ext2, where the inode density must be specified at file system creation time.

Better Disk Access Performance For small files, you will often find that both file data and "stat_data" (inode) information are stored next to each other. They can be read with a single disk I/O operation, meaning that only one access to disk is required to retrieve all the information needed.

Fast Crash Recovery Using a journal to keep track of recent metadata changes makes a file system check a matter of seconds, even for huge file systems.

JFS

JFS, the *Journaling File System* was developed by IBM. The first beta version of the JFS Linux port reached the Linux community in the summer of 2000. Version 1.0.0 was released in 2001. JFS is tailored to suit the needs of high throughput server environments where performance is the ultimate goal.

Being a full 64-bit file system, JFS supports both large files and partitions, which is another reason for its use in server environments.

A closer look at JFS shows why this file system might prove a good choice for your Linux server:

Efficient Journaling JFS follows a "metadata only" approach like ReiserFS. Instead of an extensive check, only metadata changes generated by recent file system activity get checked, which saves a great amount of time in recovery. Concurrent operations requiring multiple concurrent log entries can be combined into one group commit, greatly reducing performance loss of the file system through multiple write operations.

Efficient Directory Organization JFS holds two different directory organizations. For small directories, it allows the directory's content to be stored directly into its inode. For larger directories, it uses B^+trees, which greatly facilitate directory management.

Better Space Usage through Dynamic inode Allocation
For Ext2, you must define the inode density in advance (the space occupied by management information), which restricted the maximum number of files or directories of your file system. JFS spares you these considerations — it dynamically allocates inode space and frees it when it is no longer needed.

XFS

Originally intended as file system for their IRIX OS, SGI started XFS development back in the early 1990s. The idea behind XFS was to create a high-performance 64-bit journaling file system to meet the extreme computing challenges of today. XFS is very good at manipulating large files and performs well on high-end hardware. However, you will find a drawback even in XFS. Like ReiserFS, XFS takes a great deal of care of metadata integrity, but less of data integrity.

A quick review of XFS's key features explains why it may prove a strong competitor for other journaling file systems in high-end computing.

High Scalability through the Use of Allocation Groups
At the creation time of an XFS file system, the block device underlying the file system is divided into eight or more linear regions of

equal size. Those are referred to as *allocation groups*. Each allocation group manages its own inodes and free disk space. Practically, allocation groups can be seen as "file systems in a file system." As allocation groups are rather independent of each other, more than one of them can be addressed by the kernel simultaneously. This feature is the key to XFS's great scalability. Naturally, the concept of independent allocation groups suits the needs of multiprocessor systems.

High Performance through Efficient Management of Disk Space
Free space and inodes are handled by B^+-trees inside the allocation groups. The use of B^+-trees greatly contributes to XFS's performance and scalability. A feature truly unique to XFS is *delayed allocation*. XFS handles allocation by breaking the process into two pieces. A pending transaction is stored in RAM and the appropriate amount of space is reserved. XFS still does not decide where exactly (speaking of file system blocks) the data should be stored. This decision is delayed until the last possible moment. Some short-lived temporary data may never make its way to disk, because it may be obsolete at the time XFS decides where actually to save it. Thus XFS increases write performance and reduces file system fragmentation. Because delayed allocation results in less frequent write events than in other file systems, it is likely that data loss after a crash during a write is more severe.

Preallocation to Avoid File System Fragmentation
Before writing the data to the file system, XFS *reserves* (preallocates) the free space needed for a file. Thus, file system fragmentation is greatly reduced. Performance is increased as the contents of a file are not distributed all over the file system.

Some Other Supported File Systems

Table A.1 on the following page summarizes some other file systems supported by Linux. They are supported mainly to ensure compatibility and interchange of data with different kinds of media or foreign operating systems.

Table A.1: File System Types in Linux

`cramfs`	*Compressed ROM file system*: A compressed read-only file system for ROMs.
`hpfs`	*High Performance File System*: the IBM OS/2 standard file system — only supported in read-only mode.
`iso9660`	Standard file system on CD-ROMs.
`minix`	This file system originated from academic projects on operating systems and was the first file system used in Linux. Nowadays, it is used as a file system for floppy disks.
`msdos`	*fat*, the file system originally used by DOS, is today used by various operating systems.
`ncpfs`	file system for mounting Novell volumes over networks.
`nfs`	*Network File System*: Here, data can be stored on any machine in a network and access may be granted via a network.
`smbfs`	*Server Message Block*: used by products such as Windows to enable file access over a network.
`sysv`	Used on SCO UNIX, Xenix, and Coherent (commercial UNIX systems for PCs).
`ufs`	Used by BSD, SunOS, and NeXTstep. Only supported in read-only mode.
`umsdos`	*UNIX on MSDOS*: applied on top of a normal `fat` file system. Achieves UNIX functionality (permissions, links, long file names) by creating special files.
`vfat`	*Virtual FAT*: extension of the `fat` file system (supports long file names).
`ntfs`	*Windows NT file system*, read-only.

Large File Support in Linux

Originally, Linux supported a maximum file size of 2 GB. This was enough before the explosion of multimedia and as long as no one tried to manipulate huge databases on Linux. Becoming more and more important for server computing, the kernel and C library were modified to support file sizes larger than 2 GB when using a new set of interfaces that applications must use. Nowadays, (almost) all major file systems offer LFS support, allowing you to perform high-end computing.

Table A.2 offers an overview of the current limitations of Linux files and file systems for kernel 2.4.

Table A.2: *Maximum Sizes of File Systems (On-Disk Format)*

File System	File Size [Byte]	File System Size [Byte]
Ext2 or Ext3 (1 kB block size)	2^{34} (16 GB)	2^{41} (2 TB)
Ext2 or Ext3 (2 kB block size)	2^{38} (256 GB)	2^{43} (8 TB)
Ext2 or Ext3 (4 kB block size)	2^{41} (2 TB)	2^{44} (16 TB)
Ext2 or Ext3 (8 kB block size) (systems with 8 kB pages (like Alpha))	2^{46} (64 TB)	2^{45} (32 TB)
ReiserFS 3.5	2^{32} (4 GB)	2^{44} (16 TB)
ReiserFS 3.6 (under Linux 2.4)	2^{60} (1 EB)	2^{44} (16 TB)
XFS	2^{63} (8 EB)	2^{63} (8 EB)
JFS (512 Bytes block size)	2^{63} (8 EB)	2^{49} (512 TB)
JFS (4 kB block size)	2^{63} (8 EB)	2^{52} (4 PB)
NFSv2 (client side)	2^{31} (2 GB)	2^{63} (8 EB)
NFSv3 (client side)	2^{63} (8 EB)	2^{63} (8 EB)

Note

Linux Kernel Limits

Table A.2 on the preceding page describes the limitations regarding the on-disk format. The 2.6 kernel imposes its own limits on the size of files and file systems handled by it. These are as follows:

- *file size:* On 32-bit systems, files may not exceed the size of 2 TB (2^{41} bytes).
- *file system size:* File systems may be up to 2^{73} bytes large. However, this limit is still out of reach for the currently available hardware.

Note

For More Information

Each of the file system projects described above maintains its own home page where you can find mailing list information as well as further documentation and FAQs.

- `http://e2fsprogs.sourceforge.net/`
- `http://www.zipworld.com.au/~akpm/linux/ext3/`
- `http://www.namesys.com/`
- `http://oss.software.ibm.com/developerworks/opensource/jfs/`
- `http://oss.sgi.com/projects/xfs/`

A comprehensive multipart tutorial about Linux file systems can be found at *IBM developerWorks*: `http://www-106.ibm.com/developerworks/library/l-fs.html`

For a comparison of the different journaling file systems in Linux, look at Juan I. Santos Florido's article at *Linuxgazette*: `http://www.linuxgazette.com/issue55/florido.html`.

Those interested in an in-depth analysis of LFS in Linux should try Andreas Jaeger's LFS site: `http://www.suse.de/~aj/linux_lfs.html`.

Access Control Lists in Linux

This chapter provides a brief summary of the background and functions of POSIX ACLs for Linux file systems. Learn how the traditional permission concept for file system objects can be expanded with the help of ACLs (*Access Control Lists*) and which advantages this concept provides.

Advantages of ACLs

> **Note**
>
> **POSIX ACLs**
>
> The term "POSIX ACL" suggests that this is a true POSIX (*Portable Operating System Interface*) standard. The respective draft standards POSIX 1003.1e and POSIX 1003.2c have been withdrawn for several reasons. Nevertheless, ACLs as found on many systems belonging to the UNIX family are based on these drafts and the implementation of file system ACLs as described in this chapter follows these two standards as well. They can be viewed at `http://wt.xpilot.org/publications/posix.1e/`.
>
> **Note**

Traditionally, three sets of permissions are defined for each file object on a Linux system. These sets include the read (`r`), write (`w`), and execute (`x`) permissions for each of three types of users — the file owner, the group, and other users. In addition to that, it is possible to set the *set user id*, the *set group id*, and the *sticky* bit. A more detailed discussion of this topic can be found in the *User Guide*.

This lean concept is fully adequate for most practical cases. However, for more complex scenarios or advanced applications, system administrators formerly had to use a number of tricks to circumvent the limitations of the traditional permission concept.

ACLs can be used for situations that require an extension of the traditional file permission concept. They allow assignment of permissions to individual users or groups even if these do not correspond to the original owner or the owning group. Access Control Lists are a feature of the Linux kernel and are currently supported by ReiserFS, Ext2, Ext3, JFS, and XFS. Using ACLs, complex scenarios can be realized without implementing complex permission models on the application level.

The advantages of ACLs are clearly evident in situations like the replacement of a Windows server by a Linux server. Some of the connected workstations may continue to run under Windows even after the migration. The Linux system offers file and print services to the Windows clients with Samba.

Given than Samba supports access control lists, user permissions can be configured both on the Linux server and in Windows with a graphical user interface (only Windows NT and later). With winbindd, it is even possible to assign permissions to users that only exist in the Windows domain without any account on the Linux server. On the server side, edit the access control lists using getfacl and setfacl.

Definitions

user class The conventional POSIX permission concept uses three *classes* of users for assigning permissions in the file system: the owner, the owning group, and other users. Three permission bits can be set for each user class, giving permission to read (`r`), write (`w`), and execute (`x`). An introduction to the user concept in Linux is provided in the *User Guide*.

access ACL The user and group access permissions for all kinds of file system objects (files and directories) are determined by means of access ACLs.

default ACL Default ACLs can only be applied to directories. They determine the permissions a file system object inherits from its parent directory when it is created.

ACL entry Each ACL consists of a set of ACL entries. An ACL entry contains a type (see Table B.1 on the next page), a qualifier for the user or group to which the entry refers, and a set of permissions. For some entry types, the qualifier for the group or users is undefined.

Handling ACLs

This section explains the basic structure of an ACL and its various characteristics. The interrelation between ACLs and the traditional permission concept in the Linux file system is briefly demonstrated by means of several figures. Two examples show how to create your own ACLs using the correct syntax. In conclusion, find information about the way ACLs are interpreted by the operating system.

Structure of ACL Entries

There are two basic classes of ACLs: A *minimum* ACL merely comprises the entries for the types owner, owning group, and other, which correspond to the conventional permission bits for files and directories. An *extended* ACL goes beyond this. It must contain a *mask* entry and may contain several entries of the *named user* and *named group* types. Table B.1 provides a summary of the various types of ACL entries that are possible.

***Table B.1:** ACL Entry Types*

Type	Text Form
owner	`user::rwx`
named user	`user:name:rwx`
owning group	`group::rwx`
named group	`group:name:rwx`
mask	`mask::rwx`
other	`other::rwx`

The permissions defined in the entries *owner* and *other* are always effective. Except for the *mask* entry, all other entries (*named user*, *owning group*, and *named group*) can be either effective or masked. If permissions exist in one of the above-mentioned entries as well as in the mask, they are effective. Permissions contained only in the mask or only in the actual entry are not effective. The example in Table B.2 on the next page demonstrates this mechanism.

Table B.2: Masking Access Permissions

Entry Type	Text Form	Permissions
named user	`user:jane:r-x`	`r-x`
mask	`mask::rw-`	`rw-`
	effective permissions:	`r--`

ACL Entries and File Mode Permission Bits

Figure B.1 and Figure B.2 on the next page illustrate the two cases of a minimum ACL and an extended ACL. The figures are structured in three blocks — the left block shows the type specifications of the ACL entries, the center block displays an example ACL, and the right block shows the respective permission bits according to the conventional permission concept as displayed by `ls -l`, for instance. In both cases, the *owner class* permissions are mapped to the ACL entry *owner*. Equally, *other class* permissions are mapped to the respective ACL entry. However, the mapping of the *group class* permissions is different in the two cases.

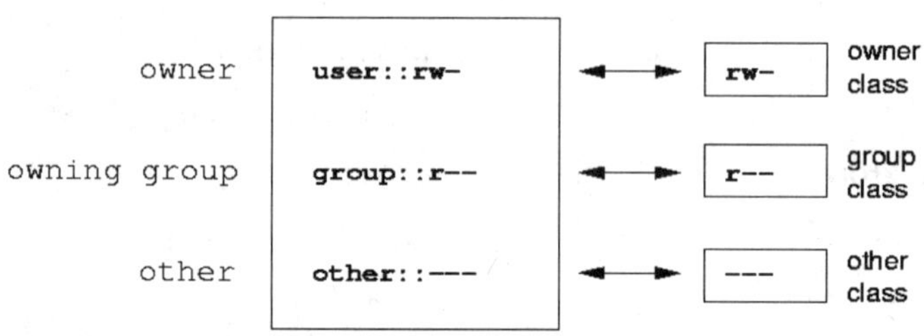

Figure B.1: Minimum ACL: ACL Entries Compared to Permission Bits

- In the case of a minimum ACL — without *mask* — the *group class* permissions are mapped to the ACL entry *owning group*. This is shown in Figure B.1.
- In the case of an extended ACL — with *mask* — the *group class* permissions are mapped to the *mask* entry. This is shown in Figure B.2 on the next page.

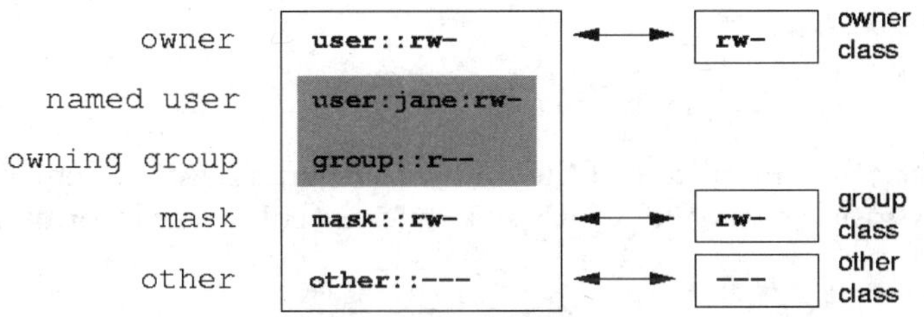

Figure B.2: Extended ACL: ACL Entries Compared to Permission Bits

This mapping approach ensures the smooth interaction of applications, regardless of whether they have ACL support. The access permissions that were assigned by means of the permission bits represent the upper limit for all other "fine adjustments" made by means of ACLs. Any permissions not reflected here were either not set in the ACL or are not effective. Changes made to the permission bits are reflected by the ACL and vice versa.

A Directory with Access ACL

The handling of access ACLs is demonstrated in three steps by means of the following example:

- Creating a file system object (a directory in this case)
- Modifying the ACL
- Using masks

1. Before you create the directory, use the `umask` command to define which access permissions should be masked each time a file object is created. The command `umask 027` sets the default permissions by giving the owner the full range of permissions (`0`), denying the group write access (`2`), and giving other users no permissions at all (`7`). `umask` actually masks the corresponding permission bits or turns them off. For details, consult the corresponding man page (`man umask`).

   `mkdir mydir` should create the `mydir` directory with the default permissions as set by `umask`. Use the following command to check if all permissions were assigned correctly:

```
ls -dl mydir

drwxr-x--- ... tux project3 ... mydir
```

2. Check the initial state of the ACL and insert a new user entry and a new group entry with `getfacl mydir`. This gives information like:

```
# file: mydir
# owner: tux
# group: project3
user::rwx
group::r-x
other::---
```

The output of `getfacl` precisely reflects the mapping of permission bits and ACL entries as described in Section B on page 490. The first three output lines display the name, owner, and owning group of the directory. The next three lines contain the three ACL entries *owner*, *owning group*, and *other*. In fact, in the case of this minimum ACL, the `getfacl` command does not produce any information you could not have obtained with `ls`.

Your first modification of the ACL is the assignment of read, write, and execute permissions to an additional user `jane` and an additional group `djungle`.

```
setfacl -m user:jane:rwx,group:djungle:rwx mydir
```

The option `-m` prompts `setfacl` to modify the existing ACL. The following argument indicates the ACL entries to modify (several entries are separated by commas). The final part specifies the name of the directory to which these modifications should be applied. Use the `getfacl` command to take a look at the resulting ACL.

```
# file: mydir
# owner: tux
# group: project3
user::rwx
user:jane:rwx
group::r-x
group:djungle:rwx
mask::rwx
other::---
```

In addition to the entries initiated for the user `jane` and the group `djungle`, a *mask* entry has been generated. This *mask* entry is set automatically to reduce all entries in the *group class* to a common denominator. Furthermore, `setfacl` automatically adapts existing *mask* entries to the settings modified, provided you do not deactivate this feature with `-n`. *mask* defines the maximum effective access permissions for all entries in the *group class*. This includes *named user*, *named group*, and *owning group*. The *group class* permission bits that would be displayed by `ls -dl mydir` now correspond to the `mask` entry.

```
drwxrwx---+ ... tux project3 ... mydir
```

The first column of the output now contains an additional + to indicate that there is an *extended* ACL for this item.

3. According to the output of the `ls` command, the permissions for the *mask* entry include write access. Traditionally, such permission bits would mean that the *owning group* (here `project3`) also has write access to the directory `mydir/`. However, the effective access permissions for the *owning group* correspond to the overlapping portion of the permissions defined for the *owning group* and for the *mask* — which is `r-x` in our example (see Table B.2 on page 490). As far as the effective permissions of the *owning group* are concerned, nothing has changed even after the addition of the ACL entries.

   Edit the *mask* entry with `setfacl` or `chmod`.

```
chmod g-w mydir

ls -dl mydir

drwxr-x---+ ... tux project3 ... mydir


getfacl mydir

# file: mydir
# owner: tux
# group: project3
user::rwx
user:jane:rwx           # effective: r-x
group::r-x
group:djungle:rwx       # effective: r-x
mask::r-x
other::---
```

After executing the `chmod` command to remove the write permission from the *group class* bits, the output of the `ls` command is sufficient to see that the *mask* bits must have changed accordingly: write permission is again limited to the owner of `mydir`. The output of the `getfacl` confirms this. This output includes a comment for all those entries in which the effective permission bits do not correspond to the original permissions, because they are filtered according to the *mask* entry. The original permissions can be restored at any time with `chmod`:

```
chmod g+w mydir

ls -dl mydir

drwxrwx---+ ... tux project3 ... mydir


getfacl mydir

# file: mydir
# owner: tux
# group: project3
user::rwx
user:jane:rwx
group::r-x
group:djungle:rwx
mask::rwx
other::---
```

A Directory with a Default ACL

Directories can have a default ACL, which is a special kind of ACL defining the access permissions that objects under the directory inherit when they are created. A default ACL affects subdirectories as well as files.

Effects of a Default ACL

There are two different ways in which the permissions of a directory's default ACL are passed to the files and subdirectories in it:

- A subdirectory inherits the default ACL of the parent directory both as its own default ACL and as an access ACL.
- A file inherits the default ACL as its own access ACL.

All system calls that create file system objects use a `mode` parameter that defines the access permissions for the newly created file system object:

- If the parent directory does not have a default ACL, the permission bits as defined by the `umask` are subtracted from the permissions as passed by the `mode` parameter, with the result being assigned to the new object.
- If a default ACL exists for the parent directory, the permission bits assigned to the new object correspond to the overlapping portion of the permissions of the `mode` parameter and those that are defined in the default ACL. The `umask` is disregarded in this case.

Application of Default ACLs

The following three examples show the main operations for directories and default ACLs:

- Creating a default ACL for an existing directory
- Creating a subdirectory in a directory with default ACL
- Creating a file in a directory with default ACL

1. Add a default ACL to the existing directory `mydir/` with:

   ```
   setfacl -d -m group:djungle:r-x mydir
   ```

   The option `-d` of the `setfacl` command prompts `setfacl` to perform the following modifications (option `-m`) in the default ACL.

   Take a closer look at the result of this command:

   ```
   getfacl mydir

   # file: mydir
   # owner: tux
   # group: project3
   user::rwx
   user:jane:rwx
   group::r-x
   group:djungle:rwx
   mask::rwx
   other::---
   default:user::rwx
   default:group::r-x
   default:group:djungle:r-x
   default:mask::r-x
   default:other::---
   ```

`getfacl` returns both the access ACL and the default ACL. The default ACL is formed by all lines that start with `default`. Although you merely executed the `setfacl` command with an entry for the `djungle` group for the default ACL, `setfacl` automatically copied all other entries from the access ACL to create a valid default ACL. Default ACLs do not have an immediate effect on access permissions. They only come into play when file system objects are created. These new objects inherit permissions only from the default ACL of their parent directory.

2. In the next example, use `mkdir` to create a subdirectory in `mydir/`, which will "inherit" the default ACL.

```
mkdir mydir/mysubdir

getfacl mydir/mysubdir

# file: mydir/mysubdir
# owner: tux
# group: project3
user::rwx
group::r-x
group:djungle:r-x
mask::r-x
other::---
default:user::rwx
default:group::r-x
default:group:djungle:r-x
default:mask::r-x
default:other::---
```

As expected, the newly-created subdirectory `mysubdir/` has the permissions from the default ACL of the parent directory. The access ACL of `mysubdir/` is an exact reflection of the default ACL of `mydir/`, just as the default ACL that this directory will hand down to its subordinate objects.

3. Use `touch` to create a file in the `mydir/` directory:

```
touch mydir/myfile

ls -l mydir/myfile

-rw-r-----+ ... tux project3 ... mydir/myfile


getfacl mydir/myfile
```

```
# file: mydir/myfile
# owner: tux
# group: project3
user::rw-
group::r-x          # effective:r--
group:djungle:r-x   # effective:r--
mask::r--
other::---
```

Important in this example: `touch` passes on `mode` with the value `0666`, which means that new files are created with read and write permissions for all user classes, provided no other restrictions exist in `umask` or in the default ACL (see Section B on page 494).

In effect, this means that all access permissions not contained in the `mode` value are removed from the respective ACL entries. Although no permissions were removed from the ACL entry of the *group class*, the *mask* entry was modified to mask permissions not set via `mode`.

This approach ensures the smooth interaction of applications, such as compilers, with ACLs. You can create files with restricted access permissions and subsequently mark them as executable. The `mask` mechanism guarantees that the right users and groups can execute them as desired.

The ACL Check Algorithm

A check algorithm is applied to all processes or applications before they are granted access to an ACL-protected file system object. As a basic rule, the ACL entries are examined in the following sequence: *owner*, *named user*, *owning group* or *named group*, and *other*. The access is handled in accordance with the entry that best suits the process. Permissions do not accumulate.

Things are more complicated if a process belongs to more than one group and would potentially suit several *group* entries. An entry is randomly selected from the suitable entries with the required permissions. It is irrelevant which of the entries triggers the final result "access granted". Likewise, if none of the suitable *group* entries contains the correct permissions, a randomly selected entry triggers the final result "access denied".

Support by Applications

As described in the preceding sections, ACLs can be used to implement very complex permission scenarios that meet the requirements of modern applications. The traditional permission concept and ACLs can be combined in a smart manner. However, some important applications still lack ACL support. Except for the star archiver, there are currently no backup applications that guarantee the full preservation of ACLs.

The basic file commands (`cp`, `mv`, `ls`, and so on) do support ACLs, but many editors and file managers (such as Konqueror) do not. When copying files with Konqueror, for instance, the ACLs of these files are lost. When modifying files with an editor, the ACLs of files are sometimes preserved, sometimes not, depending on the backup mode of the editor used:

- If the editor writes the changes to the original file, the access ACL will be preserved.
- If the editor saves the updated contents to a new file that is subsequently renamed to the old file name, the ACLs may be lost, unless the editor supports ACLs.

Note

Additional Information

Detailed information about ACLs is available at the following URLs: `http://sdb.suse.de/en/sdb/html/81_acl.html` `http://acl.bestbits.at/` and in the manual pages of `getfacl`, `acl(5)`, and `setfacl(1)`.

Note

Manual Page of e2fsck

E2FSCK(8) E2FSCK(8)

NAME

e2fsck - check a Linux second extended file system

SYNOPSIS

e2fsck [-pacnyrdfvstDFSV] [-b superblock] [-B block size] [-l|-L bad_blocks_file] [-C fd] [-j external-journal] [-E extended_options] device

DESCRIPTION

e2fsck is used to check a Linux second extended file sys tem (ext2fs). E2fsck also supports ext2 filesystems coun taining a journal, which are also sometimes known as ext3 filesystems, by first applying the journal to the filesys tem before continuing with normal e2fsck processing. After the journal has been applied, a filesystem will nor mally be marked as clean. Hence, for ext3 filesystems, e2fsck will normally run the journal and exit, unless its superblock indicates that further checking is required.

device is the device file where the filesystem is stored (e.g. /dev/hdc1).

OPTIONS

-a
This option does the same thing as the -p option. It is provided for backwards compatibility only; it is suggested that people use -p option whenever possible.

-b superblock
Instead of using the normal superblock, use an alternative superblock specified by superblock. This option is normally used when the primary superblock has been corrupted. The location of the

backup superblock is dependent on the filesystem's blocksize. For filesystems with 1k blocksizes, a backup superblock can be found at block 8193; for filesystems with 2k blocksizes, at block 16384; and for 4k blocksizes, at block 32768.

Additional backup superblocks can be determined by using the mke2fs program using the -n option to print out where the superblocks were created. The -b option to mke2fs, which specifies blocksize of the filesystem must be specified in order for the superblock locations that are printed out to be accurate.

If an alternative superblock is specified and the filesystem is not opened read-only, e2fsck will make sure that the primary superblock is updated appropriately upon completion of the filesystem check.

-B blocksize
Normally, e2fsck will search for the superblock at various different block sizes in an attempt to find the appropriate block size. This search can be fooled in some cases. This option forces e2fsck to only try locating the superblock at a particular blocksize. If the superblock is not found, e2fsck will terminate with a fatal error.

-c This option causes e2fsck to run the badblocks(8) program to find any blocks which are bad on the filesystem, and then marks them as bad by adding them to the bad block inode. If this option is specified twice, then the bad block scan will be done using a non-destructive read-write test.

-C fd This option causes e2fsck to write completion information to the specified file descriptor so that the progress of the filesystem check can be monitored. This option is typically used by pro grams which are running e2fsck. If the file descriptor specified is 0, e2fsck will print a com pletion bar as it goes about its business. This requires that e2fsck is running on a video console or terminal.

-d Print debugging output (useless unless you are debugging e2fsck).

-D Optimize directories in filesystem. This option causes e2fsck to try to optimize all directories, either by reindexing them if the filesystem sup ports directory indexing, or by sorting and com pressing directories for smaller directories, or for filesystems using traditional linear directories.

-E extended_options
Set e2fsck extended options. Extended options are comma separated, and may take an argument using the equals ('=') sign. The following options are supported:

ea_ver=extended_attribute_version
Assume the format of the extended attribute blocks in the filesystem is the specified version number. The version number may be 1 or 2. The default extended attribute version format is 2.

-f Force checking even if the file system seems clean.

-F Flush the filesystem device's buffer caches before beginning. Only really useful for doing e2fsck time trials.

-j external-journal
Set the pathname where the external-journal for this filesystem can be found.

-l filename
Add the block numbers listed in the file specified by filename to the list of bad blocks. The format of this file is the same as the one generated by the badblocks(8) program. Note that the block numbers are based on the blocksize of the filesystem. Hence, badblocks(8) must be given the blocksize of the filesystem in order to obtain correct results. As a result, it is much simpler and safer to use the -c option to e2fsck, since it will assure that the correct parameters are passed to the badblocks program.

-L filename
Set the bad blocks list to be the list of blocks specified by filename. (This option is the same as the -l option, except the bad blocks list is cleared before the blocks listed in the file are added to the bad blocks list.)

-n Open the filesystem read-only, and assume an answer of 'no' to all questions. Allows e2fsck to be used non-interactively. (Note: if the -c, -l, or -L options are specified in addition to the -n option, then the filesystem will be opened read-write, to permit the bad-blocks list to be updated. However, no other changes will be made to the filesystem.)

-p Automatically repair ("preen") the file system without any questions.

-r This option does nothing at all; it is provided only for backwards compatibility.

-s This option will byte-swap the filesystem so that it is using the normalized, standard byte-order (which is i386 or little endian). If the filesys tem is already in the standard byte-order, e2fsck will take no action.

-S This option will byte-swap the filesystem, regard less of its current byte-order.

-t Print timing statistics for e2fsck. If this option is used twice, additional timing statistics are printed on a pass by pass basis.

-v Verbose mode.

-V Print version information and exit.

-y Assume an answer of 'yes' to all questions; allows e2fsck to be used non-interactively.

EXIT CODE

The exit code returned by e2fsck is the sum of the follow ing conditions:

```
0    - No errors
1    - File system errors corrected
2    - File system errors corrected, system should
       be rebooted
4    - File system errors left uncorrected
8    - Operational error
16   - Usage or syntax error
32   - E2fsck canceled by user request
128  - Shared library error
```

SIGNALS

The following signals have the following effect when sent to e2fsck.

SIGUSR1

This signal causes e2fsck to start displaying a completion bar. (See discussion of the -C option.)

SIGUSR2

This signal causes e2fsck to stop displaying a com pletion bar.

```
REPORTING BUGS
       Almost any piece of  software  will  have  bugs.  If  you
       manage  to find a filesystem which causes e2fsck to crash,
       or which e2fsck is unable to repair, please report  it  to
       the author.

       Please include as much information as possible in your bug
       report.  Ideally, include a  complete  transcript  of  the
       e2fsck  run,  so I can see exactly what error messages are
       displayed.  If you have a writeable filesystem  where  the
       transcript can be stored, the script(1) program is a handy
       way to save the output of e2fsck to a file.

       It is also useful to send the output of dumpe2fs(8).  If a
       specific  inode  or inodes seems to be giving e2fsck trou
       ble, try running the debugfs(8) command and send the  out
       put  of the stat(1u) command run on the relevant inode(s).
       If the inode is a directory, the debugfs dump command will
       allow  you to extract the contents of the directory inode,
       which can sent to me after being first run  through  uuen
       code(1).

       Always  include  the full version string which e2fsck dis
       plays when it is run, so I know which version you are run
       ning.

AUTHOR
       This  version  of  e2fsck  was  written  by  Theodore Ts'o
       <tytso@mit.edu>.

SEE ALSO
       mke2fs(8), tune2fs(8), dumpe2fs(8), debugfs(8)


E2fsprogs version 1.34      July 2003                E2FSCK(8)
```

D

Manual Page of reiserfsck

```
REISERFSCK(8)                                          REISERFSCK(8)

NAME
       reiserfsck - check a Linux Reiserfs file system

SYNOPSIS
       reiserfsck  [  -afprVy ] [ --rebuild-sb | --check | --fix-
       fixable | --rebuild-tree | --clean-attributes  ]  [  -j  |
       --journal device ] [ -z | --adjust-size ] [ -n | --nolog ]
       [ -l | --logfile file ] [ -q | --quiet ] [ -y | --yes ]  [
       -S  |  --scan-whole-partition ] [ --no-journal-available ]
       device

DESCRIPTION
       Reiserfsck searches for a Reiserfs filesystem on a device,
       replays  any  necessary transactions, and either checks or
       repairs the file system.

       device is the special file corresponding to the device  or
              partition  (e.g /dev/hdXX for IDE disk partition or
              /dev/sdXX for SCSI disk partition).

OPTIONS
       --rebuild-sb
              This option recovers the superblock on  a  Reiserfs
              partition.  Normally  you only need this option if
              mount reports "read_super_block: can't find a reis
              erfs  file system" and you are sure that a Reiserfs
              file system is there.

       --check
              This default action checks file system  consistency
              and reports but does not repair any corruption that
              it finds. This option may be used  on  a  read-only
              file system mount.

       --fix-fixable
```

This option recovers certain kinds of corruption that do not require rebuilding the entire file sys tem tree (--rebuild-tree). Normally you only need this option if the --check option reports "corrup tion that can be fixed with --fix-fixable". This includes: zeroing invalid data-block pointers, cor recting st_size and st_blocks for directories, and deleting invalid directory entries.

--rebuild-tree
This option rebuilds the entire file system tree using leaf nodes found on the device. Normally you only need this option if the --check option reports "corruption that can be fixed only during --rebuild-tree". You are strongly encouraged to make a backup copy of the whole partition before attempting the --rebuild-tree option.

--clean-attributes
This option cleans reserved fields of Stat-Data items.

--journal device , -j device
This option supplies the device name of the current file system journal. This option is required when the journal resides on a separate device from the main data device (although it can be avoided with the expert option --no-journal-available).

--adjust-size, -z
This option causes reiserfsck to correct file sizes that are larger than the offset of the last discov ered byte. This implies that holes at the end of a file will be removed. File sizes that are smaller than the offset of the last discovered byte are corrected by --fix-fixable.

--logfile file, -l file
This option causes reiserfsck to report any corrup tion it finds to the specified log file rather than stderr.

--nolog, -n
This option prevents reiserfsck from reporting any kinds of corruption.

--quiet, -q
This option prevents reiserfsck from reporting its rate of progress.

--yes, -y
This option inhibits reiserfsck from asking you for confirmation after telling you what it is going to

```
              do, assuming yes. For safety, it does not work with
              the --rebuild-tree option.

       -a, -p These  options are usually passed by fsck -A during
              the automatic checking of those  partitions  listed
              in  /etc/fstab.  These  options cause reiserfsck to
              print some information  about  the  specified  file
              system,  check if error flags in the superblock are
              set and  do  some  light-weight  checks.  If  these
              checks reveal a corruption or the flag indicating a
              (possibly fixable) corruption is found set  in  the
              superblock,  then  reiserfsck  switches to the fix-
              fixable mode. If the flag indicating a  fatal  cor
              ruption  is found set in the superblock, then reis
              erfsck finishes with an error.

       -V     This option prints the  reiserfsprogs  version  and
              exit.

       -r, -f These options are ignored.

EXPERT OPTIONS
       DO  NOT  USE  THESE  OPTIONS  UNLESS YOU KNOW WHAT YOU ARE
       DOING.  WE ARE NOT RESPONSIBLE  IF  YOU  LOSE  DATA  AS  A
       RESULT OF THESE OPTIONS.

       --no-journal-available
              This  option  allows reiserfsck to proceed when the
              journal device is not available. This option has no
              effect when the journal is located on the main data
              device. NOTE: after this  operation  you  must  use
              reiserfstune to specify a new journal device.

       --scan-whole-partition, -S
              This option causes --rebuild-tree to scan the whole
              partition, not only used space on the partition.

EXAMPLE OF USING
       1. You think something may be wrong with a reiserfs parti
       tion  on  /dev/hda1  or  you  would just like to perform a
       periodic disk check.

       2. Run reiserfsck --check --logfile  check.log  /dev/hda1.
       If  reiserfsck  --check  exits  with  status 0 it means no
       errors were discovered.

       3. If reiserfsck --check exits with status 1 (and  reports
       about  fixable  corruptions)  it means that you should run
       reiserfsck --fix-fixable --logfile fixable.log  /dev/hda1.

       4.  If reiserfsck --check exits with status 2 (and reports
       about fatal corruptions) it means that  you  need  to  run
       reiserfsck --rebuild-tree.  If reiserfsck --check fails in
```

some way you should also run reiserfsck --rebuild-tree, but we also encourage you to submit this as a bug report.

5. Before running reiserfsck --rebuild-tree, please make a backup of the whole partition before proceeding. Then run reiserfsck --rebuild-tree --logfile rebuild.log /dev/hda1.

6. If the --rebuild-tree step fails or does not recover what you expected, please submit this as a bug report. Try to provide as much information as possible and we will try to help solve the problem.

EXIT CODES

reiserfsck uses the following exit codes:

```
   0 - No errors.
   1 - File system errors corrected.
   4 - File system fatal errors left uncorrected,
       reiserfsck --rebuild-tree needs to be launched.
   6 - File system fixable errors left uncorrected,
       reiserfsck --fix-fixable needs to be launched.
   8 - Operational error.
   16 - Usage or syntax error.
```

AUTHOR

This version of reiserfsck has been written by Vitaly Fertman <vitaly@namesys.com>.

BUGS

There are likely to be some bugs. Please report bugs to the ReiserFS mail-list <reiserfs-list@namesys.com>.

TODO

Faster recovering, signal handling, i/o error handling, etc.

SEE ALSO

mkreiserfs(8), reiserfstune(8) resize_reiserfs(8), debugreiserfs(8),

Reiserfsprogs-3.6.9 April 2003 REISERFSCK(8)

The GNU General Public License

GNU General Public License

Foreword

The licenses for most software are designed to take away your freedom to share and change it. By contrast, the *GNU General Public License* is intended to guarantee your freedom to share and change free software — to make sure the software is free for all its users. This *General Public License* applies to most of the *Free Software Foundation's* software and to any other program whose authors commit to using it. (Some other *Free Software Foundation* software is covered by the *GNU Library General Public License* instead.) You can apply it to your programs, too.

When we speak of *"free" software*, we are referring to freedom, not price. Our General Public Licenses are designed to make sure that you have the freedom to distribute copies of free software (and charge for this service if you wish), that you receive source code or can get it if you want it, that you can change the software or use pieces of it in new free programs; and that you know you can do these things.

To protect your rights, we need to make restrictions that forbid anyone to deny you these rights or to ask you to surrender the rights. These restrictions translate to certain responsibilities for you if you distribute copies of the software, or if you modify it.

For example, if you distribute copies of such a program, whether gratis or for a fee, you must give the recipients all the rights that you have. You must make sure that they, too, receive or can get the source code. And you must show them these terms so they know their rights.

We protect your rights with two steps: (1) copyright the software, and (2) offer you this license which gives you legal permission to copy, distribute and/or modify the software.

Also, for each author's protection and ours, we want to make certain that everyone understands that there is no warranty for this free software. If the software is modified by someone else and passed on, we want its recipients to know that what they have is not the original, so that any problems introduced by others will not reflect on the original authors' reputations.

Finally, any free program is threatened constantly by software patents. We wish to avoid the danger that redistributors of a free program will individually obtain patent licenses, in effect making the program proprietary. To prevent this, we have made it clear that any patent must be licensed for everyone's free use or not licensed at all.

The precise terms and conditions for copying, distribution and modification follow.

GNU General, Public License

Terms and Conditions for Copying, Distribution and Modification

0. This License applies to any program or other work which contains a notice placed by the copyright holder saying it may be distributed under the terms of this *General Public License*. The "Program", below, refers to any such program or work, and a *work based on the Program* means either the Program or any derivative work under copyright law: that is to say, a work containing the Program or a portion of it, either verbatim or with modifications and/or translated into another language. (Hereinafter, translation is included without limitation in the term "modification".) Each licensee is addressed as "you".

Activities other than copying, distribution and modification are not covered by this License; they are outside its scope. The act of running the Program is not restricted, and the output from the Program is covered only if its contents constitute a work based on the Program (independent of having been made by running the Program). Whether that is true depends on what the Program does.

1. You may copy and distribute verbatim copies of the Program's source code as you receive it, in any medium, provided that you conspicuously and appropriately publish on each copy an appropriate copyright notice and disclaimer of warranty; keep intact all the notices that refer to this License and to the absence of any warranty; and give any other recipients of the Program a copy of this License along with the Program.

You may charge a fee for the physical act of transferring a copy, and you may at your option offer warranty protection in exchange for a fee.

2. You may modify your copy or copies of the Program or any portion of it, thus forming a work based on the Program, and copy and distribute such modifications or work under the terms of Section 1 above, provided that you also meet all of these conditions:

1. You must cause the modified files to carry prominent notices stating that you changed the files and the date of any change.

2. You must cause any work that you distribute or publish, that in whole or in part contains or is derived from the Program or any part thereof, to be licensed as a whole at no charge to all third parties under the terms of this License.

3. If the modified program normally reads commands interactively when run, you must cause it, when started running for such interactive use in the most ordinary way, to print or display an announcement including an appropriate copyright notice and a notice that there is no warranty (or else, saying that you provide a warranty) and that users may redistribute the program under these conditions, and telling the user how to view a copy of this License. (Exception: if the Program itself is interactive but does not normally print such an announcement, your work based on the Program is not required to print an announcement.)

These requirements apply to the modified work as a whole. If identifiable sections of that work are not derived from the Program, and can be reasonably considered independent and separate works in themselves, then this

License, and its terms, do not apply to those sections when you distribute them as separate works. But when you distribute the same sections as part of a whole which is a work based on the Program, the distribution of the whole must be on the terms of this License, whose permissions for other licensees extend to the entire whole, and thus to each and every part regardless of who wrote it.

Thus, it is not the intent of this section to claim rights or contest your rights to work written entirely by you; rather, the intent is to exercise the right to control the distribution of derivative or collective works based on the Program.

In addition, mere aggregation of another work not based on the Program with the Program (or with a work based on the Program) on a volume of a storage or distribution medium does not bring the other work under the scope of this License.

3. You may copy and distribute the Program (or a work based on it, under Section 2) in object code or executable form under the terms of Sections 1 and 2 above provided that you also do one of the following:

1. Accompany it with the complete corresponding machine--readable source code, which must be distributed under the terms of Sections 1 and 2 above on a medium customarily used for software interchange; or,

2. Accompany it with a written offer, valid for at least three years, to give any third party, for a charge no more than your cost of physically performing source distribution, a complete machine-readable copy of the corresponding source code, to be distributed under the terms of Sections 1 and 2 above on a medium customarily used for software interchange; or,

3. Accompany it with the information you received as to the offer to distribute corresponding source code. (This alternative is allowed only for noncommercial distribution and only if you received the program in object code or executable form with such an offer, in accord with Subsection b above.)

The source code for a work means the preferred form of the work for making modifications to it. For an executable work, "complete source code" means all the source code for all modules it contains, plus any associated interface definition files, plus the scripts used to control compilation and installation of the executable. However, as a special exception, the source code distributed need not include anything that is normally distributed (in either source or binary form) with the major components (compiler, kernel, and so on) of the operating system on which the executable runs, unless that component itself accompanies the executable.

If distribution of executable or object code is made by offering access to copy from a designated place, then offering equivalent access to copy the source code from the same place counts as distribution of the source code, even though third parties are not compelled to copy the source along with the object code.

4. You may not copy, modify, sublicense, or distribute the Program except as expressly provided under this License. Any attempt otherwise to copy, modify, sublicense or distribute the Program is void, and will automatically terminate your rights under this License. However, parties who have received copies, or rights, from you under this License will not have their licenses terminated so long as such parties remain in full compliance.

5. You are not required to accept this License, since you have not signed it. However, nothing else grants you permission to modify or distribute the Program or its derivative works. These actions are prohibited by law if you do not accept this License. Therefore, by modifying or distributing the Program (or any work based on the Program), you indicate your acceptance of this License to do so, and all its terms and conditions for copying, distributing or modifying the Program or works based on it.

6. Each time you redistribute the Program (or any work based on the Program), the recipient automatically receives a license from the original licensor to copy, distribute or modify the Program subject to these terms and conditions. You may not impose any further restrictions on the recipients' exercise of the rights granted herein. You are not responsible for enforcing compliance by third parties to this License.

7. If, as a consequence of a court judgment or allegation of patent infringement or for any other reason (not limited to patent issues), conditions are imposed on you (whether by court order, agreement or otherwise) that contradict the conditions of this License, they do not excuse you from the conditions of this License. If you cannot distribute so as to satisfy simultaneously your obligations under this License and any other pertinent obligations, then as a consequence you may not distribute the Program at all. For example, if a patent license would not permit royalty--free redistribution of the Program by all those who receive copies directly or indirectly through you, then the only way you could satisfy both it and this License would be to refrain entirely from distribution of the Program.

If any portion of this section is held invalid or unenforceable under any particular circumstance, the balance of the section is intended to apply and the section as a whole is intended to apply in other circumstances.

It is not the purpose of this section to induce you to infringe any patents or other property right claims or to contest validity of any such claims; this section has the sole purpose of protecting the integrity of the free software distribution system, which is implemented by public license practices. Many people have made generous contributions to the wide range of software distributed through that system in reliance on consistent application of that system; it is up to the author/donor to decide if he or she is willing to distribute software through any other system and a licensee cannot impose that choice.

This section is intended to make thoroughly clear what is believed to be a consequence of the rest of this License.

8. If the distribution and/or use of the Program is restricted in certain countries either by patents or by copyrighted interfaces, the original copyright holder who places the Program under this License may add an explicit geographical distribution limitation excluding those countries, so that distribution is permitted only in or among countries not thus excluded. In such case, this License incorporates the limitation as if written in the body of this License.

9. The *Free Software Foundation* may publish revised and/or new versions of the *General Public License* from time to time. Such new versions will be similar in spirit to the present version, but may differ in detail to address new problems or concerns.

Each version is given a distinguishing version number. If the Program specifies a version number of this License which applies to it and "any later version", you have the option of following the terms and conditions either of that version or of any later version published by the *Free Software Foundation*. If the Program does not specify a version number of this License, you may choose any version ever published by the *Free Software Foundation*.

10. If you wish to incorporate parts of the Program into other free programs whose distribution conditions are different, write to the author to ask for permission. For software which is copyrighted by the *Free Software Foundation*, write to the *Free Software Foundation*; we sometimes make exceptions for this. Our decision will be guided by the two goals of preserving the free status of all derivatives of our free software and of promoting the sharing and reuse of software generally.

No Warranty

11. Because the program is licensed free of charge, there is no warranty for the program, to the extent permitted by applicable law. Except when otherwise stated in writing the copyright holders and/or other parties provide the program "as is" without warranty of any kind, either expressed or implied, including, but not limited to, the implied warranties of merchantability and fitness for a particular purpose. The entire risk as to the quality and performance of the program is with you. Should the program prove defective, you assume the cost of all necessary servicing, repair or correction.

12. In no event unless required by applicable law or agreed to in writing will any copyright holder, or any other party who may modify and/or redistribute the program as permitted above, be liable to you for damages, including any general, special, incidental or consequential damages arising out of the use or inability to use the program (including but not limited to loss of data or data being rendered inaccurate or losses sustained by you or third parties or a failure of the program to operate with any other programs), even if such holder or other party has been advised of the possibility of such damages.

End of Terms and Conditions

How to Apply These Terms to Your New Programs

If you develop a new program, and you want it to be of the greatest possible use to the public, the best way to achieve this is to make it free software which everyone can redistribute and change under these terms.

To do so, attach the following notices to the program. It is safest to attach them to the start of each source file to most effectively convey the exclusion of warranty; and each file should have at least the "copyright" line and a pointer to where the full notice is found.

```
<one line to give the program's name and a brief
idea of what it does.>

Copyright (C) <year> <name of author>

This program is free software; you can redistribute it and/or
modify it under the terms of the GNU General Public License
as published by the Free Software Foundation; either version 2
of the License, or (at your option) any later version.
```

```
This program is distributed in the hope that it will be useful,
but WITHOUT ANY WARRANTY; without even the implied warranty of
MERCHANTABILITY or FITNESS FOR A PARTICULAR PURPOSE. See the
GNU General Public License for more details.

You should have received a copy of the GNU General Public
License along with this program; if not, write to the Free
Software Foundation, Inc., 59 Temple Place, Suite 330, Boston,
MA 02111-1307, USA.
```

Also add information on how to contact you by electronic and paper mail.

If the program is interactive, make it output a short notice like this when it starts in an interactive mode:

```
Gnomovision version 69, Copyright (C) <year> <name of author>

Gnomovision comes with ABSOLUTELY NO WARRANTY; for details type
'show w'. This is free software, and you  are welcome to
redistribute it under certain conditions; type 'show c' for
details.
```

The hypothetical commands `show w` and `show c` should show the appropriate parts of the General Public License. Of course, the commands you use may be called something other than `show w` and `show c`; they could even be mouse-clicks or menu items—whatever suits your program.

You should also get your employer (if you work as a programmer) or your school, if any, to sign a "copyright disclaimer" for the program, if necessary. Here is a sample; alter the names:

```
Yoyodyne, Inc., hereby disclaims all copyright interest in the
program 'Gnomovision' (which makes passes at compilers) written
by James Hacker.

signature of Ty Coon, 1st April 1989 Ty Coon, President of Vice
```

This *General Public License* does not permit incorporating your program into proprietary programs. If your program is a subroutine library, you may consider it more useful to permit linking proprietary applications with the library. If this is what you want to do, use the *GNU Library General Public License* instead of this License.

Bibliography

[1] *SUSE LINUX* (*User Guide*). SUSE, 9. Edition ©2004 .

[2] EDWARD C. BAILEY. *Maximum RPM*. ©1997 . ISBN 1-888172-78-9.

[3] BRYAN COSTALES, ERIC ALLMAN, NEIL RICKERT. *sendmail*. ©1993 . ISBN 1-56592-056-2.

[4] WERNER ALMESBERGER. *LILO User's guide*. `file:///usr/share/doc/lilo/user.dvi`.

[5] OLAF KIRCH. *LINUX Network Administrator's Guide*. ©1995 . ISBN 1-56592-087-2.

[6] SIMON GARFINKEL, GENE SPAFFORD. *Practical UNIX Security*. ©1993 . ISBN 0-937175-72-2.

[7] CRAIG HUNT. *TCP/IP Netwerk Administration*. ©1995 . ISBN 3-930673-02-9.

[8] TIM O'REILLY, GRACE TODINO. *Managing UUCP and Usenet*. ©1992 . ISBN 0-937175-93-5.

[9] MATT WELSH. *Linux Installation and Getting Started*. 2. Edition ©1994 . ISBN 3-930419-03-3.

[10] LINDA LAMB. *Learning the vi Editor*. ©1990 . ISBN 0-937175-67-6.

[11] MATT WELSH, LARS KAUFMAN. *Running Linux*. ©1995 O'Reilly. ISBN 1-56592-100-3.

[12] WILLIAM R. CHESWICK, STEVEN M. BELLOVIN. *Firewalls and Internet Security* (*Repelling the Wily Hacker*). 2. Edition ©2003 Addison-Wesley Pub Co. ISBN 0-201-63466-X.

[13] BRENT CHAPMAN, ELISABETH D. ZWICKY. *Building Internet Firewalls.* ©1995 O'Reilly and Associates. ISBN 1-565-92124-0.

[14] CLIFFORD STOLL. *Cuckoo's Egg: Tracking a Spy Through the Maze of Computer Espionage* . ©2000 Pocket Books. ISBN 0-743-41146-3.

[15] BRIAN TUNG. *Kerberos: A Network Authentication System.* ©1999 Fischer-TB. Verlag. ISBN 0-201-37924-4.

Index

C

T

U

W

X

Y